T0335808

Interoperability of Enterprise Software
and Applications

Interoperability of Enterprise Software and Applications

Workshops of the
INTEROP-ESA International Conference
EI2N, WSI, ISIDI and IEHENA 2005

February 22nd, 2005 – Geneva, Switzerland

edited by
Hervé Panetto

Hermes Science
PUBLISHING

First published in 2005 by ISTE Ltd

Apart from any fair dealing for the purposes of research or private study, or criticism or review, as permitted under the Copyright, Designs and Patents Act 1988, this publication may only be reproduced, stored or transmitted, in any form or by any means, with the prior permission in writing of the publishers, or in the case of reprographic reproduction in accordance with the terms and licenses issued by the CLA. Enquiries concerning reproduction outside these terms should be sent to the publishers at the undermentioned address:

ISTE Ltd
55 Shawfield Street
London SW3 4BA
UK

ISTE USA
4308 Patrice Road
Newport Beach, CA 92663
USA

www.iste.co.uk

© Hermes Science Publishing Limited, 2005

The right of Hervé Panetto to be identified as the editor of this work has been asserted by him in accordance with the Copyright, Designs and Pattents Act 1988.

British Library Cataloguing-in-Publication Data

A CIP record for this book is available from the British Library

ISBN 1 905209 49 5

First International Conference
INTEROP-ESA'2005
Interoperability of Enterprise Software and Applications

Geneva, Switzerland, February 23rd – 25th, 2005

Organised by INTEROP NoE (FP6-IST-508011) and
Supported by IFIP and ACM-SIGAP

The interoperability in enterprise applications can be defined as the ability of a system or a product to work with other systems or products without special effort from the customer or user. The possibility to interact and exchange information with internal and external collaborators is a key issue in the enterprise sector. It is fundamental in order to produce goods and services quickly, at lower cost, while maintaining higher levels of quality and customisation. Interoperability is considered to be achieved if the interaction can, at least, take place at the three levels: data, applications and business enterprise through the architecture of the enterprise model and taking into account the semantics. It is not only a problem of software and IT technologies. It implies support of communication and transactions between different organisations that must be based on shared business references.

The INTEROP-ESA conference aimed at bringing together researchers, users and practitioners dealing with different issues of Interoperability of Enterprise Applications and Software. The conference focused on interoperability related research areas ranging like *Enterprise Modelling* to define interoperability requirements, *Architecture and Platforms* to provide implementation frameworks and *Ontologies* to define interoperability semantics in the enterprise.

General Co-Chairs
Jean-Paul Bourrières, University of Bordeaux I, France
Michel Léonard, University of Geneva, Switzerland

Program Co-Chairs:
Dimitri Konstantas, University of Geneva, Switzerland
Nacer Boudjlida, Université Henri Poincaré Nancy I, France

Workshops, Tutorials & Invited Sessions Co-Chairs:
Hervé Panetto, Université Henri Poincaré Nancy I, France
François Charoy, Université Henri Poincaré Nancy I, France

Industrial Track Chair:
Martin Zelm, CIMOSA Association, Germany

Doctoral Symposium Chair
Giovanna Di Marzo, University of Geneva, Switzerland

Local Organization Chairs
Jolita Ralyté, University of Geneva, Switzerland
Jean-Henri Morin, University of Geneva, Switzerland

Local Organization Committee
Nicolas Arni-Bloch, University of Geneva, Switzerland
Mehdi Snene, University of Geneva, Switzerland
Michel Pawlak, University of Geneva, Switzerland
Slim Turki, University of Geneva, Switzerland
Abdelaziz Khadraoui, University of Geneva, Switzerland
Jorge Pardellas, University of Geneva, Switzerland
Marie-France Culebras, University of Geneva, Switzerland

Workshops International Program Committees

Workshops General Chairs:
Hervé Panetto, University Henri Poincaré Nancy I, CRAN, France,
François Charoy University Henri Poincaré Nancy I, LORIA, France

EI2N'2005: Enterprise Integration, Interoperability and Networking
Workshops chairs:
>Ortiz Angel, University Politecnic Valencia, Spain
>Panetto Hervé, University Henri Poincaré Nancy I, France
>Molina Arturo, Tecnológico de Monterrey, Mexico

IPC Members:
>Berio Giuseppe, University of Torino, Italy
>Chapurlat Vincent (GI2P, France
>Chen David University of Bordeaux 1, LAP/GRAI, France
>Jaekel Frank-Walter IPK, Germany
>Shorter David, IT Focus, UK
>Weston Richard, University of Loughborough, UK
>Whitman Larry, Wishita State University, USA
>Zelm Martin, CIMOSA, Germany

WSI'2005: Web services and interoperability
Workshops chairs:
>Söderström Eva, University of Skövde, Sweden
>Backlund Per, University of Skövde, Sweden
>Kühn Harald, BOC Information Systems, Austria

IPC Members:
>Athanasopoulos George, National and Kapodistrian University of Athens, Greece
>Boncella Bob, Washburn University, USA
>Henkel Martin, Stockholm University, KTH, Sweden
>Johannesson Paul, Stockholm University, KTH, Sweden
>Karsten Martin, University of Waterloo, Canada
>Koutrouli Eleni, National and Kapodistrian University of Athens, Greece

Pilioura Thomi, National and Kapodistrian University of Athens, Greece
Schmitt Jens, University of Kaiserslautern, Germany
Wangler Benkt, University of Skövde, Sweden

ISIDI'2005: Interoperability Standards - Implementation, Dynamics, and Impact
Workshops chair:
Jakobs Kai, Aachen University, Germany
IPC Members:
Blind Knut, Fraunhofer ISI, Germany
Chauvel Yves, ETSI, France
Egyedi Tineke, Technical University of Deft, The Netherlands
Gerst Martina, Edinburgh University, United Kingdom
Hawkins Richard, TNO, The Netherlands
Iversen Eric, NIFU STEP, Norway
Kosanke Kurt, CIMOSA, Germany
Söderström Eva, University of Skövde, Sweden

IEHENA'2005: Towards Interoperability of Enterprise, eterogeneous Enterprise Networks and their Applications: from Industries needs to ATHENA requirements
Workshops chairs:
Li Man-Sze, IC Focus Limited, UK
Anastasiou Maria, INTRACOM, Greece
Garcia Ruben, AIDIMA, Spain
IPC Members:
Figay Nicolas, EADS CCR, France
Goncalves Ricardo, UNINOVA, Portugal
Ippolito Massimo, CR-FIAT, Italy
Lillehagen Frank, TROUX, Norway
Ruggaber Rainer, SAP , Germany

CONTENTS

Editorial – HERVÉ PANETTO 13

Enterprise Integration, Interoperability and Networks 15

PC Chairs' message – A. ORTIZ, H. PANETTO, A. MOLINA 17

Action Research as the basis to implement Enterprise Integration
Engineering and Business Process Management – R. MEJIA, L. CANCHÉ,
R. ROSAS, R. CAMACHO, M.A OCAMPO, A. MOLINA 19

An Architecture for Managing Distributed Business Processes
in Networked Organization – R. D. FRANCO, V. ANAYA, A. ORTIZ. 31

Issues for Utilizing and Enabling the Global Semantic Web for Enterprise
Integration – T. WAHL, R. MOLDEN, G. SINDRE 41

From a models translation case towards identification of some issues
about UEML – M.ROQUE, B. VALLESPIR, G. DOUMEINGTS 53

Enterprise Modelling, an overview focused on software generation
R. GRANGEL, R. CHALMETA, C. CAMPOS, O. COLTELL. 65

Enablers and Technologies Supporting Self-Forming Networked
Organizations – C-M. CHITUC, A. AZEVEDO 77

UEML : Providing Requirements and Extensions for Interoperability
Challenges – M. BERGHOLTZ, P. JOHANNESSON, P. WOHED. 89

Ontology for Enterprise Interoperability in the domain of Enterprise
Business Modelling – H. PANETTO, L. WHITMAN, K. ALI CHATHA. 103

Web Services and Interoperability . . . . : 115

PC Chairs' message – E. SÖDERSTRÖM, P. BACKLUND, H. KÜHN 117

Approaches to Service Interface Design – M. HENKEL, J. ZDRAVKOVIC . 119

Service-oriented Architecture for Business Monitoring Systems
F. BAYER, H. KÜHN, A. PETZMANN, R. SCHLOSSAR 127

Web services business values, legal and financial aspects
E. SÖDERSTRÖM. 135

A Pipelined Worklflow Framework for Frequent Scientific Data
Interaction – X. B. HUANG, J. TANG 147

A Methodolgy for Developing OWL-S Descriptions
M.C. JAEGER, L. ENGEL, K. GEIHS 153

MODTIS : System Integration Orchestrated, Dynamic and Transactional
Model – J. ABIN, F. RODRIGUEZ, ... 167

Designing Web Service Accounting System – G. ZHANG, J. MUELLER,
P. MUELLER 181

**Interoperability Standards - Implementation, Dynamics
and Impact** 195

PC Chair's message – K. JACOBS 197

Interoperability of Software: Demand and Solutions – K. BLIND 199

Current issues in RFID standardisation – M. GERST, R. BUNDUCHI,
I. GRAHAM. 211

Connection stakeholders and B2B standards life cycles
E. SÖDERSTRÖM 223

IPv6 versus Network Address Translation
J.L.M. VRANCKEN, C.P.J. KOYMANS 235

A bottom-up approach to build a B2B sectoral standard:
the case of Moda-ML/TexSpin – N. GESSA, G. CUCCHIARA,
P. DE SABATTA, A. BRUTTI 249

Standards Dynamics – T.M. EGYEDI, P. HEIJNEN 261

Standards dynamics in the mobile communication area: Three cases
E.J. IVERSEN, R. TEE 283

+ vs. - : Impacts and Dynamics of competing standards of recordable
DVD-media – S. GAUCH 299

Open Standards and Open Source Software : Similarities and differences
J. VERHOOSEL 311

Towards Interoperability of Enterprise, Heterogeneous Enterprise
Networks and their Applications: from Industries needs
to ATHENA requirements 317

PC Chairs' message – M-S. LI, M. ANASTASIOU, R. GARCIA 319

ATHENA - Advanced Technologies for Interoperability
of Heterogeneous enterprise networks and their applications
R. RUGGABER 321

Framework for training and education activities in interoperability
of ESA – R. JARDIM-GONCLAVES, R. SARAIVA, P. MALO,
A. STEIGER-GARCAO 329

Towards Interoperability of Heterogeneous Enterprise Networks
and their Applications - Requirements Handling and Validation activities
M. ANASTASIOU, M.J. NUÑEZ, O. GARCIA 341

Towards Business Interoperability Research - Requirements Gathering
and Analysis – M-S. LI, P. PAGANELLI 353

Index of Authors 363

Editorial

The INTEROP-ESA international conference, organised by the INTEROP NoE, offered a workshops program comprising four workshops. The objective of the workshops that have been hold on February 22nd, 2005, was to strengthen some key topics related to interoperability of enterprise applications and software. The workshops organisation left time slots to brainstorm between attendees in order to come out, at the end, with new research directions for the future.

It is a fact that enterprises need to collaborate if they want to survive in the current extreme dynamic and heterogeneous business world they are involved in. Enterprise integration, interoperability and networking have been disciplines that have studied how to do companies to collaborate and communicate in the most effective way. Enterprise Integration consists in breaking down organizational barriers to improve synergy within the enterprise so that business goals are achieved in a more productive and efficient way. The IFAC (International Federation for Automatic Control) Technical Committee 5.3 "Enterprise Integration and Networking" organised the Workshop "Enterprise Integration, Interoperability and Networking" (EI2N'2005) which aims to identify issues on Applications Interoperability for Enterprise Integration that will be developed in future research works.

One of the main domain related to interoperability concerns architectures. Technology such as Web services promises to facilitate the interaction between IT systems and enterprise applications. The workshop "Web services and interoperability" (WSI'2005) gathered researchers and practitioners in order to explore various aspects of web services and their benefits to the interoperability problem. However, interoperability needs common consensus through standards. The workshop "Interoperability Standards - Implementation, Dynamics, and Impact" (ISIDI'2005), organised by the NO-REST IST STREP project (Networked Organisations - REsearch into STandards and Standardisation Project) aimed at getting a better understanding of the impact ICT standards have on networked organisations. It was investigated the applicability and, specifically, the dynamics of standards and their implementations, focussing on the e-business and e-government.

In order to put in practice interoperability technologies, industry is a key focus. The ATHENA Integrated project (Advanced Technologies for interoperability of Heterogeneous Enterprise Networks and their Applications) organised the workshop "Towards Interoperability of Enterprise, Heterogeneous Enterprise Networks and their Applications : from Industries needs to ATHENA requirements" (IEHENA'2005) aiming at presenting and discussing the current results of ATHENA programme related to industry short and long term needs and requirements regarding interoperability of enterprise software and applications. In particular, the way industrial interoperability requirements are handled within the programme will be presented and specific examples of industry scenarios indicating interoperability needs and solutions will be provided.

Many thanks to all chairs for their scientific work that resulted in these workshops.

Hervé Panetto
University Henri Poincaré Nancy I, France

Enterprise Integration, Interoperability and Networks

PC Chairs' message

The EI2N "Enterprise Integration, Interoperability and Networking" Workshop was sponsored by IFAC TC 5.3 "Enterprise Integration and Networking" and INTEROP Network of Excellence. Enterprise integration, interoperability and networking are disciplines focus on how companies collaborate and communicate in the most effective way. Such disciplines are well established nowadays, with the existence of international conferences, initiatives, groups, task forces and European projects and where different branches of knowledge have being facing the problem from different point of views with different objectives (e.g. technological or managerial point of views).

The workshop attracted papers from research groups involved in these topics with the aim of present, discuss and launch initiatives that help the community to keep on working in these interesting topics, but also to provide real value to practitioners.

Two papers about UEML (Unified Enterprise Modelling Language), an ongoing European initiative, were presented. The main objective of UEML is to function as a bridge between different enterprise modelling techniques and tools facilitating model translation and hence supports model exchange and communication. The papers provide an analysis of UEML and its further development.

Business Process Management is a central point in current Networked Enterprises. **Three papers** presented in the workshop covered this topic. One of them presented a methodology to achieve the integration of enterprise modelling and business processes to create an enterprise model, a formal structure to generate business knowledge and to define a platform to achieve the interoperability between processes. Another one focused IT architecture of a business process management system that allows running inter-enterprises business process, finally, the third one focused in the automatic generation of software to automate business processes.

Plug-and-Do Business is a new paradigm devoted to promote self-forming enterprise networks, likely, one of the ways to develop dynamic business in the future. **A paper** presented in the workshop proposed an approach towards the development of a conceptual framework for a self-forming business networking environment.

Semantics is a quite important topic in the world of enterprise integration and interoperability. **Two papers** addressed this topic in the workshop. One of them presented ontology as a mean to formalise semantics of concepts within the enterprise. The other one explored the potential that Semantic Web will have in the upcoming solution for enterprise engineering and integration.

We honestly hope that the result of the workshop will be useful for all of you.

Ortiz Angel, Politecnic University Valencia, Spain
Panetto Hervé, University Henri Poincaré Nancy I, France
Molina Arturo, Tecnológico de Monterrey, Mexico

Action Research as the basis to implement Enterprise Integration Engineering and Business Process Management

Ricardo Mejía, Luis Canché, Roberto Rosas, Ricardo Camacho, Manuel A. Ocampo, Arturo Molina

Instituto Tecnológico y de Estudios Superiores de Monterrey, Campus Monterrey. Ave. Eugenio Garza Sada 2501 Sur, Monterrey, N.L., México 64849 {rimejia, luis.canche; A00561612; A00788106; A00777498; armolina} @itesm.mx

ABSTRACT. *This paper describes how Action Research (AR) provides a methodology to integrate Enterprise Integration Engineering (EIE and Business Process Management (BPM). The elements of EIE and BPM are aligned to the different stages of the AR methodology to achieve a knowledge evolutional cycle to manage change within the enterprise. The methodology is leveraged by a reference framework which helps to define strategies, evaluate performance measures, design/re-design processes and establish the enabling tools and technologies. This methodology allows the integration of enterprise modeling and business processes to create an enterprise model, a formal structure to generate business knowledge and define a platform to achieve the interoperability between processes.*

Keywords: *Action Research; Business Process Management; Enterprise Integration, Enterprise Modelling, Interoperability*

1. Introduction

Business managers in many organizations, representing a wide range of industries, are looking for ways to improve operational efficiency. For many of these companies, Enterprise Integration Engineering (EIE) and Business Process Management (BPM) looks like promising candidates.

Enterprise Integration Engineering (EIE) is the set of frameworks (reference architectures), methodologies and tools that allow to engineer different entities in an enterprise (e.g. enterprise, project, product, process). The foundation relies on the creation models of the structure, function and behavior of the different entities. EIE allows a detail description of all the key elements of an entity (activities, data/information/knowledge, organizational aspects, human and technological resources). In an enterprise model, this description provides the means to connect and communicate all the functional areas of an organizational to improve synergy within the enterprise to achieve its mission and vision in an effective and efficient manner (Molina et al, 2004).

BPM is currently defined, according to Aalst et al. (2003) as "*supporting business processes using methods, techniques and software to design, enact, control and analyze operational processes involving humans, organizations, applications, documents and other sources of information*".

The concept of business process management is not new; technologies designed to improve the efficiency of processes, such as workflow and business process re-engineering tools, have been around for well over a decade (Smith et al, 2003). BPM automates not just the flow of documents, but actions such as obtaining customer information or adding new information about a customer transaction and then generating transactions in multiple systems involved in the business process.

EIE primarily focuses on the global model of the enterprise architecture and its instantiation to partial and particular models. Then BPM, through its technologies, enable the analysis, design and execution of the particular models. However, a method is needed to provide a formal way of implementing both concepts in an interoperable and integrated manner. To underpin this issue, Action Research (AR) is proposed as the basis of the integration of EIE-BPM. As defined by Dick (Dick 2002) "Action research is a spiral process that allows action (change, improvement) and research (understanding and knowledge) to be achieved at the same time". AR is basically performed in four main stages: plan, act, observe and reflect. AR combine problem-solving and research; in this process the reflection is used to review the previous action and plan the next one.

This paper describes how Action Research (AR) provides a methodology to integrate Enterprise Integration Engineering (EIE) and Business Process Management (BPM) in order to achieve the integration of the enterprise modeling and business process to create an enterprise model; a formal structure to generate business knowledge and define a platform to achieve the interoperability between processes.

2. Action Research (AR)

AR is a spiral process and its lifecycle is constituted by the plan, act, observe and reflect stages (see figure 1). During the execution of the lifecycle AR contributes to the practical concerns of people in a problematic situation, pursuing the change and understanding at the same time. AR allows to its practitioners to create a team work environment, a collaborative research team, to be critical and self-critical and to solve problems in a responsible sense. The main characteristics of AR are (Dick 2000):

- Cyclic: Similar steps tend to recur, in a similar sequence;

- Participative: The clients and informants are involved as partners, or at least active participants, in the research process;

- Qualitative: It deals more often with language than with numbers; and

- Reflective: Critical reflection upon the process and outcomes are important parts of each cycle.

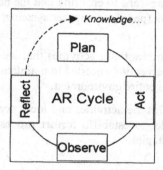

Fig. 1. Action Research cycle

The four main stages of AR are the fundamental steps in a spiraling process where participants in a team work undertake activities to (Kemmis et al,1998):

- Plan: develop a plan of a critical action to improve what is happening.

- Act: act to implement the plan visualized in the previous stage.

- Observe: observe the effects of the critical action in the contexts it occurs.

- Reflect: reflect on the effects caused by the implemented plan as the basis for further planning to start another cycle of AR.

Commonly, Action Research proceeds in this way: the researcher plans one step or complete cycle. Researchers critique their experience and based on this experience they decide what to do for the next cycle, allowing to researchers to alternate between action and critical reflection; during reflection an analysis of what has happened in previous step(s) is carried out, and then the next cycle is planned based on what the researcher is pursuing. The action research not only improved the quality of solutions to problems, but also intentionally built organizational capacity for learning and knowledge sharing.

3. EIE-BPM reference framework components

The framework proposed in this research provides a structured approach for the implementation of EIE and BPM using Action Research as an underlying process life-cycle methodology. It is focused on knowledge generation to achieve a process evolution approach.

The components of the framework are depicted in figure 2. Each of the different components is grouped inside an AR stage that defines guidelines, methodologies and tools to engineer business process changes. The stages are:

- Plan – Provides the guidelines for the structure of the enterprise business processes and how they will be deployed.

- Act – Defines the means to ensuring that the new process is carried out by all participants (people, computer systems, other organizations and other systems).

- Observe – Determines those activities that are focused on the business and technical interventions needed to maintain the health of individual processes and the entire environment.

- Reflect – Identifies the activities and tools needed to analyze business processes in order to establish further process changes based on the organization strategies.

3.1 *Planning stage*

The planning stage intends to build the formal structure of the enterprise through the use of lifecycle concept and reference models. These techniques support the planning stage of the activities that will be performed in next steps of the framework.

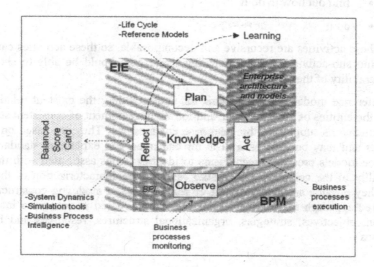

Fig. 2. Action Research's components for EIE and BPM implementation

In this stage the enterprise business processes should be developed within the concept of life-cycle engineering in order to provide an integral approach at the moment that process begin to change as the AR cycles are developed. Due to this, enterprise integration engineering (EIE) provides a set of tools that supports this stage. The concepts of Enterprise life cycle and reference models and architectures are key to set a context for the definition of the planning stage.

Enterprise life cycle engineering is the basis for most of the Enterprise Integration Architectures. A life cycle representation is an excellent model for the methodology that accompanies the architecture in order to create a complete set of tools for engineers who aims to realize an enterprise integration project (Williams et al, 1999).

Life cycle engineering will be used to analyze the entire organization based on a recursive approach. This recursion of the processes is needed due to the evolutive characteristics of AR cycle. Processes recursion can occur in two forms. The first one is the generation form, where one enterprise can produce another enterprise in a repetitive and each enterprise can be represented by its own life cycle. The second one is the hierarchical form; in this way each system is decomposed into subsystems and each subsystem can have a life cycle.

Three types of activities are required to solve issues found within each system life cycle phase. These types are:

- find out what to do.

- find out how to do it.

- do it

All these activities are recursive and decomposable, so these activities can be divided into sub-activities. Thus, modeling languages should be able to shown the interoperability of these activities.

A reference model is a framework for understanding the existent relationships among the entities of the enterprise, and for the development of consistent standards or specifications supporting the enterprise environment. They are based on unified concepts and may be used as a basis for education and explaining standards. The reference models provides mechanisms to identify issues associated with the interoperability of the company and are the base for the characterization of the enterprise; they provide an understanding of requirements, a modeling constructs and a structured approach to describe all the elements involved in enterprise integration (mission, objectives, strategies, organizational structures, resources and business processes).

3.2 *Act stage*

The act stage in BPM is performed when the business process automation is implemented. An execution component (which is mainly the BPM engine), from BPM systems is one of the most important parts of BPM. Without this module, a BPM-System (BPMS) cannot execute a process definition or enable the management of individual executions of the process. As the process flow is executed, the engine may invoke automated services or tasks that should be completed. The services may be provided by applications – legacy and new – or by other enterprises that might be trading partners or outsourcers. The runtime environment maintains the status (state) of each process instance or business event. The flow of data among participants is controlled and sent to the place it is required and in the format it is needed. Process data generated by executing processes is permanently stored, so that people or applications can query the state or structure of process.

At this stage *Business Process Integration* plays a very important role when different enterprises and applications are collaborating. It allows the flow of information and the invocation of application services following the business logic to support the management and execution of common processes that exist in and between enterprises and internal applications. There are some tools that make this happen like workflows and web-services, and also there are standards like RosettaNet, ebXML and BPML that provide a common language for interaction between enterprises and applications (Linthicum 2003).

This stage assures that the new process defined in the planning stage is carried out by corresponding participants. The BPM technical capabilities allow to adjust, to reassign the activities to another participant within the organization. This guarantee that best business practices implemented among the process are executed and not changed during the run time.

3.3 *Observe stage*

In this stage the process execution observation is carried out. This stage is mainly supported by Business Process Monitoring and Business Process Intelligence tools.

Business Process Monitoring applies to both processes and process management systems. The activities involved in monitoring are those related to maintain the health of individual processes and the entire process environment within a company. It includes the tasks needed to keep processes running well in different perspectives, such as information, resources, organizational and technical.

Business Process Intelligence (BPI) allows users to analyze the process execution from a business and information technology (IT) perspective. Business users will be focused on how the processes are successfully executed or to know about how the characteristics of processes did not meet the customer's expectations and what where the causes of it, requiring high-level information. On the other hand, IT analysts will be interested in the details of the processes execution, such as how long it takes to a process to be executed, what were the resources used to execute that process, among others. During this phase BPM solutions give tools to make monitoring on a business process and also to establish measurement rules, and then it's possible to detect bottlenecks and get numeric measurement values about the business process performance.

3.4 *Reflection stage*

During reflection stage some tools such as Business Process Intelligence are used to analyze and evaluate the performance of business processes. This analysis allows to managers to know deeply how the processes are executed and to identify opportunity areas to improve, this means, to reflect how the processes are being executed and then how they could be improved.

Business intelligence (BI) is a set of applications and technologies for gathering, storing, analyzing, and providing access to information and to help enterprise users make better business decisions; this help to predict the future impact of current decisions. The analysis capabilities of BPI can be applied to analyze, design and redesign a process model. With the resultant information it is possible to make a link with the key performance indicators and also identify the gaps between the performance of the process monitored and the business goals. Therefore the utilization of BPI tools and capabilities allow companies to observe the performance of the processes and to make a link between the as-is state and the to-be state of the company.

Analysis tools and guidelines are provided to define three propositions to achieve competitive advantage: product innovation, operational excellence and customer focus (Hope et al, 1997). Based on this statement, business process management is a means by which competitive advantage can be achieved. If so, organizations should be capable to define the guidelines by which their development process will be conducted.

In this framework systems dynamics and discrete event simulation are proposed to be used. The applied theory of system dynamics and dynamic systems modeling method (System dynamics simulation) come primarily from the work of Jay Forrester (Forrester 1980). The simulation models are built based on feedback loops of key performance measures, cause-and-effect models, feedback influences and impacts of effects. Therefore enterprise models of behavior have been developed to demonstrate the effects and impacts of best practices implementation on performance measures (Molina et al, 2003).

Simulation is, as well, a common method used to evaluate (predict) performance (Discrete event simulation). The reason for this is that a quite complex (and realistic) simulation model can be constructed using actors, attributes and events statistics accumulation. Business process simulation is used to evaluate resources usage, predict performance measures such a delivery time, capacity usage, production costs, and production rate, among other important indicators.

System dynamics provide models in such a way that key performance indicators are modeled in a cause-effect way to analyze how the different indicators are interrelated under several scenarios.

After this analysis all the guidelines that the enterprise should follow in order to achieve a competitive advantage are defined. These guidelines must be strategically oriented with the balanced scorecard in order to align these efforts with the strategic objectives.

4. Action Research cycles for knowledge generation

It is important to identify that AR is not a static methodology; in this framework AR is presented as a process evolution approach. That evolution is based in AR iterative characteristic (See figure 3), by means of this a huge amount of knowledge is generated among organization.

During the entire AR cycle, an important amount of knowledge is generated (As shown in figure 3) due to the inherent characteristics of AR, EIE and BPM. The acquired knowledge will provide a basis for the definition of the guidelines for enterprise development that will be included is the next AR cycle.

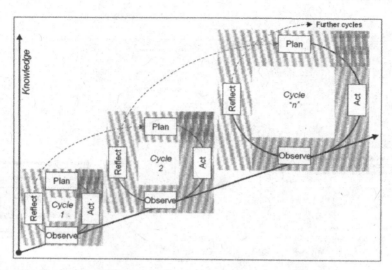

Fig. 3. Action Research cycles evolution.

5. Case Study: Asset Life Cycle Management

The achievement of EIE-BPM strategies are being implemented in a Mexican cement company through a specific project of Asset Life Cycle Management (ALM) implementation. Product Life-cycle Management (PLM) Technologies are being used for production-facilities design and a specific methodology has been instantiated for its industrial execution based on the proposed approach. The performed AR-based methodology is depicted in figure 4.

It is important to remark the location of the Engineering process within the general model of the Enterprise architecture. A *General Model* of the company is developed according to the EIE approach. A *Partial Model* of the specific plant where the project is being implemented is then instantiated, to finally obtain the *Particular Model,* which will be supported by BPM technologies to improve the engineering and design of cement production plants and supported by complementing and domain-specific PLM tools.

The different steps of the AR approach are going to be briefly detailed in the following paragraphs

1) **Plan:** In this Stage, some activities have been developed:

Activity 1. Define the company requirements and gather the information of design process where the consistency level between the drawings and the construction is identified.

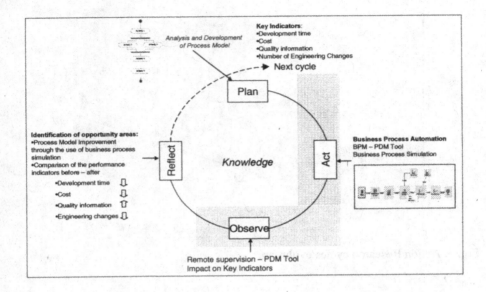

Fig. 4. Methodology for industrial plan development

Activity II. Define a reference model oriented to incorporate all the features of collaboration and coordination tools such as workflow process tools and collaborative design with the suppliers.

Activity III. Prepare a work schedule. The implementation was divided the project in 3 stages. i) Preparation of facilities to perform the project and training for people involved. ii) Gathering of plant information; transfer from 2D to 3D models of the most usual plant components. iv) Implementation of a methodology to structure all the information.

Key performance indicators have been established in order to monitor the performance of the process; these indicators are related to time, quality and information.

2) Act Stage: A Product Data Management (PDM) tool is used to support this stage. The tool provides the support to create a process model based on the reference process model defined in the plan stage. Also by using this tool it is possible to automate the designed process using the BPM engine contained in the PDM tool and to create an environment for collaborative design.

3) Observe Stage: In this stage a monitoring activity is performed based on the performance of key indicators established in the plan stage and implemented in the Act stage. These indicators improved their performance level during the project implementation: reducing costs, reducing engineering changes and improving the quality of the available information for the engineers involved.

4) Reflection stage: At this point of the *first* AR cycle a deep reflection is being carried out and the identified benefits are analyzed together with the company's responsible team. A deep analysis of the designed business process is achieved in order to identify what main changes impacted on the performance of the indicators. Business process simulation tool is used in order to validate those changes and to predict how they can impact on the performance indicators.

When reflection stage is concluded, the first cycle of AR can be closed and a new set of activities can be defined for a new cycle. Some discoveries can be obtained such as inefficient engineering procedures, which delay engineering launches or future maintenance process due to a not well structured documentation management. A final reflection is the demonstrated benefits of using parametric 3D modeling for collaborative design and engineering of cement facilities.

6. Conclusions and further research

The key element in Enterprise Integration Engineering and Business Process Management is knowledge; because of this the proposed research approach aims to create a spiral cycle where the knowledge is created in the company to manage changes and to integrate new business technologies.

There is a need for better practices of knowledge acquisition, visualization and use in manufacturing companies; it is important to develop new methodologies, strategies and tools that allow the enterprise integration through the use of reference models, documentation to evaluate possible changes in business processes. Action Research provides this approach to analyze, evaluate and combine EIE/BPM to integrate the enterprise. The four main stages of Action Research allow the integration of the reference framework of Enterprise Integration Engineering with its tools and also the integration of new technological applications such as those provided by Business Process Management.

New methods and techniques for managing change in connection with process redesign have been proposed. This paper show how participatory action research, combined with EIE and BPM offers a fruitful approach for getting the most out of work-based research and learning. In future work the results of the implementation of this approach will be presented.

The manufacturing industry is evolving from a labor intensive orientation into a knowledge-based industry, since this industry is not distinguished any more by its low wages it used to pay. This is particularly true in companies located in Mexico. Because of this, it is necessary to develop a new research approach that allows the creation of new knowledge in the enterprise in order to be competitive in the new manufacturing environment. Therefore the proposed EIE – BPM frameworks seems to be an excellent alternative to explore how a learning process can be achieved during change management process in manufacturing companies.

Acknowledgements

The research reported in this paper is part of the CEMEX's EIE-BPM Grant and Mechatronics Chair of Tecnológico de Monterrey, Campus Monterrey. The authors wish to acknowledge the support of this grant in the preparation of the manuscript, the "IBM - SUR Grant" and ECOLEAD for their funding and support in the development of the case study.

References

Aalst, W.M.P. van der; Hofstede, A. H.M. ter; and Weske, M. (2003). *Business Process Management: A Survey*. In: Conference on BMP,   Aalst, W.M.P. van der, et.al. (Ed), pp.1-12, Springer-Verlag, Berlin Heidelberg 2003.

Dick , B.(2002). "Action research: action and research" In the seminar: *"Doing good action research"* held at Southern Cross University, February 18, 2002

Dick , B.(2000). "A beginner's guide to action research" [On line].   Available at http://www.uq.net.au/action_research/arp/guide.html, 2000.

Forrester, J. (1980). Principles of systems : text and workbook. Cambridge, Mass.; MIT, 1980.

Hope J., and Hope T. (1997).   Competing in the Third Wave, Boston: *Harvard Business School Press*

Kemmis, S. and McTaggart, R (Eds.). (1988) *"The Action Research Planner"* (3rd ed.). Geelong: Deakin University. 1988.

Linthicum D (2003). *Next Generation Application Integration: From Simple Information to Web Services*. Pages 55-62. Addison-Wesley, Boston, Massachusetts, USA

Molina A. and Medina V. (2003). Application of Enterprise Models and Simulation Tools for the evaluation of the impact of best manufacturing practices implementation. *Annual Reviews in Control*, Vol 27/2, 2003, 221-228

Molina A., Garza J., Jiménez G (2004). Enterprise integration engineering as an enabler for business process management. *Proceedings og the International Conference en Enterprise Integration and Modelling*, ICEIMT.

Smith, H. and Fingar P. (2003). *Business Process Management The third wave*. pages 82-85. Meghan-Kiffer Press, Tampa, Florida, USA

Williams, T.J., Li, H. and Bernus P. (1999). The Life Cycle of an Enterprise. *In: Handbook of Life Cycle Engineering*, Molina, A. et. al.   (Ed), pp.153-180, Kluwer Academic, Dordrecht, Netherlands, 1998.

An Architecture for Managing Distributed Business Processes in Networked Organizations

Rubén Darío Franco*, Víctor Anaya*, Ángel Ortiz*

*Research Centre on Production Management and Engineering
Universidad Politécnica de la Innovación
Ciudad Politécnica de la Innovación, Edificio 8G, Acceso D
Camí de Vera S/N, Valencia, Spain

dfranco@cigip.upv.es
vanaya@cigip.upv.es
aortiz@omp.upv.es

ABSTRACT: *Service-Oriented Architectures are used for supporting inter-organizational business processes inside networks of companies by composing web services on demand.*

Although these kinds of initiatives in most of cases are lead by major companies, the INPREX project (Spanish acronym for Interoperability in Extended Processes) falls out this category. By contrast, this is an undergoing initiative leaded by a Small and Medium Enterprise (SME) and founded by a local government in Spain.

In this work, we introduce the IDIERE Platform which has been designed for supporting three major requirements of networked enterprises: openness, flexibility and dynamism when deploying and executing distributed business processes.

KEY WORDS: *Distributed BPM, Production Planning, SOA,*

1. Introduction

Collaborative Networked Organizations (CNO) are enabling new ways of conducting business transactions between their members (Franco, 2003). As organizational form, they tie together two o more companies that had understood the benefits of conducting win-win partnerships coming from such collaborative environments (Camarinha-Matos, et al, 2001, Ortiz, et. al 2003).

From this point of view, within such a collaborative environment and although every organisation keeps its independency and control over its own activities, there is always an interdependence that gives it the vision of a unique entity, but certainly increases interoperability requirements in order to preserve the vision of single entity facing new market opportunities.

When adopting this emerging approach, extended functionality needs to be designed and deployed to reach such levels of interaction. Collaborative, Extended or Distributed Business Process are terms used to name a set of activities that, in such context, need to be carried out in order to accomplish some commonly agreed business goal.

New technologies, mainly those related to the Internet are enabling the deployment of global business processes and facilitating, at the same time, the interoperability of the information systems in which they are supported.

INPREX is an undergoing initiative founded by the Office for Science and Technology of the Spanish Government One of the main objective is the deployment of a platform (called IDIERE) that, taking advantage of web services and their orchestration, enables the engineering, deployment, execution and monitoring of distributed business processes in a network of companies surrounding one SME stamping firm in the automotive sector, situated in Valencia, Spain.

Here, we are going to present a two-folded architecture that in one hand present the main tools that will compose the IDIERE platform, that is the main applications that will run over the platform to achieve the project's pursued goals; and in the other hand the software components that will be compose to form the main applications.

The paper is structured as follows: Section 2 depicts how the service-oriented architectures support Distributed Business Process Management. Then, in Section 3, the IDIERE Platform is presented, that is, its architecture and the software components that implement the architecture. Finally, in Section 4, we state some conclusions that we are gaining when developing this project.

2. Distributed Business Processes Management and Service-Oriented Architectures

We understand that the best way to manage enterprises is a process-centric approach. Although the companies that are part of the project keep a vertical organization arrangement (with a departmental splitting of the organization),

IDIERE keeps the well-know idea of end-to-end processes crossing these vertical boundaries. This approach has leaded to a new situation where inter-organizational relationships management has become a new competitive advantage by itself. Depending on how well those external relationships (mainly in terms of information flows) can be optimized, higher efficiency and reactivity degree may be expected.

In order to realise such vision, we need a paradigm shifting inside organizations in order to consider that business and technological perspectives are two faces of the same coin. Service Oriented Architectures promise capabilities for solving this dilemma.

Web Services practices can be defined as the provision of services over electronic networks (Rust, 2002). The concept, that encompasses any kind of possible electronic relationship like business to business (B2B), business to consumer (B2C) or government to any of the above, can be applied to all kinds of organisation involved in a CNO.

Relaying on emergent Internet technologies, so named Service-Oriented Architectures are allowing to see the Internet not merely as a communication channel but also as support of more complex activities tied, for instance, to purchasing, personnel recruiting or customer service, for instance.

Business requirements and the Internet are moving towards a third stage where the applications are conceived as a single user graphic interface but whose functionality is composed of computational capabilities on the client side combined with a set of invocations to provided services (Britton, 2001).

The main changes provided by service oriented architectures are:

-   The capability of narrowing down the gap existing between the modelling and the operational phases of the business process management, because we are able to reduce the gap using BPEL (synonym of BPEL4WS) to link the business process modelling world and the web-services world. BPEL is explicitly designed to work with Web services and provide coordination and integration of business services into higher-level business processes.

-   The emerging web-services technologies (mainly XML, SOAP, WSDL, UDDI and BPEL4WS) supporting the service-oriented architecture are wide-spread and well-accepted by service-oriented tool.

-   Web Services permit a loose decoupling between functionality and executors (Mowshowitz, 1999) so they provide a higher dynamicity

Based on Service-Oriented Architectures (here in after, SOA) principles, has been proposed (Franco et al, 2004) that web services interfaces are able of encapsulating activities, or sub processes, of a business process definition, and then, support composition and execution of their instances.

3. The IDIERE Platform

The IDIERE Platform relays on SOA capabilities in order to automate business process execution and monitoring. The platform provides a set of components allowing users to be involved in several business process instances of execution.

The principle is straightforward: it works as any workflow management system does but, at the same time, it provides different levels of automation when needed. Such levels of automation are supported by corresponding web services interfaces.

As was stated in (Franco et al, 2004), each web service interface that is defined inside the platform may encapsulate a whole process, a sub-process or a single activity. After that, each modelled execution unit is then assigned to several executors that will carry out them in order to reach the execution thread's goal (i.e. the process goal).

At this point, we introduce the term executor as each organizational resource that has the capability of performing some part of the process by providing a service interface that can be discovered, reached and consumed by other executors or systems. Then, a lot of executors exist inside a CNO: different companies, workers (that interact with services interfaces), machines or devices, for instance

In terms of the platform, two main building blocks have been identified: process with different abstraction levels (named execution units) and who will be in charge of their execution.

IDIERE Platform is the information system that supports distributed business process management capabilities by providing a set of components that allows creating and maintaining a centralised set of repositories of processes, executors and exchanged messages in each process's instance.

3.1. *The IDIERE Architectural View*

Although the system supports distributed business process enactment, the IDIERE Platform isn't P2P oriented. Instead of this, it is composed of two major components: a central server which stores process's definitions and orchestrate activities' execution and a set of clients which assume different roles along process' life cycle.

More precisely, inside the platform it's possible to identify:

- The IDIERE Server: it supports two major phases: process engineering and execution. It allows defining collaborative business processes structure, storing them in a common repository, registering executors, assigning execution method and executors to individual activities or sub processes, monitoring delegated activities, deploying a set of indicators for performance measurement.

- Client-side: in terms of users, there would be a set of nodes which may be connected to the platform in order to notify each assignment's status. Each node represents the instantiation of one executor for each process instance. Correspondingly, each deployed thin client, will act as Task Manager for the system but having some extended functionality.

Initially, we have defined three different kinds of users that will access the platform that is, users that will interact with the platform in order to: manage processes, accept or reject assignments, or status reporting. The types of user identified are:

- Organization: the Organization user initially will act as any company that provides some service to a process: by means of its Task Manager, it will provide a service interface that may be located and accessed by the server when needed in order to accomplish some automated task. When Workers are present, Organization is able of delegating such work to one of them.

- Workers are nodes belonging to an Organization. A Worker is a Task Manager also but with a simplified functionality in terms of capabilities for delegating tasks or accepting offers, for instance. Organization is able of adding their workers by registering them into the system. Once this process has been completed, tasks can be delegated to these nodes.

- Individual: finally, it represents individuals not belonging to any organization but, once registered, will be able of get involved in some transactions inside the platform.

Figure 1 shows a specific configuration of users that combines Organizations, Workers and Individuals accessing the IDIERE server.

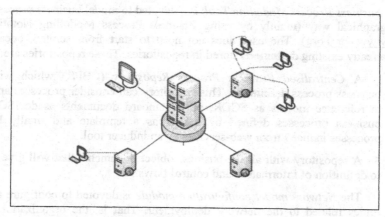

Figure 1. *Users accessing the IDIERE server*

3.2. The IDIERE Software Architecture

Figure 2 presents the building blocks (software modules, applications and databases) and the relationship between them.

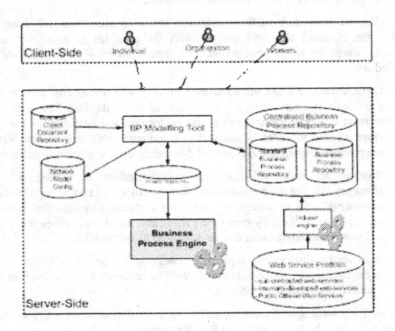

Figure 1. *The IDIERE Architectural View*

On the server-side, the architecture is mainly composed of:

- A *Business Process Modelling Tool*: it's devoted to model business processes in a graphical way (mainly by using Business Process Modelling Notation, see www.bpmi.org). The user does not need to start from scratch, because the already existing definitions stored in repositories. These repositories are:

    - A *Centralised Business Process Repository* (CBPR) which will store business process definitions. This repository can consider processes appearing in reference models as SCOR, or in standard documents as de ISO series; business processes defined by a user as a template and finally business processes induced from web-services by an inducer tool.

    - A repository with all the business object documents that will give support to definition of information and control flows.

    - The *Network model configuration module* is devoted to configure all those topics related to the network deployment. That is, the organization model, executors' permissions or additional parameters.

- The *Business Process Engine* is responsible of executing and monitoring process' instances. Consequently, it considers the enterprise models released by the business process modelling tool and it is able to execute and monitor them. By assigning each execution unit to the corresponding executor.
- *Web Services Portfolio* within which all active web services definitions that may be used to compose a business process will be registered. There will be three kind of services: sub-contracted with third parties (outside of the CNO), internally deployed (owned by the core members) and additionally those services that the CNO will able to provide to third parties to be consumed.
- The *inducer engine* is capable of inducing business process templates from existing web-services definitions.

3.3. *The IDIERE Platform Components*

In this section we depict the component design of each application running on the platform (see Fig. 3).

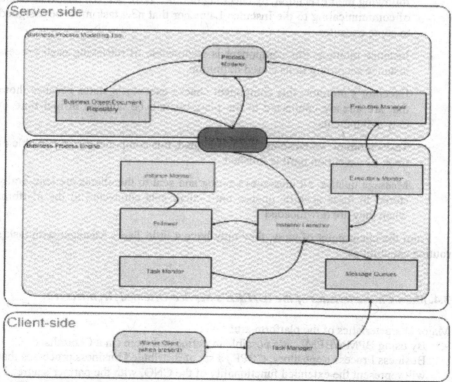

Figure 3. *Major components of the IDIERE Platform*

At the server side, major components are:

Process Modeler: mainly used at the design time in order to create business process definitions by composing web services definitions that are already stored in the WS Portfolio. Such definitions will be stored in the CBP Repository. Additionally, and depending on the parameters of the Network Model Configuration, it will be able of defining for each activity (or sub-process) the execution method and executors' selection process.

- Executors manager: this module allows to define the CNO structure in terms of roles and members which belongs to them.

- Instance Launcher: when some client requests a process execution, the Instance Launcher gets all related information (process structure and executors) from repositories and initiates it when security controls are passed.

- Follower: once instances are running, the Follower it's responsible of following their execution, by checking out the "next" step of the process and of communicating to the Instance Launcher that new task must be assigned to some executor.

- Instance monitor: this component is responsible of retrieving each process instance according to its stored definition.

- Executor's monitor: this component checks executor's status because those that are already connected to the platform will be notified in real time of new assignments.

- Tasks monitor: when some task is assigned, this component is responsible of track its execution until is finished.

- Message queues: all messages coming and sent to the clients are temporally stored in these specific queues until client gets connected to the platform when they are downloaded.

From the client point of view, they only have a little Tasks Manager with task's routing capabilities.

3.4. *Main Characteristics of the IDIERE's Service-Oriented Architecture*

Major characteristics of the platform are:
- By using BPMN/BPML, it's possible to define and store (in a Centralised Business Process Repository, CBPR) a set of distributed business processes that will represent the extended functionality of the CNO, with the partner's agreed level of abstraction.
Refinement of any previously defined activity or sub processes by replacing its

definition by a more detailed one. Validation mechanisms to cross-check interfaces are provided.

- A repository of Business Object Documents that will be used in such process definitions not only for information exchange but also for control monitoring.
- To define, for each activity, a method for selecting their executor and, correspondingly, dynamic method (direct offer, direct or reverse auction, request for quotation) for selecting them.
- Register a set of executors that will be able of operating in the system.
- Managing, by the use of the User Modeller, different kind of executors (Organization, Worker or Individual), and allowing former creation of their own internal tree of execution.
- Allow registered executors to launch and monitor some instance of a business process stored in the CBPR.
- Provide each executor of a client that plays the Task Executor's role by interfacing the Process Server with the internal clients.
- Deploying a set of Key Performance Indicators measuring the overall performance.

4. Conclusions

In this work we have presented advances in the work carried out within the IDIERE Project. We have introduced the IDIERE Service-Oriented Architecture, and have defined the main components that implement it.

The project looks for deploy a low-cost, dynamic, flexible and extensible platform within which a set of companies can be able of design and execute inter-organizational business processes by dynamically composing a sequence of services invocations.

We strongly rely on Service Oriented Architectures as a medium for enabling Small and Medium Enterprises get involved in this kind of initiatives. By adopting standards related to the Internet (Web Services stack for Communications, current initiatives like OAGIS for content and BPMN/BPML for modelling) we have composed a framework that is open, flexible and dynamic.

Regarding the project, it could be convenient to point out that currently there are a lot of initiatives concerning business process management by using web services composition, but real undergoing implementations being carried out by SMEs are not so usual. Currently, we are at the development stage of major components.

Acknowledgments

The INPREX (Interoperability of Extended Enterprise Processes) is project founded by Science and Technology inter-ministerial committee that is an agency within the research department of Spain.

5. References

Britton, C. *IT Architectures and Middleware: Strategies for Building Large, Integrated Systems.* Addison-Wesley. 2001

Camarinha-Matos, L. and Afsarmanesh, H. (2001). Dynamic Virtual Organizations, or Not So Dynamic? BASYS Proceedings pp 111-124. 2001

Franco, R.D., Ortiz, A., Anaya, V. and Lario F.C. IDR: *A proposal for managing inter-organizational business processes by using service oriented architectures.* In PRO-VE '04 Proceedings. Kluver Academic Publishers. 2004

Mowshowitz, A. The switching principle in virtual organization, *Virtual Organization Net eJOV*, vol. 1, no. 1, pp. 6-17. 1999

Ortiz, A., Franco R.D. y Alba, M. *V-CHAIN: Migrating from Extended to Virtual Enterprise within an Automotive Supply Chain.* PROVE'03 Proceedings. Processes and Foundations for Virtual Organizations. 2003

Rust, R.T. and Kannan, P.K. *E-Service: New Directions in Theory and Practice.* ME Sharpe, Armonk, New York 2002

Issues for Utilizing and Enabling the Global Semantic Web for Enterprise Integration

Terje Wahl, Rune Molden, Guttorm Sindre

Department of Computer and Information Science,
Norwegian University of Science and Technology,
Sem Sælands vei 7-9, N-7491 Trondheim, Norway
terje.wahl@idi.ntnu.no
rune.molden@idi.ntnu.no
guttorm.sindre@idi.ntnu.no

ABSTRACT: *Enterprises need Enterprise Integration (EI) of systems to stay competitive. The Web is often used to attain EI, but so far little efficiency has been achieved. The Semantic Web (SW) envisions solving many problems regarding this approach. This paper presents some important issues that must be resolved if the vision of the global SW is to become a reality. The higher layers of the SW have yet to be fully standardized, and many undecided issues exist within the areas of logic, proof, trust and security. Many of these issues arise due to the heterogeneous, highly distributed and large scale nature of the envisioned SW. Some important issues that need to be addressed are how to create semantic data sources, robust reasoning, agent coordination, semantic interoperability, trust and security. The SW definitely has potential for easing the task of EI, but has limitations on its current usability. The WISEMOD project will provide improved workflow modelling techniques and methodology to further improve the utilization of the SW for EI.*

1. Introduction

A trend in the global market is the increase of collaboration among enterprises and rapid changes in the organisational structure (ATHENA, 2005). Enterprises transform themselves into "networked organizations" in order to boost their flexibility and reduce costs (ATHENA, 2005). To achieve this, enterprises need to interact with a community of buyers, sellers and partners, and thus enterprise information systems and application need to be interoperable in order to achieve seamless business interaction across organizational boundaries (ATHENA, 2005). This further requires some effort in Enterprise Integration (EI), or more specifically in Enterprise Application Integration (EAI).

The Web is a well suited channel for interaction between different parts of an enterprise. However, it is a hinder to EI that most of the current content of the Web is understandable only to humans. In addition, it is often difficult to find relevant information when searching on the Web. Business applications are abundant on the Web, but when they want to communicate with each other autonomously, they need proprietary interconnections that are relatively difficult to develop and maintain.

The Semantic Web (SW) envisions solving these problems by transforming the Web into the SW. This will be done by adding structure and semantic information to the content of Web-pages (Berners-Lee *et al.*, 2001). This will enable machines to understand and reason about information on the Web in a generalized manner. There are however many obstacles that need to be overcome before the SW can become a reality. This paper will present some of these issues, their present status, and how they relate to EI.

Section 2 introduces the main current SW technologies, with subsections on RDF, RDF-S, ontology languages (OWL) and reasoning. Section 3 introduces the field of EI. Section 4 focuses on issues hindering the utilization of the global SW, especially within the areas of creating semantic data sources, ontologies, reasoning, agents, trust and security. Section 5 discusses implications that SW has to EI, and Section 6 relates this to the WISEMOD project. The conclusion is in Section 7.

2. Current Semantic Web Technologies

The SW is an extension of the current Web, in which information is given well-defined meaning. This will enable computers and people to cooperate in better ways (Berners-Lee *et al.*, 2001). The SW will be highly decentralized because it must be highly scalable to have a global reach. The creation/management of content may be done by almost anyone.

2.1. The Semantic Web Tower

The architecture of the SW can be represented in the form of a tower of specifications and languages layering on top of each other, like in (Patel-Schneider, 2003):

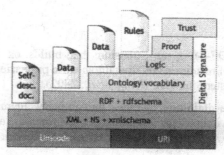

Figure 1. *"The Semantic Web Tower" as presented in (Patel-Schneider, 2003), and originally presented by Tim Berners-Lee at the XML 2000 conference*

On the bottom layer is Unicode and URI. Unicode is a standard for specifying characters and thus create a text. URI is used to specify the location of resources. XML is a standard way of structuring text with self-defined tags. Resource Description Framework (RDF) and RDF-Schema (RDF-S) is based on XML, and allows specifying semantic metadata in a document, e.g. in a HTML-document.

If terms used in RDF-descriptions are explained in ontologies, one can examine the connection between different terms in more advanced ways than with RDF-S. Logic reasoners may be built on top of this to reason on the SW, so that (more or less robust) proofs can be found when querying the SW. Trust is an issue on top of all this, because in the distributed and heterogeneous environment of the SW, it is often important to know who you can trust about the information they provide. Digital signatures should be used across many of the layers in this tower to offer a mechanism of providing trust in a secure way. Security for the SW in general is an issue that cuts across all the layers (Ferrari, 2004).

2.2. RDF

While XML is a standard mechanism to structure data, the Resource Description Framework (RDF) is a mechanism to give meaning to data by telling something about it (Ding, *et al.*, 2002).

The RDF data model consists of statements about resources, by using *object-attribute-value* triples. An object is a resource - that is anything that can be identified by a URI, e.g. a webpage, a part of a web-page or a book (URIs doesn't have to specify only resources available on the Web). Values are resources or text strings. For example, the triple "http://www.idi.ntnu.no/~terje, author, 'Terje' " would mean that Terje is the author of the webpage located at the specified URI. In this example, "author" is the *attribute*. Attributes are also called properties (Ding, *et al.*, 2002).

2.3. RDF-S

RDF-Schema (RDF-S) is an extension that builds on RDF. It allows the definition of classes of resources and domain-specific properties, and can be thought of as a simple type system for RDF (Ding, *et al.*, 2002).

RDF-S allows the definition of class and property hierarchies. It also allows *range* statements restricting legal combinations of properties and classes, and other statements like the *type* statement, which is used to declare instances of a class (Ding, *et al.*, 2002).

When combined, RDF and RDF-S can be thought of as a simple ontology language. But it is still limited with regards to areas such as the number of modelling primitives and logical semantics (Ding, *et al.*, 2002). For this, richer ontology languages should be used on top of RDF and RDF-S, like OWL, which is presented in the next section.

2.4. Ontology Languages

In (Gruber, 1993), an *ontology* is defined as "a formal, explicit specification of a shared conceptualization". The purpose of ontologies is to explain the understanding of concepts and terms relevant to a given domain (Gruber, 1993).

The markup provided by RDF and ontologies enables the creation of systems that can answer complicated questions that cannot be answered by looking at only one webpage (Berners-Lee, 2001).

Two examples of ontology languages are DAML and OIL. Features of these two languages have been combined to form the specification for OWL. OWL became a W3C recommendation in February 2004.

2.4.1. OWL

Web Ontology Language (OWL) is an ontology language intended for use on the Web. It is specifically designed for use on the SW, and uses URI and RDF as a basis. OWL allows ontologies to be distributed, it scales like the SW should do, and is an open and extensible standard.

As stated in (W3C, 2005): "OWL builds on RDF and RDF Schema and adds more vocabulary for describing properties and classes: among others, relations between classes (e.g. disjointness), cardinality (e.g. "exactly one"), equality, richer typing of properties, characteristics of properties (e.g. symmetry), and enumerated classes."

As stated in (W3C, 2005), OWL has three sublanguages: OWL Lite, OWL Description Logics (OWL DL) and OWL Full. These three specifications each add increasing expressiveness.

OWL Lite mainly supports classification hierarchies and simple constraints. OWL DL is as expressive as possible without losing computational completeness and decidability. OWL Full provides great syntactic flexibility and expressive power, but as a consequence it is probably not possible to create reasoners that provide computational guarantees when using OWL Full.

OWL Full is an extension of RDF-S. OWL Lite and OWL DL are not, because they require restricted use of RDF and RDF-S to be built on top of it.

2.5. Reasoning

Reasoning on the SW will be done by inference engines that use logic to process queries and provide (hopefully provable) results to users. Inference engines may be implemented into software agents that act autonomously and communicate with other software agents.

Inference services on the SW are equivalent of SQL query engines for relational databases, but provide more powerful support (Patel-Schneider, 2002). Two examples of inference engines are Ontobroker and FaCT (Fast Classification of Terminologies). These systems help building new ontologies and provide advanced information access and navigation (Patel-Schneider, 2002).

3. Enterprise Integration

In (Quirchmayr, 2003), Lim, Juster and de Pennington define EI as: "The task of improving the performance of complex organisations by managing the interactions among the participants. In addition, EI also concentrates on systems integration, made possible by using computer communication networks and protocols such as Ethernet and TCP/IP, as well as application integration usually based on shared data and data exchange formats". Further, they point out two principal types of EI, inter-enterprise and intra-enterprise integration. The former is concerned with the integration of locally distributed business units, while the latter deals with integration of customers, suppliers, sub-contractors and other distributed business units.

In (Croke, 2004), these important reasons why EI is necessary are pointed out:

– replacing old systems for purposes of increasing functionality or maintainability,

− restructuring of companies to optimize performance through centralising or decentralising activities,

− merging with other companies,

− companies divesting themselves of business they no longer consider core or profitable, and they also acquire new companies where they see potential,

− change of which activities are done internally and which are done by a supplier,

− change in distribution strategy, e.g. by using the Internet as a sales channel.

There are currently several technical approaches to enable EAI, which is an important part of EI. Some of these are CORBA, J2EE, .NET and Web Service technologies like BPEL4WS, and data exchange standard formats like Electronic Data Interchange (EDI) and XML-based standard formats. They are utilized for both inter and intra-enterprise integration.

4. Issues

This chapter goes through some issues that need to be solved before the SW can be fully utilized on a global scale.

4.1. Creating Semantic Data Sources

Data sources for the SW may be represented in several ways, but the most common method will probably be enriching HTML-coded documents with semantic information in the form of RDF tags, and some times referring to ontologies contained in external documents.

The effectiveness of software agents that process information from the SW will increase exponentially as more semantically annotated webpages and automated services become available (Berners-Lee, et al., 2001). At the same time, the incentive to semantically enrich webpages and to create agents depends of the relative immediate usefulness of it. This may create a "vicious circle".

There are several ways to create data sources for the SW. One might semantically enrich Web-pages by manual adding of semantic information, but this consumes a lot of time and resources. In addition, there is the issue of user friendliness. Non-technical or untrained users need simple methods and GUI to perform this task. Fully automatic or semi-automatic methods for semantically enriching Web resources are being researched (Rinaldi, et al., 2003). In (Handschuh, 2003), a framework is presented for support of semantic annotation of both static and dynamic webpages. Their approach for annotation of dynamic webpages assume that web sites wish to make their information available on the SW, and thus they see little difficulty in requiring some server-side programming to annotate webpages that are e.g. generated based on some database information. However, further discussion of this topic is beyond the scope of this paper.

4.2. Ontologies

It will be easier to cooperate between agents if a common representation model is decided upon (Aberer, *et al.*, 2004). Currently there exist many standards for writing ontologies. It is possible to implement translations between these languages, but the W3C recommendation of OWL is helpful to speed up the deployment of the SW.

There is a trade-off between expressive power and efficiency among different modelling languages in large scale distributed systems such as the SW. It is difficult to support robust reasoning over schemas such as OWL, which has relatively powerful expressiveness. The simpler RDF-standard makes it easier to do reasoning, but is still quite flexible and support rich semantics (Aberer, *et al.*, 2004). Reasoning based on RDF might therefore be an alternative until more robust reasoners for OWL emerge.

4.3. Reasoning

The SW will be as decentralized as possible. This versatility will lead to paradoxes and unanswerable questions when trying to reason based on the SW. SW researchers accept that this is a price that has to be paid to achieve versatility (Berners-Lee, *et al.*, 2001). But this makes it much harder to do robust reasoning on the SW.

Reasoning on the SW has not yet been fully realized. Current prototypes seem to compromise on either Knowledge Representation principles and capabilities, or scale and distributiveness (Kalfoglou, *et al.*, 2004). To fully utilize the SW, one must successfully provide robust reasoning over distributed resources.

Robust reasoning is closely related to *soundness* and *completeness*. First-order logic (FOL) is well established in the field of knowledge representation and reasoning (KRR), and has had some success of providing robust reasoners for these earlier systems. Standardisation of SW technologies has so far resulted in the ontology-language OWL (among other standards), which is also based on this foundation of FOL (Kalfoglou, *et al.*, 2004). But this might be a problem because of the envisioned size and diversity of the SW. Without centralized control, inconsistency will exist. It must probably be accepted that reasoners sometimes will give a wrong answer to a query. Also, it will be hard to require answers to queries to be complete, because we can seldom spend the time or resources to examine *all* the information on the SW to answer each query. Thus incompleteness must probably also be accepted (Matthews, 2004)). Locality is a component of the emergent SW, because it will be gradually built up from a large number of small local interactions. Many agents operating on the SW are going to be autonomous and not centrally coordinated. The SW will also have a lot of randomness, because nodes may change, fail or disconnect at different times. This locality, autonomy and randomness make robust reasoning harder, because they affect global integrity and completeness of the SW (Aberer, *et al.*, 2004).

Automated reasoners must be able to deal with broken or dead semantic links, because they are bound to exist on the SW with its many diverse information providers. Inference engines must be able to handle this if they are to be successful at providing quality answers to queries.

If we can know which resources we can trust (and hence which resources are the most useful) on the SW, it would be simpler to build a robust reasoner. For the SW, this might be implemented by some sort of automated mechanism for trust. The literature suggests that this issue of trust can be solved in combination with the use of software agents (Kalfoglou, *et al.*, 2004). But there are many issues associated with these aspects, as seen in the next chapters.

4.4. Agents

Software Agents in various forms will be used to collect and process information on the SW (Berners-Lee, *et al.*, 2001). They will be able to communicate and cooperate by exchanging information containing semantic markup (Berners-Lee, *et al.*, 2001). It may however be challenging to accomplish this task. This problem is associated with semantic interoperability, because if two agents with two separate representations of the domain want to communicate, they need some kind of mapping between their vocabularies and their meaning (Kalfoglou, *et al.*, 2004). As stated in (Kalfoglou, *et al.*, 2004), "This must be done automatically if the agents are to cooperate autonomously in the SW".

4.4.1. Semantic Interoperability

There exist several suggestions on how to overcome this problem of semantic interoperability. One solution might be to use a standard upper ontology, or to provide mapping or merging between some terms in two or more ontologies (Kalfoglou, *et al.*, 2004).

Several suggestions for such "top-level" ontologies have been created. Examples are Cyc and IEEE's Standard Upper Ontology. These are especially helpful for smaller applications, but if some of these standard upper ontologies were to be used for the SW, it would limit its distributiveness and decentralisation. This suggests that the use of ontology mappings would be preferable for the SW (Kalfoglou, *et al.*, 2004). Ontology mappings may however not be enough to achieve successful knowledge sharing between agents. Erroneous results may be produced if the inference engines of two communicating agents are based on different logic systems, e.g. inference logic versus relevance logic. Such an error may therefore arise even if the agents use the same ontologies on their knowledge bases (Kalfoglou, *et al.*, 2004). A suggested solution to this issue is that agents negotiate or at least communicate which logical system is used. Another suggestion is to use an information-theoretic approach, e.g. that of Barwise and Seligman's channel theory. Their suggested approach takes into account different understandings of semantic terms, and allows ontology mappings explaining different use of terms in different contexts related to local concepts (Kalfoglou, *et al.*, 2004).

4.4.2. Agent Communication Infrastructure

To be able to communicate and reason about semantic information, one must be able to locate resources at the network. The mechanism for doing this should be decentralized, since the SW itself aims at being so, to facilitate good scalability (Aberer, *et al.*, 2004). P2P-systems use more or less decentralized communication infrastructures, and consequently the architecture of agent communication infrastructure might be inspired by these systems' architectures. There are three main directions of design in P2P-systems to do decentralized resource location (Aberer, *et al.*, 2004):

1. Unstructured P2P-systems that are based on gossiping techniques.

2. Hierarchical P2P-systems that have specialized superpeers responsible for routing.

3. Structured P2P-systems based on distributed hash tables.

The third approach combines efficient search and maintenance without using centralized components. But it is still an open issue what method(s) will be used for the SW in the future. Load balancing is also an undecided issue regarding these P2P-systems (Aberer, *et al.*, 2004).

4.5. Trust

Traditionally, trust has not been an issue in knowledge-based systems, because these systems have not been highly distributed. But on the SW, where almost anyone or anything can be a source of information, trust becomes an issue (Kalfoglou, *et al.*, 2004). Matthews (2004) asks: "How can trust be modelled and exchanged between agents and SW services? Where should trust annotations be stored and made available? What kind of knowledge is required to measure trust and where will this knowledge come from? What trust features need to be considered (e.g. subjectivity, propagations, transitivity)? And how do they affect trust in general?" Some work has been done to create a conceptual model of trust (Kalfoglou, *et al.*, 2004). This is helpful, but how should this be used to implement trust in the SW? This is still an open issue, but there exist some suggestions. One approach is to implement trust as an extension of an existing system, but this might not be very efficient. It is argued that trust needs to be added to the system design process, and that "there is a clear need for semantic language support for representing trust" (Kalfoglou, *et al.*, 2004). There exist some emerging standards (such as SOAP security extension), but none of this work has reached far enough to be able to represent trust in an efficient manner (Kalfoglou, *et al.*, 2004).

4.5.1. The Source of Trust Information

It is not yet decided if trust should be centrally controlled and managed, or if it should be distributed such that many agents may contain trust information and share this among them. There have been several prototypes that suggest some kind of centralized server for storing trust information. This raises the questions if the agents or users providing information regarding trust to this service can be trusted, and if the trust service itself can be trusted. Another issue is that centralized systems in a highly distributed setting tend to have limitations to scalability (Kalfoglou, *et al.*, 2004).

4.5.2. How to Measure Trust

The question of how to measure trust is still an open issue. Such a measurement could be based on the experience of agents, but the concrete measure of this and how this information can be distributed is still an open issue (Kalfoglou, *et al.*, 2004). Also, when you want to measure trust in a diverse system like the SW, trust needs to be measured in a context. For example, you may trust an agent to recommend a good restaurant, but not to perform payment services on your behalf. This makes the measure of trust even more complex and harder to compute (Kalfoglou, *et al.*, 2004).

4.6. Security

Little research has been conducted on security for the SW, in contrast to many other areas within the SW (Ferrari, 2004). There is a need to establish methods to avoid unauthorized access and malicious modifications on the SW. Privacy also needs to be retained. In (Ferrari, 2004) it is argued that security needs to be inserted into the system from the beginning, and not added to it afterwards. If the SW is to be secure, all its layers (as shown in Figure 1) need to be secure. Secure interoperability must also be ensured. There currently exist security mechanisms for TCP/IP, sockets and HTTP. But for the higher layers of the SW, security is still an open issue. XML needs to be secure, for example by controlling access to various portions of a document. RDF needs to be secure with regards to interpretations and semantics, because one might want to specify security relative to a context. Ontologies should be able to have security levels attached to them. Secure reasoning by information integration is a big challenge. As stated in (Ferrari, 2004), information on the SW should be "managed, integrated and exchanged securely" (Ferrari, 2004).

Privacy is a closely related issue. Some documents or parts of them may be private, while other parts may be public or partially public. It is an important issue to examine how the SW may reach its visions without losing the ability to maintain privacy and anonymity when wanted (Ferrari, 2004). If no restrictions are applied to security or privacy on the SW, it is easy to imagine possible abuse of private information if it is semantically enriched and searchable by anyone on the distributed SW.

5. Implications of Semantic Web to Enterprise Integration

Many integration models and new standards have been developed to try to solve the problem of Enterprise Application Integration (EAI), but little has been achieved so far (Quirchmayr, 2003). The SW definitely has potential for easing the task of EAI, thus enabling EI. With regards to SW technology, the main enabler for EAI is the *standardisation* that the SW promises to provide for communication and integration of systems and applications, and the high degree of *automation* of these processes, including automatic exchange of semantically enriched data. However, the issues relating to the current state of the art in SW (as discussed in the previous section) put clear limitations on the immediate usability of SW technologies for EAI. All the above mentioned issues apply when an enterprise system wants to communicate with various other enterprise systems in an ad-hoc way. However, if an enterprise system/application would like to employ SW technologies to cooperate with a set of fixed and stable enterprise systems or business partners, one might avoid many problems of the unfinished SW, but at the cost of greatly reduced flexibility. For example, one might manually create ontology mappings between the ontology of two enterprise applications and create a local, closed SW to avoid many of the problems associated with semantic interoperability, automated ontology mapping, agent communication infrastructure, trust, security and (to a degree) robust reasoning. Such a limited "SW" system might not be very practical initially, but it might prove to be a useful step on the way to prepare oneself for the SW of the future.

6. The WISEMOD Approach

If the SW is to catch on as a technology for EAI, we believe that it must be simple to use for non-technical business users. This means that business users must themselves be able to semantically enrich data-sources that are not automatically enriched, and perform work by composing SW Services into business processes and executing them. This will require a strong user-friendly framework as a basis for work, and a robust methodology to guide users in their work. The beforementioned issues regarding SW technologies also need to be solved. The Web Information Service Modelling (WISEMOD) project[1], funded by the Research Council of Norway (NFR), aims to address some of the issues mentioned above. This project will result in a new approach for workflow modelling tailored for the needs of the SW. By utilizing SW resources - both services and information - in the context of workflow modelling, EAI will be achieved in a more efficient way.

7. Conclusion

The basic layers of the SW contain well specified standards, like Unicode, URI, XML, RDF and RDF-S. OWL has appeared in 2004 as a W3C recommendation for an ontology language designed for use with the SW. The higher layers of the SW have yet to be fully standardized, and many undecided issues exist within the areas

---

[1] http://www.idi.ntnu.no/~guttors/wisemod

of logic, proof, trust and security. Many of these issues arise due to the heterogeneous, highly distributed and large scale nature of the envisioned SW.

Some important issues that need to be addressed are how to create semantic data sources, robust reasoning, agent coordination, semantic interoperability, trust and security. It may take some time to resolve all these issues, but if the SW is realized according to its vision, it will be a revolutionary and powerful tool to search for and share semantically enriched information on a global scale, processable by both humans and machines.

The SW definitely has potential for easing the task of EI. There are however clear limitations on the immediate usability of SW technologies for EI. An enterprise might ready itself for the future SW by partially implementing SW technologies to do integration with relatively fixed and stable systems, thus avoiding a number of the issues related to the unfinished SW technologies. The WISEMOD project will provide improved workflow modelling techniques and methodology to further improve the utilization of the SW for EAI.

References

ATHENA Public Website, What is ATHENA: http://www.athena-ip.org, 2005

Berners-Lee, Hendler, Lassila, The Semantic Web. *Scientific American*, 2001

Croke, Enterprise Business Integration in 2010A.D. *LNCS 3095*, pp. 1-10, Springer-Verlag Berlin Heidelberg, 2004

Ding, Fensel, Klein, Omelayenko, The Semantic Web: Yet Another Hip? *Data and Knowledge Engineering*, 2002

Ferrari, Thuraisingham, Security and Privacy for Web Databases and Services. *EDBT 2004*.

Gruber: A Translation Approach to Portable Ontology Specifications. *Knowledge Acquisition*, 1993

Handschuh, Staab: Annotation of the Shallow and the Deep Web. *Volume 96 Frontiers in Artificial Intelligence and Applications, IOS Press*, 2003.

Harmelen: How the Semantic Web will change KR: Challenges and opportunities for a new research agenda. *The Knowledge Engineering Review, 17*, 2002

Kalfoglou, Alani, Schorlemmer, Walton: On the Emergent Semantic Web and Overlooked Issues. *ISWC 2004*, 2004

Karl Aberer et al.: Emergent Semantics Principles and Issues. *DASFAA 2004*, 2004

Lim, Juster, Pennington: The Seven Major Aspects of Enterprise Modelling and Integration: A Position Paper. *SIGGROUP Bulletin*, Vol. 18, No. 1, April 1997, 1997

Matthews, Dimitrakos: Deploying trust policies on the Semantic Web. *iTrust'04*, 2004

Patel-Schneider, Fensel: Layering the Semantic Web: Problems and Directions. *ISWC 2002*

Quirchmayr, Toja: Enterprise Application Integration - Future Revisited? *EC-Web 2003, LNCS 2738*, pp. 445-450, 2003

Rinaldi, Kaljurand, Dowdall, Hess: Breaking the Deadlock. *CoopIS/DOA/ODBASE*, 2003

From a models translation case towards identification of some issues about UEML

Matthieu Roque — Bruno Vallespir — Guy Doumeingts*

LAPS/GRAI University Bordeaux 1
351, Cours de la Libération
33405 Talence cedex
France

matthieu.roque@laps.u-bordeaux1.fr
bruno.vallespir@laps.u-bordeaux1.fr
guy.doumeingts@laps.u-bordeaux1.fr

* ADELIOR / Itrec gestion
62bis, Avenue André Morizet
92100 Boulogne-Billancourt
France
doumeingts@itrec.com

ABSTRACT: *Nowadays, one of the most important research topics in the domain of enterprise modelling is the development of a unified language, often called UEML (Unified Enterprise Modelling Language). UEML is expected to be a pivot language in order to make the large amount of enterprise modelling languages able to communicate and then to increase the interoperability in the domain of enterprise modelling. The paper is focused on one of the more illustrating points about UEML: the translation of models. We will present a simple example of model translation between the SADT activity and the GRAI activity of a GRAI net. On the basis of this translation case, we shall derive a set of issues concerning the development of UEML..*

KEY WORDS: *Interoperability, enterprise modelling, models translation, constructs, UEML.*

1. Introduction

Since the first development in the area of enterprise modelling started in the US during 70's (ex. SADT, SSAD, IDEF0, Data Flow Diagram, ...), a lot of enterprise modelling languages have been elaborated world-wide. We can mention for example, Entity-Relationship model, MERISE, GRAI grid and nets, CIMOSA constructs and building blocks, OMT, IEM, ARIS method, IDEFx,... (Chen *et al.*, 2002), (Petit, *et al.* 2002), (Vallespir, 2003), (Vernadat, 1996). It is generally recognised that, at the time being, there are too many heterogeneous modelling languages available in the "Market" and it is difficult for business users to understand and choose a suitable one.

The main problems related to this situation are (Doumeingts *et al.*, 1999):

– difficulties (impossibility in some case) to translate one model built using a language to a model expressed in another one; and

– difficulties for an enterprise to use a software tool if it is based on languages which are different from the ones adopted by the enterprise.

However, it seems that the elements behind these various languages are similar or slightly different in details. Thus, it is natural to think about the development of a Unified Enterprise Modelling Language. One of the principal benefits to have a Unified Enterprise Modelling Language is to be able to translate a model of an enterprise built in a language in another one (Chen *et al.*, 2002), (Doumeingts *et al.*, 1999), (Panetto *et al.*, 2004), (Roque *et al.*, 2002), (Vallespir *et al.* 2001), (Vallespir 03), (Vernadat, 1999), (Vernadat, 2001). Moreover, requirements about UEML have been stated during the UEML project (IST – 2001-34229) (Knotte *et al.*, 2003). The third most important requirement stated was the expectation for an "invariant and unique behavioural semantic" language.

The purpose of this paper is not to justify the interest of UEML. It is not either to discuss about the approach and the principles usable to develop UEML. The contain of the paper is to present a very pragmatic case of translation between parts of two different languages of enterprise modelling in order to identify some issues related to UEML. This example has been already presented but this presentation is enhanced and enriched. We present here a better explanation of what we call an elementary construct and a more precise definition of the corresponding rules between the languages and UEML (Roque *et al.*, 2002), (Roque *et al.*, 2004).

2. The translation example

Let us assume that we want to deal with the translation between only two pieces of languages: the SADT and the GRAI activities, as presented figure 1.

Practically speaking, GRAI and SADT have not really the same domain of application. However, if this methodological aspect is not taken into account it is clear that many concepts are similar in both languages. That is why to translate one of this language into the second one has a sense.

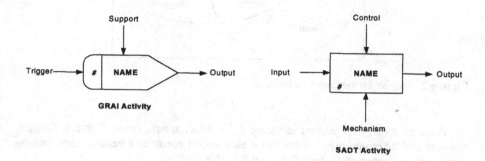

Figure 1. *GRAI and SADT activities*

2.1. *The unified model*

The analysis of GRAI and SADT activities into constructs may be expressed such as:

– SADT Activity = {Name, Number, Input, Output, Control, Mechanism},

– GRAI Activity = {Name, Number, Trigger, Output, Support}.

The term "Activity" exists in both formalisms but it must be concluded that it is not formally a common concept. Neither the "SADT activity" concept nor the "GRAI activity" concept exit in the same manner in the two languages. Thus, we shall say that they are not elementary constructs.

Definition: *A concept is an elementary construct if it exists completely or not at all in all considered languages.*

The application of this notion to our translation issue leads to the identification of constructs as shown figure 2.

This puts in evidence that the "Activity.min" construct belongs completely and simultaneously to the two languages.

$$Activity.min = \{Name, Number, Output\}$$

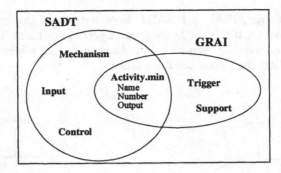

Figure 2. *Search for common constructs*

Then, all constructs present in figure 2, i.e. Mechanism, Input, Control, Trigger, Support and "Activity.min", seem to be elementary constructs because they belong completely or not at all to the GRAI and SADT activities.

However, if we go deeper in detail, it comes up that an Input, a Control and a Mechanism in SADT could be a Support in GRAI and a Trigger in GRAI is a Control in SADT. Then, because a SADT Control may be a GRAI Support and a GRAI Support may be a SADT Control, a "partial overlap" appears between these two concepts. In order to represent such a situation, we have to add another elementary construct. This construct is called "No triggering Control". It corresponds to the overlap between Support and Control (figure 3). This new construct is internal for UEML because it does not appear as such neither in SADT activity nor in GRAI activity.

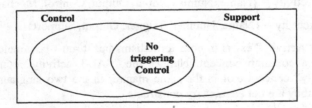

Figure 3. *"No triggering Control" as construct representing the overlap between "Control" and "Support"*

Thus, we can conclude that finally, we have only five elementary constructs:

- Activity.min,

- Trigger,

- Input,

- Mechanism, and

- No triggering Control.

These elementary constructs compose UEML and allow recomposing all the concepts of the considered languages. These constructs are organised as represented by figure 4.

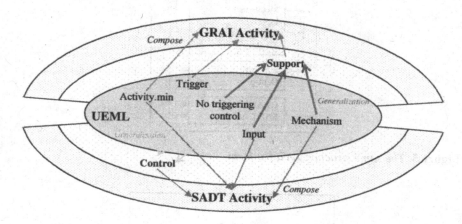

Figure 4. *The resulting structure*

More precisely, it could be noticed that, first, generalization relationships allow to rebuild local constructs (i.e. construct belonging to only one language) from elementary constructs and, second, composition relationships enable to get the language considered. These generalisation and composition relationships represent the correspondences rules between UEML and the GRAI and SADT activities.

We shall consider this organization of constructs as our unified model, the core of which is composed of UEML. Figure 5 proposes the unified model on a list form.

2.2. Translation SADT → GRAI

In this case, information is given in SADT format as shown figure 6.

If we translate this information into the unified model, we get the figure 7. It may be noticed that the GRAI activity is automatically built up. However, there is an uncertainty about the composition of GRAI activity because Trigger is not specified, however D is eligible as Trigger. This situation comes from the fact that D was allocated to Control but not to any of the specializations of Control (among which Trigger).

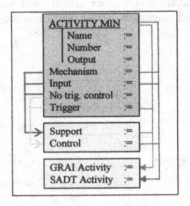

Figure 5. *The same structure on a list form*

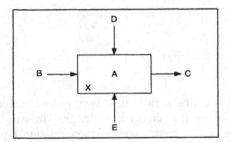

Figure 6. *Information in a SADT format*

Thus, if we want to project the unified model onto the GRAI activity, we obtain two possible cases (the two specializations of Control). There is no information in the model enabling to decide. Then, more information is required from the modeller to complete the model by asking him the following question:

Is D a No triggering Control or a Trigger?

If D is finally a no triggering Control, it becomes a Support (through the second generalization relationship) and is added to the GRAI activity as such. The structure is updated as shown figure 8 and, finally, the translation of the SADT activity into the GRAI activity gives the result also presented figure 8.

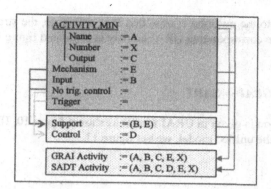

Figure 7. *Translation of SADT activity into the unified model*

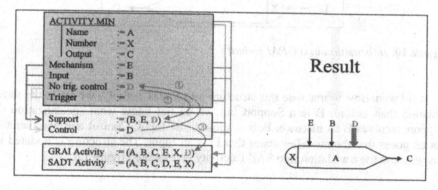

Figure 8. *The result in the case where D is not a Trigger*

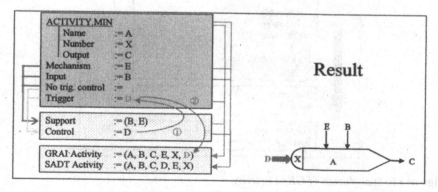

Figure 9. *The result in the case where D is a Trigger*

If the answer to the question is now that D is a Trigger, the structure is updated as figure 9 and the corresponding GRAI activity is presented figure 9 as well.

2.3. *Translation GRAI → SADT*

The information is given in GRAI format as shown figure 10. If we translate this information into the unified model, we get figure 11.

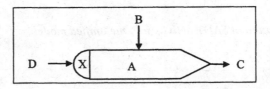

Figure 10. *Information in a GRAI format*

If we want now to translate this structure into SADT activity, we are in the same situation than before: B is a Support but we do not know what specialization of Support receives B as instance. B is eligible to be Input, Control and Mechanism. Let us guess that the modeller states that D is an Input. The structure is updated in this way and the translation into SADT activity is presented figure 12.

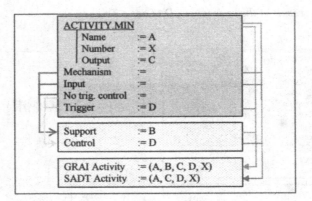

Figure 11. *Translation of GRAI activity*

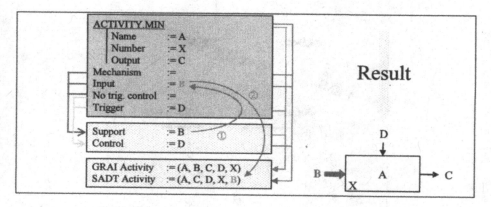

Figure 12. *The result in the case where B is an Input*

3. Conclusion coming up from the translation example

This simplified example makes some specific points concerning the translation process to appear.

3.1. *Definition of elementary constructs*

The definition of elementary constructs (as defined in this paper) appears to not be so easy. The issue is to find a trade-off between:

– the respect of the definition that can lead to go deeper in detail than what could be assumed at initially (i.e. the example of the no triggering Control),

– the search for constructs as big as possible (i.e. the example of the activity.min) in order to avoid a too large number of constructs and thus a model too huge to handle.

A general (and obvious) rule comes up: The search for common constructs between several languages needs to go deeper in detail than the detail needed to define one language. Moreover, this level of detail goes deeper with the number of languages. Then, we may imagine that the problem will be harder when an UEML will be developed for more languages than only two.

Practically, this rule leads to get elementary constructs belonging to UEML that enable to rebuild constructs of languages (so-called local constructs) by generalization. Since these local constructs are obtained, they can be composed to get the whole language (figure 13).

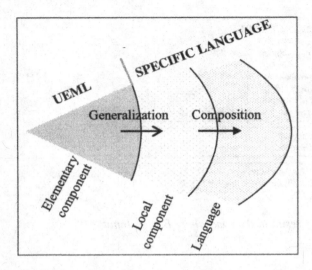

Figure 13. *Relationships between elementary constructs, local constructs and languages*

3.2. Hierarchies and relationships between constructs

It appears from our example that hierarchies exist between constructs in term of generalization. Moreover, multi-generalizations are possible (such as no triggering Control which is a Control and a Support as well).

These relationships lead to complex situations. The situation is even much complex in a real case because of semantics relationships between constructs, that have not been taken into account in our example. Meta-models built during the UEML project show these relationships (Berio, *et al.* 2003).

3.3. Languages as projections of UEML

We have right seen that the definition of UEML can lead to go deeper in detail than what could be assumed at initially. This situation leads to several points:

– There is a possibility that some pieces of information are not translated from the UEML model to any of the languages; more precisely, they are not translated as such but as a part of a construct of the language.

– The UEML model is richer than any other models, this comes from the fact that UEML is built up as a union of langugages; conversely, that leads languages to be some projections of the UEML model (figure 14).

– Then, generally a language can inform only partially the UEML model.

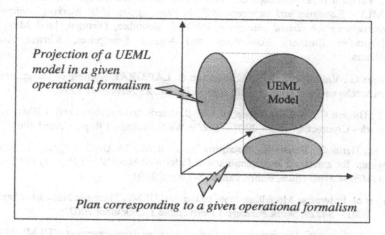

Figure 14. *Languages as projections of UEML*

4. General conclusions

The example presented in this paper is very simple from many sides. First, only a part (the activity) of the languages which are addressed (GRAI nets and SADT) is presented. Second, the analysis of each language is expressed into a list of constructs. Then, the relationships between constructs are not presented and so nor syntactic neither semantic issues are not addressed.

However, the pragmatic case of translation presented in this paper enables to identify some issues related to UEML. Working on these issues could constitute the first step towards the definition of UEML. But it is obvious that following steps, dealing with the true size of the problem (complete languages, more languages than two, taking syntactic and semantic aspects into account) will be very more difficult and will be very effort consuming.

5. References

Berio G., et al. Requirements analysis: initial core constructs and architecture, UEML Thematic Network - Contract n°: IST – 2001 – 34229, Work Package 3 Deliverable 3.1, May 2003.

Chen D., Vallespir B., Doumeingts G., "Developing an unified enterprise modelling language (UEML) – Roadmap and requirements", *in Proc. of 3rd IFIP Working conference on infrastructures for virtual enterprise*, PROVE, Sesimbra, Portugal, 1st-3 May 2002 – Collaborative Business Ecosystems and Virtual Enterprises, Kluwer Academic Publishers.

Doumeingts G., Vallespir B., UEML : Position du LAP/GRAI, Seminar of Groupement pour la Recherche en Productique, GRP, Nancy, France, 25 November 1999.

Knotte T., Busselt C., Böll D., Report on UEML (needs and requirements), UEML Thematic Network - Contract n°: IST – 2001 – 34229, Work Package 1 Report, April 2003.

Panetto H., Berio G., Benali K., Boudjlida N., Petit M., "A Unified Enterprise Modelling Language for enhanced interoperability of Enterprise Models", *in Proc. of the 11th IFAC INCOM2004 Symposium*, Bahia, Brazil, 5-7 April 2004.

Petit M., et al. Enterprise Modelling State of the Art, UEML Thematic Network, Contract n°: IST – 2001 – 34229, Work Package 1 Deliverable 1.1, October 2002.

Roque M., Vallespir B., Doumeingts G., Contribution au développement d'UEML : Principes et projet, Seminar of Groupement pour la Recherche en Productique, GRP, Tarbes, France, 24-25 October 2002.

Roque M., Vallespir B., Doumeingts G., "Modélisation d'entreprise : traduction et méta-modélisation", *in Proc. of 5th Conférence Francophone de Modélisation et Simulation*, MOSIM, Nantes, France, 1-3 September 2004.

Vallespir B., Doumeingts G., Chen D., Problem and research orientation on UEML: A point of view, IFAC-IFIP interest group on UEML, Vienna, Austria, 19 September 2001.

Vallespir B., Modélisation d'entreprise et architecture de conduite des systèmes de production, Thesis for Habilitation à Diriger des Recherches, University Bordeaux 1, December 2003.

Vernadat F., *Enterprise modelling and integration: principles and applications*, Chapman & Hall, 1996.

Vernadat F., Unified Enterprise Modelling Language (UEML), IFAC-IFIP Task force Interest group on UEML, Paris, France, 16 December 1999.

Vernadat F., UEML: "Towards a Unified Enterprise Modelling Language", *in Proc. of 3rd Conférence Francophone de Modélisation et Simulation*, MOSIM, Troyes, France, 25-27 April 2001.

Enterprise Modelling, an overview focused on software generation

Reyes Grangel, Ricardo Chalmeta, Cristina Campos, Òscar Coltell

Grupo de investigación en Integración y Re-Ingeniería de Sistemas (IRIS)
Dep. de Llenguatges i Sistemes Informàtics
Universitat Jaume I
12071 Castelló Spain

grangel@uji.es
rchalmet@uji.es
camposc@uji.es
coltell@uji.es

ABSTRACT: *Nowadays, enterprises face to an economic environment controlled by global competitiveness. In this context, enterprises must be more agile and be able to interoperate with their partners, in order to align their objectives with the market needs. Enterprise Modelling can become a way that enables enterprises to know and understand much better their business to achieve these objectives. However, some aspects as the great quantity of existing Enterprise Modelling Languages or the weak connection between Enterprise Modelling and software generation do not make easy this task. In this paper, we present an overview of the current state of the art in Enterprise Modelling Languages from software generation point of view. The main objective is to analyse the existing Enterprise Modelling Languages in order to establish how they can be useful to generate software.*

KEY WORDS: *Enterprise Modelling, Enterprise Modelling Languages, Overview, Software Generation, Model Driven Architecture (MDA), Computation Independent Model (CIM).*

1. Enterprise Modelling

In the 70s the first concepts of modelling were applied to the computer systems (E/R Model, DFD, etc.), but the concept of Enterprise Modelling appears in the USA at the beginning of the 80s, with the initiative Computer Integrated Manufacturing (CIM). Examples of this initiative are the projects Integrated Computer Aided Manufacturing (ICAM) carried out by the US Air Force or the Integrated Computer Aided Manufacturing-International (CAM-I). In the middle of the 80s, different Enterprise Modelling Languages emerge in Europe like for instance GRAI or CIMOSA. Numerous commercial tools appear in the 90s for giving support to a great number of different modelling languages (ARIS ToolSet, FirstSTEP, METIS, KBSI Tools, CimTool, MO2GO, e-MAGIM, etc.).

Enterprise Modelling is defined in (Vernadat 96) as the art of 'externalizing' enterprise knowledge, which adds value to the enterprise or needs to be shared, i.e., representing the enterprise in terms of its organisation and operations (processes, behaviour, activities, information, objects and material flows, resources and organisation units, and system infrastructure and architectures). This art consists of obtaining enterprise models, whose role should be to obtain a design, analysis and operation of the enterprise according to the model, i.e., driven by the model (model-driven) (Fox et al., 98).

Therefore, Enterprise Modelling can be used to select and develop computer systems, to better understand and improve business processes, etc., but the most important benefit of enterprise models is the capacity to add value to enterprise (Vernadat 96). Since, such models are able to make explicit facts and knowledge, which can be shared for users and different enterprise applications in order to improve enterprise performance (EXTERNAL 02).

2. Enterprise Modelling Languages

An Enterprise Modelling Language (EML) is a language with an accurate sintaxis and semantics, which can be interpreted and managed by a computer (Fuentes et al., 04), and it can generate graphical models that represent several dimensions of an enterprise. EMLs should allow building the model of an enterprise according to various points of view such as: function, organisation, process decision, economic, etc. in an integrated way.

Moreover, EMLs define the generic modelling constructs for Enterprise Modelling adapted to the needs of people creating and using enterprise models, according to the definition provide by GERAM (GERAM 99). In particular EMLs will provide construct to describe and model human roles, operational processes and their functional contents as well as the supporting information, office and production technologies.

Enterprise models are normally composed of submodels such as organisational models, process models, data models, configuration models, etc. The purpose of these models is to provide a common understanding among users about enterprise operations and structure, and decision-making support. In this context, the basis of the standards in Enterprise Modelling should be to achieve the following requirements (Berio et al., 99):

- To enable three fundamental types of flow inside and among enterprises: material, information and decision or control.

- To enable four modelling views: functional, informational, resources and organisational.

- To enable three levels of modelling: definition of requirements, specification of design and implementation description.

Many modelling methods and techniques have been established since 90s, besides there are a great number of initiatives and groups of standardization in Enterprise Modelling (Kalpic et al., 02). The greatest part of the standards related to Enterprise Modelling have been developed for the CEN TC310/WG1 (European Standardisation Committee) and ISO TC184/SC5/WG1. They are needed for enterprise integration and interoperability, but they have had really little or null industrial impact.

Next, we show a brief summary of existing EMLs in order to provide a general perspective of existing EMLs. Then, the main weaknesses in the context of EMLs are presented.

2.1. Overview of existing EMLs

Nowadays, there exists a great quantity of EMLs and they are widely detailed in several states of the art in Enterprise Modelling carried out in the framework of European Projects, as IDEAS (IDEAS 05), UEML (UEML 05), ATHENA (ATHENA 05), and INTEROP (INTEROP 05). Next, we present an overview of EMLs raise in these projects (see tables 1, 2, 3). These tables show the Enterprise Modelling Tools (EMT) associated with these EMLs, the Enterprise Modelling Methodologies (EMM), approaches or standards supported by them, their owner enterprise and their website.

The table 1 shows the EMLs, which enable to represent the three fundamental types of flow among enterprises, the four modelling views and the three levels of modelling above mentioned. This kind of languages could be called traditional EMLs. Next, a brief description of them is shown:

1. **ARIS (ARchitecture of Integrated information Systems)** conceptual design is based on an integration concept which is derived from a holistic analysis of business processes. The result is a highly complex model which is divided into individual views in order to reduce its complexity: data view, function view, organization view and control view.

2. **CIMOSA (CIM Open System Architecture)** is an architecture for enterprise integration consisting of a framework for Enterprise Modelling (reference architecture), an EML and an integrating infrastructure for model enactment all to be supported by a standards based on common terminology.

3. **GRAI** is the set of twelve Methodological Modules. These modules cover the following areas: Re-Engineering and elaboration of target enterprise, Audit, Choice of Information Technology (IT) solutions, Implementation of IT solutions, Performance Indicators, Benchmarking, Business Plan, Relationships between GRAI TM Methodology and quality approach, Management of design department, Management of enterprise evolution, Knowledge management.

4. **IDEF (Integrated DEFinition methodology)** methods are used to create graphical representations of various systems, analyse the model, create a model of a desired version of the system, and to aid in the transition from one to the other. Depending on the IDEF method used, different syntaxes exist to represent the models. The most representative construct of IDEF methodology is the generic IDEF0 diagram (a meta-model). IDEF0 allows the user to depict a view of the process including the inputs, outputs, controls and mechanisms (which are referred to generally as ICOMs).

5. **IEM (Integrated Enterprise Modelling)** allows different views (information model, process chain, etc.) on one consistent model, in which an enterprise is described by objects, its relations and its behaviour. The generic object classes that can be used are 'product', 'order' and 'resource'. An additional element is the action and a class structure can be defined for it. In the process chain the action connects the input, output states, the controlling order and the necessary resources to perform the process. The modelling of bill of materials and part of relations is also supported.

6. **ITM** is used to implement the four leading EA methodologies. The ITM template also has expressiveness to start modelling of most other enterprise needs, such as project models, business and impact analysis models. BPM is a new template aimed at the BPM market and implements most of the BPMN constructs plus integrates it with IDEF and other process modelling language yielding the expressiveness required in practical situations. UML implements nine of the diagrams described by OMG as part of the UML version 2.0 specifications, but all has expressiveness to start modelling of most other enterprise needs, such as project models, business and impact analysis models.

7. **MEML (EEML from EXTERNAL and MEML 1.0, UEML compliant)** is made to support process and enterprise modelling across a number of layers. The four layers of interest are: Generic Task Type, Specific Task Type, Manage Task

Instances, Perform Task Instances. The modelling language currently includes four modelling domains, in addition to general modelling mechanisms and primitives provided in METIS, like swimlane-diagrams: Process modelling, Resource modelling, Goal modelling, Data modelling (currently implemented with UML Class Diagram).

8. **Petri nets** were initially developed by CA Petri for the specification of concurrent (parallel) systems. The recognised benefits in the context of Enterprise Modelling of Petri Nets are modelling power (resource sharing, conflicts, mutual exclusion, concurrency, non-determinism, visual modelling); analysis (deadlock detection, bottleneck analysis, animation, simulation); and code generation for Controlling Manufacturing Systems.

EML	EMT	EMM	Owner	www
ARIS Language	ARIS Process Platform	ARIS UML 1.4	IDS Scheer AG	www.ids-scheer.com
CIMOSA			CIMOSA Association e.V.	www.cimosa.de
	First step designer			www.interfacing.com
	CimTool			www.rgcp.com
GRAI	GraiTools	GIM	LAP/GRAI	www.graisoft.com
IDEF	IDEF Tools	IDEF Method.	KBS	www.kbsi.com
	Business Modelling Workbench			www.idefine.com
	System Architect			www.popkin.com
IEM	MO2GO	IPK Procedure	IPK	www.ipk.fhg.de
ITM/BPM UML	Metis	Zachman Framework TOGAF 8 UML 2.0 DoDAF (C4ISR) TEAF/FEAF	Computas AS	www.computas.com
MEML	Metis	EEDO Method.	Computas AS	www.computas.com
Petri Nets	www.daimi.au.dk/PetriNets/tools		Petri Nets Steering Committee	

Table 1. *Overview of the traditional EMLs (I)*

The table 2 shows languages than could be considered like EMLs, but they have created in order to make easy different kinds of interchanges. Next, a brief description of them is shown:

1. **BPML (Business Process Modelling Language)** is a meta-language for the modelling of business processes, just as XML is a meta-language for the modelling of business data. BPML provides an abstracted execution model for collaborative transactional business processes based on the concept of a transactional finite-state machine.

2. **PIF (Process Interchange Format)**, a PIF process description consists of a file of objects, such as ACTIVITY, ACTOR, and RESOURCE objects. Each object in the file has a unique id that other objects can use to refer to it. Each object type (or class) has a particular set of attributes defined for it; each attribute describes some aspect of the object.

3. **PSL (Process Specification Language)**, the goal of PSL is to create a process interchange language that is common to all manufacturing applications, generic enough to be decoupled from any given application, and robust enough to be able to represent the necessary process information for any given application. This representation would facilitate communication among the various applications because they would all have a common understanding of concepts to be shared.

4. **UEML (Unified Enterprise Modelling Language)**, the main objective of the UEML is to provide industry with a unified and expandable enterprise modelling language. The concept of UEML was born in 1997 in the frame of ICEIMT (Torino conference) organised in cooperation with NIST.

5. **XPDL (XML Process Definition Language)**, the WfMC has identified five functional interfaces to a workflow service as part of its standardization program. This interface includes a common metamodel for describing the process definition (this specification) and also an XML schema for the interchange of process definitions.

EML	Owner	www
BPML	BPMI	www.bpmi.org
PIF	PIF Working Group	ccs.mit.edu/pifwg.html
PSL	NIST	www.mel.nist.gov/psl
UEML	UEML European Project	www.ueml.org
XPDL	WfMC	www.wfmc.org

Table 2. *Overview of the main EMLs created to make easy exchange (II)*

Languages showed in the table 3 are based on standards as XML or UML, and they can be used like EMLs. Next, a brief description of them is shown:

1. **BPDM**, this meta-model provides a common language, for describing business processes in an implementation independent manner. This is not to say that the models are abstract from execution details, on the contrary it is our aim to describe executable processes, these models are intended to be abstract from the detailed implementation (platform) mechanisms. The standardization is still in progress.

2. **ebXML (Electronic Business using eXtensible Markup Language)** is a modular suite of specifications that enables enterprises of any size and in any geographical location to conduct business over the Internet. Using ebXML, companies now have a standard method to exchange business messages, conduct

trading relationships, communicate data in common terms and define and register business processes.

3. **UML Profile for EAI (Enterprise Application Integration)** intends to solve the EAI problem by defining and publishing a metadata interchange standard for information about accessing application interfaces. The goal is to simplify application integration by standardizing application metadata for invoking and translating application information.

4. **UML Profile for EDOC (Enterprise Distributed Object Computing)** provides a modelling framework for describing how objects are used to implement enterprise systems. It is based on UML 1.4 and conforms to the OMG Model Driven Architecture.

EML	EMM	Owner	www
BPDM		OMG	www.omg.org
ebXML	XML	OASIS	www.ebxml.org
UML Profile for EAI	UML 1.4	OMG	www.omg.org
UML Profile for EDOC	UML 1.4	OMG	www.omg.org

Table 3. *Overview of the main EMLs based on XML and UML (III)*

2.2. Problems related to EMLs

Conclusions about EMLs pointed out in the states of the art of mentioned European Projects (IDEAS, UEML, ATHENA, INTEROP 05) are:

- There exist a great quantity of EMLs and they are overlapped.
- EMLs provide constructs to describe and model the people roles, operational processes and functional contents, as well as support information and production and management technologies.
- The integration of the models generated with these languages is complicated, since tools do not exist to integrate models generated with different languages.

Another European Project, EXTERNAL, provides the main weaknesses related to EMLs, as the following ones (EXTERNAL 02):

- **Support to enterprises in dynamic environments:** especially for dynamic roles, cooperation in time and supporting of specific processes. Permanent changes in this kind of enterprises require a controlled way for managing the maturity of structures and processes. Nowadays, Enterprise Modelling Methodologies are not able of dealing with different levels of maturity. Besides, the EMLs are weak in easy and transparent externalization of dynamic roles and policies in extended enterprises.

- **Maintenance of enterprise models:** enterprise models are not updated after its first implementation, which reduces the value for improving the performance of the business processes.

- **Link with software generation:** Enterprise Modelling has the objective to support software implementation. However, few and isolated solutions exist that can link the conceptual level of Enterprise Modelling with the implementation level.

Therefore, the main problems that concern to EMLs can be located on two axis:

- **Horizontal:** the lack of interoperability between EMLs and their corresponding Enterprise Modelling Tools. Almost all kinds of these languages are proprietary specifications and can only be implemented with specific tools designed for this purpose. This problem complicates the interoperability of enterprises at conceptual level. The main solutions provided by the research community to address this problem are focused on defining a common exchange language that can become a standard among the existing EMLs. This is for instance the goal of the UEML Project (UEML 05) and one of the objectives of the ATHENA Project (ATHENA 05).

- **Vertical:** the weak connection between enterprise models and the generation of software is one of the major reasons why enterprises only develop few models, which moreover are rarely updated and therefore are not very successful in accomplishing their initial purpose. Initiatives, such as MDA (MDA 03) promoted by OMG intend to solve this kind of problems.

3. MDA framework

One of the weaknesses of Enterprise Modelling is the difficulty to software generation from enterprise models. In this section, MDA (Model Driven Architecture) of OMG (MDA 03) is described as a reference framework.

MDA was proposed by the OMG (Object Management Group) in 2001 as an architecture for software applications development. This initiative intends to promote the use of models as fundamental way for designing and implementing systems. One of the main objectives of MDA is to separate the operation specification of a system from the details of implementation in a specific platform; so that the computer systems and enterprise can be able to evolve with fast technological changes. In this context, MDA establishes a framework for:

- Specifying a system independently of the platform that supports it.
- Specifying platforms.
- Choosing a particular platform for the system.
- Transforming the system specification into one for a particular platform.

3.1. Benefits of MDA

MDA is focused on functionality and behaviour of systems independently of the technology in which they will be implemented. The main advantage of MDA is that it is not necessary to repeat the modelling process of behaviour or functionality of an application or system each time that a new technology appears. Other architectures are connected with a specific technology, with MDA operation and behaviour is modelled only once. The three most important benefits of the use of MDA for enterprises are:

- An architecture based on MDA is always prepared to respond to the future needs.

- MDA makes easy to integrate applications through the boundaries of the middleware.

- The specific facilities of domain in MDA defined by the OMG's Domain Task Force will provide an extensive interoperability, being available on a particular platform or in multiple platforms when necessary.

3.2. Components of MDA

A system in MDA can include among others: a program, a single computer system, some combinations of parts of different systems, a federation of systems, people, an enterprise, a federation of enterprises, etc. And a system model is defined as a description or specification of that system and its environment for certain purpose. A model shows often a combination of graphics and text. The text can be in an EML or in natural language.

MDA is focused on the use of models for system development. Therefore, MDA encourages the use of certain classes of models and the relationship among themselves. A system can be observed and analysed from different points of view; MDA specifies three points of view: an independent point of view of the computation, an independent point of view of the platform and a dependent point of view of the platform. In this way, MDA defines three conceptual levels:

- **Computation Independent Model (CIM):** to represent domain and system requirements in the environment in which it is going to operate, concerning business models and a holistic point of view about enterprises.

- **Platform Independent Model (PIM):** to model system functionality but without define how and in which platform will be implemented, centred in information and from a computational point of view.

- **Platform Specific Model (PSM):** the PIM is transformed in a platform dependent model according to selected platform, focused on technological point of view.

CIM specifies the requirements, and the PIM and PSM specify the system design and implementation. The PIM and PSM must not violate the CIM (Hendryx 03). The most interesting idea of this approach is the possibility of model transformation by means of tools that automate the transformation process until code generation.

4. CIM characterisation

A CIM describes the domain and requirements of the system in a model that is independent of computation representations and is expressed in the vocabulary of the domain practitioner. The CIM corresponds to the conceptualization perspective and might consist of a model from the informational viewpoint, which captures information about the data of a system.

CIM is an emerging model, not yet formally defined or supported by OMG standards and tools. Using a CIM, an enterprise can capture, manage, and better use some of its most valuable assets: knowledge of its resources, policies, rules, terminology, and processes. Also, enterprises can specify, in an EML, the requirements of their systems and validate that the system design satisfies these requirements. CIM is made up two main subdivisions, which analyse enterprises and their environment from different point of views (Hendryx 03):

– **Business Model:** focused on the scope and goals of the business, and the terminology, resources, facts, roles, policies, rules, processes, organizations, locations, and events of concern to the business.

– **Business Requirements for Systems:** based on the purpose, scope, and policies for the system. Business Requirements can be divided into Functional Requirements, Interaction Requirements, and Environment Contract.

In (Berrisford 04), two kinds of CIM are proposed. The first one is a model of a business enterprise, a stand-alone CIM, independent of data processing and of potential software systems. A purely conceptual or domain model of this kind is interesting per se. It can be used to define some business rules. But forward engineering transformation is problematic.

The second one is definitively related to one or more data processing systems. It can be transformed into software systems that consume input data and produce output data. Such a CIM may be thought of as a very abstract PIM. And given there are degrees of PIMness, there must surely be degrees of CIMness.

Some authors (Berrisford 04) do not envisage forward engineering from a purely conceptual CIM. However, they are more optimists about forward engineering from a CIM that abstracts from data processing systems. This kind of CIM can be recognised because it will:

– Acknowledge the divisions between data in discrete loosely-coupled data stores.

- Define what units of work clients invoke or require on each distinct data store, with the preconditions and post conditions of each unit of work.

- Define what data must persist in each discrete data store for those units of work to be completable.

Finally, a standard model framework is required to support the pragmatic association of CIMs with PIMs and PSMs, in order to specify the separation of concerns between different models that make up a complete specification. It will be helpful for MDA to establish normative mappings between other popular frameworks and the standard framework, to promote reuse of models by projects that use different frameworks (Hendryx 03).

5. Conclusion

Enterprise Modelling must become for enterprises a way for better understanding business, not a final goal. One of the main weaknesses of Enterprise Modelling is the lack of strong links between enterprise models and software generation. A lot of Enterprise Modelling Languages, Standards and Tools exist, but enterprises carried out few enterprise models and it is very hard to maintain them, to use them in order to generate software, or to exchange them among different enterprises.

The main conclusions about state of the art in Enterprise Modelling Techniques, Tools and Standards, in order to understand how it can be useful to software generation from enterprise models, are:

- There is a great number of Languages, Standards, Frameworks, Methodologies and Tools concerning Enterprise Modelling, which cover different parts of the dimensions defined in GERAM and even they are overlapped.

- Enterprise Modelling Tools usually support a particular Enterprise Modelling Language and Methodology; and only a few ones allow the definition of a new language or some adaptation of the languages that implement. Moreover, there not exist tools that can integrate their models with models carried out with other Enterprise Modelling Tools. Therefore, mechanisms for the exchange of enterprise models among enterprise do not exist.

- Enterprise Modelling Standards are necessary for enterprise integration and interoperability, and there are a lot of them concerning Enterprise Modelling. But they have had really little or null industrial impact due to they are associated with a specific platform or technology; which can not be achieved by a great number of enterprises.

- Many works are being performed related to PIMs, PSMs, UML Profiles, QVT, etc., in the MDA framework, but the characterisation of CIMs and the features that a enterprise model must satisfy to be considered CIM and generate appropriate software are still in progress.

Acknowledgments

This work has being founded by CICYT DPI2003-02515. Also, it is partially supported by the European Commission within the 6th Framework Programme (INTEROP Network of Excellence, (IST-2003-508011), www.interop-noe.org). The authors are indebted to WP7.

References

"ATHENA (Advanced Technologies for interoperability of Heterogeneous Enterprise Networks and their Applications) Project (IST-2003-2004)", http://www.athena-ip.org, 2005.

Berio G., Vernadat F. B., "New developments in enterprise modelling using CIMOSA", Computers in Industry, vol. 40, no. 2-3, 1999, p. 99-114.

Berrisford G., "Why IT veterans are sceptical about MDA", Second European Workshop on Model Driven Architecture (MDA) with an emphasis on Methodologies and Transformations, Kent, 2004, Computing Laboratory, University of Kent, p. 125-135, http://www.cs.kent.ac.uk/projects/kmf/mdaworkshop/submissions/Berrisford.pdf.

"EXTERNAL (Extended Enterprise MEthodology) Final version 1-12-D-2002-01-0 (IST-1999-10091)", http://research.dnv.com/external/default.htm, 2002.

Fox M. S., Gruninger M., "Enterprise Modelling", AI Magazine, vol. 19, no. 3, 1998, p. 109-121.

Fuentes L., Vallecillo A., "Una introducción a los perfiles UML", Novática, vol. marzo-abril, no. 168, 2004, p. 6-11.

"GERAM: Generalised enterprise reference architecture and methodology. Technical Report Version 1.6.3", 1999, http://www.cit.gu.edu.au/ bernus/taskforce/geram/versions.

Hendryx S., "Integrating Computation Independent Business Modeling Languages into the MDA with UML 2", http://www.omg.org/docs/ad/03-01-32.doc, 2003.

"IDEAS (Interoperability Development for Enterprise Application and Software) Project", http://www.ideas-roadmap.net, 2005.

"INTEROP (Interoperability Research for Networked Enterprises Applications and Software) Project", http://interop-noe.org, 2005.

Kalpic B., Bernus P., "Business process modelling in industry - the powerful tool in enterprise management", Computers in Industry, vol. 47, no. 3, 2002, p. 299-318.

"MDA Guide Version 1.0.1", 2003.

"UEML (Unified Enterprise Modelling Language) Project (IST-2001-34229)", http://www.ueml.org, 2005.

Vernadat F. B., Enterprise Modeling and Integration: Principles and Applications, London , Chapman and Hall, 1996.

Enablers and Technologies Supporting Self-Forming Networked Organizations

Claudia-Melania Chituc, Americo Lopes Azevedo

Faculty of Engineering of the University of Porto (FEUP) and INESC Porto
Campus da FEUP, Rua Dr. Roberto Frias 378
4200-365 Porto
Portugal
{cmchituc, ala}@fe.up.pt

ABSTRACT: *The rapid evolution of the information and communication technologies and the changing client's demands determined enterprises to adapt their business from traditional practices to e-business, and to participate in new forms of collaboration, such as networked organizations. Peer-to-Peer, Web services, agents, workflow become core technologies supporting enterprise integration, streamlining transactions while supporting process coordination and consistency. This paper presents the most relevant enterprise integration reference models, frameworks, standards and technologies as potential candidates to the development of a self-forming business networking environment and proposes an approach towards the development of a conceptual framework for a self-forming business networking environment based on Plug-and-Do Business paradigm.*

KEY WORDS: *Self-Forming Networked Organizations, Enterprise Integration Plug-and-Do Business Paradigm.*

1. Introduction

Nowadays, in the information age, agility and flexibility are key characteristics for enterprises' business success. Current business trends determined new forms of collaboration, such as "supply chain enterprises", "extended enterprises", "virtual enterprises", "smart organizations" or "networked organizations". In this context, technologies such as Peer-to-Peer (P2P), Web services, workflow systems, intelligent agents emerge as core solutions for enterprise integration (EI), streamlining transactions while supporting process coordination and consistency. However, actual information and communication technology (ICT) solutions do not guarantee a true natural operational environment. They often separate and isolate particular departments, companies, supply chains, authorities, research institutions and each individual of their surroundings. Therefor, it is required to compile concepts and develop new applications, frameworks, paradigms, information system architectures and operating environment models in a speedy manner which than facilitate the achievement of flexible business ICT infrastructure support and can serve as basis for EI, offer outcome-driven and problem-oriented solutions and tie organizations in the short-term without hindering their agility. The urgent need for such new business ICT solutions is also shown in several research projects, such as VOSTER (http://voster.vtt.fi) or THINKcreative (http://www.thinkcreative.org).

Reference architectures, ontologies, Plug & Play interoperable service architecture for collaboration at work, interaction among peers, utility-like computing capacity and connectivity, group-level security, privacy and trust, mobility at work were indicated as research challenges for future enabling technologies supporting e-activities, concerning the next generation of collaborative working environments (European Commission, 2004). The current research project addresses these issues and contributes to the realization of a full-flagged collaborative working environment that answers the needs of the current e-activities and contributes to the development of new technologies in ICT area.

The aim of this paper is to concisely present the main enterprise integration reference models, frameworks, standards and technologies, and to propose an approach towards the development of a conceptual framework for a self-forming business networking environment based on Plug-and-Do-Business interoperability paradigm.

For the purpose of this research project, the term self-forming networked organizations refers to networked organizations where the detection of service providers as well as their contracting is done in an automated form (Bussler, 2003).

The paper is organized in four sections. After a brief introduction to the topic of the paper, several integration models, frameworks, standards and relevant technologies are succinctly presented. The third section proposes the methodology to be followed, proposing an approach towards the development of a conceptual framework for a self-forming business networking environment based on Plug-and-

Do Business interoperability paradigm. The fourth and last section contains the conclusions of the paper.

2. Enterprise Integration

2.1. *Needs for Enterprise Integration*

The complex and sometimes hostile business environment, the new forms of collaboration, and the autonomy and heterogeneity of enterprises require innovative solutions able to handle distributed business processes that cross the borders of various enterprises in a networked environment. EI aims at developing solutions and computer-based tools that facilitate the coordination of work and information flow across organizational boundaries. "EI is concerned with facilitating information, control and material flows across organizational boundaries by connecting all the necessary functions and heterogeneous functional entities (information systems, devices, applications, and people) in order to improve communication, cooperation, and coordination within this enterprise so that the enterprise behaves as an integrated whole, therefore enhancing its overall productivity, flexibility, and capacity for management of change (or reactivity)" (Vernadat, 1996). EI does not represent a new issue. Evolving from physical integration to application and later business integration, EI has been a challenge for both information technology (IT) and manufacturing industries for several decades.

Despite the existence of a significant number of computer-based tools claiming to support EI, and the scientific results in the business networking area and on the so-called "collaborative work", it is generally accepted that more work needs to be done since available solutions are usually cumbersome and lack in flexibility to respond to the most recent technological outcomes, focusing on very specific aspects and do not provide or tackle all aspects related to EI. The scientific community agrees that questions related to the formalization, conceptual development and semantic integration (namely concerning the formal description of the domain, ontology, behavior, etc.) are fundamental research topics waiting for a consistent development (Camarinha-Matos, 2003).

Major motivations identified for EI are (Vernadat, 1996): the need for real information sharing, and not just data exchange among systems (i.e. application systems or information systems), or to partner companies; the need for interoperability (i.e. the need to harmonize the operational environment, which is characterized by a wide variety of more or less incompatible operating systems, communication networks, application systems, data files, database systems, etc., and the need for improving task coordination or inter-working between organization units, individuals, and systems in interaction within an enterprise.

In order to be competitive in a collaborative business networked environment, enterprises must adopt a bipolar approach, which allows them to fully benefit from the specific competences of each partner of a collaborative business network: to develop a compatible organizational infrastructure allowing them to join their competences while supporting the operations and functions to be performed, and to build up new management methodologies based on the most recent ICT developments, assuring high performance of the business activities with a minimum of human interaction. The management methodologies refer also (in the case of self-forming networked organizations) to the rules and procedures that enable an enterprise to join a formed networked organization in a natural way.

2.2. Integration Reference Models, Frameworks, Standards and Technologies

Several reference models, frameworks and standards have been developed, aiming at organizing EI knowledge and serve as guide in EI programs. A reference model represents a (partial) model which can be used as a basis for particular model developments or for evaluation of particular models; very often it can be used for comparing something to a reference (Vernadat, 1996). The term 'framework' refers to a collection of elements (i.e. principles, methods or tools), put together for a certain purpose relevant for a given domain of application (adapted after (Vernadat, 1996)). Standards can be considered objects (i.e. hardware, software, processes, date, function, protocol, etc.), which are accepted and shared within a community (i.e. business unit, value chain, sector or geographical region) (Caragill, 1989) (Buxmann, 1996).

This section concisely presents some integration reference models, frameworks, standards referring to B2B domain and relevant infrastructures and technologies supporting EI.

A. Reference Models and Frameworks

SCOR *(Supply Chain Operations Reference Model)* (www.supply-chain.org) is a process reference model developed by the Supply-Chain Council as cross-industry standard for supply-chain management used to describe, measure and evaluate supply-chain configurations. The users are able to address, improve and communicate supply-chain management practices within and between parties. SCOR model is organized around five primary management processes (plan, source, make, deliver and return) that allow it to be used to describe, measure and evaluate very simple or very complex supply chains by using a common set of definitions.

GERAM *(Generalized Enterprise Reference Architecture and Methodology)* (GERAM IFAC/IFIP, 2000) defines a tool-kit of concepts for designing and maintaining enterprises for their entire life-history. GERAM refers to the methods, models and tools, which are needed to build and maintain the integrated enterprise, a single enterprise or a network of enterprises (virtual or extended enterprises).

GERAM is not reference architecture; it is aimed at organizing enterprises' existing integration knowledge, and unifies two distinct approaches of EI: based on product models and based on business process design.

Zachman's Framework for enterprise architecture (Zachman, 1987) describes a holistic model of an enterprise information infrastructure from six perspectives: planner, owner, designer, builder, subcontractor and the working system. Its focus is to ensure that all aspects of an enterprise are well-organized and exhibit clear relationships that will ensure a complete system.

Workflow Reference Model (Workflow Management Coalition, 1999) provides the general architectural framework that identifies interfaces and covers broadly various areas of functionality between a Workflow Management System and its environment.

B. Business-to-Business (B2B) integration standards

As defined by (Bussler, 2003), B2B integration is the enabling technology and the necessary infrastructure (referred to as B2B integration technology) to make automated supply chain integration possible, to send XML-formatted messages over the Internet, to send messages in a P2P pattern to trading partners or to exchange messages with marketplaces.

According to (SWWS, 2003), B2B standards' scope can be roughly separated into: catalogue and classification standards (such as BMEcat, eCX (Electronic Catalog XML), OCP (Open Catalog Protocol) as catalogue systems, and Ecl@ss or UNSPC (United Nations Standard Products and Services) as classification standards); document exchange (such as EDI (Electronic Data Interchange), EDIFACT (Electronic Data Interchange For Administration, Commerce and Transport), XML (eXtensible Markup Language), xCBL (XML Common Business Library), cXML (commerce eXtensible Markup Language), OAGIS (OAGI Integration Specification), RNIF (RosettaNet Implementation Framework), SWIFT (Society for World-wide Interbank Financial Telecommunications) Standard Modeling) ; collaboration (that includes ebXML (Electronic Business XML Initiative), UBL (Universal Business Language), RosettaNet); and business processes.

Relevant developments for enterprise integration are also OBI, bolero.net, eCo, BTP (Business Transaction Protocol), XAML (Transaction Authority Markup language) and Microsoft BizTalk.

Networked organizations require advanced infrastructures supporting features such as multi-level support for interoperability, multi-level security, reconfiguration and recovery mechanisms, and they should be as much technology independent as possible (Camarinha-Matos et al., 2004). The section below presents some relevant platforms and technologies sup-porting EI.

C. Infrastructures and Technologies

Message-Oriented Middleware (MOM) is a client/server infrastructure that increases the interoperability and flexibility of an application by allowing it to be distributed over multiple heterogeneous platforms. MOM enables applications to exchange messages with other programs without having to know on what platform or processor the other application resides on, within the network.

Agent technologies brought a promising contribution to the development of infrastructures and services supporting collaborative networked organizations (Camarinha-Matos *et al.*, 2004). The conceptual approach behind any kind of solution design and development for agent-based architectures strongly relies upon the notion of interaction of autonomous processes that dynamically coordinate their actions by communicating with each other. Several efforts were mad by FIPA (The Foundation for Intelligent Agents) (www.fipa.org) in order to produce standards specifications of generic agent technologies in an internationally agreed mode, usable across a large number of applications, and achieving a high level of interoperability across applications (i.e. FIPA-OS - http://fipa-os.sourceforce.net).

Internet and Web technologies, mainly in the area of **Web services** and **Semantic Web,** seem to have a big potential for networked organizations. Web services are self-contained, self-describing, modular applications that can be published, located and invoked across the Web. Semantic Web is an extension of the current Web in which information is given well-defined meaning.

Peer-to-Peer networking technology allows the development and secure deployment of business solutions supporting several communication capabilities, such as: transparency, awareness, adaptability or mobility.

Several analytical comparisons are available concerning EI standards and technologies, based on different criteria. For example, related to B2B standards, it is possible to find an analytical comparison of ebXML and RosettaNet in (Pusnik *et al.*, 2000), and (Kotinurmi, 2002) compares XML-based B2B integration frameworks.

3. Towards a Self-Forming Business Networking Environment

3.1. *Pug-and-Do Business Paradigm*

Plug-and-Do-Business paradigm refers to the natural integration of an enterprise in a networked environment, meaning that the inter-enterprise integration should be at least as natural as in an intra-enterprise environment, the integration infrastructure being transparent to the users.

European Commission's Information Society Technologies R&D Program (Bacquet *et al.*, 2002) hosted an expert group with a view to providing a framework for the development of a radically new basis for interoperability of Internet-enabled business (applications).

The group is aiming at building a wide consensus on the strategy and approaches, which could be implemented through a research initiative supporting the vision of "Plug and Do Business". The technology-oriented themes identified were: Model-ling Internet-worked organizations; Open architectures supporting inter-enterprise collaboration and Ontologies. The current research project tackles these areas of research.

Plug-and-Do-Business paradigm for self-forming networked organizations can be regarded from different perspectives. The business processes within an enterprise can be coordinated (integrated) using a tool (that could be a distributed workflow, for example). The "plug" with another enterprise can be made by a public component offered by an enterprise and it is determined by the current necessities. The selection is made considering several requirements. The search can be based on different technologies, such as P2P or intelligent agents. Plug-and-Do-Business paradigm for self-forming networked organizations addresses also issues related to integration semantics, trust, enterprise' transparency and contract negotiation. Few similar approaches have been made. IBM developed and promoted On Demand Business (ODB). ODB represents "an enterprise whose business processes-integrated end-to-end across the company and with key partners, suppliers and customers – can respond with speed to any customer demand, market opportunity or external threat" (http://ibm.com/ondemand). It relays on three levels of integration and focuses on business transformation; operating environment made of application environment; systems environment, and utility-like services.

The research project under development will assure just-in-time just-in-place business process execution, trust-based B2B integration, transparent inter-enterprise business processes access, seamless contract- and ontology-based access to a networked organization (self-forming networked organization) by focusing on semantic integration on top of B2B standards, and distributed workflow technology will be used for coordination activities. Semantic integration encompasses data semantics and behavior semantics (Bussler, 2003). Data semantics and ontologies are used to establish a formal semantic description of business domain concepts that allow an automatic transformation between them, without a human integration modeler. Process semantics concerns the match between communicating interfaces processes, so that their execution results in a consistent state after their execution is finished.

3.2. Main Research Questions

The research project under development will provide an improved understanding of critical issues related to EI and networked organizations, which could eventually lead to answers to questions such as:

- *Question 1:* Which are the differences and similarities of the current existing (or still under development) frameworks for business networking?

- *Question 2:* Are the available technical solutions and conceptual frameworks competing or are they complementary?

- *Question 3:* Which criteria must be used to compare the available integration frame-works and standards?

- *Question 4:* Which is the most effective methodology allowing the integration, in a natural way, of one or more networked organizations?

- *Question 5:* Which are the organizational, functional and technological requirements for the implementation of an integration paradigm suited for a Plug-and-Do-Business environment?

- *Question 6:* Which are the requirements for the semantic integration among heterogeneous and autonomous business partners that are part of a network?

- *Question 7:* Which are the elements allowing an effective strategic alignment among all entities participating in an operational network?

By answering all these questions, it will be possible to respond the main research question: *how is it possible to achieve self-forming collaborative networks?*

3.3. *Proposed Methodology*

The research project in progress aims at developing a conceptual framework for self-forming networked organizations and implementing the supporting infrastructure. The outcomes will be validated by designing and implementing two concept proto-types.

The main phases of the research project are: **Phase 1** - Foundations (research basis and business orientation); **Phase 2** - Development (business model, infrastructure, and prototypes development), and **Phase 3:** Evaluation.

Conceptual framework development, and infrastructure and prototypes implementation represent the core activities of the project and they continue throughout the research project lifetime. Thus in Phase 1 of the project research results are intended to give input to the development phase, development tests can also inform what is feasible in terms of research and business goals. Similarly, Phase 3 of the research project intends to apply the output to the development process, which will lead to improved output to test. In this way, the research and

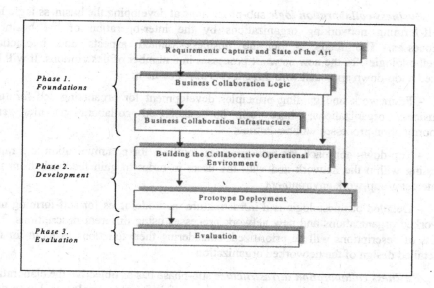

Figure 1. *Methodology Phases*

development activities and outcomes are combined. Phase 1 provides requirements, models and specifications to Phase 2, while Phase 2 infers outcomes which will focus research. Similar relation-ships hold between all three phases. Figure 1 illustrates a brief overview of the main phases of the methodology to be followed by the current research project. In parallel with the activities described, dissemination activities will be also performed in order to best disseminate the research project concepts, and to achieve an improved aware-ness of the research project results among industrial and public sectors.

3.3.1. *Foundations*

Phase 1 (Foundations) provides the research basis and business orientation for the research project. It contains the following sub-phases: requirements capture and state of the art; business collaboration logic; business collaboration infrastructure.

Requirements capture and state of the art sub-phase aims at identifying, representing and structuring the requirements related to the research project domain by using requirements engineering methodologies. It is under development a state of the art survey of the main technologies and available tools, presenting their advantages and disadvantages and it will be elaborated a comparison of the main integration frameworks according to the criteria defined. This analysis will constitute the basis for the development of the conceptual framework for self-forming networked organizations. Framework application and receptive industrial sectors will be also identified.

Business collaboration logic sub-phase aims at developing the business logic for self-forming networking organizations by the inter-operation of the business processes. The focus is on the business-oriented aspects and interaction methodologies for the new network processes in a number of descriptions. It will be used a top-down approach with three levels of refinement:

- Framework and guiding principles development for organizing self-forming business organizations; there will be established collaboration rules, and coordination processes will be defined

- Top-down approach for new processes outline, for communication and rapid testing within the network and with the users in order to gain feedback from the interest group-work environment

- Detailed business logic and infrastructure methodologies for self-forming net-worked organizations and new network processes using different descriptions. The sets of descriptions will be prioritized, considering their functions as input for the detailed design of the networked organization

Business collaboration infrastructure sub-phase has as objective the elaboration of a roadmap for the implementation and usage of different technologies. Up-to-date technologies concerning networked organizations, such as: intelligent agents and domain ontologies, P2P, Web services, Workflow, mobile technologies will be analyzed.

3.3.2. *Development*

Phase 2 (Development) aims at the implementation of the business model, supporting infrastructure, and of two concept prototypes that will validate the results obtained. It contains the following sub-phases: building the collaborative operational environment and prototype deployment.

Building the collaborative operational environment sub-phase aims at specifying the operational environment for self-forming business networks (the development of the collaborative infrastructure). This will be achieved through two levels of de-sign: high-level design and detailed design. The detailed design of the business processes refers to the refinement of the rough distributed processes; detailed methodologies for handling the difficult parts of the processes will be also designed here. The 'use-cases' will be grouped and prioritized for implementation. The high-level design concerns the design of a flexible and extendable system architecture for distributed business processes in dynamic networked organizations. The ontology building process will be finalized during this sub-phase.

Prototype deployment sub-phase aims at designing and implementing two concept prototypes, only with limited features that will validate the concepts developed. It is intended to build the concept prototypes mainly from commercially available software tools. The most suitable software tools will be selected. Their availability will be determined and possible gaps that require specific developments will be identified. Both explicit and implicit metrics will be quantitatively and qualitatively synthesized to ensure that the implemented software meets the scope of the research project.

3.3.3. *Evaluation*

Phase 3 (Evaluation) aims at assessing project results. There will be designed and developed several scenarios, and the infrastructure will be installed at pilot sites. The concept prototypes will allow valuable feedback from potential users. It is expected to foster acceptance among project manager and responsible of self-forming networked organizations, and to provide reference cases demonstrating the benefits of the results. Every partial result will be looked at with the view to improve it.

4. Conclusions and Further Work

The need to support enterprise integration (EI) is increasing. Several conceptual frameworks, integration standards and technologies are being developed. Although there are available several tools claiming to support EI and numerous scientific results in the business networking area and on the so-called "collaborative work", it is generally accepted that more work needs to be done, mainly concerning networks' creation or setting-up, support and implementation.

The current research project proposes an approach towards the development of a conceptual framework for a self-forming business networking environment based on Plug-and-Do Business paradigm, exploring issues on semantic integration and analyzing collaboration technologies, such as Peer-to-Peer, Web services, Semantic Web, agents and Workflow for the development of the supporting infrastructure.

Further work will be developed towards the development of a self-forming networking environment, in order to achieve the objectives proposed by the research project, while making methodology and concept tuning.

Acknowledgements

The authors would like to thank to FCT (Fundacao para a Ciencia e a Tecnologia) for funding the participation in EI2N Workshop and for the PhD scholarship.

5. Bibliography/References

Azevedo, A., Decision Support for the Negotiation of Orders in Enterprise Networks, PhD Thesis – Faculty of Engineering of the University of Porto, 1999

Bacquet, J; Naccari, F., "Plug and Do Business and The European R&D Programmes", Kluwer Academy Publishers, 2002

Bussler, C., *B2B Integration – Concepts and Architectures*, Springer, 2003

Buxmann, P., *Standardisierung betrieblicher Informatiossysteme*, Gabler, Wiesbaden, 1996

Camarinha-Mathos, L.M., "New Collaborative Organizations and Their Research Needs" in *Process and Foundations for Virtual Organizations*, Kluwer Academy Publishers, 2003

Camarinha-Matos, L.M.; Afsarmanesh, H., "*Collaborative Networked Organizations: A Research Agenda for Emerging Business Models*", Kluwer Academic Publishers, 2004

Crargill, C.F., *Information Technology Standardization: Theory, Process, and Organization*, Digital Press, Bedford, 1989

European Commission: Next Generation Collaborative Working Environments 2005-2010. In 1st Report of the Expert Group on Collaboration @ Work, 2004

Goranson, H.T.: "Architectural Support for the Advanced Virtual Enterprise". In *Computers in Industry*, 2003, 51 (p.113-125)

GERAM: Generalized Enterprise Reference Architecture and Methodology, IFAC/IFIP Task Force on Architectures for Enterprise Integration, 2000

Jagdev, H.S., Thoben, K.D.: "Anatomy of Enterprise Collaborations". In *Production Planning and Control*, (2003) Vol. 12, no. 5 (437-451)

Kotinurmi, Paavo, Comparing XML Based B2B Integration Frameworks, 2002 (White paper)

Pusnik, M.; Juric, M.B.; Rozman, I.; Sumak, B.: A Comparison of ebXML and RosettaNet, 2000 (white paper)

SWWS – Semantic Web Enabled Web Services: Analysis of B2B Standards and Systems, 2003, Deliverable D1.1

Tolle, M.; Bernus, P., "Reference Models Supporting Networks and Virtual Enterprises". In *International Journal of Networking and Virtual Organizations*, 2003, Vol. 2, No. 1

Vernadat, F., *Enterprise Modeling and Integration - Principles and Applications*, Chapman & Hall, 1996

Workflow Management Coalition, The Workflow Management Coalition Specification: Terminology and Glossary, 1999

Zachman, J.A., "A Framework for Information Systems Architecture". In *IBM Systems Journal*, 1987, Vol. 26, No.3

UEML: Providing Requirements and Extensions for Interoperability Challenges

Maria Bergholtz * — Paul Johannesson * — Petia Wohed **

* Department of Computer and Systems Sciences
Stockholm University / The Royal Institute of Technology
Forum 100, 164 40 Kista, Sweden

maria@dsv.su.se
pajo@dsv.su.se

** Centre de Recherche en Automatique de Nancy,
CRAN, Université Henri Poincaré, Nancy 1/CNRS
BP239, 54506 Vandoeuvre-les-Nancy, France

petia.wohed@cran.uhp-nancy.fr

ABSTRACT: *Addressed in this paper is the domain of interoperability and interoperable information systems. Enterprise analysis and modelling is an essential tool for achieving interoperability. However, the big number and diversity of enterprise modelling tools and techniques available today challenges the usefulness of enterprise modelling. Addressing this problem, a Unified Enterprise Modelling Language is under development. The aim of this language is to function as a bridge between different enterprise modelling techniques and tools facilitating model translation and hence support model exchange and communication. The work presented here is an analysis of UEML and its further development. A number of requiems are identified and extensions to UEML for capturing these requirements are proposed.*

1. Introduction

The growth of the number of information systems developed and in operation, as well as the development of techniques like the web facilitating communication and data exchange during the last couple of decades, has raised the need for developing interoperable information systems. By interoperable information systems is usually meant information systems which not only can operate in isolation for a single organisation's needs, but which are open and can also interact and function in co-operation with systems outside the organisational unit for which they were initially developed or procured (Ouskel and Sheth, 1999).

As this puts focus on the technical aspects and a lot of solutions, e.g., communications and data exchange standards were developed, the attention paid on interoperable information systems has been broadened into the more general concept of interoperability. While interoperable information systems refer to the capability of information systems for physically receiving and processing data from outside and sending data in required format to external sources, interoperability refers to interoperable information systems imbedded in well integrated environments. For achieving this, integration on an organisational level where different actors' businesses and processes are interplayed was focused on.

As enterprise modelling was a well recognized and widely applied technique for enterprise analysis, attention was paid on the communication problems caused by the big number and diversity of enterprise modelling techniques and focused was on "unification" or model translation and exchange between these. Diverse initiatives for facilitating enterprise model exchange were undertaken.

One of these initiatives was the UEML project (UEML, 2003), the goal of which was the development of a Unified Enterprise Modelling Language (UEML), which should act as an *Interlingua* between different enterprise modelling techniques and tools. For the development of UEML, three enterprise modelling languages, GRAI, IEM and EEML, were cross-analysed and a shared meta-model for them built (Panetto, *et al.* 2004). In this meta-model, only concepts which appeared in at least two of the analysed languages were included. The choice of the analysed languages, GRAI, IEM and EEML, was not definite but only constituted a first step of the work. The development of the UEML language is therefore not considered to be completed. On the contrary, the intention is to further develop it by gradually analysing and adding new languages into it. Addressed in the work presented here are hence extension areas of UEML. The analysis is provided through identification of new requirements for UEML. We have followed the main principle that a construct shall only be added into UEML language if it appears in at least two other modelling languages.

The presentation starts by first introducing UEML. After that a number of new requirements are identified and discussed. For every requirement examples of the languages supporting it is presented and a possible extension of UEML suggested. The analysis is summarised by a presentation of an extended UEML meta-model.

2. UEML

In this section the UEML language is briefly introduced. The intention has been to keep the description as close to the original as possible. Many of the definitions are, therefore, directly copied from (Berio, *et al.* 2002). The meta-model is presented in Figure 1.

An Activity represents a generic description of a part of enterprise behaviour that produces outputs of a set of inputs. An Activity may be decomposed into other Activities. An Activity may require one or several ResourseRoles played by Resources. An Activity has at least one InputPort and at least one OutputPort, to which flows representing inputs or outputs of the activity are connected.

There are two ways to represent the fact that Resources are used in an Activity. It is either through the definition of a role (i.e. ResourceRole), that a Resource plays in an Activity (which is meant to be used when the origin of the Resource is not explicitly represented), or through a Flow, connected to the InputPort of the Activity, which carries the Resource (this is meant to be used when the origin of the Resource is explicit or if the Resource to be used is the result of some decision or grouping or decomposition of some other Resource(s) through a ConnectionOperator).

A Flow represents the flowing of an object from one origin to a target. The origin and target of a Flow are Anchors that can be InputPorts, OutputPorts or ConnectionOperators. Furthermore, a Flow is an IOFlow, a ResouceFlow or a ControlFlow.

- An IOFlow represents the flowing of an Object between two activities. If the Object is an input, then the IOFlow is connected to an InputPort of an Activity and this means that the Object is needed for the Activity to be executed. The Object can possibly be consumed or modified by the Activity. If the object is an output of an Activity the IOFlow is connected to the activity's OutputPort and this means that the Object has been produced by the Activity.

- A ResourceFlow represents the flowing of a Resource between two Activities. The Flow then connects an OutputPort of an Activity that produces it and an InputPort of the Activity that requires it.

- A ControlFlow represents either the precedence relationship between Activities (i.e., a ControlFlow without carried Objects); or the triggering of an Activity after another (i.e., an TriggerFlow, carrying an InformationObject that represents the event triggering the second Activity); or the flowing of an InformationObject that is used to constraint the execution of the Activity (i.e., ConstraintFlow carrying a constraining

InformationObject such as e.g. a description of a procedure to be followed to execute the Activity).

As mentioned above, an Anchor is an InputPort, an OutputPort, or a Connection-Operator. An InputPort represents the entry of a Flow in an Activity. An OutputPort represents the exit of a Flow in an Activity. A ConncetionOperator represents the grouping or splitting (Join and Split) of Flows between two Activities. A ConnectionOperator of type "Join" is target of at least two Flows and is origin of exactly one Flow. A ConnectionOperator of type "Split" is origin of at least two Flows and is target of exactly one Flow.

Furthermore, a ResourceRole defines a Role played by a Resource in an Activity. A Resource may be a MaterialResource or a HumanResource. Finally, an Object is anything that can be attached to a Flow. In other words it is anything that may be needed or produced by an Activity. It can be an InformationObject or a Resource.

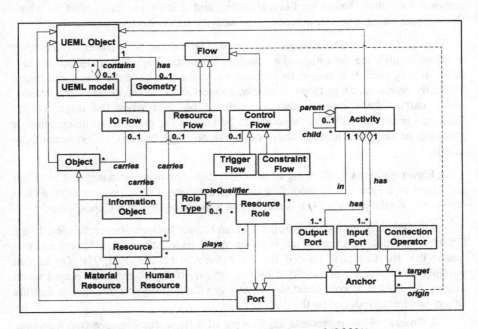

Figure 1. *UEML meta-model (reprinted from (Berio, et al. 2002))*

3. New requirements and extension areas for UEML

In this chapter a number of new requirements are presented. The basic reason for each requirement is that it introduces concepts that occur in several other enterprise modelling languages. These concepts should therefore also be included in UEML.

As motivation for every requirement a number of languages supporting it are given. The requirements are divided into three groups: dynamic aspects, modelling aspects, and social/institutional/organisational aspects.

3.1 Dynamic Aspects

In this sub-section we consider requirements for dynamic aspects, in particular how to handle events and different kinds of activities.

3.1.1 Distinguishing between different kinds of activities

UEML should distinguish between two kinds of Activities. The concept of Task (i.e. an atomic, not further decomposable unit of work) shall be distinguished from the concept of Process (a unit of work consisting of a number of steps, where each step is either a task or a sub-process which in turn can be decomposed into a number of steps). Tasks and Processes have several properties in common, e.g., they both have inputs and outputs and someone responsible for their execution. Therefore, the class Activity, capturing these common properties, shall be used as a generalization of them (see the shaded classes in Figure 2). The reason for distinguishing Tasks from Processes is the basic difference in that a process orchestrates a number of activities (i.e. shows the control flow between these), while a task does not (but is still important to introduce as it represents units of work). Note that this also implies that the aggregate relationship from class Activity to itself can now be more accurately drown from class Process to class Activity.

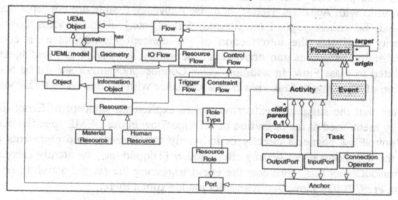

Figure 2. *Extension of UEML with concepts such as Process, Task and Events*

The distinction between atomic and compound activities is made in several languages. In UML (OMG, 2003) *Action* and *Activities* are used for atomic and compound activities, respectively. In BPMN (BPMI, 2004) the constructs *Task* for atomic activity is separated from the constructs of *Process* and *Sub-process* for representing compound activities. In BPEL4WS (Andrews, *et al.* 2003) the constructs used are *Basic Activity* and *Process* and in YAWL (van der Aalst and Hofstede, 2005) *Task* is distinguished from *Composite Task* and *Process*.

3.1.2 Capturing events

UEML should include an Event concept (see the shaded and doted classes in Figure 2). An Event is something that happens outside the system but that has effects on the system. Hence, an Event is something that (from the perspective of the system) happens instantaneously, as apposed to an Activity, which has duration. An Event is triggered by a source outside, while an Activity is executed by resources within the system. Examples of Events are timeouts and the receiving of a message. When an Event occurs it affects the control flow of the process. For example, an external agent sending a message, e.g. a purchase order, into the system would result in a number of steps being executed, e.g. for processing and delivering the purchase order. A timer signalling a timeout would often result in a reminder sent or in an interruption and, possibly reset, of the process. The concept of Event is present in several process modelling languages: BPMN (BPMI, 2004) (*Event with Message or Timer triggers*), ebXML/BPSS (ebxml, 2003)) (*Responding/Requesting Activity*), AOR (Wagner, 1999)) (*External Events* as opposed to *Internal Events*).

UEML should, therefore, be able to distinguish between instantaneous activities (i.e., Events) happening outside the system and Activities with duration within the control of the system. Furthermore, as Events influence the execution of the system, it should be possible to define and model the effects of an event as well as their relationship with Activities. Hence, likewise Activities, Events are concepts that can and shall be choreographed (sequenced, forked, etc.) in the process flow. This similarity motivates the introduction of the concept FlowObject as a common generalisation of Events and Activities in the model, see Figure 2. FlowObjects are associated to class Flow. In addition, class ConnectionOperator should be a specialisation of FlowObject. This view is in accordance with the one taken by BPMN.

Note that the suggested extension makes explicit the concept of Event. It was actually mentioned in the definition of a TriggerFlow in the UEML specification, i.e. "A ControlFlow connects directly or indirectly two Activities and represents either [...], the triggering of an Activity after another (TriggerFlow, eventually carrying an InformationObject that represents the **event** triggering the second activity), or [...]." (Berio, *et al.* 2002). However, it was not made explicit there.

3.2 Modelling Aspects

In this sub-section we consider requirements concerning general modelling constructs, in particular type levels and control flow constructs.

3.2.1 Capturing advanced control flow constructs

UEML should support a wide variety of control flow constructs. It should not only support basic control flow constructs (like those of sequence, parallel split, synchronisation, merge, exclusive choice, and multi choice) as described by the Workflow Management Coalition (WfMC, 1999)) and supported by the majority of enterprise modelling and workflow management tools. It should also support more advanced control flow constructs as identified and described in the workflow patterns (van der Aalst, *et al.* 2003; Worlflow, 2005).

An example of a more advanced control flow construct is Deferred Choice. There is a distinction between Decisions and Deferred Choices. A Decision operator can be seen as a question that will be answered based on process data. In contrast, "A Deferred Choice operator represents a branching point in the process where the alternatives are based on events that occur at that point in the process rather than the evaluation of expressions using process data" (BPMI, 2004). The Deferred Choice is hence implicit, which is different from a Decision, which represents an explicit choice. An example where the Deferred Choice concept is needed is when a sales process waits for a customer confirmation. Either a message with a confirmation will arrive from the customer or a time-out will occur. The process proceeds in different ways in these two cases and the actual choice is deferred to runtime. Examples of process languages that support Deferred Choice are: YAWL (van der Aalst and Hofstede, 2005) (*Deferred Choice*), BPMN (BPMI, 2004)) (*Event Gateway*), BPEL4WS (Andrews, *et al.* 2003)) (*Pick*).

Another example of an advanced control flow construct is the presence (creation, management and possibly synchronization) of Multiple Instances running in parallel for the same task within one and the same case. For instance[1], for an insurance claim, a number of witnesses need to be interviewed. The number of witnesses is different from case to case and it may not even be known at run-time when the initial interview task starts as new witnesses may appear as the result of already running interviews. Some recent languages supporting the concept of arbitrary multiple instances are YAWL and BPMN. Therefore, UEML should support the run time creation and synchronisation of arbitrarily many Multiple Instances.

3.2.2 Capturing knowledge and operational levels

UEML should support the modelling of concepts on both the knowledge and operational levels. The *operational level* models concrete tangible individuals in a domain, while the *knowledge level* models information structures that characterise categories of individuals at the operational level (McCarthy, 2004)). An example of the distinction between knowledge level and operational level is the one given by Martin and Odell (1994), who employ the concept of power type to refer to the difference between knowledge level and operational level. A *power type* is a class

---

[1] This example is taken from the Workflow Patterns Homepage (Workflow, 2005)

whose instances are subtypes of another class. A UEML example can be taken for the class Resource. This class contains concrete tangible individuals such as a particular car with registration number ABS125, a particular agent with name Stephen Dahl, etc. A class Resource Type added to the model would then model the different categories of cars, e.g. trucks, wagons etc and different kinds of agents, e.g. teachers, students, graduate students, etc. Examples of approaches that support the distinction between knowledge level and operational level are REA (McCarthy, 2004)), UMM (BRV) (UN/CEFACT, 2004)), Fowler's analysis patterns (Fowler, 1996)), and Coad's et al. components (Coad, *et al.* 2000).

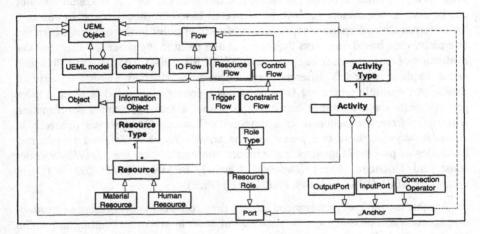

Figure 3. *Distinguishing between classes at knowledge and operational level*

Most UEML classes today are on the operational level only. These could be split so that they are represented at the knowledge level as well. See Figure 3, where such distinction is suggested for the classes Resource and Activity.

- Resource should be associated to a corresponding ResourceType class, in order to be able to model both individual resources and describe the distinctions or constraints that apply to certain types of resources. Example: properties of class ResourceType may be isbn-number, author, publisher, title, year etc. The corresponding properties of Resource are owner, id-number, place-in-library, condition etc.

- Class Activity should be associated with a corresponding ActivityType in order to model categories of activities as well as individual activities. Example: class ActivityType may contain properties like terms that may initiate or terminate an activity, delay-allowed or not, description, priority, etc. The corresponding properties of class Activity are responsible, id-number, delay-time, start-time, end-time, priority, state, etc.

3.3 Social/Institutional/Organisational Aspects

Human actions may be viewed as taking place in three different worlds; the physical world, the communicative world, and the social/organisational/institutional world. In the *physical world* people carry out physical Activities – they carry goods, utter sounds, wave their hands and send electronic messages. In the *communicative world* people express their intentions and feelings – they tell other people what they know and they try to influence the behaviour of others by communicating with them. Communicative Activities are performed through Activities in the *physical world*. In the *Social/Institutional/Organisational* world people change the social and institutional relationships among them – people become married, people acquire possession of property. People change social and institutional relationships by performing Activities in the *communicative world*. In this sub-section we consider requirements for social/institutional/organisational aspects, in particular how to handle agents, values, and social relationships.

3.3.1 Capturing Agents

UEML should be able to distinguish between active and passive objects. UEML should include the Agent concept for capturing active objects as well as the Passive Objects as the opposite of the Agent concept, see Figure 4. Agents can perform Activities, exercise rights and have responsibilities and obligations towards other Agents. Passive Objects, on the other hand, cannot perform Activities on their own accord, nor can they possess rights versus other Resources or have duties towards them. Passive Objects are used in and acted upon in Activities. They may be physical objects or social objects like Contracts and Commitments.

Furthermore, UEML should make explicit what kinds of Agents there exist. Human agents, Organisations, and artificial agents, e.g. Software, are some examples, but several can possibly be identified and added accordingly. The Human-Resource concept, which is present in UEML 1.0 as a specialisation of the Resource concept, will then only be one of several specialisations of the Agent concept (see Figure 4). The MaterialResource concept, which is the other Resource specialisation in UEML 1.0, will become a specialisation of the Passive Object concept, as it partially captures it. Other examples of Passive Objects are Commitment and Contract. They are further explained in the following subsection.

Examples of approaches where the distinction between active and passive objects is explicit are AOR (Wagner, 2003) and FRISCO (Falkenberg, et al. 1998)).

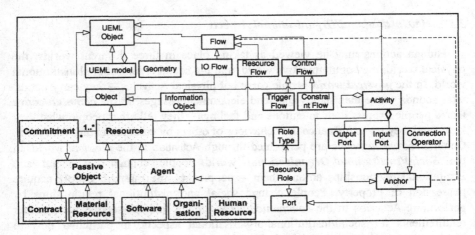

Figure 4. *Extension of UEML with Agent and Passive Object concepts*

3.3.2 Capturing social effects

UEML should include business oriented concepts including economic, value, and service aspects. I.e.,

- UEML should include a Commitment concept (see Figure 5). A Commitment is an obligation between two or more Agents, i.e. that of performing some kind of Activity. An example of a Commitment is a promise from a Supplier to a Customer to deliver an agreed upon quantity of goods. The corresponding Commitment on the Customer's behalf is to pay the Supplier. Examples of ontologies that include the Commitment concept are REA (McCarthy, 2004), AOR (Wagner, 2003) and UMM (BRV) (UN/CEFACT, 2000).

- UEML should include a Contract concept. A Contract is an aggregation of Commitments. An example of a Contract is an order which aggregates a number of order lines. Each order line represents two reciprocal Commitments between Agents. Examples of ontologies that include the Contract concept are REA (McCarthy, 2004) and UMM (BRV) (UN/CEFACT, 2000).

- UEML should include a Service concept. A Service provides value to one or several Agents and is realised through a Process. A Service may be realised through several different Processes and a Process may realise many Services. For instance, both Amazon.com and Ebay.com provide the service of supplying books online. This is however achieved by different processes. This requirement was inspired by the approach presented in (Klein and Bemstein, 2002).

UEML should relate the suggested social concepts with existing UEML concepts. By including these concepts, UEML will be able to bridge to business modelling languages and ontologies such as Gordijn's e3 (Gordijn, 2004)) and Pigneur's and Osterwalder's ontology (Osterwalder, 2004).

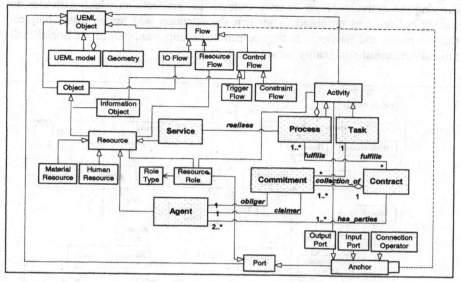

Figure 5. *Capturing social effects in UEML*

4. Summary

In this paper addressed were extensions of Unified Enterprise Modelling Language. A number of requirements for the language were identified and extensions for fulfilling these requirements were proposed. In order to justify the work, for every requirement examples of approaches supporting it were presented. The final result is shown in Figure 6. In this UEML meta-model, the suggested extensions are highlighted by shading the corresponding classes.

The requirements were divided into three groups. The first group, focusing on the dynamic aspects, resulted in the introduction of the class Event, as well as the separation of the concept of Task from this of Process.

The second group of requirements focused on the modelling aspects. Extension areas for modelling advanced control-flow constructs were suggested. They are however not, for the moment, graphically shown in Figure 6. This would require a rather detailed discussion and falls therefore outside the scope of this paper. Furthermore, a requirement for explicit distinguishing between knowledge and operational level was discussed. This is in the model exemplified by separating the classes Activity Type and Resource Type from the classes Activity and Resource.

The third group of requirements focused on capturing Social/Institutional/-Organisational aspects in enterprise modelling. Firstly, distinguishing Agents carrying out activities, from Passive Objects, i.e. artefacts on which activities are carried out on, was proposed. After that the attention was turned into Contracts, Commitments, and Services, as they constitute an important part of the Social/Institutional/Organisational reality we are in.

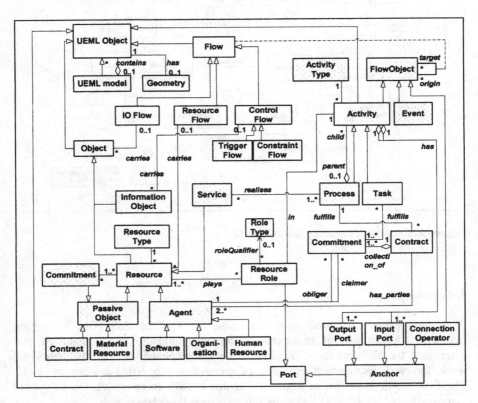

Figure 6. *The extended UEML meta- model*

References

van der Aalst W.M.P. and ter Hofstede A.H.M., "YAWL: Yet Another Workflow Language", *Information Systems*, 30(4):245-275, 2005

van der Aalst W.M.P., ter Hofstede A.H.M., Kiepuszewski B., and Barros A.P., "Workflow Patterns", *Distributed and Parallel Databases*, 14(3), pages 5-51, July 2003

Andrews T., et al, "Business Process Execution Language for Web Services, Version 1.1", at http://www.ibm.com/developerworks/library/ws-bpel/, 2003

Berio G., et al. D3.1: Requirements analysis: initial core constructs and architecture, UEML TN IST 2001 34229. http://www.ueml.org, 2002.

BPMI.org, "Business Process Modeling Notation (BPMN), Version 1.0", downloadable from www.bpmi.org, 2004

Coad P., LeFebvre E., and De Luca J., *Java Modeling In Color With UML: Enterprise Components and Process*, Prentice Hall, 2000

ebXML, "Electronic Business eXtensible Mark-up Language (ebXML)",Valid on 20030328, http://www.ebxml.org/specs/index.htm

Falkenberg E.D. et al., "FRISCO – A Framework of Information System Concepts", Technical Report, ISBN 3-901882-01-4, IFIP, 1998

Fowler M., *Analysis Patterns: reusable object models*, Addison Vesley, 1996

Gordijn J., url: http://www.cs.vu.nl/~gordijn/research.htm, accessed Dec 2004

Klein M. and Bernstein A., "Searching for Services on the Semantic Web Using Process Ontologies", in *Proc. of the 1st International Semantic Web Conference (ISWC)*, 2002

Martin J. and Odell J., *Object-Oriented Methods. A Foundation*, Prentice Hall 1994

McCarthy W.E., "REA Enterprise Ontology", http://www.msu.edu/user/mccarth4/rea-ontology/, accessed Apr 2004

McCarthy W.E., "The REA Accounting Model: A Generalized Framework for Accounting Systems in a Shared Data Environment", *The Accounting Review*, 1982

OMG, "UML 2.0 Superstructure Specification. OMG Draft Adopted Specification, ptc/03-08-02", http://www.omg.org/cgi-bin/doc?ptc/2003-08-02, Aug 2003

Osterwalder A., homepage url: http://www.hec.unil.ch/aosterwa/article.php?sid=12, accessed Dec 2004

Ouskel A. M. and Sheth A., "Semantic Interoperability in Global Information Systems: A brief introduction to the research area and the special section", *SIGMOD Record Special Issue on Semantic Interoperability in Global Information Systems*, vol.28, no.1, Mar 1999

Panetto H. et al., "A Unified Enterprise Modelling Language for enhanced interoperability of Enterprise Models", in *Proc. of the 11th IFAC INCOM2004 Symposium*, Apr 2004.

Unified Enterprise Modelling Language (UEML) project, 2003, homepage url: www.ueml.org, accessed Dec 2004

UN/CEFACT, "UN/CEFACT Modeling Methodology, 2000 (UMM-N090 Revision 10)", http://webster.disa.org/cefact-groups/tmg/doc_bpwg.html, Apr 2004

Wagner G., "The Agent-Object Relationship metamodel: towards a unified view of state and behaviour", *Information Systems*, 28(5), pp 475-504, 2003

WfMC, "Workflow Maganement Coalition Terminology & Glossary", Document Number WFMC-TC-1011, Technical report, Feb 1999

Workflow Patterns, http://is.tm.tue.nl/research/patterns/, accessed Apr 2005

Ontology for Enterprise Interoperability in the domain of Enterprise Business Modelling

Hervé Panetto* — Larry Whitman** — Kamran Ali Chatha***

*Université Henri Poincaré Nancy 1, CRAN, BP 239
F-54506 Vandoeuvre-Lès-Nancy, France

Herve.Panetto@cran.uhp-nancy.fr

**Dept. of Industrial & Mfg Eng, Wichita State University
Wichita, KS 67260-0035, USA

Larry.Whitman@wichita.edu

Department of Manufacturing Engineering
Loughborough University
Loughborough, Leicestershire, LE11 3TU, UK

K.A.Chatha@lboro.ac.uk

ABSTRACT: Enabling applications' interoperability to facilitate the true and seamless exchange of business process models within enterprises applications or between networked enterprises is referred to as enterprise integration. In this discipline of enterprise integration there is a growing need to setup pivotal languages expressing the enterprise models' knowledge to be exchanged. However, knowledge implies the semantic representation of concepts. Thus, ontology, being a means to formalise semantics of concepts and their inter-dependences, could serve as the technology for specifying such knowledge in completing the enterprise business models with the required semantics. This paper outlines what enterprise ontology will bring to the enterprise integration problem.

KEY WORDS: Enterprise Ontology, Interoperability, Business Modelling

1. Introduction to Ontology

Ontology is defined by Vernadat (1996) as "a formalization of some knowledge in terms of abstract concepts (entities made of a list of properties) and axioms (predicates on the properties)". Poli (1996) states that "*ontology is the theory of objects. And it is so of every type of object, concrete and abstract, existent and non-existent, real and ideal, independent and dependent. Whatever objects we are or might be dealing with, ontology is their theory. 'Object' is used in this sense as synonymous with the traditional term 'being'"*. Gruber (1993) defines Ontology as "a specification of a conceptualization." Ontology is an explicit specification of some topic. For our purposes, it is a formal and declarative representation which includes the vocabulary (or names) for referring to the terms in that subject area and the logical statements that describe what the terms are, how they are related to each other, and how they can or cannot be related to each other. Ontologies therefore provide a vocabulary for representing and communicating knowledge about some topic and a set of relationships that hold among the terms in that vocabulary.

In that sense, Poli (1996) postulates three theses:

THESIS 1: An ontology is not a catalogue of the world, a taxonomy, a terminology or a list of objects, things or whatever else. If anything, an ontology is the general framework (structure) within which catalogues, taxonomies, terminologies may be given suitable organization. This means that somewhere a boundary must be drawn between ontology and taxonomy.

THESIS 2: An ontology is not reducible to pure cognitive analysis (in philosophical terms, it is not an epistemology or a theory of knowledge). Ontology represents the 'objective' side (on the side of the object), and from the theory of knowledge, the 'subjective' side (on the side of the knowing subject) of reality. The two sides are obviously interdependent, but this is not to imply that they are the same (exactly like the front and rear of a coin). In order to conduct ontological analysis, it is necessary to 'neutralize', so to speak, the cognitive dimension, that is, to reduce it to the default state. We assume that the default state is the descriptive one, where the dimensions of attention, of interest, etc., are as neutral as possible (natural attitude). It is of course possible to modify the default state and construct ontologies of the other cognitive states as well, but this involves modifications of the central structure.

THESIS 3: There is nothing to prevent the existence of several ontologies, in the plural. In this case too, ontological study is useful because, at the very least, it renders the top categories explicit and therefore enables verification of whether there are reasonable translation strategies and of which categorization can serve best to achieve certain objectives.

Analysing these theses, applied to the enterprise domain, let us postulate that:

Thesis 1 focuses on the definition of a framework. In that way, enterprise ontology defines a kind of reference model that could be derived or refined to express an enterprise business process model. There is then a strong need to take into account the many kind of architecture and reference models to build a common enterprise domain ontology;

Thesis 2 shows that an enterprise ontology expresses the enterprise knowledge closely linked with the "enterprise objects" such as resources, processes, and activities In order to let enterprise applications interoperate, there is a need of a unified language to express enterprise knowledge and exchange of models. Such a Unified Enterprise Modelling Language (UEML) (Panetto, *et al.*, 2004a) would serve as an interlingua between enterprise applications that use specific enterprise models.

Thesis 3 postulates that a common enterprise ontology is not possible to be built, and is also not desirable. However, model transformations together with ontology alignment could be an answer to the need of cooperation between networked enterprises by facilitating applications interoperability. Enterprise ontologies have to be aligned and architectures and their supported technologies such as Model-driven architectures could help in formalising model transformations from *Enterprise Models* (EM) through *Computation Independent Models* (CIM) and *Platform Independent Models* (PIM) to Platform Specific Models (PSM) (Mellor, *et al*, 2004).

As an extension of these theses, applied to the enterprise domain, this paper outlines what an enterprise ontology should bring to the enterprise integration problem. The broader perspective in which we are working requires that there should be one enterprise wide ontology. And any system which is developed based on this enterprise wide ontology will be able to interoperate with other systems which are also developed based on the same enterprise wide ontology. General Ontology, if it exists, will provide a framework for conceptualising an enterprise. It will aim to identify general categories of concepts, their organisation relative to one another and their inter-relationships that will facilitate understanding the nature and working of enterprises and their constituents. The domain ontology will focus on populating these categories of concepts with domain specific semantics and their organisation. The framework could be applicable to an enterprise as a whole or a part of it.

2. Enterprise Integration Background

Enterprise Engineering is defined by The Society for Enterprise Engineering (SEE) as "that body of knowledge, principles, and practices having to do with the analysis, design, implementation and operation of an enterprise"[1]. Business Process Reengineering began in the 1990s with Hammer and Champy (1993) and these concepts are still practiced throughout the world (albeit with many different names; lean manufacturing, process improvement, TQM, and others). Reengineering recognizes that an organization's business processes are usually fragmented into sub processes and tasks that are carried out by several specialized functional areas within the organization. Reengineering maintains that optimizing the performance of sub processes can result in some benefits, but cannot yield dramatic improvements if the process itself is fundamentally inefficient and outmoded.

A key enabler of Enterprise Engineering focuses on is Enterprise Integration which consists in connecting and making interoperable all the functional areas of an organization to improve synergy within the enterprise to achieve its mission and vision in an effective and efficient manner (Molina, *et al.*, 2004). It requires a unique blend of skills of many different professionals today. For the purposes of this paper, enterprise engineering and integration is comprised of three pillars (Interop NoE, 2003; Panetto, *et al.* 2004b):

- Enterprise Modelling
- Enterprise Architecture
- Enterprise Ontology

These pillars are described in this section.

Enterprise Modelling – A model is an abstract representation of reality. This representation is necessary to provide a basis for common understanding and for improvement. Models are useful to provide a focus for discussion and a means to evaluate the design of a new process. The modeller, based on the goal of the model, determines which aspects of the real system are of interest and which system elements are to be modelled. An enterprise model is defined as "a symbolic representation of the enterprise and the things that it deals with. It contains representations of individual facts, objects, and relationships that occur within the enterprise" (Presley, 1997). The above definition entails the kinds of items that are of interest to the modeller. The use of symbols to represent the enterprise presents these facts, objects, and relationships in an easy to understand manner.

Enterprise integration needs model repositories. A survey showed that less than a quarter of the enterprises had models that were updated more frequently than once a quarter (Whitman and Huff, 2001). Enterprise model repositories and better methods of interoperability will significantly improve the currency and reusability of the models.

Enterprise Architecture – An architecture is made useful by providing components that define the complete system. "An architecture is that set of design artefacts, or descriptive representations, that are relevant for describing an object

---

[1] http://www.iseenet.org

such that it can be produced to requirements as well as maintained to the period of its useful life." (Zachman, 1987). Formal reasoning concerning the current state is enabled by architectures. Architectures, as the name implies, provide a complete view in which an organization works right from the stage of raw material procurement through product building until shipping the final goods to the customer (Inmon, W., *et al.*, 1997). An enterprise architecture is a tool which can be used for developing a standard method for viewing the system in which the enterprise operates in a very broad range. Architectures provide the key building blocks for an effective strategy, which in turn is the basis for a successful business strategy.

Enterprise Ontology – The purpose of an Enterprise Ontology (Fox, *et al.* 1996) is to complete models to make interoperability operational, including research, methodological and in-practice points of view. The nowadays widely distributed and obviously heterogeneous enterprise living and operating environment (variety of "enterprise cultures", business rules, supporting technology, dynamics of enterprise structures through new alliances or enterprise merging and acquisition, etc.) increases the needs for making explicit (i.e. modelling) enterprise structure and organization, enterprise processes, intra and inter-enterprise communication and so on, while ensuring fast enterprise adaptation to the changing environment together with preserving enterprise privacy, autonomy and communication security. Founding enterprise modelling and support on commonly agreed enterprise ontology will obviously impact modelling techniques and will improve intra and inter-enterprise entities connectivity. Moreover, it will very probably impact the underlying supporting architecture and technology by making them more knowledge-based.

3. Need for an Enterprise Ontology

A key hindrance in exchanging enterprise information is that inter- and intra-enterprise applications frequently associate different meanings to the same terms or use different terms to represent the same information. Direct mapping between the two terms is a "heroic" challenge and would likely still leave much confusion. A precisely defined terminology, relevant for exchanging enterprise information, can enable accurate information integration in the inter-enterprise efforts. This combination of terminology and definitions will constitute an enterprise ontology. For any interoperability to occur, a clearly defined conceptualization of that domain must exist. A proper ontology will also aid in achieving consensus among enterprise partners concerning the meaning of terms. The lack of coordination between departments within an organization can lead to failure of implementing change methods (Kim, 2000).

The following is an overview of the intended uses of an Enterprise Ontology (Uschold, *et al.*, 1998):

- "The major role of the Enterprise Ontology is to act as a communication medium, in particular, between:

  - different people, including users and developers, across different enterprises;

  - people and computational systems;

  - heterogeneous computational systems.

Also, and very importantly, an Enterprise Ontology is intended to assist:

  - acquisition, representation, and manipulation of enterprise knowledge; such assistance is via the provision of a consistent core of basic concepts and language constructs;

  - structuring and organising libraries of knowledge;

  - the explanation of the rationale, inputs and outputs.

The following are potential future uses of the Enterprise Ontology:

  - the transition of research knowledge and systems into operational prototypes;

  - the analysis of the internal structures, algorithms, and inputs and outputs of implemented systems, in theoretical and conceptual terms.

Enterprises rely on diverse information and interoperable environments for successfully surviving in competitive customer oriented market, where speed and flexibility play an important role in quickly responding to changing customer needs. For efficient enterprise operation and effective communication, a shared domain involving ontologies to capture semantics of the heterogeneous resources, thereby providing definitions for terms used in data sources is needed (Cui, *et al.*, 1999). Ontology is an "explicit specification of terms and their relationships, where terms are characterized by attributes". This shared domain model will be helpful to dynamically locate and integrate relevant data sources based on information resources. The main purpose of an Enterprise ontology in this model is to provide the foundation for building "collaborative information systems that meet the information requirements of flexible enterprises". To attain an enterprise flexibility system, syntax, structure and semantic heterogeneity should be overcome. Systems would become interoperable if conceptual entities, being exchanged between two system share same structure, semantics and syntax. Thus ontology for interoperability would be the identification, specification and organisation of structure, semantics and syntax of these conceptual entities. Ontologies are used to overcome these heterogeneities. Ontology uses agent communications, horizontal dynamic information integration, contents and capability descriptions, abstraction, and system integration for effectively communicating across various domains. One of the main uses of an ontology is to reduce misunderstanding by sharing semantics of the terms used in data sources. An additional goal of an ontology is to represent the domain model and vocabulary "in a way that enables programs to derive the intended meaning of the terms with minimum human intervention during their execution". Several tools like, Ontolingua[2], OWL,[3] CLASSIC (Borgida and Patel-Schneider, 1994), have been used for developing ontologies for efficient knowledge sharing and reuse of information.

A domain ontology management environment (DOME) has been developed by (Cui, *et al*, 1999) using CLASSIC to utilize ontologies in building corporate knowledge shops. The DOME architecture consists of four main components they are, generic ontology, ontology repository, mapping database and ontology reasoner.

3.1. *Towards an Enterprise Domain Ontology*

Ontology can be informally regarded as a set of general terms with specification of their meanings about a universe of discourse under study. Ontology does not only question the existence of entities in that universe of discourse but also develops a set of general terminology regarding those entities, helps to specify their structural attributes and their interrelationships. A middle-out approach to ontology development for a specific domain may save time, effort and re-work and provide an ontology that would be general enough to be applicable in most similar domains. Whether applications are federated inside an enterprise or among supply-chain (the extended enterprise), if they are developed using a general ontology they will have same semantics which should be the first condition to satisfy in order to attain inter-operability. Developing such an ontology requires a thorough understanding of an enterprise.

Consider two manufacturing organisations as shown in Figure 1. Based on the type of decisions to be taken and their time-frames, and objectives to be fulfilled, each organisation can be decomposed into three classes of process namely: Strategic Class, Tactical Class, and Operational Class (Doumeingts, *et al.*, 1998). Each class of process may be further decomposed into domain processes, business processes, and enterprise activities using CIMOSA like decomposition principles. Any manufacturing organisation can be configured by combining these classes of processes; and any process can be organised by combining business processes or enterprise activities. The basic constituent of any business process, domain process or process class is that an activity is a conceptualisation of reality not reality itself (Chatha, 2004). A process instance is an initialisation of a general process for a particular product or for a particular horizon.

---

[2] http://www.ksl.stanford.edu/software/ontolingua/
[3] http://www.w3.org/2004/OWL/

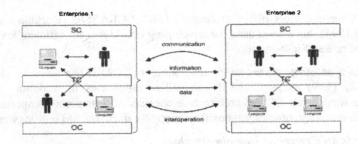

Figure 1. *Working among Enterprises*

It can be further argued that the process-based form of organising resources allows functional and team-based forms to be coupled to it. Any process may involve 'human', 'mechanical' and 'software application' resources in order to carry it out. These resources will need to interact with one another during their operation. This interaction may take the form of exchanging data, information, communications among humans, technical and software applications, and interoperation among humans, among technical resources, and among software applications. These interactions will not only exist among resources within a process but also between any two process-classes and even between two organisations.

Any class of processes will involve three types of activities namely: core activities, support activities, and managing activities where managing can be further divided into planning and controlling activities. Each class of processes will have its specific core activities. However, each class will involve similar support activities. Process also need, besides actors, the information/data and material resources.

3.2. Enterprise Domain Ontology for Enterprise Integration

Jasper and Uschold (1999) have compiled four scenarios of ontology application that are given below.

Neutral Authoring: An information artefact is authored in a single language, and is converted into a different form for use in multiple target systems. Benefits of this approach include knowledge reuse, improved maintainability and long-term knowledge retention.

Ontology as Specification: An ontology of a given domain is created and used as a basis for specification and development of some software. Benefits of this approach include documentation, maintenance, reliability and knowledge (re)use.

Common Access to Information: Information is required by one or more persons or computer applications, but is expressed using unfamiliar vocabulary, or in an inaccessible format. The ontology helps render the information intelligible by providing a shared understanding of the terms, or by mapping between sets of terms.

Benefits of this approach include interoperability, and more effective use and reuse of knowledge resources.

Ontology-Based Search: *An ontology is used for searching an information repository for desired resources (e.g. documents, web pages, names of experts). The chief benefit of this approach is faster access to important information resources, which leads to more effective use and reuse of knowledge resources.*

Of these *neutral authoring, ontology as specification* and *common access to information* are the types which will benefit enterprises at different ways as shown in Figure 2. It can be seen that each application scenario will be fulfilling a specific purpose in the manufacturing organisation and its scope will be limited to that purpose. Hence the ontology developed to support that application scenario will also be limited to fulfilling that purpose. Such a situation requires us to take a step back and see whether this will allow seamless interoperability between two organisations. How many different types of ontology will need to be developed?

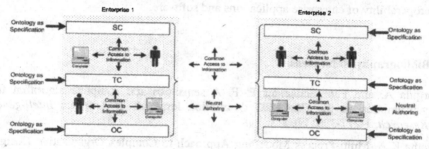

Figure 2. *Ontology based Interoperability*

It will describe the concepts that should be taken into consideration for the identification of entities. The framework will provide a general structure which can be exercised on a specific domain to build Domain Ontology. The Domain Ontology would be a General Ontology framework populated with domain specific attributes and concepts. The general ontology will also guide the development of domain ontology.

4. Summary and Future Directions

The paper presented an overview of what an enterprise domain ontology could bring to Enterprise Integration by means of applications interoperability related to Business Process modelling. Enterprises rely on diverse information and interoperable environments.

In order to be able to exchange not only data, by using syntactic languages and representations, but also information related the enterprise knowledge, a unified enterprise modelling language needs formalising the semantics of enterprise objects.

A common enterprise domain ontology describes the concepts that should be taken into consideration for the identification of entities and then provides a kind of reference model that could be derived or refined to express an enterprise business process model.

However, such common enterprise ontology is not possible to be built, because of the various types of enterprises and different kind of organisations. Thus, model transformations together with ontology alignment could be an answer to the need of cooperation between networked enterprises by facilitating applications interoperability. In that way, a Unified Enterprise Modelling Language based on enterprise ontology alignment tightly linked to model-driven architectures (MDA) is a research direction that could, at least partially, answer to the problem of interoperability of enterprise applications and software.

5. Bibliography/References

Borgida A. and Patel-Schneider P. F. A semantics and complete algorithm for subsumption in the CLASSIC description logic, *J. of Artificial Intelligence Research*, 1:277-308, 1994.

Chatha K.A. Multi-Process Modelling Approach to Complex Organisation Design. PhD Thesis, Loughborough University, 2004

Cui Z., Tamma V. A. M. and Bellifemine F. Ontology management in enterprises. *BT Technology Journal*, 17, (4), 98-107, 1999

Doumeingts G., Vallespir B. and Chen D. Decision modelling GRAI grid, in: *Handbook on architecture for Information Systems* (Peter Bernus, Kai Mertins, Gunter Schmidt. Eds.), Springer, 1998

Fox M. S., Barbuceanu M. and Gruninger M. An organisation ontology for enterprise modeling: Preliminary concepts for linking structure and behaviour, *Computers in Industry* 29/1-2, July, 123-134, 1996

Gruber T. R. A translation approach to portable ontologies. *Knowledge Acquisition*, 5(2), 199-220, 1993

Hammer M. and Champy J. *Reengineering the Corporation: A Manifesto for Business Revolution*, HarperBusiness, New York, 1993, ISBN: 088730687X

Inmon W., Zachman J.A. and Geiger J.G. Data stores data warehousing and the Zachman framework, *Managing enterprise knowledge*. McGraw-Hill, 1997

INTEROP NoE IST-508 011 Network of Excellence, Interoperability Research for Networked Enterprises Applications and Software, http://www.interop-noe.org, November 2003

Jasper R. and Uschold M. A Framework for Understanding and Classifying Ontology Applications. *Proceedings of IJCAI Workshop on Ontologies and Problem Solving Methods*, Stockholm, Sweden, August 2nd, 1999

Kim H.W. Business process verses coordination process in organizational change. *The International Journal of Flexible Manufacturing Systems*.12, 275-290, 2000

Mellor S.J., Kendall S., Uhl A. and Weise D. *Model Driven Architecture*, Addison-Wesley Pub Co, March 3, 2004, ISBN: 0201788918, 2004

Molina A., Chen D., Panetto H., Vernadat F. and Whitman L. Enterprise Integration and Networking: Issues, trends and vision. *IFIP International Conference on Enterprise Integration and Modeling Technology (ICEIMT'04)*, Kluwer Academics Publisher, October 9th-11th, 2004, Toronto, Canada

Panetto H., Berio G., Benali K., Boudjlida N. and Petit M. A Unified Enterprise Modelling Language for enhanced interoperability of Enterprise Models. *Proceedings of the 11th IFAC INCOM2004 Symposium*, April 5th-7th, 2004a, Bahia, Brazil

Panetto H., Scannapieco M. and Zelm M. INTEROP NoE: Interoperability Research for Networked Enterprises Applications and Software. Proceedings of the On the Move to Meaningful Internet Systems 2004 International Workshops. Agia Napa, Cyprus, October 25-29. 2004b, *Lecture Notes in Computer Science*, Springer-Verlag Heidelberg, Vol. 3292, 866-883, ISSN: 3-540-23664-3

Poli R. Ontology for knowledge organization, in R. Green (ed.), *Knowledge organization and change*, Indeks, Frankfurt, 313-319, 1996

Presley A. R. A Representation Method to Support Enterprise Engineering. Doctoral dissertation, Department of Industrial Engineering, The University of Texas at Arlington, Arlington, TX), 1997

Uschold M., King M., Moralee S. and Zorgios Y. The Enterprise Ontology. *The Knowledge Engineering Review*, 13/1, 31-89, March, Special Issue on Putting Ontologies to Use (eds. Mike Uschold and Austin Tate), 1998

Vernadat, F.B. *Enterprise Modelling and Integration: Principles and Applications*, Chapman & Hall, London.

Whitman, L. and Huff B. On the use of Enterprise Models. *International Journal Of Flexible Manufacturing Systems* - Special Issue on: Business Process Design, Modeling, and Analysis. 13(2), 195-208, 2001

Zachman J. A Framework for Information Systems Architecture. *IBM Systems Journal*, 26(3), 276-292, 1987

Web Services
and Interoperability

PC Chairs' message

The first Workshop on Web Services and Interoperability (WSI'05) was held in conjunction with the INTEROP – ESA'05 conference in Geneva on the 22nd of February. WSI'05 consisted of two sessions in which seven papers were presented. We had approximately 15 attendants throughout the workshop. This means that we had a number of attendants who were interested in the topics without presenting any material of their own. We interpret this as a success and hence we feel that the workshop had a good breakthrough. We wish to thank all authors and participants for making WSI'05 a success.

In order to enhance the discussion of each paper the workshop was organised so that each paper had an appointed discussant whose task was to get the discussion about each presentation started. This scheme worked out well and all presentations were followed by active discussions.

The workshop was organised into two sessions. In *session one*, there were four papers. The **first** concerned three fundamental approaches to service interface design; method centric, constrained and message centric interface design. We discussed how each approach impact the use of web service standards. The **second** paper presents the need to observe changing crucial success factors and complex business processes and their interrelationship to corporate strategy. Meta-modelling was used to develop proper monitoring concepts. A case study explained the application of the proposed service-oriented architecture. The **third** paper highlights business value for web services, possible challenges to achieving these benefits, and on legal and financial aspects that may arise. The result is in terms of a survey, and includes implications on issues that need to be elaborated and enhanced. The **fourth** paper of session one presents how data used in a scientific workflow may be located at different websites. Interaction between services at different sites often consumes a large proportion of time and network band width in such workflows. A new pipeline web services and scientific workflow framework was presented which can greatly reduce frequent data interaction between sites and mitigate network traffic incurred by huge scientific data transmission during the course of its execution. More processing time will be saved when more complex workflows are processed.

Session two included three papers. The **first** proposes a methodology to develop the semantic description about Web services using OWL Services (OWL-S). The implementation of a prototype revealed that development of such a description is not easily done and requires the support of a software tool. A methodology was proposed for how to develop an OWL-S, to be used as a basis for a software tool. The **second** paper discusses system integration as a central issue given the diversity of sources of information (internal or external), technologies and suppliers in current organisations. Environmental changes must be added, which are required to maintain competitiveness and provide solutions tailored to customers' needs. The adaptation directly impacts information systems, and the services these provide. A model was presented which aims to solve central problems, by contributions in three essential areas: orchestration / choreography of services, their transactional management, and a detector of change and re-configuration of choreographies. The **third** paper proposes a Web Service Accounting architecture, where accounting is the process of collecting Web Service usage information for the purpose of charging and billing. Through accounting service providers can cover costs and make profit from their provided Web Services.

Söderström Eva, University of Skövde, Sweden
Backlund Per, University of Skövde, Sweden
Kühn Harald, BOC Information Systems, Austria

Approaches to Service Interface Design

Martin Henkel* — **Jelena Zdravkovic****

* *Royal Institute of Technology and Stockholm University*
Forum 100, 164 40 Kista
Sweden
martinh@dsv.su.se

** *Royal Institute of Technology and University of Gävle*
Forum 100, 164 40 Kista
Sweden
jzc@dsv.su.se

ABSTRACT: *Services can be seen as an extension of the component and object oriented paradigms. Just like objects and components services need well defined, well documented interfaces. However, unlike most components and objects, services must be designed to work in a wide range of computing environments. Service design must cope with problems ranging from the integration of remote-procedure based legacy systems to the use state-of-art message based orchestration servers. In this paper we provide an overview of three fundamental approaches to service interface design; method centric, constrained and message centric interface design. Furthermore, we briefly discuss how each approach impact the use of web service standards and conclude with future research directions.*

KEY WORDS: *software services, design, service interface*

1. Introduction

Many view web services as a next step of evolution from components and object-oriented development. This view is not surprising since components are often described as providing services via their interfaces (Allen *et al., 1998*). Components separation of interface from implementation (Cheesman *et al., 2001*) is also one aspect that corresponds with web services separation of interface description (WSDL) from its implementation. However, even if components, objects and services do share some basic concepts many authors consider it to be a mistake to design web services in the same way as components and objects (Allen *et al., 1998*), (Monday 2003), (Piccinelli *et al., 2001*).

Web services as a technology have been in use a couple of years now. Knowledge on how to (and how not to) design web services is starting to be documented. One specific skill that a web service architect need to posses is the ability to design the interfaces to a web service. This task includes the selection of a service's operations, and their input and output parameters. To most experienced architects this might be a routine task, while novices struggles with the various "best practice" design descriptions in literature and as found on the World wide web.

The design of a web service interface (it's operations and their parameters) can vary widely depending on the fundamental design principle that is applied. The problem of selecting an approach is further complicated by that some of the design principles found in the literature are widely agreed upon as being "best practice", while other principles are popular, but controversial.

This paper gives a high-level overview of the fundamental approaches to service interface design. We also provide a brief discussion on how the use of each described design approach influences the use of XML schema, and the WSDL and SOAP web service standards.

2. Designing Interfaces

From the beginning the basic web service protocol SOAP was designed to be a simple way to do remote procedure calls (RPC) over the Internet. The similarity between SOAP and earlier distributed communication protocols such as CORBA and DCOM made SOAP easier to understand and implement. This similarity also affected the design of web service interfaces, services where designed with "RPC style" or "method centric" interfaces, with clearly separated operations and well-defined parameters (Vogels 2003). However method centric interface design is not the only design approach suggested as a "good" way to design interfaces. Other "message centric" approaches suggest that the design should focus more on the design of the messages in the system, and that the interfaces should contain a comparable small set of operations (Prescod, 2004). This discussion about method versus message centric design has caused some controversy. Some authors argue that the method centric design should not be applied when designing web services

(Arsanjani 2002). Others argue that a mixture between method and message centric design is appropriate, this third approach is called a constrained design (Orchard 2003).

In the following sections we describe the three basic approaches to service design.

2.1. *Method Centric Interfaces*

As mentioned earlier, method centric, or RPC style design, is the common way to design interfaces in distributed systems based on components or distributed object technology. RPC style design results in relatively large set of operations for each service interface, each operation performing a certain function. Figure 1 shows a simple example of a method centric interface to a library system. The simple example interface can be utilized to get information about a book (the getBookDetails operation), and to register that a book is loaned (the regBookLoan operation).

The RPC style design of interfaces has several drawbacks when applied in an environment where several separated applications need to communicate (Chappel 2002). The RPC style design can cause tightly coupled interfaces, where each client needs to know the exact definition of the service interface. When the interface changes all service clients need to be updated, which might cause a lot of extra work in large systems. For example, adding a parameter to the method regBookLoan in Figure 1 require that all the clients of the interface must be recompiled and re-deployed.

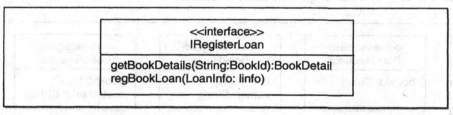

Figure 1. A method centric interface (parameter structure omitted)

The web services standards WSDL and SOAP are central for describing method centric interfaces, while the use of XML schema to describe the parameter structures is "optional". WSDL files are important when using method centric interfaces, because they describe the operations that the interface supports and the parameters that the operations can handle. Most development tools support the creation of WSDL files from a language specific definition of the service interface (e.g. a Java interface). The need for using XML schemas can be considerably lessened by using standardized XML object serialization ("SOAP Section 5 encoding"). For example, the parameters and return values in the IRegisterLoan interface can automatically be serialized into XML by using the standardized SOAP object encoding. The need for a domain specific XML schema is then alleviated completely.

The SOAP standard also got specific support for transferring calls made to method centric interfaces. The SOAP/RPC message style specifies where in the SOAP message operation names and parameter data should be encoded. This makes it possible for middleware servers and development tools to separate operations and their parameters, messages can thus be handled in a "method centric" way.

2.2. Message Centric Interfaces

Message centric design promotes the use of message structures instead of operations. The call semantic is then embedded in the messages sent to the web service. A message centric interface could be viewed as a method centric interface with only one operation, "send(msg)". This means that all information about a service request is embedded in the message structure. This approach has several advantages. Firstly, the interface is fixed, changes are only made to the message structure. Secondly, messages can be handled by intermediate parties (such as message queues) without them having to know the details of the interface. However, a message centric design makes it difficult to interpret and understand the functionality provided by a service. To understand the functionality of a service, a developer has to examine the structure of the messages that the service can handle. In a method centric interface the developer can get a simple overview of the functionality by examining the available operations.

Figure 2. *A message centric interface, consisting of message definitions*

The usage of message centric interfaces requires that all message structures (Figure 2) are described, for example by using XML schema. Therefore, schema design is a central activity when designing message oriented systems. However, WSDL plays a minor part when dealing with pure message oriented interfaces. In the extreme case there simply are no operations that need to be described by using

WSDL. Note that this is precisely the opposite of method centric interfaces, where WSDL plays a major role, and XML Schema a minor.

Just as for method centric interfaces the SOAP standard has support for message centric interfaces by virtue of the SOAP/Document message style. By using the SOAP/Document style developers are free to structure messages in (almost) any way possible, without the need to define operation and parameter names explicitly.

2.3. *Constrained Interfaces*

Constrained interfaces (Orchard 2003) are interfaces that contain a fixed set of standardized operations. Figure 3 shows a simple constrained interface for a library service. The operations in the interface depicts the basic operations needed for requesting information (the get operation) and creating entities (the create operation). The generic parameters contain information about what information to retrieve or create. This kind of interface can be used for a wide range of requests, for example the get operation in Figure 3 might fetch information about books or customers, depending on the contents of the data parameter. A common way to define a constrained interface is to include all the CRUD operations (Create, Read, Update and Delete). However, common operations like performing access control might also be included (for example by adding the operation "checkAccess(data, userId)").

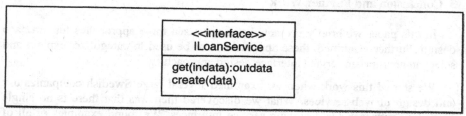

Figure 3. *A constrained interface for the service (parameter structure omitted)*

A (well known and controversial) example of an architecture entirely relying on constrained interfaces is Representational State Transfer (REST) (Fielding 2000). REST promotes the use of HTTP and its basic operations for building large-scale distributed systems. In this architecture the HTTP operations PUT, POST, GET and DELETE form a standardized, constrained interface. These operations are then applied to resources, located with Unified Resource Locators (URLs). By using only the four operations it is possible to build large distributed systems.

Since a constrained interface is standardized across an entire system, this design has the same advantages as the message centric design. This means that the interfaces operations are not affected by changes. Instead, changes affect the operation parameter structures. However, compared to the message centric approach constrained interfaces do provide a coarse grained overview of the service functionality. For example, it's easy to identify if a system (or subsystems) support deleting entities if the constrained interface has a Delete operation. A detailed examination of a constrained interface requires the examination of the parameter structures passed to and from the operations, just like the examination of message centric interfaces requires this.

WSDL can be used to define constrained interfaces. However, most effort of defining constrained web service interfaces must go into the definition of the XML schema that defines the parameter structures. A single system might only need a single WSDL file containing the operations of the constrained interface, and link to the used XML schemas.

The three presented design approaches are in no way exhaustive for representing possible service interface designs. The three approaches should rather be viewed as a scale where on one side the notion of operations are paramount (the method centric approach), and on the other side the notion of operations dissolves and all focus is put on the messages definitions (the message centric approach). On this scale, constrained interfaces can be put in the middle, since they do use the notion of operations, but only in a limited, tightly standardized way.

3. Conclusion and Further Work

In this paper we briefly presented and discussed three approaches for interface design. Further examined, these approaches can be used to categorize, explain and select an appropriate service interface design approach.

We started this work when we examined several large Swedish companies use and design of web services. What we discovered then was that there is no single prevailing approach for designing service interfaces. We found examples of all of the three design approaches, some companies even employed several different approaches for their services. This view was confirmed when studying literature on service design, some sources advocated a "message centric" design, some (often more developer centric) sources gave examples of "method centric" web services, others argued heavily for the REST architecture (thereby pointing towards the use of constrained interfaces).

Providing a rough classification of service interface design approaches is just the first step in providing a framework for choosing an appropriate service interface design. Beside the approach classification we identify the definition of service properties and the examination of technology support as important research areas:

Definition of desirable service properties. These properties define in which environment and under which requirements the service should work. For example a desired property of a service oriented system might be that it should be "loosely coupled", this means that the services should be independent. The desire to create loosely coupled systems might steer an architect towards the use of message centric interfaces. Other desirable properties of services must be identified, and the support for the property must be examined for each design approach. These properties form the basis for explaining why a certain design is preferable in a particular situation.

Further examination of technology support for the design approaches. In this paper we briefly discussed how each approach could impact the use of technologies such as SOAP and WSDL. However, we must also consider how other common technologies such as message oriented middleware and process orchestration engines affect the service design. Examining the technical limitations and possibilities will provide the fundament for explaining how a design approach can be supported, and well as how it is influenced by technology issues.

This work is a part of the Serviam project, partly funded by the Swedish Agency for Innovation Systems.

4. References

Allen P., Frost S., *Component-Based Development for Enterprise Systems: Applying the Select Perspective*, Cambridge University Press, 1998.

Arsanjani A., Developing and Integrating Enterprise Components and Services, *Communications of the ACM*, vol. 45 no. 10 , 2002.

Chappell D., Asynchronous Web Services and the Enterprise Service Bus, WebServices.org June 2002, www.webservices.org/index.php/article/articleprint/352/-1/24/, Accessed 15 Dec 2004.

Cheesman J., Daniels J., *UML Components*, Addison-Wesley, 2001.

Fielding R. T., Architectural Styles and the Design of Network-based Software Architectures, Doctoral dissertation, University of California, Irvine, 2000.

Monday P.B, *Web Service Patterns: Java Edition*, Apress, 2003.

Orchard D., The four Major Constraints to Loosely Coupled Web Services, Webservices.org 2003, http:///www.webservices.org/index.php/article/articleprint/1246/-1/24/, Accessed 15 Dec 2004.

Piccinelli G., Salle M., Zirpins C., "Service-Oriented Modelling for e-Business Application Components", HP Labs Technical Report HPL-2001-123, 2001.

Prescod P., "Second Generation Web Services", www.xml.com/pub/a/2002/02/06/rest.html (2002), accessed 13 Dec 2004.

Vogels W., "Web services are not distributed objects", *IEEE Internet Computing*, vol. 7 iss. 6, 2003, p. 59- 66.

Service-oriented Architecture for Business Monitoring Systems

Franz Bayer — Harald Kühn — Alexander Petzmann — Reinhard Schlossar

BOC Information Systems GmbH
Rabensteig 2
A-1010 Vienna
Austria

franz.bayer@boc-eu.com
harald.kuehn@boc-eu.com
alexander.petzmann@boc-eu.com
reinhard.schlossar@boc-eu.com

ABSTRACT: *For successfully managing a corporation in a state of changing crucial success factors and complex business processes, the interrelationship to the corporation's strategy has to be observed. Data provided by information systems are often heterogeneous, isolated and applicable in a difficult manner within decision-making processes. This is a result of heterogeneous information systems and their restricted architecture. Additionally, the variety of data provided by information systems is taken out of context in many instances and therefore difficult to interpret. The solution provided in this paper follows a service-oriented approach to overcome the restrictions of the underlying applications and data sources and allows open and maintainable system architecture. Additionally, metamodeling concepts are used for the characterization of the resulting Business Monitoring System. Interchangeable Services are specified on different layers from data extraction to the presentation of indicators. Finally, a case study explains the application of the proposed service-oriented architecture.*

KEY WORDS: *Service, Service-oriented Architecture, Business Monitoring, Business Monitoring System.*

1. Introduction

To keep business information systems in coherence with the business strategy of a corporation is one of the main goals in enterprise systems development. On the other side, tracking business execution and business evolvement - online or "just" offline - is no more possible without using adequate information systems. Performance Management is a management approach focusing on monitoring and controlling the key success factors of an organization (Kueng, Wettstein *et al.*, 2001; Kueng, Meier *et al.*, 2001; Neely 2002). Systems supporting these tasks are called Business Monitoring Systems (BMS).

Service-oriented concepts are core concepts designing open and maintainable information systems. This article applies service orientation in Performance Management and presents a service-oriented architecture of BMS. The remainder of the article is structured as follows: Chapter 2 classifies monitoring concepts and introduces a metamodel for BMS. Additionally, important approaches, techniques and implementation aspects for business monitoring are explained. Chapter 3 presents a service-oriented architecture of a BMS. Chapter 4 describes a real case of a service-oriented BMS. The article ends with chapter 5 describing related work and future developments in BMS with their impact on Performance Management.

2. Characterication of Business Monitoring Systems

BMS can be characterized in many different ways, normally in accordance with the underlying management approach. For example, the Balanced Scorecard Approach (Kaplan, Norton 1999) uses "perspectives" as main criteria, BPMS (Business Process Management Systems) uses "core elements" (Karagiannis 1995; Junginger *et al.*, 2004), Business Activity Monitoring (BAM) normally uses "core processes and activities" and the like. In chapter 2.1 some general ideas are considered to characterize the foundations of BMS. The results are refined in chapter 2.2 as a metamodel representing the basic requirements. Finally, in chapter 2.3 some implementation aspects provide ideas for the derivation of a service-oriented architecture.

2.1. *Foundations of a Monitoring System*

Starting from a business monitoring point of view, the designers of the monitoring system have to know what they are aiming for: Objectives and goals of the monitoring system have to be identified. This is the first dimension of characterization aggregated in table 1. According to the goals, the corresponding levels respective approaches of consideration are derived. After the selection of relevant approaches, the KPIs (Key Performance Indicators) and their probes in accordance with the monitoring scope have to be defined by means of time and events or a combination of both. This leads to a pre-selection of business monitoring scopes. The scopes may have their focus on the past, real time or treat with simulation of systems behavior to explain ex post system interdependencies, to trigger events or notifications in real-time monitoring systems or to give predictions of the future. Each combination of approaches, probes and scopes uses different techniques for data extraction, processing and presentation. Using proper techniques leads to an appropriate interpretation of monitoring information and the efficient deployment of measures.

Table 1. *Dimensions and characteristics of Business Monitoring Systems*

Dimension	Characteristics					
Objectives and goals	qualitatively			quantitatively		
Level	strategic		tactical		operational	
Approach	strategy driven	business type driven	business activity driven	data driven		
Probe	ex post consideration	ex post simulation	real time monitoring	prediction		
Scope	time based		event driven		comination of time based and event driven	
Techniques	execution	extraction	categorization	condensation	conceptualization	presentation
Interpretation	analyzing		controlling		decision support	acting

2.2. Requirement engineering for Business Monitoring Systems

The presented dimensions and their characteristics mentioned in table 1 are the most important for the derivation of a metamodel used to describe requirements for a generic Business Monitoring System. Figure 1 specifies the metamodel of the Business Monitoring System represented in this paper. Each dimension of table 1 is a particular view on the metamodel.

Among other aspects the metamodel describes the generic interrelationships of all dimensions and characteristics to find useful combinations during the instanciation of the metamodel for designing a single Business Monitoring System. The combination of the different views leads to a useful set of combinations and constraints. Particular scopes for instance "one year" may not lead to short-term actions on the operational level. On the other hand time-critical systems require short-term escalations and even short-term adjusting of target values.

Additionally, Enterprise Model Integration concepts (Kühn et al., 2003) can be applied to integrate the Business Monitoring System in existing modeling standards or model-driven architectures.

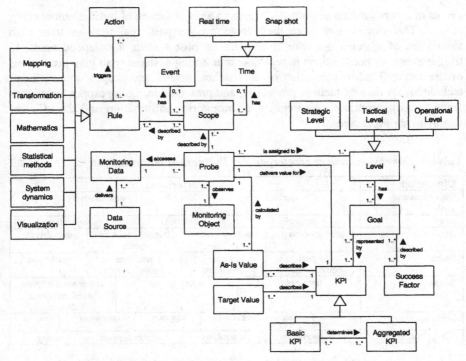

Figure 1. *Metamodel extract of the generic BMS*

2.3. Implementation Aspects

The implementation of Business Monitoring Systems severely depends on the complexity of the metamodel requirements and the architecutre of the underlying execution systems. To get an open and maintainable information system different service layers have to be considered. Additionally, each service layer and each service should be self-sufficient and interchangeable to set up opportunities for changing portal services, using condensation mechanisms of middleware systems or applying adaptors of database systems.

3. Business Monitoring Systems

The proposed service-oriented architecture of BMS consists of 6 categories of services. These categories are called macro services and represent the building blocks of BMS. A macro service is not (directly) an executable service and is therefore bound – depending on the specific requirements of each BMS application

– to a concrete implementation. These implementations are called micro services. Figure 2 shows these services and their interrelationships.

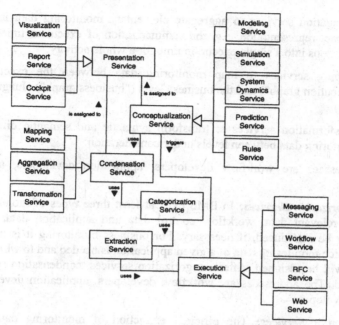

Figure 2. *Service oriented Architecture of BMS*

Presentation Services: All relevant business monitoring information has to be delivered in an appropriate form, facilitating quick and understandable access. More and more BMS provide the concept of "monitoring cockpits". The monitoring cockpit represents a service which can be compared to the cockpit of an airplane or ship. A monitoring cockpit uses visualization techniques such as tachometers, thermometers, pie charts, bar graphs, trend charts, model graphs, tables etc. The addressees are the strategic and operational management.

Conceptualization Services: To map, analyze, optimize and implement BMS applications several conceptualization services are applied. Modeling services for items such as company goals, business processes, organizational issues, workflows, applications, system infrastructures etc. provide the basic understanding of complex interrelationships and dependencies. Dynamic evaluation services such as system dynamics, simulation and optimization are used to get further insight into the "execution behavior" of a certain business (Jain 1991). Especially by using simulation services, business monitoring scenarios can be evaluated before implementing a monitoring system, e.g. by using concepts such as simulation agents to represent probes in the simulation environment. The addressees are business analysts.

Condensation Services: During business monitoring, most monitoring-relevant data has to be condensed into a higher level of abstraction. Some typical services are:

- Aggregation services to aggregate elementary monitoring data into a more compact representation, e.g. the summarization of execution times of single work steps into a single execution time for a whole activity.

- Mapping services to map monitoring data between the execution level ("execution graph") and the business level ("business graph") (Junginger *et al.*, 2004).

- Transformation services to transform syntactic and semantic differences of monitoring data between levels under consideration.

The addressees are workflow developers, application developers, and system developers.

Categorization Services: In BMS exist at least three types of monitoring data: workflow-relevant data, workflow control data and application data. Additional types may be introduced, if necessary. For business monitoring it is important to clarify which monitoring data of a given application is needed and to which category the data will be assigned. After categorization services, condensation services will be applied. The addressees are workflow developers, application developers, and system developers.

Extraction Services: The efficient extraction of monitoring data from the business execution environment is a crucial factor for BMS. In "pure" workflow-based execution environments, data sources such as file-based audit trails and audit databases deliver directly monitoring-relevant data. But often, workflow management systems are only a part of the business execution environment and other systems provide monitoring relevant data as well (see "Execution Services"). In this situation special adapters for each system involved in business execution are needed (as in integrating several data sources in data warehouse applications). These adaptors may be used via standard API, native API, XML etc. The addressees are workflow developers, application developers, and system developers.

Execution Services: For the execution of business applications various target environments such as WFMS, ERP systems, CRM systems, Groupware systems, legacy systems, web-based systems etc. exist. Each target environment produces monitoring-relevant data. Often, WFMS are used for the integrated execution of complex processes spanning various target systems (WFMC 2000; WFMC 2002). The resulting runtime data must then be extracted and categorized for being used for monitoring purposes (McGregor 2002). The addressees are all people concerned executing business processes.

4. Case Study

In 2004 BOC Information Systems GmbH implemented a BMS at together internet services GmbH, which is an Austrian internet platform for handling business between agents and insurance companies. The platform started in 2001 and serves several major insurance companies in Austria wich have a combined market share of about 60% calculated in premium.

The BMS was introduced to provide cockpit services to those insurance companies for monitoring business transactions which are processed by the platform. Different types of business transactions are implemented as processes (like applications or claims) using a light-weight workflow engine.

KPI's are categorized by processes, products and organizational units, following the core elements of BPMS (Karagiannis 1995; Junginger *et al.*, 2004). An interesting KPI shows for example numbers of applications (process) for car insurances (product) in Vienna (organizational unit) in December 2004 (scope – time). This as-is value is compared with an appropriate target value. Out of this the system can calculate the degree of reaching the goal in selling (compare with metamodel shown in figure 1).

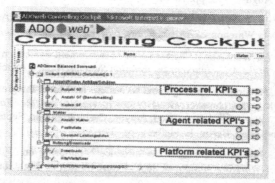

Figure 3. *Main levels of navigation in the KPI's tree list*

Figure 3 shows a screenshot with a collapsed KPI navigation tree. The above example can be found, drilling down into process related KPI's.

The BMS in this case study implements a SOA by encapsulating mainly the services shown in figure 2. Data extraction is done directly in the platforms core application. This data is condensed for usage in KPI-models, which calculate aggregated KPI's from basic KPI's. Those KPI-models are used by score-models, which calculate scores in reaching predefined goals on operational and strategic level. Finally, those models are published using web-enabled controlling cockpits within the platforms web-portal as an integrated service to authorized insurance company users.

5. Summary and Perspectives

The paper described the service-oriented development of BMS by the use of metamodeling concepts. A static metamodel was described with characteristics and requirements which was refined by a service-oriented architecture. For the future work the service architecture will be refined by introducing additional standards of the SOA community providing e.g. WSDL, WSCI, BPEL, Service Policies, QoS.

6. Bibliography/References

Jain R., *The Art of Computer Systems Performance Analysis: Techniques for Experimental Design, Measurement, Simulation and Modeling*, John Wiley & Sons, 1991.

Junginger S., Kühn H., Bayer F., Karagiannis D., Workflow-based Business Monitoring, In: *Workflow Handbook 2004*, Future Strategies Inc. Edited by Fischer L. (2004), pp. 65–80.

Kaplan R. S., Norton D. P., The Balanced Scorecard: Translating Strategy into Action, *Harvard Business School Press*, 1999.

Karagiannis D., BPMS: Business Process Management Systems, In: *ACM SIGOIS Bulletin*, Vol. 16, Nr. 1, August 1995, pp. 10-13.

Kueng P., Wettstein T., List B.: A Holistic Process Performance Analysis through a Performance Data Warehouse, *7th Americas Conference on Information Systems*, 2001.

Kueng P., Meier A., Wettstein T.: Performance Measurement Systems must be engineered, *Comunications of the Association of Information Systems*, Vol. 7, Article 3, 2001.

Kühn H., Bayer F., Junginger S., Karagiannis D., Enterprise Model Integration, In: Bauknecht K., Tjoa A. M., Quirchmayer G. (Eds.), *Proceedings of the Fourth International Conference EC-Web 2003 – Dexa 2003*, Prague, Czech Republic, September 2003, LNCS 2738, Springer-Verlag, Berlin, Heidelberg, pp. 379-392.

McGregor C., The Impact of Business Performance Monitoring on WfMC Standards, In: Fischer L. (Ed.), *Workflow Handbook 2002*, Future Strategies, Lighthouse Point, 2002.

Neely A. (Ed.), *Business Performance Measurement*, Cambridge University Press, 2002.

Workflow Management Coalition (WFMC), Workflow Standard – Interoperability Wf-XML Binding, Document Number WFMC-TC-1023, Document Status – Official Version 1.0, May 2000. http://www.wfmc.org/standards/docs/Wf-XML-1.0.pdf.

Workflow Management Coalition (WFMC), Workflow Process Definition Interface –XML Process Definition Language, Document Number WFMC-TC-1025, Document Status – Version 1.0 Final Draft, October 2002. http://www.wfmc.org/standards/docs/TC-1025_10 _xpdl_102502.pdf.

Web services business values, legal and financial aspects

Eva Söderström

School of Humanities and Informatics, University of Skoevde
Box 408, 541 28 Skoevde
Sweden
eva.soderstrom@his.se

ABSTRACT: *Web services are a hot topic, and there is much research and much industrial effort going into developing and enhancing them. The focus is, however, often technical. This paper highlights some business aspects, in focusing on business value for web services, possible challenges to achieving these benefits, and on legal and financial aspects that may arise. Material is gathered both from a literature perspective and an empirical effort in terms of a project including several WS-using organisations. The result is more in terms of a survey, and includes implications on issues that need to be elaborated and enhanced.*

KEY WORDS: *web services, business value, challenges, legal and financial aspects.*

1. Introduction

"Web services isn't about technology; it's about successful business strategy." (Dunn, 2003).

The quotation above describes how web services really are not foremost about technology, but equally about management and strategic issues. There has been a lot of attention to and hype surrounding the concept of Web Services (WS) lately. Most large organisations have some form of attitude or position towards this phenomenon (Azzara, 2002), and there will be a basic change in how applications are created and disseminated (Wong, 2002). True values with WS, however, are still to come, and expectations are great. It is furthermore still a lack of empirical studies regarding actual measurements of real-life experienced values, and how businesses are affected. This paper is a first step towards such an understanding, and includes three parts: business values, challenges, and legal and financial aspects of WS. The purpose is to enhance the current knowledge on web services business values and effects. The empirical material was gathered through a Swedish project concerning WS, where a number of industry companies interested in, using, and creating WS were involved. The paper is organised as follows: Chapter 2 will introduce findings on business values, while Chapter 3 is focused on challenges for the same. Chapter 4 investigates legal and financial aspects, before Chapter 5 concludes the paper.

2. Business values

There are different types of business values regarding web services (WS). This chapter will summarise both values and challenges identified in the project.

There are many promises for what WS can help achieve, for example that they enable considerable cost savings within six to twelve months, while only requiring minor investments (Hagel, 2003). WS are supposed to help organisations to focus on creating and delivering services to customers, employees and partners without concern for systems compatibility (Roby, 2003). It is possible to describe the aforementioned change by comparing WS technology. Traditional solutions are firstly often expensive and complex, for example due to scaling of point-to-point solutions (Race, 2003; Murphy and Stoyanova, 2003; Colan, 2003). Web services solutions, on the other hand, enable data from existing systems to be connected to higher levels, which enables loosely coupled solutions (Race, 2003; Colan, 2003). Furthermore, traditional systems used to require changes to connections when incorporating application changes (Smolnicki, 2004). WS uses standardised interfaces, which remain functional even during application rework (Smolnicki, 2004). In summary, the number of WS values identified can be grouped into 10 categories: providing and consuming services; business information exchange; increasing revenues and enhancing competition; integration; automation; time-to-market; middleware and applications; enhanced productivity and efficiency;

application development; and cost reduction. The primary source for identification of the groupings is literature, but our empirical material fits into them as well. Each perspective will now be presented in a sub-section each.

2.1. *Literature business values*

10 groupings of business values were identified. In the list below, each grouping will be explained what each category covers based on the literature sources.

– Providing and consuming services includes access to services without concern for technical platforms (Race, 2003; Marshman, 2002), exposure of legacy system functionality (Estrem, 2003), and out- and insourcing of services depending on the needs at hand (Smolnicki, 2004; Marshman, 2002; Estrem, 2003; Syntegra, 2002).

– Business information exchange includes using standards for information exchange (AmberPoint, 2002), for rapid response to new possibilities and opportunities (Dunn, 2003; Barry, 2003), increasing opportunities to co-operate for reducing costs and time cycles, and to enable the use of business information embedded in applications (AmberPoint, 2002).

– Increasing revenues and enhancing competition includes possibilities for new business and co-operation models to increase market shares (Clabby, 2002), and better utilise the intellectual capital and competition from others (Dunn, 2003; Fletcher and Waterhouse, 2002).

– Integration includes integration of applications, both internally and externally in order to stream-line the business (Dunn, 2003; Smolnicki, 2004; Clabby, 2002; Cape Clear, 2002; Thelin and Murray, 2002). It should be conducted in co-operation between organisational management, and through the use of standards. WS are also easier to create, configure and reuse, which facilitates integration and reduces compatibility problems (Roby, 2003; Fletcher and Waterhouse, 2002).

– Automation includes ways of creating stronger business relationships that enable a quicker response to market needs (Smolnicki, 2004; Clabby, 2002), reduce the number of errors, and to automate previously manual processes.

– Time-to-market includes getting products to the market fast, by quick responses to new opportunities (Smolnicki, 2004; AmberPoint, 2002; Clabby, 2002).

– Middleware and applications includes tying systems and transactions together across organisational borders through, for example, a more flexible access to applications (Smolnicki, 2004; Syntegra, 2002; Fletcher and Waterhouse, 2002; Clabby, 2002). The middleware can in this case be used as interfaces, which incorporate WS standards to define how data will be requested and passed.

– Enhanced productivity and efficiency includes a chance to increase productivity for a number of personnel types. Examples are application developers (AmberPoint, 2002), end users (Fletcher and Waterhouse, 2002; Clabby, 2002) and

IT departments (Syntegra, 2002; Barry, 2003). Maintenance, administration and service costs can also be reduced in benefits and payroll management (Dunn, 2003).

– Application development includes faster development of applications, through for example the reuse of code and a simplified development process for inexperienced people (Wong, 2002; Marshman, 2002; Estrem, 2003; AmberPoint, 2002; Barry, 2003; Fletcher and Waterhouse, 2002; Valtech, 2001).

– Cost reduction includes time reduction, code reuse (Barry, 2003), connecting information for an increased value (Syntegra, 2002), reduced administration (Dunn, 2003), and a reduction of the number of unnecessary software functions (Estrem, 2003). Another benefit may be better and cheaper customer service (Clabby, 2002).

Using the same groupings, the next sub-section will further explain empirical findings with respect to business values for web services.

2.2. Empirical business values

During the project, several visits were made to the main offices of the participating organisations. A number of business values, were derived from these visits, showing where the organisations have experienced an increased value. The same categories as identified in literature can be used to compare the findings.

– Providing and consuming services includes the possibilities to expose legacy system functionality as well as functionality from other existing systems, as a way to increase customer value.

– Business information exchange includes packaging information in a new way, e.g. in the form of catalogues to offer to customers. This contributes to service reuse on a higher level.

– Increasing revenues and enhancing competition includes primarily an increased customer adaptation through web services, which also increases the value for both customers and the organisation itself.

– Integration includes many aspects. Examples are reduction of problems with redundancy storage and updates, as well as being able to preserve internal systems through the use of a web services interface.

– Automation includes primarily uniformity in the way of working, and consistent results from for example calculations. This increases for example the quality in a long term perspective.

– Time-to-market was not mentioned by either of the participating organisations within the project.

– Middleware and applications includes a central solution for achieving web services functionality, and enabling correct scaling and levelling of applications.

– Enhanced productivity and efficiency was not mentioned by either of the participating organisations within the project.

– Application development includes for example component thinking in both applications and in development methodology. Development can also be distributed, at the same time as reuse of both code and services is enabled.

– Cost reduction includes primarily that costs decrease following a reduction of internal organisational administration. Customers can themselves conduct many simpler tasks directly towards the systems.

2.3. Summarising the business values for web services

Literature and industry have both mentioned several business values for web services (see table 1). Both perspectives view legacy system functionality exposure as important, accompanied by the comments on preservation of internal systems and application integration. This is related to packaging information according to new needs and depending on the co-operation at hand, which further increases flexibility and adaptability. The number of errors is reduced, bringing more consistent results. A central solution is also enabled, which for example takes place using middleware.

Value category	Literature	Empirical
Providing and consuming services	Exposure of legacy system functionality	Exposure of legacy system functionality
Business information exchange	Enabled use of embedded business information	Re-packaging of information to customers
Increasing revenues and enhancing competition	Possibilities for new business and co-operation models	Adaptation according to customer needs
Integration	Integration of applications; Simplified creation, configuration and reuse	Reduced redundancy and updating problems; Preservation of internal systems
Automation	Reduce the number of errors	Consistent results increase quality
Time-to-market	No similarities	No similarities
Middleware and applications	Using middleware as interfaces	A central solution enabled
Enhanced productivity and efficiency	No similarities	No similarities A
Application development	Faster development of applications through reuse of code; A simplified development process	Distributed development is enabled; Reuse of code and services
Cost reduction	Reduced administration	Reduced administration

Table 1. *Comparison of business value aspects in literature and industry*

Due to code reuse, application development can be both faster and distributed. All similarities between the aspects are presented in table 1. Comments are inserted where the two perspectives share opinions regarding the values. One remark is that administration in-house to organisations can be reduced. These administrative tasks are instead placed in the hands of customers, while the organisation itself can focus on other, more competence-focused tasks. So far, the business values for web services have been in focus. However, the web services arena also faces a number of challenges if the business values are to be achievable. These challenges will be presented in the next section.

3. Problems and challenges

Web services bring major promises, but there are some aspects that may cause problems. These should hence be viewed as challenges and potential pitfalls. This section will focus on five such challenges that were identified in literature: standards-related challenges; inter-operability challenges; challenges for new opportunities; challenges for knowledge and skills; and legal and financial challenges. Similar to the business values, challenges can also be divided according to literature information and empirical material.

3.1. *Literature challenges*

Let us start with *standards-related challenges*. Standards for web services (WS) are still rather immature and incomplete, with the exception of the core standards (SOAP, WSDL and UDDI). Aspects that still need to be resolved are security, transactions, process flows, user interaction etc. (Dunn, 2003; Wong, 2002; Smolnicki, 2004; Estrem, 2003). The standards that are used must also be possible to manage internally within organisations. A related challenge is the category of *Interoperability challenges*. These refer to that software being developed cannot handle the opportunities built into the standards, and the software is therefore only focused on a limited part of the standards. Different software vendors also offer different types of web services environments, and promise inter-operability between them at the same time. Other promises are mobile applications, code reuse, scalability, security, etc. However, it remains to be seen whether these promises can be kept to 100 percent.

Web services are also said to bring *new possibilities*, which is our next challenge category. Each organisation about to start using WS must consider which new possibilities they may launch using the new technology, and how they can reach new markets. A focus is therefore needed on solutions of the kind not previously possible. The challenge lies in being able to financially motivate such efforts to the organisational management. WS are not only about technology, which has been said earlier in the paper. There are therefore also challenges regarding *skills and knowledge* for employees. Many of those currently working with IT are rather inexperienced with regards to incorporation of WS (Smolnicki, 2004). Without human competence, the technology cannot be utilised as desired, which makes education a necessity. At the same time, organisations need control of what to use WS for, which is a long term perspective.

Finally, there are *legal and financial challenges*. A few examples are to protect customer integrity, intellectual capital, to achieve effective cost sharing and payment models, web services ownership, etc. (Govern and Weagraff, 2003).

3.2. Empirical challenges

The same grouping will be utilised as with literature challenges. Here, *standards-related challenges* refer to immaturity in standards, the lack of a comprehensive web services security standard, or that the standards cannot manage organisational needs to a full extent. Furthermore, existing systems and protocols can prevent the full usage of new standards. Regarding *inter-operability challenges*, system changes and updates are problematic. Firstly, it is difficult to change in old systems due to much of the embedded business logic, and because it is difficult to know how the changes will affect other systems. Some of the existing technologies cannot manage the organisations' demand for, for example, schema levels. *Challenges for new possibilities* include that most organisations emphasise that the technology should not be leading or guiding the web services effort, but that needs must be the driver. Organisations must know which information to expose and why they do so, as well as which aspects and services that are important to prioritise. For challenges regarding *knowledge and skills*, it is difficult to know how much administration of, for example, password formation that can be transferred to customers without causing problems in the business relations. The organisations do not want to burden the customers, while at the same time wishing to reduce as much of the internal administration as possible. Finally, *legal and financial challenges* refer primarily to that it is difficult to maintain an overview of service ownership and service definitions, as well as of Service Level Agreements (SLAs) and legal aspects. These aspects will be further discussed in chapter 4.

3.3. Summarising challenges for web services

Both literature and industry have mentioned several challenges to successful and profitable web services usage. The perspectives both view problems in standards as important, where immaturity and incompleteness are highlighted. Concerns for software (and technology in general) problems are also shared, in that all aspects desired by organisations are not covered or managed. More strategic aspects are also emphasised, such as organisations needing to know why they are using web services and what for, such as for reaching new markets. Human competence is also essential, since organisations without it cannot fully exploit web services and the value they may bring. Finally, web services ownership is not a simple task, nor is agreements between companies regarding for example service levels or cost sharing. The similarities between the perspectives are shown in table 2. Two aspects are interesting to note with regards to challenges. Firstly, inter-operability challenges are in literature more clearly related to standards challenges, while they in the empirical material refer more to embedded business logic. It thus seems that the two perspectives have a slightly different focus here.

Challenge category	Literature	Empirical
Standards-related challenges	Immature and incomplete standards	Immature and incomplete standards
Inter-operability challenges	Software cannot handle the opportunities built into the standards	Some existing technologies cannot manage all demands made by organisations
Challenges for new possibilities	How to reach new markets	Know which information to expose and why; which services to prioritise
Challenges for knowledge and skills	Human competence is important	Human competence is important
Legal and financial challenges	Web services ownership Effective cost sharing and payment models,	Web services ownership and service definitions Service Level Agreements (SLAs) and legal aspects

Table 2. *Comparison of challenges in literature and industry*

The same applies for knowledge and skills challenges, which in literature are more focused on organisation-internal skills, while the organisations in the project are more concerned of the competences of their customers. There is therefore a need to meet and resolve issues in both inter-operability challenges and challenges for knowledge and skills. A common understanding of the differences in perspectives should at least be resolved during such meetings, so that awareness of them is raised.

4. Legal and financial aspects of web services

Aspects in focus in literature and in organisations are often of a technical nature. However, there are many considerations to make that relate to a strategic and business perspective as well. This chapter will therefore elaborate on the findings concerning the legal and financial aspects of web services. The material is gathered from the project, and is hence empirical.

4.1. *Legal aspects*

The organisations taking part in the web services project claim that legal aspects are important, but in many cases difficult to manage. Three main issues were raised:

– Contracts: These are an essential part of the contact between the organisation and its customers. These contracts regulate which information the customer is allowed to ask for and get access to. One common strategy is to use authentication registries, against which comparisons are made when requests are submitted for information.

– Identification and authentication: Trust is a very important concept, but a difficult one at the same time. One reason is that it is difficult to know what to identify when a service is requested, for example if it should be a specific person or a legal entity. The answers may require different solutions. One common approach is to use server certificates for identification, which then are compared to the aforementioned authentication registry.

– Problems related to governmental organisations: Such problems concern the different and more encompassing set of laws regulating state-owned organisations. The primary problem highlighted is that laws are not updated and developed in the same pace as technology.

The importance of considering legal aspects is clear to all participating project organisations. One point made was that knowledge of legal aspects will be essential in the future, such as when developing new web services.

4.2. *Financial aspects*

WS also bring financial implications for organisations. So far, direct profits and benefits or values have been difficult to measure, while still being highlighted as important. Comments raised within the project have mainly concerned three aspects:

– Costs: WS cost to develop and maintain, for example since they bring new ways of working. These ways of working must be incorporated into the organisation. Furthermore, follow-ups for the sake of maintenance take time. The time of developing web services cannot be too long either, since costs for the same must be possible to motivate.

– Profits: Customer adaptation is the primary reason highlighted for increased profits. At the same time, it is emphasised that the profit emerging from using WS is greater than potential risks the profit must be weighed against. To create a WS before your competitors is also important. Furthermore, WS availability in itself is viewed as something that actually increases the demand for WS.

– Payment models: The models mentioned and in use are: authority servicing; one-time payments; and yearly fees. Payment per unit has been mentioned as being one possibility. This is, however, not in use, due to the difficulty of ascertaining justice in the approach.

5. Summary and discussion

This paper has reported on a study regarding web services business values, complemented with challenges for the same, and with legal and financial aspects. The purpose was to enhance current knowledge on web services business values and effects. Furthermore, the business perspective of web services needs to be highlighted and researched to a greater extent. Quite a large mass of information exists about the technological aspects of WS, but its business and strategic implications are still not well investigated. This paper is one step towards increasing the understanding, for technicians as well as for business managers and legal experts. Taking the example of legal experts, new technology is rarely developed by or with them. Therefore, legal problems are discovered already when they have occurred. Law has historically had a problem with discussing technical solutions in detail, and the result has often been an exaggerated belief in law as being technology-free or technology-neutral. New technology may not require new laws, but certainly new technical interpretations. Technicians in turn need to be aware of the bigger perspective, and perhaps to include both legal experts and business managers in order to discuss the solution to a problem before it has occurred.

Acknowledgements

The author would like to thank the Serviam project for valuable input, and the Knowledge Foundation for partial sponsorship of the research.

6. Bibliography/References

AmberPoint: Gaining Real-Time Business Value from Web Services Management: Leveraging the Content and Context of XML Web Applications, White paper, AmberPoint (2002), available at: http://www.amberpoint.com/solutions/foundation.shtml

Azzara, C.: Web Services: The Next Frontier: A Primary Research Opportunity Study, Topical report: Enterprise Findings, Hurwitz Group, Inc. (2002)

Barry, D.: *Web Services and Service Oriented Architectures: the Savvy Managers Guide*, San Francisco, Calif.: Morgan Kaufmann: Elsevier Science, ISBN: 1-55860-906-7 (2003)

Cape Clear: Creating Web Services From WebSphere Applications Using Cape Clear Software, Cape Clear Software Ltd (2002), available at: www.capescience.com/articles/content/ CapeClearandWebSphere.pdf

Clabby, J.: *Web Services Explained: Solutions and Applications for the Real World*, Upper Saddle River, NJ: Prentice Hall, ISBN: 0-13-047963-2 (2002)

Colan, M.: The business value of Web services: improving IT stability, agility and flexibility – Achieving ROI, WebSphere Developer's J., Sys-Con Publications Inc. and Gale Group, January (2003)

Dunn, B.: A Manager's Guide to Web Services, *EAIJournal*, January (2003), pp. 14-17

Estrem, W.: An evaluation framework for deploying Web Services n the next generation manufacturing enterprise, *Robotics and Computer Integrated Manufacturing*, 19 (2003), 509-519

Fletcher, P. and Waterhouse, M. (eds.): *Web Services: Business Strategies and Architectures*, UK: Expert Press Ltd., ISBN: 1-59059-179-8 (2002)

Govern, M. and Weagraff, S.: Web Services: Provider Threat or Opportunity?, Convergys Corporation, September (2003)

Hagel, J.: The CEO and IT Relationship: Harnessing the Value of Web Services Technology, *Internetworld*, April 1 (2003) available at: http://www.internetworld.com/

Marshman, W.: Web Services within the corporation, Hewlett-Packard Company, May (2002)

Murphy, T. and Stoyanova, D.: Optimize the Business Value of Web Services, Computer Associates International Inc., *CA World*, July 13-17 (2003), Las Vegas, Nevada, USA

Race, S.: What is the Value of Web Services?, *EACommunity.com*, as is: 2003-12-10, available at: http://www.eacommunity.com/articles/openarticle.asp?ID=1820

Roby, T.: Web services: Universal integration powers seamless, long sought after business servives, Accenture April (2003), available at: http://www2.cio.com/consultant/report1641.html

Smolnicki, J.: *How XML and web services will change your business*, PriceWaterhouseCoopers, as is: 2004-01-08, available at: http://www.pwcglobal.com/Extweb/ncinthenews.nsf/docid/2C9CB295270D752DCA256DD5006D122D

Syntegra: Deploying web services to integrate the enterprise, White Paper, Syntegra (2002), available at: http://www.syntegra.com/webservices/integration_white_paper.pdf

Thelin, J. and Murray, PJ.: CORBA and Web Services, Cape Clear Software Ltd (2002)., available at: http://capescience.capeclear.com/articles/content/CORBA%20and%20Web%20Services.pdf

Valtech: The Value of Web Services, Valtech seminar by C. Larman (2001), available at: http://roots.dnd.no/2002/speakers/speaker_material/Larman_Craig/The%20Value%20of%20Web%20Services.pdf

Wong, S.: Success With Web Services, *EAIJournal*, February (2002), pp. 27-29

A Pipelined Workflow Framework for Frequent Scientific Data Interaction

Xiao Bing Huang 1 — Jian Tang 2

Computer Science Department
Memorial University of Newfoundland
St. John's, NL, A1B3X5
Canada

xbhuang@cs.mun.ca
jian@cs.mun.ca

ABSTRACT: *Data and relative processing tools for a typical scientific workflow are usually located at different websites. The interaction between services in different sites often consumes a large proportion of time and network bandwidth in such workflows. After reviewing some exiting endeavours, this paper will present a new pipeline web services and scientific workflow framework which can reduce frequent data interaction between sites and mitigate network traffic incurred by huge scientific data transmission during the course of its execution. In the full version paper Xiao et al., 2005 we also show that more processing time will be saved when more complex workflows are processed.*

KEY WORDS: *scientific workflow, pipelining, web services*

1. Introduction

High-throughput experimental methods provide data collection techniques on a large number of molecular experiments (Ziauddin *et al.*, 2001, Fey *et al.*, 2001). Data on the transcription level of 100,000 different mRNA species from a given tissue can be produced in a single experiment (Baker *et al.*, 1999). These new experimental methods have increased the data size exponentially. Since scientists often need to compare, integrate, exchange, and analyze data from different sites, frequent data interaction and the heterogeneous processing tool integrations have generated great challenges to bioinformatic scientists. In addition, since some analytical algorithms (e.g. hierarchical clustering method) need to be run iteratively and recursively, it is important to keep the state and values for the intermediary data appropriately when the evolutional track of a set of data is necessary to the data analysis (Matthew *et al.*, 2003). Within the challenges, the key issue is incorporating the semantics into the model with minimum modification to existing systems.

The remainder of this paper is organized as follow: the related work part will review some exiting endeavours and frameworks; the SPL model is then described and the main problems that are tackled will be discussed; the conclusion section summarizes our present work and indicates the future research directions.

2. Related works

BPEL4WS (Wohed *et al.*, 2003) stems from IBM's WSFL and Microsoft's XLANG. Although it has abilities to express complex web services composition, it does not support arbitrary cycles (Wohed *et al.*, 2003). However, in bioinformatics workflow, sometimes, a portion of web services need to be executed repeatedly without imposing restrictions on the number, location, and nesting of these points. Hu *et al.*, 2004 propose a toolkit SeqVISTA to accommodate the needs to integrate computational tools scattered over the Internet for analyzing transcriptional regulation; this framework allows users to perform batch data analysis with multiple programs on a selected set of sequences. In this manner, SeqVISTA provides certain convenient pipelined process. However, this pipeline function is rather limited. For example, user intervention is needed if one analysis needs multiple inputs from the outputs of several other services. New *et al.*, 2001 propose two similar methods for Web services pipelining; both methods utilize a Call Sequence (CSeq) to describe all the services that are to be executed. In these methods the CSeq will pass through involved sites, which issue those services. Unfortunately, it is unclear that how the structural/semantic information of a workflow is expressed. Our system is based on a web services framework (SPL) which has full carrying ability of the workflow semantics and utilizes pipeline services to establish a visual pipeline between the input and output data, when a certain scientific function which we treat as a web service in our context is executed. Through this visual pipeline, data automatically flow from the beginning site to the end site according to the workflow structure without any intervention of the service requester; thereby the network traffic and intermediary data storage problems are both mitigated. Furthermore, since our system adopts the XML storage structure, the message that carries the data information is highly scalable: if the data size is relatively small, the data can be directly embedded into XML message and transmitted, otherwise, only the workflow structural information and parameters will be included in the XML message and real data are stored in an integrated database published with UDDI, another advantage of using XML is that the embedded information can be extracted in a standard query using tools when the data size is large.

3. Service Pipeline Logic (SPL)

A typical scientific workflow usually describes the implementation of a scientific analysis procedure. For instance, a gene regulatory pathway may be: 1. Establishing the model. 2. Making the prediction with training set. 3. Inputting real experimental data. 4. Evaluating the model. 5. Modifying the model. 6. Going back to step 3 until the output data converge to a given threshold. 7. Drawing conclusions and storing the results. Each step is connected to the next step through their input/output data and parameters. The whole procedure can be executed many times and each step can invoke services issued by different remote sites. Since frequently the output of one service will be the input of another service, how to handle the automatic data flow is critical. To tackle the problem, we add a new web service Pipeline Service Logic (SPL) as one part of the middleware at each service provider's site (Xiao 04). The SPL is the underpinning basis for the successful flow of the top SOAP message. It can be shown that the output of one service is directly sent to its next service as the next service's input. This way, frequent interaction between service requesters and service providers is avoided and the network bandwidth is saved. The SPL is responsible for maintaining a pipeline between services and transmitting input/output data through the pipeline according to the workflow logic; with the SPL, a complex workflow can be directly executed among remote sites without interaction with the service requester unless some errors are encountered (Xiao 04). A typical Bioscience workflow will have three basic structures (sequence, branch, and iteration) in its services route; we will illuminate how SPL handles such a workflow.

1. The service requester submits the whole workflow information in a SOAP message format (we name this message as SWD - Service Workflow Description) to the site in which the first service is to be executed. The SWD message includes FPS (the first pipeline service), CPS (the current pipeline service), CS (the current service to be executed), and the information of all services in the workflow as a sequence. Besides the basic service name, Service ID, port type and URL, the information also include: the iteration number, the iteration condition, the input parameters, the relation of the output parameters of current service and the input

parameters of the next service, the relation condition, appended parameters, last service information in an iteration, branch condition, next pipeline service address, next service ID;

2. The SPL will extract the SWD message once it is received: first, if the FPS field is null, the SPL recognizes itself as the first pipeline service in the workflow and set its address into the FPS field. Then the current service is executed (recorded in the CS field); after the execution, its next service ID will be set into the CS field, and the next pipeline service address is set into the CPS field; The execution results of the service will be set into the input parameters field (to be used by the next service); The whole modified SWD SOAP message will be then forwarded to the next PS (note now the address of the next PS is in the CPS field);

3. Repeat step 2 until all services in the workflow have been executed; the SWD message from LPS (last pipeline service) is then sent back to the FPS, the FPS forwards the result to the service requester (note LPS does not directly send the result to the service requester, the reason is explained in Xiao *et al.*, 2005).

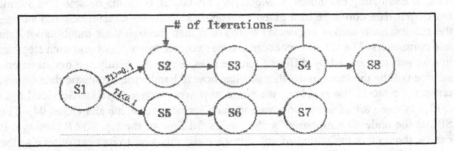

Figure 1. *A Typical Service Workflow*

We now explain the process with a example shown in Figure 1. Suppose a workflow includes iteration, branch, and sequence executions of a set of services. We assume that when the value of T1 >= 0.1 (an randomly threshold), the service will follow the upper route and the serial services 2, 3, 4 will be executed some times and end at Service 8; otherwise, the route will be service 1, 5, 6, 7. Without losing the generality, we assume the service ID and PS address is given as

Service Name: S1...S8; *Service ID:* 000001...000008;

PS Address: 100001...100008;

Input Parameters: Inp 1...Inp 8; *Output Parameters:* Oup 1...Oup 8.

Due to space limitation, the full version XML code of the initial SWD message is shown in Xiao *et al.*, 2005; we will only explain the main idea of the service pipelining process here.

At the beginning stage, the service requester submits the SWD message to the first Pipeline service (FPS). All the corresponding fields are in its initial status. When the FPS receives the SWD, it will find that the FPS field is null, then it sets its own PS address into this field and extract the service in the CS field (which has the current service that is to be executed) and the corresponding CPS field (since the service might be located at other sites, thus CPS field is also necessary). Then the input parameters and data Inp 1 will be used to execute the current service (here the CS is S1) at CPS. When the execution of S1 finishes, the PS will check the value of T1, if T1 >= 0.1, the first branch will be executed and the next PS (Pipeline service) 100002 is chosen, otherwise the second branch will be executed and the next PS 100005 is chosen. This PS is set into the CPS field and the next service ID is set into the CS field. Then, the output Oup 1 of the execution is set into the Input Parameters field of the new CS (current service). Afterward, the whole updated SWD message is sent to the next PS (which is indicated by CPS field). Suppose at some moment Service 4 is executed, the value of the part "Last Service in the Iteration" in the above SWD message is "yes" (which indicates S4 is the last service in an iteration); then, at the beginning, the value of Iteration number is replaced with (Iteration Number - 1); if after the replacement, the Iteration Number is not zero, the following service to be executed will be S2 and the corresponding CPS and CS will be set (this way, an iteration will be continuously executed). If the Iteration is finished (after repeating some times, the Iteration Number is zero), the following service will be S8 and the corresponding PS and Service ID will be extracted. As marked in the service route figure 1, we simply assume the Iteration simply repeat some times. In fact, it is also possible that the iteration terminates while a special condition is achieved (e.g. a presetting threshold is arrived). In this case, the Iteration Number is useless (a "null" will be set in the field); instead, the Iteration Condition field will be set to be the corresponding condition to quit the loop. It is also possible that the input of one service (e.g. service Si) are the aggregation of the output of some (more than one) previous services (e.g. service S1, S2,..., Sn). In such a case, the Relation will be Oup S1 +... + Oup Sn == Inp Si and each of the not-finish-yet output Oup Sk (k= 1...n) will be set into the Appending Parameters field of the corresponding service after the service finishes; The service Si can be executed only when the last Oup Sn is obtained;. In any time, once some unpredictable error occurs, the corresponding service ID and error ID will be collected in the Error List field. In addition, the whole pipelining process is asynchronous; once one PS finishes a job, it is available to accept another requirement. Due to space limitation, we will not discuss the experimental analysis section here; interested readers are referred to Xiao et al., 2005.

4. Conclusions

We have proposed a framework that heterogeneous data and services in different sites can be seamlessly integrated into a workflow. Comparing with the large-scale data set, the additional SPL will consume just a small part of the network bandwidth while greatly increase the efficiency. Since all the jobs are controlled by the SPL, we can standardize the design of SPL and adjust it independently. Any other changes in the whole service framework will not affect SPL. Moreover, each service provider can handle many parallel service requirements simultaneously to increase the throughput with different instances. Another potential improvement is that when errors occur, the workflow does not need to be restarted from the beginning; instead, once the problems are solved, the workflow can be recovered from up to the site where the error occurred. In addition, if we hope to make the SOAP message lighter, we can put a reference at the data referring area and store the real /initial/intermediary/final data in a sharable database. Given many advantages we explain above about our SPL framework, the model can suffer from some potential problems. For instance, if one service needs many large data sets to be the Input Parameters, these data will accumulate in the Appending Parameters field and transmit all the way until the last service. This may induce network traffic and needs to be investigated with more simulation experiments.

References

Baker P.G., Goble G.A., Bechhofer S., Paton N.W., Stevens R., Brass A., "An ontology for bioinformatics applications. Bioinformatics", *Nature*, Vol. 15., 1999, p. 510-520.

Fey S.J., Larsen P.M., "2D or not 2D. Two-dimensional gel electrophoresis", *Current Opinion in Chemical Biology*, Vol 5. 2001, p. 26-33.

Hu Z., Fu Y., Halees A.S., Kielbasa S.M., Weng Z., "SeqVISTA: a new module of integrated computational tools for studying transcriptional regulation", *Nucleic Acids Research, Web Server issue*, Vol 32, 2004, W235-W241.

Matthew A., Justin F., Mark G., Peter L., Darren M., Tom O., Anil W., "Experiences with e Science workflow specification and enactment in bioinformatics". *Proceedings of UK e-Science All Hands Meeting*, 2003, p. 459-466.

New M., Sriram K., Vimal K. V., Arul. S., "Web service pipelining", *International. Conference on High Performance Computing*, 2001.

Wohed P., van W.M.P., Dumas M., and Hofstede A.H.M., "Analysis of Web Services Composition Languages: The Case of BPEL4WS", *the 22nd International Conference on Conceptual Modeling , Lecture Notes in Comp. Science*, Vol 2813, 2003, p. 200-215.

Xiao Bing H., "BIWSP: a Web services Framework for the Integration of Heterogeneous Genetic Data and Services", http://www.cs.mun.ca/~xbhuang/biwsp.doc, 2004

Xiao Bing H., Jian T., "A pipeline service framework for complex scientific workflow". http://www.cs.mun.ca/~xbhuang/wsi05full.doc, 2005.

Ziauddin J., Sabatini D.M., "Microarrays of cells expressing defined cDNAs", *Nature*, Vol. 411. 2001, p. 107-110.

A Methodology for Developing OWL-S Descriptions

Michael C. Jaeger[1], Lars Engel[1] and Kurt Geihs[2]

[1]*TU Berlin, Institute of Telekommunication Systems,*
SEK FR6-10, Franklinstasse 28/29, D-10587 Berlin
mcj@cs.tu-berlin.de
sral@cs.tu-berlin.de

[2]*Univ. Kassel, FG Verteilte Systeme, FB 16,*
Wilhelmshöher Allee 73, D-34121 Kassel
geihs@uni-kassel.de

ABSTRACT. *This work proposes a methodology to develop the semantic description about Web services using OWL Services (OWL-S). In a preceding paper we have introduced a matchmaker algorithm for OWL-S and its prototype implementation to match semantic service descriptions of service requesters and providers. The experience from this work has revealed that the development of such a description is not easily done and requires the support of a software tool. Consequently, we propose in this work a methodology for how an OWL-S description is developed. The purpose of this proposal is to build a software tool upon this. The methodology is divided into three main steps. In the first step a software generates automatically an abstract template from existing descriptions (such as a software model or a WSDL file). In a second step, suitable ontologies or classification systems are identified for the semantic description of the service elements. And as the third step, the classification of the relevant elements is performed. This paper discusses the problems that may occur and introduces research findings, which can support our approach.*

KEYWORDS: *Semantic Web Services, Service Discovery, Service Matchmaking, OWL Services*

1. Introduction

The Semantic Web initiative of the W3C develops languages and technologies for the semantic description of the Web. Their goal is to make the Web understandable by machines and to increase the level of autonomous interoperation between computer systems [KOI 01]. Several standards and languages were already introduced to address this objective. The most relevant are the *Resource Description Framework (RDF)* [Fra 04] and the *Web Ontology Language (OWL)* [MCG 04]. The primary purpose of RDF is to structure and describe existing data. Thus, RDF is also called a metadata language. RDF Schema is a vocabulary extension to RDF to describe a semantic network. OWL is based on RDF Schema and is the successor of the combination of the DARPA Agent Markup Language and the Ontology Inference Layer (DAML+OIL). OWL is generally used to develop a formal specification of an ontology.

These languages are primarily used for the description of content. The next logical step is to describe the semantics of services in order to improve their platform- and organisation-independent interoperability over the Internet. Referring to the Semantic Web, the research field addressing this objective is named *Semantic Web Services* [MCI 03]. Its vision is the application of semantic description for Web services in order to provide relevant criteria for their automated discovery. Based on OWL, an upper ontology for the description of Web services named OWL Services (OWL-S) had been introduced [The 04]. This upper ontology defines the basic elements of a Web service. It can be used to define classifications of these elements and the binding to existing interface information including operations and their parameters.

The use of OWL-S for the description of Web services can increase the ability of computer systems to discover eligible services autonomously. This is important in open environments where provided services can appear and disappear dynamically. Basically, a service provider describes his advertised services in an OWL-S compliant description and a service requester queries for services using such a description expressing his requirements. In a preceding paper we have introduced a matchmaking algorithm and its implementation for matching OWL-S descriptions [JAE 05]. During this work, we have realised that the development of such a description (to test our algorithm) is unhandy and error-prone.

Consequently, we now propose a methodology for the development of OWL-S descriptions. The intention of this work is to provide a foundation for a software tool, which supports the development of OWL-S descriptions. In the next section, a scenario is introduced, which explains how the development of OWL-S descriptions fits into the world of Web services. A short overview about the three-staged methodology is given is section 3. After this, each step is presented in detail in sections 4, 5 and 6. In the remainder of the paper a discussion and information about the related work are provided. The paper ends with conclusions about this work and an outlook about future research opportunities.

2. Scenario

When service descriptions are used to identify matching, two descriptions usually exist: one of the service requester, which defines requirements to a service, and another of the service provider, which defines the capabilities of a service. A methodology must distinguish these two cases and thus a tool should be capable of creating OWL-S descriptions from existing services or the description of requirements without concrete available services.

Looking at the usage scenarios which are provided by the recommendations from the W3C, a service provider will publish the Web services. A requester will perform a chain of processes starting with a discovery, then proceeding with a selection of the discovered services, and finally, the service will be bound to be able to invoke it [Dav 04]. For the provider, the creation of the OWL-S description is a new part of the efforts to publish a Web service. The intention of the OWL Services Coalition, the group that has proposed the OWL-S, is to make the semantic description available for published Web services just as the interface description WSDL is [The 04].

A service requester will use his semantic description to find suitable Web services in a discovery. Thus, he needs to develop the OWL-S description to perform this discovery. Different methods were already identified to perform a discovery using OWL-S. For the discovery of Web services, originally a specification called *Universal Discription, Discovery and Integration*, in short UDDI, has been proposed to provide a centralised repository for capturing descriptions about Web services [TC 03]. The basic idea of UDDI is to conform to a common standard for a functional and organisational description of Web services in order to let service requesters find the desired services. Akkiraju et al. [AKK 03] and Trastour et al. [TRA 02] have already proposed to extend the UDDI specification with semantic description. In this scenario a requester passes his query including the semantic description of the requirements to a UDDI service. Then the UDDI service performs a matchmaking between requested and advertised service descriptions.

2.1. *OWL-Services*

The OWL-S upper ontology defines three basic elements: (1) a service profile to describe the functionality of a service, (2) a process model to describe the structure of the service, and (3) grounding definitions to map the semantically described interface to concrete binding information such as a WSDL file. As the focus of this work is on the discovery of Web services, we will concentrate on the service profile which provides the necessary elements for performing a matchmaking of service requirements and capabilities.

The profile is divided into three main sections: (*a*) a textual description and contact information, which is mainly intended for human users, (*b*) a functional description of the service. This functional description provides the input and output of a service.

Additionally, two sets of conditions are defined, namely preconditions, which have to hold before the service can be executed properly, and effects, which are conditions that hold after the successful execution of the service, i.e. postconditions. These four functional descriptions are also referred to as *IOPE* (Input, Output, Precondition, and Effects). For identifying matches, generally all four types of elements are suitable. However, since we are adapting our methodology to an existing matchmaking algorithm, only the input and outputs are covered. We find that preconditions and effects are not yet sufficiently standardised for being considered by a matching algorithm.

The third section (*c*) is a set of additional properties that are used to describe the features of the service. From these properties we use the service category, which is used to classify the service with respect to some ontology or taxonomy of services. On an optional basis, other properties can also be taken into account, such as a description about the service quality, or custom defined properties, such as the duration of the execution.

3. The Steps of the Methodology

The proposed methodology is split into three main steps. It is presented using flowchart symbols in Figure 1. The methodology will be explained briefly in this section and a detailed description for each step in the subsequent sections will be given:

Step 1: Generation of a OWL-S template. In the first step, a basic OWL-S document is created, which will be enriched and extended during the further parts of the methodology. The basic idea is to generate – as much as possible – automatically from existing formalisation of the provided or desired Web service. In this work such a document is called *template*.

Depending on whether the process is performed by a service requester or provider, an OWL-S template is generated by two different approaches. In the case of a provider a WSDL is available, available tools can be used and generate an OWL-S document from an existing WSDL file. A service requester does not have a WSDL file of his desired Web service. However, a tool can also create an OWL-S template which contains the basic fixed elements. The output is an OWL-S file, which can be extended further in this methodology.

Step 2: Identification of Available Ontologies. The classification must perform by using some ontology which defines the common terms and concepts that are considered for the classification. For a matchmaking algorithm the ideal situation occurs, when a service requester and provider refer their classifications to a common ontology. Thus any effort of service classification shall take existing ontologies into account. Then, it should be considered, whether existing ontologies could be extended. Only if existing ontologies are not adequately covering the domain of desired concepts, a new ontology should be created. The out-

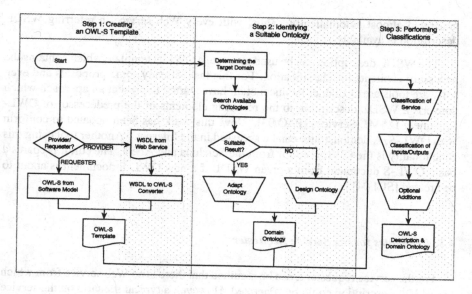

Figure 1. *General Methodology*

put of this phase is an ontology that contains the concepts used by the referring domain. It can be extended with necessary concepts used by the Web service.

Step 3: Performing Classification. In the preceding work of matchmaking algorithm we identified that for classification the service category, the input and the output parameters are most suitable. Accordingly, in this phase these three elements are subject to classification. For the first Version of the tool we see the classification as a manually performed process. Please note at his point that the trapezoidal boxes in the flowchart indicate a manual task and rectangular boxes an automated task. The output of this phase is an OWL-S description and the referring ontology.

4. The OWL-S Template

First of all, a template can be automatically created when it is based on existing information about the Web service. It can be assumed, that a service provider has got a WSDL description of his service. This description can be used to generate the referring elements of an OWL-S document. In general, the WSDL description is a platform-independent interface description of the service and thus a cornerstone of the Web service idea. With existing frameworks (such as the Apache Axis SOAP Implementation or the Sun Web Service Development Pack), the WSDL file can be generated almost automatically. Thus, with every Web service, a referring WSDL description is available.

The WSDL description can be used to create a OWL-S template which contains the necessary elements for classification. For this task, already some proposals and even software tools are available. Paolucci et al. have started to present an approach which converts a WSDL description to the referring elements of the predecessor of OWL-S, namely DAML-Services [PAO 03]. Now, this work has been updated to conform with OWL-S. A demonstrator can be accessed in the Internet.[1] Another tool using this functionality is the OWL-S editor from the Scicluna and Abela. The editor prepares a basic OWL-S document from a given WSDL if a new OWL-S document is about to be created [SCI 04].

4.1. *Templates for the Service Requester*

For the service requester it can be assumed that there is no Web service from which the WSDL description could be generated. However, a typical scenario on the service requester side is a Web service needed for the integration in a software system, a workflow management system or in a Web service composition. For developing software systems, designing workflows or Web service compositions, a common approach is to use models with specific modelling languages to define structure, dynamic behaviour, architecture etc. Newest development methodologies use the created software models to automate the generation of interface descriptions, source code, parts of it, or a parameterisation for execution environments. Such a model-centric approach to develop software is characterised as Model-Driven-Architecture (MDA). In this approach, graph transformations are used to transform platform independent software models into platform dependent models along with interface description. Different approaches have been already presented, which provide WSDL as the target interface description within a MDA environment. Therefore, this mechanism can be used to provide a WSDL file, which can used to generate the OWL-S template. Then, a WSDL description can be used the same way for the generation of an OWL-S template as described for the service provider.

If the service requester does not have the facilities available to generate a WSDL description from a software, workflow or process design, a tool can provide basic templates. As the very basic level of support, a general OWL-S template that is prepared for being extended in subsequent phases of this methodology. Based on this, different prepared OWL-S templates can be provided depending on the type of service that is desired. Either it has been created as preparation for the classification process, or it can be taken from previous matchmaking efforts. However, in these cases, the number of inputs or outputs of the service must be determined manually.

---

1. The demo of the tool can be found at http://www.daml.ri.cmu.edu/wsdl2damls/

4.2. *Template Elements*

The referring matchmaking algorithm considers only a subset of the available OWL-S elements. For the creation of a template document, only elements are considered which are covered by the matchmaking algorithm. Figure 2 at the end of this paper shows a schematic view of such a template: the light grey boxes *(boxes number 1, 2 and 5)* show elements which can be generated first, by an existing WSDL file of the Web Service, and/or are default for an OWL-S description. The two dark grey boxes *(number 3 and 4)* show the elements which are relevant for the classification phase: service category as well as the inputs and outputs. The tag to determine the service category can be generated by default as well. Regarding the inputs and outputs, their occurrence and number depends on the design of the service. Thus, either these elements must be derived from an existing WSDL description or other information, for example a software model of the service requester. At this point the benefit of the support by software tools becomes clear: elements that cover the inputs and outputs occur at several places within the XML document. A manual creation process does not automatically cover all occurrences and is thus error-prone. A tool can easily synchronise different occurrences of such elements.

Such a template is only a preliminary document for creating a semantic description. Existing WSDL to OWL-S conversion tools generate only a subset of the OWL-S description as well. It should be noted that a generator tool cannot derive a semantic description from a WSDL file unless it uses any approaches for semantic mining. The nature of the WSDL description is just the syntactic definition of the interface which is mapped into a OWL-S description. The semantics of the elements must be provided by an additional step.

5. Identifying Ontologies

For the classification two main types of elements must be covered by a domain ontology: the service itself and the elements that are handled by the service. The goal of this phase is to identify an ontology that covers these elements in order to perform a classification. The general question of matchmaking is whether service requester and provider do use the same ontology for the classification. In this case, a reasoning task can easily identify the relation between each of the elements of the requester and provider. If requester and provider do not use the same ontology or the used concepts do not refer to some common upper ontology, other matchmaking approaches – such as finding similarities in the string representation – must be used. These approaches can only identify matches with a limited correctness or by using a probability.

To increase the performance of the matchmaking process, provider and requester should therefore try to adopt existing ontologies by first searching for a published ontology that covers the domain of interest. If existing ontologies do not contain the concepts which are needed to perform the classification, the ontology could be extended. If no domain ontology has been found, as the next step an upper ontology

```xml
<?xml version="1.0" encoding="UTF-8"?>
<rdf:RDF
  xmlns:owl= "http://www.w3.org/2002/07/owl#"
  (...)>

      <service:Service rdf:ID="AbstractTemplateService">
            <service:presents rdf:resource="#AbstractTemplateProfile"/>
            <service:describedBy rdf:resource="#AbstractTemplateProcessModel"/>
            <service:supports rdf:resource="#AbstractTemplateGrounding"/>
      </service:Service>

   <profile:Profile rdf:ID="AbstractTemplateProfile">

            <service:isPresentedBy rdf:resource="#AbstractTemplateService"/>
            <profile:serviceName xml:lang="en">Abstract Template Service</profile:serviceName>
            <profile:textDescription xml:lang="en">(...)</profile:textDescription>

            <profile:serviceCategory rdf:ID="(...)">
                  (...)
            </profile:serviceCategory>

            <profile:hasInput rdf:resource="#InputString"/>
            <profile:hasOutput rdf:resource="#OutputString"/>

   </profile:Profile>

   <process:ProcessModel rdf:ID="AbstractTemplateProcessModel">
            <service:describes rdf:resource="#AbstractTemplateService"/>
            <process:hasProcess rdf:resource="#AbstractTemplateProcess"/>
   </process:ProcessModel>

   <process:AtomicProcess rdf:ID="AbstractTemplateProcess">
            <process:hasInput rdf:resource="#InputString"/>
            <process:hasOutput rdf:resource="#OutputString"/>
   </process:AtomicProcess>

   <process:Input rdf:ID="InputString">
            <process:parameterType rdf:resource="http://www.w3.org/2001/XMLSchema#datatype"/>
            <rdfs:label>Input Parameter</rdfs:label>
   </process:Input>

   <process:Output rdf:ID="OutputString">
            <process:parameterType rdf:resource="http://www.w3.org/2001/XMLSchema#datatype"/>
            <rdfs:label>Output Parameter</rdfs:label>
   </process:Output>

   <grounding:WsdlGrounding rdf:ID="AbstractTemplateGrounding">
            <service:supportedBy rdf:resource="#AbstractTemplateService"/>
            <grounding:hasAtomicProcessGrounding rdf:resource="#AbstractTemplateProcessGrounding"/>
   </grounding:WsdlGrounding>

   <grounding:WsdlAtomicProcessGrounding rdf:ID="AbstractTemplateProcessGrounding">

            <grounding:owlsProcess rdf:resource="#AbstractTemplateProcess"/>
            <grounding:wsdlDocument>http://.../AbstractTemplate.wsdl</grounding:wsdlDocument>
            <grounding:wsdlOperation>
                  <grounding:WsdlOperationRef>
                        <grounding:portType>http://.../Ab...te.wsdl#Ab...PortType</grounding:portType>
                        <grounding:operation>http://.../Ab...te.wsdl#operation01</grounding:operation>
                  </grounding:WsdlOperationRef>
            </grounding:wsdlOperation>

            <grounding:wsdlInputMessage>http://.../Ab...te.wsdl#Ab...teRequest</grounding:wsdlInputMessage>
            <grounding:wsdlInputMessageParts rdf:parseType="Collection">
                  <grounding:WsdlMessageMap>
                        <grounding:owlsParameter rdf:resource="#InputString"/>
                        <grounding:wsdlMessagePart>http://.../Ab...te.wsdl#inputString</grounding:wsdlMessagePart>
                  </grounding:WsdlMessageMap>
            </grounding:wsdlInputMessageParts>

            <grounding:wsdlOutputMessage>http://.../Ab...te.wsdl#...</grounding:wsdlOutputMessage>
                  (...)
   </grounding:WsdlAtomicProcessGrounding>

</rdf:RDF>
```

Figure 2. *Elements of an Abstract OWL-S Template*

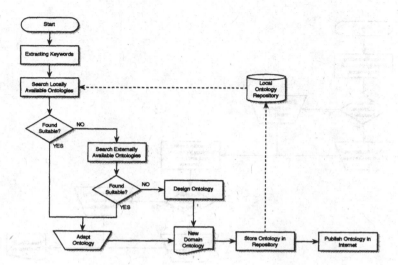

Figure 3. *Methodology for Identifying Suitable Ontologies*

should be searched for that covers the basic elements of interest. Only if nothing at all is available, a service provider should develop a new ontology. Seen from the perspective of a service requester, it can be assumed that if no suitable ontology can be found that covers the elements of interest, no service provider offering these might exist.

A tool can support the process of identifying ontologies by considering the name of the web service itself, its operations and parameters and its URL. Often these elements show already relations to the referring domain. For example, a weather forecast service might use an appropriate URL and service name that contains the words *weather* and *forecast*. These elements can be used as keywords to perform a search on existing ontologies. Nevertheless ontologies can be found in the Internet, a service provider or requester might have an appropriate ontology already locally available – developed in previous efforts. Figure 3 shows the methodology of this phase as a flow chart.

6. Classification

After the domain ontology has been determined, the classification of the service elements can be performed. For this step, we can basically distinguish two cases: (1) either appropriate concepts already exists in the ontology or (2) they do not. If the concepts exist already this step is trivial. A tool must only provide the functionality to add a reference into the OWL-S description. In case that the ontology must be extended with a new concept that relates to the existing concepts, this step can take advantage of existing service attributes such as the name or the names of its parameters.

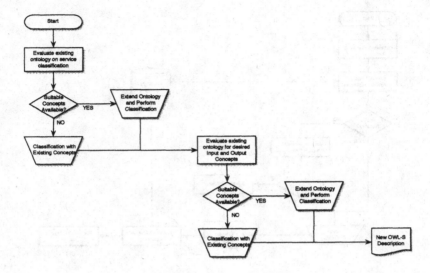

Figure 4. *Steps to Perform Classification*

For the classification of the service it is likely that some domain ontology does not provide the appropriate concepts. In a domain ontology concepts of entities from this domain might be described instead of services dealing with them. For this case, the developers of OWL-S propose to perform the classification according to some existing service ontologies or taxonomies such as the United Nations Standard Products and Services Code (UNSPSC) from the United Nations Development Council or the North American Industry Classification System (NAICS). The disadvantage of using such a classification system is that matchmaking algorithms cannot reason easily over such a classification as they could do with using OWL ontologies. We believe that the matchmaking process runs optimally if an OWL reasoner component is able to identify the relation of all elements of the service. Using the UNSPSC or NAICS in their current specification (i.e. not as an OWL ontology) this would result in a more restricted matchmaking process, because only the matching of a specific value can be determined. In addition to the services, the inputs and outputs of the OWL-S service profile must be classified as well. For a service provider the number of inputs and outputs is already known from the OWL-S template, which is based on the found inputs and outputs of the WSDL file. All the steps that are needed to be performed in this phase are displayed in Figure 4.

7. Discussion and Related Work

For describing the elements of services semantically, there are not many alternatives to the service category, the inputs and the outputs. Other aspects of the service such as the used communication protocols are technical parameters and thus a semantic description would not be beneficial. We believe that the issue which requires a broad discussion is about the used classification system – either an OWL ontology or a different approach. The main issues are the following:

– In this work, it is proposed to entirely use classification systems that are specified using the OWL. A matchmaking algorithm that is capable of processing OWL-S would also benefit from processing ontologies in OWLs, because otherwise the implementation gets more complex to support another ontology languages or classification systems.

Existing classifications for services or entities are already available from bodies or organisations such as the United Nations Development Programme, which provides the UNSPSC or the cooperation of different governmental organisation of Canada, Mexico and the United States. These countries have developed the above mentioned NAICS. So the desired ontology for creating a OWL-S description might exist already. However, it is not using the OWL for specification. This leads to the problem, that existing matchmaking implementation might not support these. Moreover, this issues also leads to the general problem about what would be the ontological languages that are supported by common matchmakers.

– Presuming that a consensus exists on the used matchmaking approaches and ontology languages, there is still the problem to identify appropriate domain ontologies or even ontologies that are already used for service description. The problem is different for requesters and providers, but it affects both. For the requester, the search for appropriate domain ontologies might be difficult. Common search engines might find a lot of different content besides a domain ontology in the Internet. How could a user or even a software system efficiently perform the search for ontologies in the Web?

As a provider, who is interested in developing his own domain ontology, the question raises how to publish the domain ontology in the Internet. Currently, used domain ontologies for the semantic description of services are placed on web pages, marked by HTML tags. Thus, potential users might not efficiently find them.

7.1. Related Work

Two software projects have already been introduced, which support the creation and modification of DAML-S [KLE 03] and OWL-S descriptions [SCI 04]. We see our work as an extension to the existing efforts, because the methodology discusses these efforts in the context of developing an OWL-S description from the perspective of service requesters and providers. Similar to the existing software projects, a tool for the description of CORBA components based on Conceptual Graphs was developed for the AI Trader in an earlier project of our research group [PUD 97].

We have mentioned above how existing transformation approaches can be used to realise our methodology. Gronmo et al. have explained how UML models can be the basis for the generation of interface description to different target platforms including

WSDL [GRO 04]. The transformation of WSDL files into a DAML-S file has already been introduced by Paolucci et al. [PAO 03]. This work has been upgraded to support OWL-S. Gannod and Timm have also introduced an approach to generate the OWL-S service model from existing models using the UML [GAN 04]. The difference to our approach is that Gannod and Timm discuss the development of OWL-S description in the context of an MDA environment.

8. Conclusions

The paper has introduced a methodology to develop OWL-S descriptions and also points out the differences between its steps that can be easily automated by a software tool and tasks that must be performed manually by the user. The methodology described in this work provides the foundation for a software tool to develop such a description. The proposed tool could also support the search for available ontologies in the Internet and it could reduce the efforts to add further OWL-S elements to provide a finer service matchmaking.

With this work we have explained how existing research results and tools from other parties can be integrated into this methodology. The approach has been kept rather simple, consisting of three stages to provide clear vision about the necessary tasks for developing an OWL-S description. Of course, several extensions and refinements are possible, but we believe that a methodology should provide a framework identifying the basic steps. Besides the realisation of a software tool, we plan – as the next steps – to refine the search for existing ontologies. We believe that for the semantic description of service it is crucial to share domain ontologies. However, currently neither a mechanism nor a platform is focussing on this issue.

9. References

[AKK 03] AKKIRAJU R., GOODWIN R., DOSHI P., ROEDER S., "A Method for Semantically Enhancing the Service Discovery Capabilities of UDDI", *In Proceedings of the Workshop on Information Integration on the Web*, August 2003, p. 87–92.

[Dav 04] DAVID BOOTH ET AL., "Web Services Architecture", report , 2004, W3C, http://www.w3.org/TR/ws-arch/.

[Fra 04] FRANK MANOLA ET AL., "RDF Primer", report , 2004, W3C, http://www.w3.org/TR/rdf-primer/.

[GAN 04] GANNOD G. C., TIMM J. T. E., "An MDA-based Approach for Facilitating Adoption of Semantic Web Service Technology", *Proceedings of the 8th International Enterprise Distributed Object Computing Conference (EDOC 2004), Workshop on Model-Driven Semantic Web*, Monterey, California, September 2004, IEEE Press.

[GRO 04] GRONMO R., SKOGAN D., SOLHEIM I., OLDEVIK J., "Model-Driven Web Services Development", *Proceedings of 2004 IEEE International Conference on e-Technology, e-Commerce and e-Service (EEE'04)*, Taipei, Taiwan, March 2004 2004, IEEE Press, p. 42–45.

[JAE 05] JAEGER M. C., ROJEC-GOLDMANN G., MÜHL G., LIEBETRUTH C., GEIHS K., "Ranked Matching for Service Descriptions using OWL-S", *n Kommunikation in verteilten Systemen (KiVS 2005), Informatik Aktuell*, Kaiserslautern, Germany, February 2005, Springer (accepted for publication).

[KLE 03] KLEIN M., KOENIG-RIES B., "A Process and a Tool for Creating Service Descriptions based on DAML-S", *Proceedings of 4th International Workshop Technologies for E-Services, TES 2003*, Springer, September 2003, p. 143–154.

[KOI 01] KOIVUNEN M.-R., MILLER E., "W3C Semantic Web Activity", *Semantic Web Kick-Off in Finland*, November 2001, p. 27–44.

[MCG 04] MCGUINNESS D. L., VAN HARMELEN F., "OWL Web Ontology Language Overview", report , 2004, W3C, http://www.w3.org/TR/owl-features/.

[MCI 03] MCILRAITH S. A., MARTIN D. L., "Bringing Semantics to Web Services", *IEEE Intelligent Systems*, vol. 18, 2003, p. 90-93.

[PAO 03] PAOLUCCI M., SRINIVASAN N., SYCARA K., NISHIMURA T., "Towards a Semantic Choreography of Web Services: from WSDL to DAML-S", *roceedings of the International Conference on Web Services (ICWS 2003)*, Las Vegas, Nevada, June 2003, IEEE Press, p. 22–26.

[PUD 97] PUDER A., GEIHS K., "Meta-level Service Type Specifications", *Proceedings of the IFIP/IEEE international conference on Open distributed processing and distributed platforms*, Toronto, Canada, 1997, Chapman and Hall, p. 74-84.

[SCI 04] SCICLUNA J., ABELA C., MONTEBELL M., "Visual Modelling of OWL-S Services", *Proceedings of the IADIS International Conference WWW/Internet*, Madrid, Spain, October 2004.

[TC 03] TC U. S., "UDDI Version 3.0.1", report , 2003, OASIS, http://www.oasis-open.org/committees/uddi-spec/doc/tcspecs.htm.

[The 04] THE OWL SERVICES COALITION, "OWL-S: Semantic Markup for Web Services", report , 2004, http://www.daml.org/services/.

[TRA 02] TRASTOUR D., BARTOLINI C., PREIST C., "A Semantic Web Approach to Service Description for Matchmaking of Services", *Proceedings of the 11th international conference on World Wide Web*, Honolulu, USA, May 2002, ACM Press, p. 89–98.

MODTIS: System Integration Orchestrated, Dynamic and Transactional Model

Jorge Abin * — Fernando Rodríguez *

* Laboratorio de Integración de Sistemas, INCO
Facultad de Ingeniería - Universidad de la República
Julio Herrera y Reissig 565, Montevideo 11300, Uruguay
jabin@fing.edu.uy
frodrig@fing.edu.uy

ABSTRACT: *System integration has become a central issue given the diversity of sources of information (internal or external), technologies and suppliers in current organizations. To this we must add the necessary adaptation to environmental changes required to maintain competitiveness and provide solutions tailored to customers' needs. This adaptation impacts directly on information systems, and thus on the services they in turn provide. Changes of this sort impinge directly on all consumers of the said service. The model presented in this paper aims to solve the problems that are considered central in this reality, by contributions in three essential areas: orchestration / choreography of services, their transactional management, and a detector of change and re-configurator of choreographies.*

KEY WORDS: *system integration, choreography, soa, web service. ontology*

1. Introduction

Reality in the technological sector poses a constant challenge in cost reduction and the maximization of use of the existing technology (special in South America and other developing countries), without leaving aside the need to provide an increasingly better service to clients while maintaining competitiveness of the business and responding to strategic priorities.

Two key elements characterize this reality: *diversity* and *change*.

Regarding the first element, we currently are facing a situation that is repeated in organizations: multiple sources of information are available, as in the case of in house applications developed in different technologies or architectures, systems from other suppliers or clients with whom it is necessary to interact, or services available through the Internet that must be integrated to the "technological umbrella" the company offers to internal users and even to the Web. It is practically impossible to count with a single and isolated solution provided by one technological supplier alone that does not need to interact with other systems. Even in the best of cases, time will show the need for integration with more modern systems implemented in other technologies.

As for change, this factor controls the globalize world in which we live. In order to be competitive and maintain short product life cycles, it is necessary to rapidly adapt to the environment. By this we mean optimizing the internal logistics of the company, with the possibility of incorporating solutions for new customer requirements in an

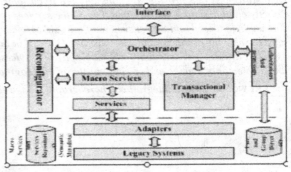

Figure 1. *The Modtis Model*

agile manner and/or having the possibility of generating comparative advantages vis a vis competitors. In all these items the IT sector of the company plays an increasingly important role, in spite of the fact that it must go hand in hand with continual improvements of the available technologies and in the capacity to adapt to them.

Service Oriented Architecture (SOA) is being backed both by the academic sector and by the main companies devoted to software development as the correct procedure for working in the previously described reality.

This paper thus presents a model based on service oriented architecture, and supported by this architecture's resilience to facilitate problems related to diversity and change. Among its assets we have low coupling, transparent location of systems and independent protocol access for clients. The client shouldn't mind if the interaction occurs with a system implemented in J2EE or .NET platforms.

We consider the systems resulting from operations with this model as Cooperative Information Systems (CIS). Using Carlo Batini's definition of a CIS, i.e. a set of system components acting in cooperative manner on a diverse group of computers belonging to a network so that, by cooperating through the contribution of software, data, restrictions and business rule mechanisms they are capable of solving a set of problems belonging to the organizations' domain.

Figure 1 shows the model proposed in this paper: System Integration Orchestrated, Dynamic and Transactional Model (MODTIS), also known as Orchestrator-Adapter Model. It is based on three essential pillars: i) a service orchestrator with a language defining choreographies called Thalia (Abin 2001); ii) a transactional manager for the management of data integrity; iii) a re-configurator capable of maintaining software integrity, detecting changes in the interfaces provided by them, and operating pro-actively to make the necessary corrections in the service orchestration so that the cooperative system continues to function.

We speak of "Legacy Systems" to refer to re-utilized applications or services (developed in the past) that shall be integrated to compose a CIS using the MODTIS. In a more formal sense, we consider all indispensable applications for the normal functioning of a company, also including the acquired systems or those related with strategic partners in an organization, covering the needs of one or more of its critical sectors, whatever the time elapsed since they were included in production as legacy systems .

The main complexities we aimed to solve with the MODTIS are related with two areas where little progress has been made at the level of standards and concrete solutions implemented at industrial level: transactionality at the business transaction level, when they use uncoupled services distributed by and using low coupling networks; and, the detection of changes in those services (resulting from changes in the inherited systems that support them) and the later corrective action so that the resulting cooperative system continues to function (all business activity utilizing the modified service).

The specificity of the modifications is related to the fact that changing systems impact on services used by people external to the CIS ambit, and who may know nothing about them. In the case of changes, and because the services are developed and maintained by third parties (unknown to those developing the CIS), we hereby propose a manner of metadatizing semantic descriptions of each service. When change occurs in any system, this semantic metadata should be used to analyze its impact. Options such as DAML-S and OWL-S were studied to this aim.

2. State of the Art

The research for this paper was based on four important areas: Web Services (WS) and their standards / non-standards, service orchestration, transactionality of highly uncoupled services, and last, the area less frequented by the industry and by the academic sector: identification of change (and posterior automatic re-configuration) in services using ontologies.

2.1. Web Services

In the ambit of WS the present reality is that standarization has not been achieved, in spite of being sought for; although there is consensus in various areas, there are other areas in which there are two possible choices: companies that follow Microsoft and companies that follow IBM. Nevertheless, the WS concept is already five years old, and there are multiple WS-* specifications that addressed diverse problems. Nevertheless, inside companies the use of the WS has been directed to the utilization of simple resources, and has not always focused on the specifications. Among the most interesting specifications related with this paper we find: WS-Business Activity, WS-Transactions, WS-Coordination and WS-Discovery (Vinoski S. 2004).

The main problem with the WS is that there is no standard architecture gathering all the WS-* specifications. What we do have is partial views of how this architecture should be: Microsoft, for example, has presented a model that at least integrates the specifications with which they are involved (Cabrera L.F., et al 2004).

By manner of reference, we now present a brief description of some of the specifications:

- *WS-Coordination*: describes a framework that may be extended to provide protocols to coordinate actions of distributed systems. This protocol coordination is used to support a series of applications, including those that need to reach a result by common agreement regarding the exit of distributed transactions.
- *WS-Transaction*: provides the definition of two types of coordination including their respective protocols. Atomic Transaction (AT) is used to coordinate short duration activities executed within limited confidence domains. One Business Activity (BA) is used to coordinate activities of long duration and that want to apply the business logic to manage business exceptions.

Most of the analyst agrees that only the most basic WS standards (SOAP, WSDL and UDDI) need to be used, see (WS-IBasic Profile).

2.2. Orchestration

Regarding what was said in the previous item, there are two ways of solving the WS coordination: HP-WST by HP and WS-Transaction by IBM, BEA and Microsoft (WS-T).

Coordination languages are another important area related with orchestration. The most currently well-known for WS are based on the WS-C. BPEL4WS model based on WSFL and XLANG; WSCI; BPML initiated by BPMI.org; ebXML supported by OASIS and UN/CEFACT; and also BPSS (part of ebXML), another new standard similar to the rest.

The most widespread is BPEL4WS. It is a language that enables the development of a composition of Web Services (synchronic and non-synchronic) within the business flow. The language introduces mechanisms to define how an individual or compound activity within the process may be compensated for in the case of exceptions or when the partners turn back the requests. All the resources and partners are represented as WSDL services.

2.3. Transactionality and Web Services.

Environments such as those related with the WS require the same coordination behavior as that provided by a traditional mechanism for transactions to control operations and the application's output. This requires more flexible forms of transaction – those that do not need to strictly maintain the ACID properties – as for example, collaborations, Workflow, real time processes, etc.

The problems that are introduced by making WS transactionable are: granularity, durability, reversibility, recoverability, concurrence and synchronization. However those problems can be solved imposing certain restrictions. For example, related to durability: usually the problem is that it is not know how long a transaction with WS is going to take, so in that case a timeout could contribute to solve this issue. Also in case of reversibility, it is possible to use a compensation mechanism to avoid those cases where rollback can not be done.

The BTP (Business Transaction Protocol) is a transaction coordination protocol based on the XML language that allows the management of complex business transactions in the Web, together with the organization of the exchange of XML messages among commercial partners from the beginning to the end of any B2B (Business-to-Business) process.

The BTP was specifically designed to coordinate interactions inside a transaction, while the WS-C was designed to define a generic coordination framework, and thereby make it much more flexible. On the other hand, BAs from WS-T do not follow exactly a 2PC protocol, and when there are failures in order to return to a consistent state they execute compensatory actions.

2.4. Ontologies and Changes

According to Neches, Ontology defines the terms and basic relationships to enable us to understand an area, together with the rules to combine the terms in order to define extensions of the vocabulary.

The search thus led to a language describing the ontologies related with the WS. OWL-S (see (OWL-S W3C org)) is the most important standard in this sense, and presents a semantic description of the services. It describes what a WS does at application level, and not only how it does it. When we say "at application level", we mean that the mechanism to publish, discover, describe both at conceptual and functional level, and transport the information from a WS has been solved.

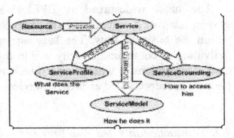

Figure 2. *Structure of the OWL-S*

OWL-S provides WS suppliers with a basic set of markup language constructors (Fig. 2) that enable the description of WS properties and capacities in a non-ambiguous manner that may be consumed by automats. In this way, the use of OWL-S will facilitate the automatization task of services such as discovery of services, execution, inter-operation, together with their composition and monitoring.

3. MODTIS Architecture

The architecture model proposed to approach the issues posed is based on the scheme shown in Figure 3, based on the classic model (Arsanjan A.) of a Service Oriented Architecture (SOA). This architecture model is essentially designed to allow the conditions to host a collection of

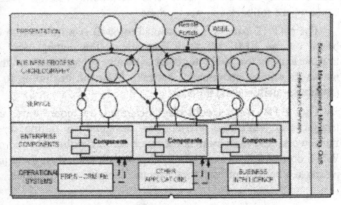

Figure 3. *The Modtis Architecture model*

services and grant them the capacity of communicating among themselves and with the exterior in a safe manner and according to the quality service conditions agreed upon. Communication may vary from simple data exchange to, in the other end of the complexity spectrum, having two or more services interacting with each other to carry out coordinated activities. Integration is shown in Figure 4.

We speak of the "enterprise components" layer to refer to all the components that may be accessed to integrate a business process. These components may be obtained from functionalities of inherited systems by means of adaptors or originate

from other systems in the same organization. This paper will not analyze this layer in detail, as it is not central for the study of the three main pillars (Orchestration, Management of Change and Transactionality); for more details see (Fernández D. et al

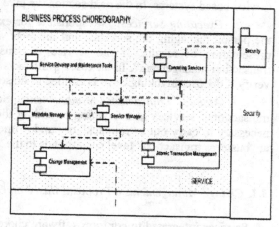

Figure 4. *The Service Layer Architecture*

2001). The following items describe the central layers in this model. Service Layer

The "service" layer contains and exhibits the services, presents facilities for discovering and invoking in static manner. They may be directly invoked from the introductory layer or otherwise compose business processes using software choreographies. This layer includes interfaces presented as service descriptions. It is important to note that the mentioned services may be both atomic and compound. Service logic may be based on the company's components or on those of WS external to the organization.

At the level of this layer we find a series of services necessary to: administer metadata; manage the configuration; administer security related to the services, basically everything related with rights of usage; monitoring services for the layer interface – Figure 4 shows the diagram of components that solve it. These functionalities are offered as services and are defined in the metadata proper. Now we will describe the main components of this layer:

-       *Service Manager*: It is the main component, and its fundamental functions are: supplying the interfaces to interact with this layer, receive and coordinate the interaction with the other components in this layer.

-       *Metadata Management*: Metadata is the item that describes the properties of each service. This component is devoted to execute the services; it obtains the information necessary to be able to "run" each service from the metadata. In cases where the services are external, this component establishes the relationships with the UDDI. It provides support and easy-use of the information needed by the different components of this layer. The services offered by the metadata are described in the metadata itself.

- *Change Management*: Management of change and management of the configuration are two of the most important aspects to ensure the functioning of the service-based systems. In the next section we give further details regarding this item.

- *Executing Services*: Is responsible for executing the services requested by the person managing the services, and interacts with it in everything regarding the presentation of results. If the service is transactional it invokes the "atomic transaction management". In all cases it interacts with the security layer in order to verify if the user invoking them is entitled to do so.

- *Atomic Transaction Management*: Solves the problems related to transactional services in everything regarding the management of the information necessary to carry out a "rollback" or "undo" operation. Transactional management at "business transaction" level corresponds to the "business processes logic" layer.

3.1. Change Management: a Proposal Based on Ontologies

Services integrated to conform software choreographies (Business Transactions) are of diverse origin, some belong to the organization and others do not. Whoever exhibits a service as a WS do not have the possibility of analyzing the impact of the changes implemented by its consumers. They two characteristics make change management a central problem of difficult solution. This model presents a solution based on semantic descriptions using ontologies.

WS' changes can be classified in two main areas: changes in the metadata related to the service, or changes in the input/output parameters. The types of changes in metadata (service's attributes) are the following: change in the transactionality, state, timeout, synchronism, service version or to the id of the rollback service. Among the type of changes with the input/output parameters, we have the addition of input/output parameter, the removal of input/output parameter (with or without a default value) or a change in the nature of one of the input/output paramenters (with or without a default value).

The management of change is achieved in two stages: first, the detection of the change carried out by the developer of the services used by the Orchestrator, and second, the analysis of the impact produced in the choreographies (Business Activity) that use them. To achieve this we have chosen to enrich the semantic descriptions of services using ontologies. The semantic description at service level allows to infer the changes produced at this level, while the semantic at choreography level (expressed in the same language used to describe choreographies – in this case Thalia) enables the analysis of the impact of change and the provision of elements to determine the feasibility of the adaptation.

To all practical effects, this model proposes that the services utilized publish a semantic description file in OWL-S format, describing the semantics of the service attributes and parameters. Given the extensibility of OWL, we are therefore proposing the extension of the "ParameterDescription" class defined in OWL-S, adding to it a new property called "defaultValue". The latter may contain any type of element, an ideal condition to assign values by omission in the definition of a parameter. This extension is obtained with the following statement in OWL:

```
<owl:Property rdf:ID="defaultValue">
  <owl:domain
   rdf:resource="&profile;#ParameterDescription"/>
  <!-- <owl:range rdf:resource="&owl;#Class"/> -->
</owl:Property>
```

In this statement there is a comment regarding the range of the property, it is therefore clearly specified that its value may be any ontological concept. The complete description of this implementation may be found in (Dalchiele S, et al. 2003).

3.2. *The Business Processes Choreography Layer*

The "logic of business processes" integrates part of all the elements related to orchestration. Compound services or choreographies (business processes belonging to the organization) of services exhibited in the previous layer (Item 3.1), are defined here.

- Orchestrator: The component responsible for organizing and coordinating the activities related with the choreographies that represent business processes. It specifically obtains its properties from the "Business Process Metadata" and "Metadata Management" in the case of services; it interacts with the security layer, carries out confirmations of integrity face to changes by means of the "Business Process Change Management", invokes "Execute Choreographies", and interacts with the user.

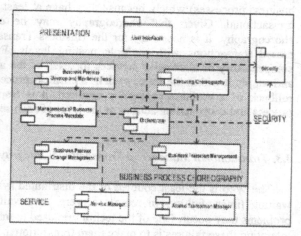

Figure 5. *Business Process*

- *Management of Business Process Metadata*: Metadata is the instrument used to describe and store business process properties, including the description of its choreography and binding mechanisms. It also provides the proper functionalities for metadata management.

- Business Process Change Management (Re-configurator of choreographies *affected by changes in the services)*: This component is essentially designed to provide elements to contribute to maintain the integrity of software choreographies face to changes that may originate in the services composing them. Its activities are: i) to determine what choreographies are affected by the changes detected in the services; ii) alter, when possible, the description of the affected choreographies to avoid or minimize the impact; iii) notify the persons responsible for the choreographies and for the system; iv) change the state of the choreographies when tests or inhibitions of their use are required.

-   *Executing Choreographies*: Is responsible for carrying out the execution of software choreography. Is initiated by the orchestrator and interacts with the users through it. If the choreography is transactional (i.e. contains at least one transactional service), it invokes the "Business Transaction Manager". If necessary, it invokes the execution of compensatory activities or choreograhies. Information about service metadata and choreographies is obtained from the specific components via the orchestrator.

-   *Business Transaction Management*: Deals with the activities needed to provide the transactional management software choreographies (macro services or business processes) which, because they have at least one transactional service, are transactional. Given that choreography may be considered as a service by choreography, it is necessary for the Business Transaction Manager to implement nested transactions with multiple nesting levels. Furthermore, it must manage compensatory or alternative services for each of the atomic services that require it, and supply it within the framework of a business process or choreography. When the rollback of a business process is required, it is responsible for carrying out this process and coordinating actions at the level of each service involved.

3.3. Transactional Manager: a Transactional Integrity Proposal in the Web

The Web is the least coupled of the distributed systems due to the fact that long waiting times, failures in remote servers, non-availability of WS or connection problems may occur. One of the techniques used to make the applications capable of tolerating these failures is to make them transactional.

Insofar as a service is an abstraction of the functionalities it offers, it is of essential importance from the architectural point of view to exhibit its properties in order to enable the framework to "adapt" the execution of a choreography as a function of the properties of its components.

Special interest has been therefore granted to the development of semantic metadata describing services and Business Activity. We will now describe some of the main elements of the metadata characterizing a service and supporting the resolution of the problems of transactionality and management of change:

-   *Transactional character of the service*: This property indicates if the service modifies data while it is being executed. It only refers to the transactionality of the service; it is important to note that not all the systems that sustain WS implement transactions at the level of the systems that exhibit them, and the manner how they solve the transactional integrity is not homogeneous. The service property that implements the rollback is included in order to solve this problem.

- *The Service implementing the rollback*: Each transactional service must present a method to implement the rollback. Thus, the Transactional Manager invokes this method when it requires the rollback.

When the need to invoke the rollback is due to the impossibility of connecting with the server sustaining the WS, it is necessary to be able to apply other methods to ensure that it will be possible to restore the information, even if it be in manual form; the failure notification property is included to this aim.

- *Failure Notification*: It a prolonged failure preventing the appropriate realization of the rollback were to occur, a failure notification is sent via e-mail to the address specified in this parameter.

- *Timeout*: This property indicates to both participants that the time to provide a response has expired and that it is therefore considered that the service failed, and, if required, that it must carry out the rollback.

Compensatory or alternative activities are other instruments utilized by the transactional manager to avoid the rollback of the business activity. We speak of compensatory o alternative activity when, according to the author of the choreography, they present functionalities analogous to those provided by the service being compensated. Compensatory activities are properties of a service at choreography level; the same service may have different compensatory activities in another context. Compensatory activities are mentioned in a statement in the Thalia language; this allows a service to have multiple compensatory activities, in (Ezquerra M, et al 2003) we will find details of the language and examples showing these statements. If the transactional manager detects the failure of a service, it invokes the first compensatory activity, if this were to fail, it will continue with the next; if they were all to fail, or if this service does not count with compensatory activities, it initiates the Business Activity rollback process invoking in sequence the methods to do this as stated in each service.

The scope of this paper does not allow us to give further details regarding other in this design; for a complete description of this implementation, see (Ezquerra M, et al 2003).

4. Comparison

It is not possible to compare the architecture presented here with another one, because it was not found one that could handle all the same issues and features. So the comparison can be done partially, topic by topic. For example, OASIS is working on a WS Coordination Framework Specification, see (Chapman Martin). In particular, here there is a comparison between the choreography specification languages used by our architecture, Thalia, and one of the standards that are being promoted in the industry: BPEL4WS.

FEATURES	THALIA	BPEL4WS
Language and simplicity	Describes services based on the composition of others, that already exists. Very easy to be used by no-technical users.	Also allow composition, but with stress on a workflow-style model with multiple users taking part of it. More complex.
Flow-control structure	Describes routes based on the logic of the business process (graph) – uses logic conditions to select the correct route.	Has many options to control the flow – it's similar to a programming language.
User interaction	Allows interactions with the users, even within the processes but only with the user that initiate the process.	Allows interactions with more than one user. It's oriented to workflow-type of processes.
Roles and permissions to use each service	Let each service handle that, after previously being validated as an user.	Uses special structures to identify roles and specified which attributes are visible, etc
Error handling	Yes, both for processes and services.	Same
Compensatory operations	Yes	Yes
Specification of special functions	Yes	Yes
Intensively use service properties and metadata	Yes, strongly based on the metadata to do an abstraction of the services.	Weak, only what is declared in the WDSL.
Allows multiple concurrent versions	Yes	?

5. Summary and Conclusions

This project started following the research started in Abin's thesis, bearing the title "Integration of encapsulated applications for the development of cooperative information systems" (Abin J. thesis 2001), where the main elements of the architecture described are proposed together with a language to describe software choreographies (Thalia), and setting the bases for future research. Their development within the different thesis of graduated projects during the 2002 – 2004 period at the Instituto de Computación de la Facultad de Ingeniería (InCo, UdelaR), together with the "project SICO: Information systems in a cooperative environment" (Motz.R. et al 2002) and the studies and papers prepared in the framework of the Laboratorio de Integración de Sistemas (Lins), are the main elements that have contributed towards the development of this project.

Several prototypes in J2EE and .NET were developed based on this architecture. The current model is developed for the .Net platform; it is totally operative but, to date, does not provide the possibility of administering the repositories, nor management, service monitoring and administration of users and permits; these functions will be incorporated soon.

In summary, we will highlight the following conclusions:

-       The model proposed provides a complete solution for the problem of integrating heterogeneous systems in uncoupled environments using a SOA.

- An orchestrator including a processor of choreographies described in its own language (Thalia) is introduced.

- A solution for transactions in a Business Activity based on the properties of services described in the metadata (including a reference to rollback methods proper to each service) and compensatory activities described at the level of choreographies is provided.

- It was possible to detect changes in the services and re-configure the Business Activity in a dynamic manner.

- The solution presented is based on technologies and standards from the industry, with specific implementations in two of the main platforms (j2ee and .Net). Among the standards used we find WSDL, UDDI, Ws-Transaction, OWL-S and Ontologies, among others.

6. References

Abin J.; "Thalia, un lenguaje para la descripción de coreografías de software" (2001), http://www.fing.edu.uy/inco/grupos/lins/modtis/thalia

Abin J.. "Integración de aplicaciones encapsuladas para el desarrollo de sistemas de información cooperativos"; Universidad de la República – Montevideo Uruguay, 2001; http://www.fing.edu.uy/~jabin/papers/TesisMaestria.pdf

Arsanjan A. i, Ph.D.; "Service-oriented modeling and architecture" http://www-106.ibm.com/developerworks/library/ws-soa-design1

Cabrera L.F., Christopher K., Box D.; "An Introduction to the Web Services Architecture and Its Specifications, version 1.0," Microsoft, 2004; http://msdn.microsoft.com/library/default.asp?url=/library/en-us/dnWebsrv/html/introwsa.asp

Chapman Martin; Web Services Coordination Framework Specification, draft ver 0.2 http://www.oasis-open.org/committees/download.php/10889/WSCF-Working-12-22.pdf

Dalchiele S, D\íaz C., Gerchicov D., Rettich A.; "Diseño de la metadata semántica para un orquestador de operaciones encapsuladas"; Universidad de la República – Montevideo Uruguay, 2003; http://www.fing.edu.uy/~pgmetsem/

Ezquerra M., Pereira S., Revello S., Silva L.; "Transacciones Distribuidas en la Web"; Universidad de la República – Montevideo Uruguay, 2003; http://www.fing.edu.uy/~pgtdistr/

Fernández D., Uslenghi C., Caceres P.; "Integración de Sistemas Legados como Web Services"; Universidad de la República – Montevideo Uruguay, 2001; http://www.fing.edu.uy/inco/grupos/lins/modtis/sistleg

Motz R., Ruggia R., Abin J., Marotta A., Peralta V., Carpan F.; "Proyecto SICO: Sistemas de Información en un entorno Cooperativo" 2002;
http://www.fing.edu.uy/inco/grupos/csi/esp/Proyectos/Sico/SICO.pdf

OWL-S; http://www.w3.org/2004/OWL/

Vinoski S., "WS-Nonexistent Standards". IEEE Internet Computing 1089-7801/04 © 2004
IEEE Published by the IEEE Computer Society, Vol. 8, No. 6

WS-IBasic Profile; http://www.ws-i.org/Profiles/BasicProfile-1.1-2004-08-
24.html#philosophy

Designing Web Service Accounting System

Ge Zhang — Jochen Mueller — Paul Mueller

University of Kaiserslautern
Paul Ehrlich Strasse Geb. 36
67663 Kaiserslautern, Germany
{gezhang, jmueller, pmueller}@informatik.uni-kl.de

ABSTRACT: *Web Service technology is attracting increasing attention not only from academy and institutes for study and research purposes but also from commercial areas for business purposes. How to reasonably reflect the value of the Web Services is a very important concern must be considered. Web Service Accounting is the process of collecting Web Service usage information for the purpose of charging and billing. Through accounting service providers can cover costs and make profit from their provided Web Services. This paper introduces a Web Service Accounting system architecture and explains the detail techniques about the entities of the accounting system.*

KEY WORDS: *Web Service, Accounting.*

1. Introduction

The emergence of Web Service provides a standard platform facilitating the interoperability among applications residing in heterogonous environment. Through XML based message communication mechanism and abstracted Web Service interfaces, software systems developed with different programming language, running in different operating systems, or in different hardware platform can easily cooperate with each other. Now the Web Service technology is attracting increasing attention not only from academy and institutes for study and research purposes but also from commercial areas for business purposes. The Web Service architecture can be considered as the next generation multi-service integration platform supporting future business operations modes on the basis of Internet. From checking the UDDI registries of IBM, Microsoft etc. we can find more and more commercial Web Services are being registered offering value added services in the Internet.

The brilliant economical prospect of the Web Services depends not only on the contribution from more enterprises through migrating their business processes into the Internet Web Service platform, but also on the support from Web Service related techniques such as security, accounting, billing etc. In order to stimulate more commercial transactions, such as B2B, B2C, taking advantage of the Web Service techniques and efficiently assist the business processes supported by Web Service plat-form, how to reasonably reflect the value of the Web Services is a very important concern must be considered. On the one hand, the traditional flat-rate pricing model and the free usage model may be unreasonable or even unacceptable for the commercial Web Services. Therefore usage based, content based, or transaction based charging models should be introduced for the purpose of covering costs and earning revenue of the services consumption. On the other hand, the new characters of the Web Service architecture requires also new accounting, charging and billing model and techniques to be applied adapting to the new variation. The distributing nature of the Web Services components, the scattering around the world of the Web Service users arise the challenges to the accounting for Web Services.

Accounting, according to the definition of IETF in (Aboda, et al., 2000), is the process of collecting the resource usage information for the purpose of billing, trend analysis etc. Here only accounting for the financial purpose, i.e. billing, is considered. The Web Service Accounting can be defined as the process of collecting Web Services usage related in-formation for the billing purpose. Accounting, charging, billing are normally regarded as the three phases of a billing process. Charging is the process of calculating the cost of the services or resources usage according to the pricing strategies and the accounting information. And billing is the process of converting the gathered charging information of a customer to deliverable bill (Stiller, et al., 1998). This paper concentrates on the accounting technique for the Web Service, and detailed discussion about charging and billing is beyond the scope of this paper.

In this paper we present a Web Service Accounting system architecture and analyze the technique issues concerning entities in this architecture. The rest of this paper is organized as follows: in section 1.1 some related works are introduced; in section 2 a Web Service usage scenario is studied to reveal the requirements for Web Service Accounting; in section 3 a Web Service Accounting architecture is suggested and explained in detail; and at the end conclusion and future work are described.

1.1 Related Works

Although Web Service has been extensively discussed in recent years, few works concerning Web Service accounting were reported. (Kuebler, 2001) suggested a simple Web Service meter architecture. In this architecture the meter is designed as meter Web Service, which can provide time based Web Service usage measurement according to the SLA contract. Many issues concerning Web Service accounting such as accounting protocols, inter-domain data collection, composite Web Services metering etc. are not addressed. (Agarwal, et al., 2002) discussed three possible models of integrating meter services into the OGSA accounting system architecture. Especially the metering information ex-change among composite Grid Services in different models was analyzed. The authors have also developed a prototype e-Service accounting system managing composite services provided by a financial portal (Agarwal, et al., 2003). Their work concentrated also on the meter layer and concerned only limit issues of a Web Service Accounting system.

Regardless of few efforts on Web Service Accounting, there exist many accounting technologies, principle and standards that can be applied to the Web Service Accounting. Content and usage based accounting techniques provide finer granular service measurement mechanism. The TINA Service Architecture (Abarca, et al., 1997) separates the service with resource in different layer, therefore separating service and resource metering and accounting becomes possible. This layer architecture can not only provide a clear view for service consumption but also facilitate outsourcing accounting management. Accounting protocols such as RADIUS, DIAMETER, SNMP etc. can be extended for Web Service accounting purpose. Inter-domain accounting requirement mentioned in (Aboda, et al., 2000) also needs to be adopted for composite Web Services spanning in different AADs. Federated Accounting (Bhushan, et al., 2001) is a solution for accounting composite Web Services. With policy based accounting techniques (Radisic, 2002) business requirements such as SLA defined in contracts can be easily mapped to the control of the Web Service Accounting. In spite of these now existing accounting solutions, they may need to be extended, enhanced, and modified to be integrated into the Web Service Accounting system. New mechanism such as effective Web Service metering, new standards such as Web Ser-vice Accounting Usage Record are needed to be developed.

2. Travel Agency Scenario Study

Below a classical Web Service usage scenario - Travel Agency example[1] - is inspected to outline the issues related to Web Service Accounting.

A Travel Agency utilizes a Web Service based system providing customers with travel reservation services. With that the Travel Agency can earn money through charging fees from the sold travel packages. Two service providers, providing Hotel reservation service and Flight reservation service respectively, join in the travel reservation sys-tem through offering corresponding Hotel and Flight reservation Web Services. Additionally a credit company supplies on-line payment service for the travel reservation transactions. Figure 1 depicts the relationship between these Web Services. The travel reservation system utilized by the Travel Agency makes travel reservation for the customers through the Travel Reservation (TR) Web Service, which may be offered by another service provider, e.g. a travel information service company. The TR Web Service exploits Hotel Reservation (HR) and Flight Reservation (FR) Web Services to make reservation for hotel rooms and flight tickets respectively. And a Credit Card Payment (CCP) Web Service is employed to support the TR, HR and FR Web Services for payment. A travel package for a customer can be sold by the travel agency in several steps:

1.   A customer calls to the travel agency for a travel reservation. After under-standing the requirement, e.g. destination, time, etc., of the customer, the travel agency utilizes the travel reservation system that takes advantage of the TR Web Service to make travel reservation.

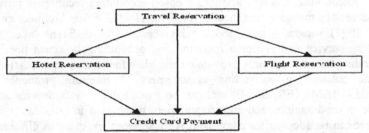

Figure 1 *Relationship among travel reservation related Web Services*

2.   The TR Web Service calls the HR Web Service to reserve a hotel room for the customer, and calls the FR Web Service to book a flight ticket for the customer.

3.   After successful reservation, the TR, HR and FR Web Services all utilize a CCP Web Service for payment. Certainly the TR, HR and FR Web Services can require CCP Web Service from different service providers.

From the above described process, we can find several characters that may affect the Web Service Accounting processes, therefore corresponding requirements should be considered for the Web Service accounting:

---

[1] http://www.w3.org/2002/04/17-ws-usecase

- A travel reservation transaction may involve several Web Services instead of only one Web Service. Accounting for the usage of one Web Service may concern several other Web Services, therefore a transaction based or session based accounting mechanism should be introduced to handle this situation.
- The involved Web Services may scatter in different Accounting Administration Domains (AAD) instead of only in one domain. Hence how to aggregate and correlate the metered Raw Data Records (RDR), which attributes should be measured reflecting the different Web Services usage, and what kinds of format should be used for the RDRs or a uniform format should be suggested as standard for RDRs are all issues aroused from this situation.
- Although several Web Services are involved in the travel reservation transaction, only the TR Web Service is directly called by the travel agency, whereas the TR Web Service is the direct user of HR, FR and CCP Web Ser-vices.
- The usage charge of all these involved Web Services may depend on the commercial purposes of the corresponding services. The application and designed purpose of the provided Web Service plays an important role in determining the behaviour of the accounting system. The application purpose of the Web Services decides the billing strategy, which will be mapped to the charging policy. The charging policy in turn is mapped to the accounting policy, which controls the behaviour of the accounting processes and the accounting information exchange. If the usage of the Web Service is free of charge, then no billing strategy is applied, and therefore no accounting process is needed to be executed. Otherwise the billing strategy will be mapped to the accounting policy to control the accounting system's behaviour, for example, which attributes of the Web Services should be measured, how the RDRs can be formatted and gathered.

From this sample scenario we can find that new challenges to the accounting technology arising with the emergence of Web Service need new mechanisms to meet their requirements.

3. Web Service Accounting

In this section the detailed Web Service Accounting mechanisms are discussed in order to explain the construction of a Web Service Accounting system. Figure 2 depicts a Web Service Accounting system architecture that is constructed with two layers. The function layer aggregates the accounting function modules that fulfil the accounting tasks. The control layer consists of policies and control managers that control the behaviours of different accounting modules in function layer. This architecture concentrates on the accounting level techniques, whereas the charging and billing related mechanisms are not addressed here. But this accounting architecture still provides "Distributor" as interface for the charging and billing systems.

3.1 Meter

Meter is responsible for measuring the usage of the Web Services and generating RDRs from the measured data. Meter location, measured attribute metrics and RDR format are issues concerning the design of the meter for Web Services.

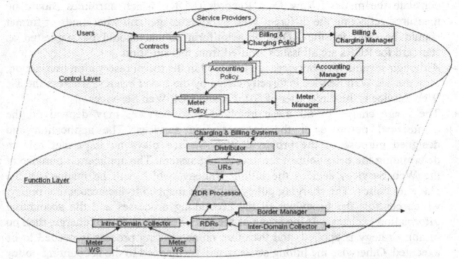

Figure 2 *Web Service Accounting system architecture*

3.1.1 Meter location

Meter for the Web Service can be located in or outside the measured Web Services. If a meter resides in the measured Web Service, all the activities of the Web Service can be monitored by the meter. Outside the Web Service a meter can intercept the SOAP messages in the SOAP router to measure the usage of the Web Services. Figure 3 depicts the two locations of the meter. According to the different placement of meter in Figure 3, the measurement mechanism of the meter can be realized with intrusion or non-intrusion method.

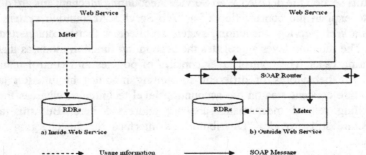

Figure 3 *Meter location inside and outside the measured Web Service*

The intrusion method is integrating the measurement function into the measured Web Services, with that the measured data can be gathered. This is usually done during the development of the Web Services through inserting the measurement related code. The Web Service developer can insert their own defined measurement related code, or insert the measurement APIs manually. The measurement related code can also be integrated into the Web Services through the development platform automatically.

So far there exists neither this kind of measurement APIs nor development platform supporting automatically measurement function integrating, and there is no standard for Web Service measurement issues, such as attributes, format etc., therefore only the developers' own measurement code can be manually inserted into Web Service for measurement purposes. The measurement functions can be implemented either fixed or dynamic. The fixed or static measurement functions are designed to measure the predefined attributes and the measured attributes will not be changed in the future. The dynamic measurement functions can measure different attributes according to the meter policy. In other words the dynamic measurement functions support a predefined super set of attributes, and for every Web Service measurement only a sub set of at-tributes is needed, hence flexibility and efficiency of the measurement can be enhanced. But, no matter static or dynamic measurement mechanisms the intrusion methods have a disadvantage that the change of the accounting requirement may cause the Web Service to be modified. For example, if CPU usage attribute is neither a pre-defined attribute nor an attribute of a predefined super set of attributes, then in order to measure this attribute the new measurement code must be inserted into the Web Service through modifying the code of the Web Service. Another disadvantage is that the measurement code cannot be integrated into the measured Web Services in some cases. For example, the legacy Web Services or the Web Services that were developed by other companies and no source code is available. Comparing with the non-intrusion measurement method, the advantage of this method is that this method can provide more detailed usage information due to its tightly coupled with the measured Web Services.

The non-intrusion method does not need to insert the measurement related code into the measured Web Services. Usually the meter is implemented as a stand alone application or component. Figure 3 b) shows how to measure the Web Service usage out-side the Web Service. The SOAP Router is a message distributor that delivers messages from SOAP clients to the receivers. Monitoring the messages through the SOAP Router the Web Services usage information can be collected. In order to monitor the SOAP messages the meter intercepts the SOAP messages and extracts corresponding attributes to generate RDRs. This measurement process is outside the scope of the measured Web Services. This non-intrusion method can also be guided by the ac-counting policy to filter the non interested messages to improve the measurement efficiency, and to control the measured attributes. The advantage of this method is obviously that the measurement code needs not be inserted into the measured Web Services, and consequently the measured Web Services need not be modified to adapt the change of the measurement requirement. Therefore this method is suitable for measuring legacy Web Services or Web Services without available source code. But this method has also disadvantages. One disadvantage is that it can not provide finer granular or accurate measurement results, since some attributes can only be measured inside the Web Services and some context information, which may be important for billing, cannot be obtained outside the Web Services. Another disadvantage is the central position of the meter may become a bottleneck. On the one hand the meter needs monitor all SOAP messages crossing the SOAP Router. Hence the processing ability and the performance of the meter is an issue must be considered. On the other hand, since the centralized meter is usually responsible for monitoring many or even all Web Services in a Web Service system, the failure of the meter may cause more meter data loss.

3.1.2 Attribute metrics

Attributes are the parameters need be measured to reflect the Web Service usage. A Web Service usage can be measured in two layers: one is the resource layer and the other is the service layer. The resource layer provides required resources to support the supply of the Web Ser-vices. The resource layer measurement reflects the resource consumption corresponding to Web Service usage. Network resource and computing resource are two types of resources.

Network resources usage measurement has been researched extensively for a long time. There are many attributes should be measured in the network resource level measurement. They are determined by the accounting purpose and policy. For example, time duration and traffic volume are two frequently measured attributes concerning network resources usage. Delay, bandwidth etc. are attributes required for QoS based accounting. The network resource consumption measurement is usually independent of the Web Service measurement. If the network resource consumption is required to be calculated as one part of the Web Service consumption, the key issue is how to correlate the network resource usage records with corresponding Web Service usage records. This needs correlation attributes, e.g. source, destination IP addresses, ports, start and end time etc., to join the network resource usage records and Web Service usage records together.

Web Service usage consumes not only network resources but also computing re-sources. Computing resource refers to the CPU, memory, storage etc. computing ability related resources. The computing resource consumption can be divided into two categories. One is the computing resource consumption accompanying with the Web Service usage. For example, a Web Service searches database will cause some computing resource consumption. In this case the search results instead of the consumed computing resources are the service content provided by Web Service. The other is the Web Service providing computing resources as the service content. For example, the computational Grid can organize computers spanning in different domains to fulfil a computing resources relied job. The computing resources usage can be measured with performance tools supplemented by the OS or performance measurement soft-ware vendors. The challenge of using these tools for meter purposes is how to configure them to provide suitable and enough computing resources usage information. Correlating the computing resource usage with the corresponding Web Service is also an issue should be considered.

The service layer offers the Web Services that are interested by the customers. The contents of different Web Services vary widely. Therefore the accounting attributes for one Web Service may be totally different with another Web Service. For example, for the TR Web Service in section 2 maybe only "how many successful travel package sales are made through the TR Web Service by which users" needs to be counted, whereas for a VoD Web Service "which video films are demanded by which users" should be recorded. Because of the variety of the attributes of Web Services, no standard attributes metrics or super set can be defined for all Web Services, though an attribute super set defined for some types of Web Services may be possible. A common attribute that is indispensable for accounting composite Web Services is Transaction Identification (TID), which is the key index for joining RDRs generated from different Web Services usages for a common transaction. The generation of TID and the Transaction concept for composite Web Services will be explained in section 3.3.

3.1.3 Raw data record format

Raw data records are measured results and generated by the meters. The format of RDRs depends on the accounting protocols. Accounting protocol is used to convey data for accounting purposes. Till now there exists no accounting protocol specified for Web Service accounting and there is no standard record format for RDRs. RADIUS (Rigney, 2000), DIAMETER (Calhoun, *et al.*, 2003), TACAS+ (Finseth, 1993) and SNMP (Case, *et al.*, 2002) are frequently used ac-counting protocols. These accounting protocols can be chosen for the Web Service Accounting purposes. Surveying these accounting protocols (Brownlee, 2000) we can find the record formats can be divided into several categories: ASN.1, e.g. SNMP; Binary, e.g. RADIUS, DIAMETER; Plain Text; Tagged Text, e.g. XML based formats. If an accounting protocol is chosen for conveying the RDRs, the RDRs' format must be compatible with the requirement of the accounting protocol. Otherwise the RDRs must be converted before transmission. Certainly proprietary formats may be used or defined by different vendors, but this may cause compatible problem in exchanging accounting information with different formats.

3.2 Raw data records collector

Meters are distributed in different places in which Web Services reside. The RDRs may also scatter in different meter systems. A RDRs collector belongs to one accounting administration domain. The RDRs collector gathers RDRs from different meters in its own AAD. It may also collect RDRs in other AADs according to the accounting policy. The ability of collecting RDRs spanning several AADs is a requirement for accounting composite Web Services that are offered by different service providers. Therefore the RDRs collectors can be classified into two categories: Intra-Domain Collector and Inter-Domain Collector. Intra-Domain

Collectors gather RDRs in their local AADs. The behaviour of the collectors, such as data gathering intervals, data gathering filter settings etc., is controlled by policies or rules configured by the accounting manager. In order to collect the RDRs suitable accounting protocols should be used for Web Service Accounting purposes. Currently existing accounting protocols can be chosen for this purpose. But before they are applied for Web Service Accounting they must be extended to adapt the new attributes of Web Service Accounting. Extensibility is the most important factor that must be considered in selecting the now existing ac-counting protocols for Web Service Accounting. Considering the possible variety of the accounting attributes of different Web Services, the accounting protocol should be flexible and extensible to accommodate the variety requirement. RADIUS, as an ex-ample, has limited extensibility, because the type identifier of RADIUS is limited to a single octet and consequently only 256 types can be supported for this protocol. The SNMP, on the contrary, is an extensible framework protocol which supports private MIBs. From this point of view SNMP is suitable for Web Service accounting purposes. If the SNMP is chosen for Web Service Accounting purpose, corresponding Web Service Accounting MIB extension should be made.

Inter-Domain Collectors gather RDRs from outside local AADs. This needs a federation data collection mechanism to negotiate the data gathering process cross several AADs. Figure 4 illustrates an inter-domain RDRs collection model.

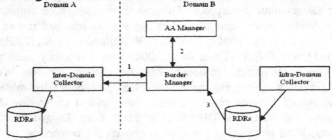

Figure 4 *Inter-Domain RDRs collection*

The Inter-Domain Collector in domain A can neither directly access the RDRs nor directly collect RDRs from meters in domain B. It can collect RDRs in domain B only through the help of the Border Manager (BM). The BM provides interface to Inter-Domain Collectors outside its AAD for gathering RDRs. If the Inter-Domain Collector in domain A needs to collect RDRs in domain B, it sends a request to the BM in domain B. The request may include authentication information, key indexes such as transaction ID for retrieving RDRs etc. When the BM in domain B receives the collection request, it requests the Authentication and Authorization Manager (AAM) to authenticate this Inter-Domain Collector. Security is a very important factor must be taken into consideration for federated accounting. Inter-Domain Collectors must be authenticated before they can collect RDRs from local AAD. In order to simplify the authentication and authorization process, Single Sign On (SSO) or other federation authentication mechanism can be applied (Goetze, 2004). After authentication the Inter-Domain Collector can acquire corresponding authorization in collecting local RDRs. The BM retrieves the required RDRs from the RDRs database, and then sends these RDRs to the Inter-Domain Collector in domain A. After that the Inter-Domain Collector stores the RDRs in local RDR data-base. In order to coordinate the interaction between Inter-Domain Collector and BM, contract between domain A and domain B should be agreed in advance. The contract can be used as guidelines for Inter-Domain RDRs collection, since contract can be converted into accounting policies controlling RDRs collection. For example, SLAs defined in contract may be required to generate the accounting policy to control the behaviour of the Intra-Domain Collectors.

3.3 Raw data records processor

After data collection the RDRs need to be further processed to generate Usage Re-cords (URs) for charging and billing purposes. Processing procedures such as validation, aggregation, correlation, filtering, normalization etc. are needed to convert RDRs into URs. All these processing procedures are controlled by accounting policy, which is generated or determined by charging and billing policies. The difficulty of RDRs processing for Web Service Accounting is the correlation processing of the composite Web Services RDRs. Since the Web Services may reside in different AADs and their usages maybe measured by different meters, how to correlate the RDRs scattered in different AADs with each other becomes a challenge. An-other challenge for correlation is to combine service level usage RDRs with network and computing resource usage RDRs for a Web Service transaction together. At first we should define a concept: Web Service Transaction (WST). A Web Service Transaction is defined as one time Web Service operation that involves one or more Web Services. A Web Service Transaction's lifecycle begins with a request to a Web Service operation, and is ended with the requested operation finished with or without response message sent back to the caller. A Web Service Transaction can be assumed as the basic unit for Web Service charging. A Web Service operation may fulfil its task alone, or it may require other Web Services in local AADs to help fulfilling the task, or it may even require helps from other Web Services in different AADs. There-fore a Web Service transaction may link a group of Web Services together in a hierarchical tree structure, and root is the first called Web Service. Consequently their corresponding RDRs measured by meters distributed in different places need a correlation mechanism to rebuild a complete image of a Web Service Transaction. The correlation processes are based on Web Service Transaction. RDRs of service, network resource and computing resource consumption related to one Web Service Transaction will be consolidated to generate a Usage Record reflecting this Web Service Transaction. In order to correlate these RDRs Transaction ID (TID) can be used as an index to indicate to which Web Service Transaction a RDR belongs. A TID uniquely identifies a Web Service Transaction. It is used not only for correlating RDRs but also for guiding inter-domain RDRs collection. A Web Service Transaction can be regarded as a whole even if it involves several Web Services. In this case only one TID is needed for metering related Web Services. The TID is generated by the first called Web Ser-vice related meter, and this TID will be handed on to the subsequent called Web Ser-vices' meters. This TID information will be logged as an item in all generated RDRs concerning this Web Service Transaction. This is the only one index to link related RDRs together. For collecting RDRs in different AADs, BMs in different AADs can directly send all gathered RDRs with the same TIDs in its own AADs to the Inter-Domain Collector that belongs to the AAD of the first called Web Service, since AAD information can be integrated into the TID. Another view of a Web Service transaction is that a Web Service Transaction consists of several sub-Web Service Transactions, therefore a Web Service Transaction can be described as: WST=WST1+WST2+¡-+WSTn. WST1 is the first called or root Web Service Transaction. Other Web Services Trans-action may not exist for WST if this Web Service Transaction includes only one Web Service operation. A WST may have a parent WST if its related Web Service is called by the Web Service of the parent WST, and this WST is called as a child WST of the parent WST. Under this pattern every WST related meters can generate its own TIDs for corresponding WSTs. The TID generation and transfer in this situation have several different schemes. One is that a WST's meter records all its child WSTs' TIDs in RDRs. Through that collection and correlation of RDRs can be fulfilled with a for-ward traversing tree like method. Another is that a WST's meter records the parent WST's TID in RDRs. Therefore a retrospection method is needed for collecting and correlating RDRs. Another issue in RDRs processing worth consideration here is the normalization, which is responsible for converting processed RDRs into different formats according to the requirements of charging and billing layers. Due to the variety of the Web Ser-vices application purposes, the format of URs should adapt to this requirement. IPDR has proposed several service-oriented record format schemas. It can be chosen for defining Web Service Accounting usage record format[2].

3.4 Policies for Web Service Accounting

Web Service Accounting systems should be flexible to meet different Web Service providers' requirements. Accounting functionalities may need to be customized to adapt different customers' needs. Especially for the commercial Web Services providers the flexible billing strategy is a competitive means in the market. Therefore policy based accounting mechanism should be adopted for Web Service accounting. Policies play very important role in controlling the Web Service Accounting behaviours. Con-tracts negotiated between customers and Web Service providers will be converted to corresponding policies. For example, meters, collectors, RDRs processors etc. ac-counting components all have their appropriate policies to provide adaptive and automatic accounting management. In order to support policy based accounting policy conversion mechanism, policy language and

---

[2] Ipdr.org, *"Network Data Management - Usage(NDM-U) for IP-Based Services"*, version 3.1.1, October 2002

policy enforcement mechanism are required. Concrete discussion about these elements is out of the scope of this paper.

4. Conclusion and future works

In this paper we used a Web Service scenario to reveal the requirements for Web Service Accounting. Then a Web Service Accounting architecture was suggested. Entities in this architecture are explained. Especially many considerations about the meter mechanism are discussed. Concerning composite Web Service a Web Service Transaction concept is used to coordinate the metering and correlation processes. Policy based accounting was suggested for Web Service Accounting.

The suggested Web Service Accounting architecture is designed to be applied to our VoIP Web Service project "Venice" (Hillenbrand, 2004). In the "Venice" project all VoIP functions and supplementary services are implemented as Web Service. The Web Service Ac-counting will also be implemented as Web Services, which may consist of Meter Web Service, Accounting Protocol Web Service and Accounting Web Service etc. Through this way the Web Service Accounting system can be served not only for Venice project but also for more other Web Services after extension or adding plug-ins components.

References

Abarca C., et al., *"Service Architecture Version 5.0"*, TINA, June 1997

Aboda B., Arkko J., D. Harrington, *"Introduction to Accounting Management"*, RFC2975, October 2000

Agarwal V., Karnik N., Kumar A., *"Architectural Issues for Metering and Accounting of Grid Services"*, 2002

Agarwal V., Karnik N., Kumar A., *"Metering and Accounting for Composite e-Services"*, Proceedings of the IEEE International Conference on E-Commerce (CEC'03), June 2003

Bhushan B., Tschichholz M., Leray E., and Donnelly W., *"Federated Accounting: Service Charging and Billing in a Business-To-Business Environment"*, IEEE/IFIP International Symposium on Inte-grated Network Management (IM 2001), May 2001

Brownlee N., Blount A., *"Accounting Attributes and Record Formats"*, RFC2924, Sept. 2000

Calhoun P., Loughney J., Guttman E., Zorn G., Arkko J., *"Diameter Base Protocol"*, RFC3588, September 2003.

Case J., Mundy R., Partain D., Stewart B., *"Introduction and Applicability Statements for Internet Standard Management Framework"*, RFC3410, December 2002

Finseth C., *"An Access Control Protocol, Sometimes Called TACACS"*, RFC 1492, 1993

Goetze J., "Single Sign On in Web Service Scenarios", Diplomarbeit, July 2004

Hillenbrand M., Zhang G., *"A Web Services Based Framework for Voice over IP"*, 30th EUROMICRO, Rennes, France, August 31st - September 3rd, 2004

Kuebler D., Eibach W., *"Metering and Accounting for Web Services"*, http://www-106.ibm.com/developerworks/library/ws-maws/, July 2001

Radisic I., *"Using Policy-Based Concepts to Provide Service Oriented Accounting Management"*, Proceedings of the 8th International IFIP/IEEE Network Operations and Management Symposium (NOMS 2002), 2002

Rigney C., *"RADIUS Accounting"*, RFC2866, June 2000

Stiller B., Fankhauser G., Plattner B., Weiler N., *"Charging and Accounting for Integrated Internet Services"*, INET'98: The Internet Summit, Geneva, Switzland, 21-24 July, 1998

Interoperability Standards
Implementation, Dynamics and Impact

PC Chair's message

The Workshop aimed at getting a better understanding of the impact ICT standards have on networked organisations, striking a balance between academic rigor and practical relevance. Researchers and practitioners (from both industry and standards setting bodies) attended and presented their ideas and views.

To this end, the presentations first discussed interoperability issues and their relation to standardisation. A general overview was followed by papers discussing the different dimensions of software interoperability, from an economic perspective. Subsequently, issues in RFID[1] standardisation were discussed. With RFID being an extremely hot topic, such standards issues are rather high on the agenda of everyone wishing to promote this technology.

Other papers discussing specific cases followed. These included B2B standardisation, both sectored and general, and IPv6 addressing issues. Although these topics are rather dissimilar, all studies highlighted the importance of standards in the quest for interoperability.

The approach to achieve interoperability through standards is further complicated by the fact that standards, once passed, are not set in stone. Rather, they can develop over time, either by means of e.g., new versions or addenda, or through implementation and use. The sources of such standards dynamics were thoroughly discussed. An analysis of the effects of the dynamics of JTC1[2]'s standards maintenance process highlighted the former, and different cases on mobile communication standards analysed the changing dynamics associated with standards in the larger context of the evolution of mobile communications. This was complemented by an analysis of the 'standards skirmish' (not really a battle) about DVD formats.

Many (most?) hard technical interoperability problems have been solved already. Now we are moving up to interoperability at the semantic level. This problem was discussed from the point of view of a European standards body. Subsequently, the relation between standards and the open source movement was addressed. After all, Open Source Software (OSS) is considered by many as a complement,

---

[1] Radio Frequency Identification
[2] Joint Technical Committee 1, a committee jointly ran by ISO and iEC, which is responsible for the ICT and e-business sectors.

or even an alternative, to standardisation. Differences and similarities between standards and OSS were identified and discussed, and an example of how to introduce OSS and standards into the government sector was given.

The workshop participants engaged in lengthy and interesting discussions during and after the individual presentations. It seems to be safe to say that everyone learned quite a bit, got new insights, and maybe even new ideas for future research.

The workshop was organised on behalf of the NO-REST[3] project. For more information on this project please see www.no-rest.org.

Jakobs Kai, Aachen University, Germany

---

[3] Networked Organisations – REsearch into STandards and Standardisation

Interoperability of Software: Demand and Solutions

ABSTRACT: *This paper presents empirical evidence on the demand for interoperability among German software companies. We test a set of hypotheses in the empirical analyses. The findings confirm that the interoperability with the software of their customers is most important. The multivariate analysis shows that the demand for interoperability increases with company size, confirming the concept of network externalities, especially between users. In addition, for companies trying to achieve lead-time advantage, interoperability is also of high importance to secure the installed user base. Finally, the demand for interoperability depends on the characteristics of specific software products. The most important instrument to achieve interoperability is the disclosure of interfaces, the second preference is the use of standardised architectures*

KEY WORDS: *software, interoperability, interfaces, standards.*

1. Introduction

From an economic perspective, it is well known in theory (Shy 2001) that the greater the interoperability of two complementary components, like software and hardware, the greater too is the diversity of complementary inputs, like further software products, which are at the user's disposal. However, the empirical evidence on the interrelationship between interoperability and variety in the software market is not very broad, but some examples do exist (David 1990).

Another question, which is not extensively dealt with either in the theoretical literature or in empirical studies, is the demand for interoperable solutions. Since we observe an increasing complexity of the software development process, various dimensions regarding interoperability for companies producing software emerge. First, a software developing company thinks immediately about the need to produce software which is inter-operable with the software its customers uses, which they may have even developed themselves. However, software developing increasingly takes place within a complex value chain, which may also require integrating software from other supplying companies. This will be facilitated, if interoperability is realised with the supply side. The demand for own software depends also on its relation to other products on the market. Here we have to distinguish two dimensions. First, the interoperability of own software with complementary software products, which are used by potential customers, increases the demand and the value of the own product. Second, interoperability with the software products of competitors is ambivalent. Dominant players have little interest in interoperability with competing products, because price competition especially will drive down their profits (Besen, Farrell 1994). Small companies or companies entering the market should have a stronger interest to provide products which are interoperable with the products of the incumbents or the dominant players, in order to use their so-called installed base of users. The need to join installed bases of users is higher for software, which requires both high development costs and which is characterised by strong positive network externalities. In total, whether companies desire interoperability with the software products of competing products depends on several factors.

The empirical data allows us to demonstrate different preferences for the interoperability in the four dimensions discussed above. Furthermore, we will estimate four demand functions for interoperability depending both on firm and software characteristics.

In a second step, we have to discuss how interoperability is achieved. In mainstream economic literature, interoperability is either not used at all (Shy 2001) or is used more or less synonymously with compatibility. And compatibility is achieved simply via standardisation (compare for an overview of empirical studies Blind 2004). In economics literature, we find also the option to develop gateways between technologies (David, Bunn 1988). However, gateway technologies are more appropriate to achieve interoperability or compatibility between hardware components in order to generate mostly direct network externalities, e.g. in the case of telecommunication. In software, gateway solutions do not play a significant role. In our study we distinguish between three different standardisation strategies. First, companies may use in their software the specifications of standardised sector-wide architectures, which are open and transparent. Second, they may orient their software towards the de facto standards of the market leader. In contrast to the two passive standardisation strategies, software companies may try to get their own specifications accepted as de facto standards. A step towards interoperability, which is a pre-stage of standardisation, is the disclosure of interfaces or even of the complete source code. Both strategies are closely related to the promotion of the specifications towards de facto standards. Finally, the problem of interoperability can already be tackled at a very early stage by cooperating in the joint development of software or at least of common interfaces. In the same way as for the demand for interoperability in the four dimensions discussed above, we will develop hypotheses that will determine the demand for these instruments, which includes also for which interoperability dimension they are used.

The remainder of the paper is organised as follows. In the next section, we will develop a set of hypotheses regarding first the demand for interoperability regarding customers, suppliers, and competitors providing complementary or substitutive software. Based on these hypotheses, we will construct a general demand function for interoperability. In chapter three, we present the data source and the main characteristics of the companies surveyed. Chapter four presents descriptive statistics regarding the demand for the four dimensions of interoperability. Besides the descriptive statistics, we present the results of multivariate ordered Probit models, which allow us to determine the driving forces for the demand for interoperability. In chapter five, we present descriptive statistics regarding the use of various instruments to achieve interoperability. The paper concludes with a summary of the results and an outlook regarding the needs for future research.

2. Hypotheses

In this chapter, we develop a set of hypotheses, which will be tested on the basis of the empirical data. Some tests will be based on simple descriptive statistics, others require multivariate regression methods.

The first set of hypotheses concern the importance of interoperability of a firm's software within the value chain and regarding its competitors:

- H1a: The interoperability of own software with the software used by their customers is most important for companies.
- H1b: Since customers use numerous other software, which is complementary to the own software, interoperability of the own software

with complementary software provided by competitors is certainly more important than interoperability with the software of suppliers.
- H1c: Interoperability with the software of competitors supplying competitive products is desirable only for some companies.

The second set of hypotheses focuses on the influence of company characteristics on the demand for interoperability:

- H2: With increasing company size interoperability becomes more important, because of economies of scale in the software production process, although very large companies may be able to set specifications which are accepted both by their suppliers and customers.
- H3: Companies with high R&D intensities try to restrict interoperability in order to avoid unintended knowledge spillovers, whereas companies with low R&D intensities are forced depend on the interoperability of their products.
- H4: Independent software developers attribute a high importance especially to substitutive and complementary software.
- H5: Companies trying to achieve lead-time advantage have a high preference to secure interoperability in order not to lose their installed base (backward compatibility).
- H6: Demand for interoperability also depends on the functionality of software.

In chapter 4, we present the results of empirical analyses testing the hypotheses listed above after a brief description of the main characteristics of the software companies surveyed.

3. The Database and Major Characteristics of the Sample

3.1. The Database

The data for testing the hypotheses regarding the demand for interoperability and the means to achieve it originates from a survey of German software developing companies performed in the year 2001 (Blind et al. 2003; see the English version Blind et al. 2004). A basic hypothesis of a former empirical study (Stahl et al. 2000) pre-supposes significant differences between enterprises whose main corporate aim is to develop and sell software (primary sector), and enterprises of the so-called secondary sector, which besides a traditional main business also produce software for their "hardware". Software, which is irrevocably integrated in hardware components and can only function together with them, such as e.g. specific control software in mechanical engineering or vehicle construction, we refer to as embedded software. For this reason the presentation of the descriptive statistics is differentiated according to these two groups.

In the survey, enterprises belong to the primary sector whose corporate objective is the development of software, according to the generally accepted classification NACE (NACE 72.202), supplemented by a number of independent software developers, be-cause these micro-companies play a considerable role in the software area (Stahl et al. 2000). The industries of the so-called secondary sector were vehicle construction (NACE 34), electro-technology (NACE 30-32), telecommunications (NACE 64) and mechanical engineering (NACE 29). The survey was conducted in May and June 2001 by approaching software companies or companies developing also software via an online questionnaire. In total 149 questionnaires from companies of the primary sector, 39 questionnaires of independent software developers and 68 questionnaires from companies of the secondary were available for the analysis. Since the companies were asked first for the general willingness to participate at the survey, before they have been requested to fill out the questionnaire, two response rates have to be reported. From the companies signalling their willingness to participate, 47% filled out the questionnaire in the primary sector and 22% in the secondary sector. Related to the number of companies approached in the first step, the response rate is significantly lower at 16% in the primary and less than 4% in the secondary sector.

3.2. Types of Software Developments and their Significance

Since the need for and the instruments to achieve interoperability is depending on the type of software being developed, the firms were first of all asked how their turnover was distributed among various types of software. A first dimension hereby is the independence of the developed product, which ranges from the so-called stand-alone solutions and complete integration in other software, respectively hardware. The average turnover share with independent software products amounts to somewhat over 58% in the primary sector, in the secondary sector to somewhat more than 35%. For the turn-over share of so-called "embedded software", that is, software which is an integral part of hardware and only functions in conjunction with it , this ratio is reversed, as expected.

In the primary sector, the average share of embedded software amounts to only 7%, while it accounts for nearly 36% in the secondary sector and thus corresponds mainly to the share of independent software. This distribution corresponds to the claims about own production of hardware: 85% of the enterprises in the secondary sector and 44% of the firms in the primary sector develop, respectively also produce hardware. These differentiations according to primary and secondary sector are both statistically significant. These distributions mean that the particular problems of embedded software do not play an essential role for the primary sector, whereas for the secondary sector not only the specifics of independent software, but also the idiosyncrasies of embedded software are relevant. Furthermore, in both sectors hardware producers also increasingly produce embedded software.

As the demand for and the means to achieve interoperability will depend on the functionality of their products, the sample was asked about the various application areas of their software products (Figure 3.1). It appears that the secondary sector has the largest share of turnover with systems-related software, followed by approximately equal shares of user software from the areas business management, technical applications, automatic control engineering and multi-media. In the primary sector, on the other hand, the user software plays a greater role (with business administration software in the lead), systems-related software takes third place here with only 11%.

Figure 3.1: *Turnover Shares with Software of Different Functionality*

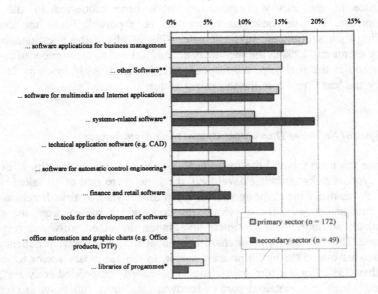

A final differentiation among the firms regarding their products distinguishes according to what extent they develop their products as individually tailored software solutions for single customers, respectively small groups of customers. The underlying assumption is that the patenting of products for the mass market is of greater significance than for custom-made articles. The results show that in the secondary sector most often small series are developed for certain customer groups, whereas the primary sector is more strongly polarised and clearly more than a third of their turnover stems either from client-specific, customised developments or from products for the mass market.

4. Demand for Interoperability

In a first step, we present the results relating to the hypotheses about the importance of interoperability with suppliers or customers, or with competitors.

One idiosyncrasy of software development in contrast with other products is the interoperability necessary between systems and applications or between various applications. As argued above, four dimensions must be differentiated regarding interoperability. Figure 4.1 shows that the interoperability with customer software is by far the most important criterion for both sectors. The interoperability with supplier products is of medium importance and is approximately as significant as the interoperability with products of complementary suppliers. The significantly higher figure of the primary sector in the interoperability with competitive products reveals the importance attributed to the functional compatibility of the own product with others on the market. On the other hand, this strategic motive is not pronounced in the secondary sector.

Figure 4.1 *Significance of Interoperability with Software of Various Actor Groups (1 = very low, 5 = very high)*

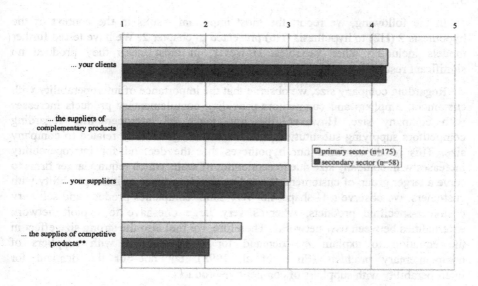

In order to test the hypotheses about the factors, i.e. company or product characteristics, influencing the demand for interoperability, we apply the following approach. Multivariate ordered Probit analyses allow us to determine the influence of single variables on the assessment of the importance of interoperability, controlling for all explanatory factors simultaneously. The general ordered Probit model equation, which we apply for the four different categories of interoperability (Figure 4-1), is specified as follows:

$$OProbit(Importance\ of\ Interop) = f(Company\ Characteristics;$$
$$Company\ Strategy;$$
$$Product\ Charcteristics)$$

The company characteristics we have included in our various models are:

- company size measured by the number of employees
- R&D intensity as percentage of R&D expenditures of turnover
- dummy variables for companies of the primary sector or independent software developers with the companies of the secondary sector as base category.

The company strategy is characterised as:

- the importance to achieve lead-time advantage regarding competitors.

The product characteristics are defined according to the differentiation in Figure 3.1.

In the following, we report the most important results in the context of the hypothesis 2 (H2) to hypothesis (H6) presented in chapter 2. We have tested further models including other variables. However, in most cases they produce no significant results.

Regarding company size, we observe that the importance of interoperability with customers, suppliers and competitors providing complementary products increases with company size. However, the importance of interoperability regarding competitors supplying substitutive products is not significantly related to company size. This result confirms our hypotheses that the demand for interoperability increases with company size due to economies of scale, which require larger firms to serve a larger group of customers. Regarding the importance of interoperability with customers, we observe a U-shape, i.e. very small companies produce and sell very customer-specified products, whereas very large oneshave to exploit network externalities between user networks. Therefore, we find also the strong size effect in the equation to explain the demand for interoperability with suppliers of complementary products (Succi et al. 1998), but not for the demand for interoperability with suppliers of competitive products.

The R&D intensity does not explain the importance of interoperability regarding customers and competitors providing complementary products. However, it turns out that companies with higher R&D intensity have a lower demand for interoperability, respectively their suppliers and their competitors supplying substitutive products. This result confirms the trade-off between R&D intensity and interoperability. Companies with lower R&D activities try to benefit either from the input of their suppliers or from the network effects of their direct competitors.

The independent software developers reveal a higher demand for interoperability with products of suppliers both of complementary and substitutive products. This observation is in line with the traditional picture and philosophy of the Open Source community.

The hypothesis that companies trying to achieve lead-time advantage respective to their competitors is impressively confirmed, because they have a higher demand for all four types of interoperability. The compatibility with the existing installed base is obviously very crucial for those companies trying to be at the leading edge.

In our final hypothesis, we postulate that the characteristics of software products have an influence on the importance of interoperability. Indeed, we find the following product-related results. The companies especially developing computer games and tools for software development have a lower demand for interoperability. In contrast, companies developing office products have a higher demand for interoperability, respectively their customers. Companies developing business administration software have lower demand for interoperability with suppliers of substitutive products, whereas companies developing finance and retail software have higher demand for interoperability with suppliers of substitutive products.

In general, we find supporting empirical evidence for our hypotheses presented in chapter 2. However, the results indicate that further investigations are required, based on more theoretical and model-based approaches.

5. Means to Achieve Interoperability

Since there are different options to achieve interoperability, we must ask first of all how interoperability can be established at all. For all the relationships depicted in Figure 4.2, there are no significant differences between the two sectors. However, it makes sense to differentiate between the vertical level of clients and supplier relationships (Figures 5.1) and the horizontal level of competing and complementary products (Figures 5.2).

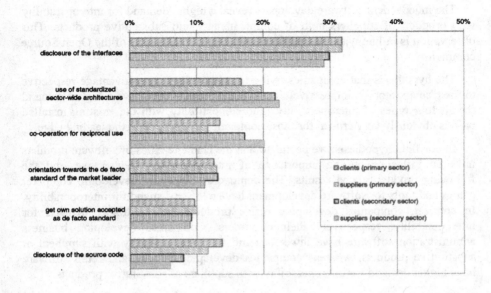

Figure 5.1: *Securing Interoperability to Clients and Suppliers*

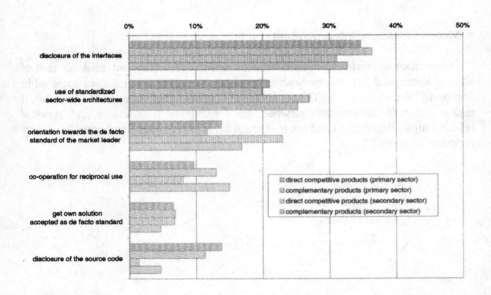

Figure 5.2: Securing Interoperability with Competitive and Complementary Products

By far the most frequently mentioned instrument for all four dimensions is the disclosure of interfaces, followed by the use of standardised sector architectures, which is obviously somewhat more widespread within the secondary sector. The same relation applies to contractual co-operations, which is accorded slightly less importance. On the other hand, code disclosure plays rather a subordinate role, above all in the secondary sector. It is surprising that, by comparison to the orientation to the de facto standard of the market leader, only slightly fewer firms attempt to have their own specifications accepted as a de facto standard.

If one leaves the vertical level of client and supplier relationships and turns to the direct competitive relations divided according to suppliers of complementary and competitive products, similar structures emerge. On the one hand, the disclosure of relevant interfaces is the preferred strategy of around one third of all enterprises, not only for complementary, but also for competitive products. Further, a quarter of the firms in the secondary sector use standardised sector architectures. Only a fifth does so in the primary sector. It is remarkable that regarding the direct competitive products above all in the secondary sector, an orientation to the sector standard takes place, while direct legally contracted co-operations are entered into especially with suppliers of complementary products. The enterprises obviously have greater difficulties cooperating with suppliers of direct competitive products on a contractual basis, as in certain circumstances conflicts can be caused in competition law by this. In the case of complementary products, these and other risks are less, on the other hand, the incentives for direct co-operations are obviously more pronounced. The disclosure of own code does not play a role in either sector finally and within the primary sector is only practiced by the independent developers.

6. Summary

This paper is another attempt to present some insights on the demand for interoperability in the software sector and on the means to achieve the different dimensions of interoperability. The basis for the empirical analysis was a sample of German software companies. We have analysed the factors influencing the demand for interoperability. In a separate chapter, we have presented the use of different means to achieve interoperability. Further investigations require both the derivation of more theoretic and model based hypotheses, but also an integrated empirical approach to combine the demand for interoperability with the means to achieve interoperability.

7. References

Besen, S.M.; Farrell, J. (1994): Choosing How to Compete: Strategies and Tactics in Standardization. In: Journal of Economic Perspectives, 8 (2), pp. 117-131.

Blind, K.; Edler, J.; Nack, R.; Straus, J. (2003): Software-Patente: Eine empirische Analyse aus ökonomischer und juristischer Perspektive, Heidelberg: Physica-Verlag.

Blind, K. (2004): The Economics of Standards: Theory, Evidence, Policy, Edward Elgar (ed.): Cheltenham.

Blind, K.; Edler, J.; Friedewald, M. (2004): Software Patents - An Empirical Analysis from an Economic Perspective, Stuttgart: Fraunhofer IRB Verlag.

David, P.A. (1990): The Economics of Compatibility Standards: An Introduction to Recent Research. In: Economics of Innovation and New Technology, 1, pp. 3-41.

David, P.A.; Bunn, J.A. (1988): The Economics of Gateway Technologies and Network Evolution. In: Information Economics and Policy, 3, pp. 165-202.

Shy, O. (2001): The economics of network industries, Cambridge, New York, Melbourne: Cambridge University Press.

Stahl, P.; Friedewald, M.; Rombach, H.D.; et al. (2000): Analyse und Evaluation der Software-Entwicklung in Deutschland. Eine Studie für das Bundesministerium für Bildung und Forschung, Nürnberg: GfK Marktforschung, Karlsruhe: ISI, Kaiserslautern: IESE.

Succi, G.; Valerio, A.; Vernazza, T.; Succi, G. (1998): Compatibility, Standards and Software Production. In: StandardView, 6 (4), pp. 140-146.

Current issues in RFID standardisation

Martina Gerst* — Raluca Bunduchi* — Ian Graham**

*RCSS, University of Edinburgh, High School Yards, Edinburgh, EH1 1LZ, UK

martina.gerst@ed.ac.uk
r.bunduchi@ ed.ac.uk

** *School of Management, University of Edinburgh, 50 George Square, Edinburgh, EH8 9JY*

i.graham@ed.ac.uk

ABSTRACT: RFID technologies significantly reduce costs, increase the transparency and hence improve the visibility of the entire supply chain, leading one step further towards the achievement of the truly integrated and virtual supply chain. This paper seeks to provide an overview of the current situation of RFID standardisation issues, with a particular focus on the different, and often competing, interests of the actors involved in the two standard life cycle stages: standard creation and standard use in order to unveil the challenges surrounding the standardisation issue.

KEY WORDS: RFID technology, standards creation, standards use

1. Introduction

According to professional journals, Internet information services and consultants, RFID (Radio Frequency Identification) seems to be "the new technology hype" which "will revolutionise business performance across supply chains" (www.accenture.com). While low-frequency RFID has been used in some areas in the industrial world for more than a decade (source), the recent decision by Wal-Mart and the U.S. Department of Defence (DoD) to mandate to all its suppliers the adoption of ultra-high frequency RFID as a logistics and inventory management tool by January 2005 (Brewin, 2003) is driving a widespread interest in RFID technology throughout other industry areas and in academia.

The supporters of the technology argue that RFID significantly reduces costs, increases the transparency and hence improve the visibility of the entire supply chain, leading one step further towards the achievement of the truly integrated and virtual supply chain. In contrast, the critics draw the attention on the huge technical challenges such as integration with the existing IT infrastructure and the even more substantial organisational changes required by the adoption of RFID such as the changes in the business processes, let alone the high costs of the RFID tags that hamper the implementation and use of RFID. Another major obstacle for the widespread adoption of RFID are RFID standards. In a global business environment, the lack of interoperability between systems based on RFID technology in different parts of the world deter users to make large investments in a technology that has to be used on a global basis.

This paper seeks to provide an overview of the current situation of RFID standardisation issues, with a particular focus on the different, and often competing, interests of the actors involved in the two standard life cycle stages: standard creation and standard use. The analysis is based on extensive documentation (company information, newspaper articles) and interviews with experts involved in RFID standardisation, as well as representatives of companies involved in RFID development and use.

After a brief section describing the RFID technology and identifying a number of issues related to the development and use of the technology, the following two sections analyse the two RFID standardisation stages: standard creation and standard use in order to unveil the challenges surrounding the standardisation issue. The conclusions summarise the observed phenomena and identify areas of further research.

2. Background

2.1. *Technology*

RFID is defined as a method of identifying unique items using radio waves (http://www.rfidjournal.com). RFID technology allows the automatic collection of product, place, time and transaction data quickly and easily without human intervention. An RFID system includes a reader (or interrogator), a transponder (or a tag), and their associated antennas. The reader transmits the radio signal, through its antenna, that the transponder receives via its own antenna. The transponder converse with the reader to verify and exchange the data. Once the reader receives and eventually verifies the data, it sends it to a computer for processing and management. This process is illustrated in the figure below:

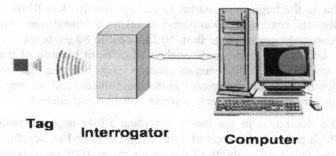

Tag   **Interrogator**   **Computer**

Figure 1. RFID system

RFID readers are automatic locks, fixed or mobile hand held scanners. They are usually connected to a computer and serve the same purpose as a barcode scanner. The transponder, also called tag, smart card or smart label, consists of a chip containing a processor and a receiver, and an antenna to broadcast and receive data via radio frequency. Dependent on the installation size of the antenna and the air interface protocol, the coverage reaches up to several meters. In contrast with the barcode, the transponder can be read without direct visibility and is contact-free. Additionally, transponders can store more information and are safer in terms of staining or abrasion. A huge advantage of RFID is the parallel data collection: a RFID reader can read up to 200 tags. Active and passive transponders are available. The antenna connected to the RFID reader activated the RFID tag and transfers data by emitting wireless pulses.

2.2. *Issues*

The issues surrounding RFID technologies can be categorised in five main categories:

1.   The RFID market is congested, with a massive amount of diverse players such as chip makers, transponder manufacturers, system integrators or consultancies, all of whom offer different, and generally proprietary, products and services. Available systems consist of different frequency ranges, transfer modes, etc. For a potential customer, it is difficult to acknowledge the distinct benefits and disadvantages of these different RFID solutions.

2.   Currently RFID technologies cannot offer a so-called "killer application" which is an off the shelf standard solution . A selection of different RFID systems has to be done by the users depending on the organizational specific process and technological requirements.

3.   Due to the fragmented market (a variety of individual RFID products and services), the total costs of RFID implementation are not transparent. Apart from the fact that transponder prices range from 50 Eurocent to 80 Eurocent, the exact price calculation as part of a cost-benefit analysis is difficult because of the number of unknown variable. A RFID implementation cost analysis has to take into consideration not only the investment in the transponders and readers, but also the other cost drivers, such as peripheral systems, software and integration effort.

4.   The discussion in the media regarding RFID implementations often is driven by high promises in terms of what can be expected as benefits, that is cost reduction and improved visibility of the supply chain. If these expectations are not fulfilled, potential customers defect from the "RFID vision". Additionally, there are a number of privacy and health issues concerning the wide spread adoption of RFID.

5.   RFID technologies require a huge effort in terms of standardisation. RFID standards are a major issue in securing the high investments in RFID technology on different levels (e.g. interface protocol, data structure, etc.). Not only different standards co-exist in parallel, but also different actors with sometimes divergent interests influence the standardisation life cycle.

This paper addresses the last of these issues – the challenges surrounding the standardisation of RFID technologies. The standardisation life cycle is conceptualised as formed of two different, yet deeply interrelated stages: standard creation and standard use. The next section discusses the existing approaches to RFID standard creation, and focuses on two competing initiatives, the EPC Global approach and the ISO process. EPC Global is a commercially driven initiative dominated by the large end users, in particular retailers. In contrast, ISO adopts a more global (cross industry) perspective following a generic approach to standards. The implications that RFID standardisation has for the user organisations are discussed in the second part of the paper.

3. RFID standards creation

There are two competing initiatives in the RFID standardisation arena: ISO and EPC Global. Additionally, there are also a number of special interest groups including industry specific such as the American Trucking Association in the transport industry, the NFC forum in the in consumer electronics, mobile devices and computer industry or the Automotive Industry Action Group in the automotive industry that seek to influence RFID standards development. This section will compare the two major approaches to RFID standardisation, unveiling the underlying conflict that shape the RFID standards creation process, and consequently, the future development of the technology.

3.1. *The ISO approach*

RFID standards first come to scene during the early 1990s, when the (newly created) CEN TC225 committee on bar coding focused the attention on automatic ID techniques in general. During the early 1990s, the standardisation activity on automatic ID techniques was mainly carried out in Europe within the CEN standard body (TC225 committee),, with little involvement from the US. However, during the 1995, a joint ISO IEC JTC1 committee – the SC31 – was set up for standardisation of automatic identification techniques generally drawing from the earlier work on RFID standards within CEN. Another influence on the RFID work within ISO was the work on the GTag initiative for RFID standardisation of asset tracking and logistics which was launched by UCC and EAN in 2000 along with input from international companies including Philips Semiconductors, Intermec, and Gemplus.

The members of the SC31 committees are the representatives of the national standard bodies such as the BSI IST34 committee on bar coding in UK, including the same people who tend to participate in CEN TC225. They represent either internal consultants within large corporations, or external consultants which are representing different companies. Their work on the committees is primarily voluntary. As a result, three different levels of representativeness (and thus interests) can be identified in the ISO process: the individual, the organisational, and the national level.

RFID ISO standards cover 4 different areas: technology (e.g. ISO 18000 series including the air interface standards, which are developed within the SC31 committee), data content (e.g. ISO 15418), conformance and performance (e.g. ISO 18046), and application standards (e.g. ISO 10374). The ISO standards are defined at a very high level, focusing on the interface rather than on the data which is transported. As a result, ISO standards are generic, being able to be supported by any system and in any context, irrespective of the data that is being carried.

3.2. *The EPC Global approach*

In parallel with the ISO standardisation efforts, MIT and UCC together with a number of industrial partners including Procter & Gamble, Gilette and Wal-Mart set up the Auto-ID consortium in 1999 to research RFID technologies and standards. The members included end users, primarily from consumer packaged goods, large retailers and solution providers, including hardware and software providers and consultants. The Auto-ID members included large retailers such as Wal-Mart, Gilette, Coca Cola, Unilever, Tesco, Carrefour and Ahold (http://archive.epcglobalinc.org/aboutthecenter_oursponsors.asp).

As the membership of Auto-ID became larger and more diverse, and with the increasing need for global "legitimate" standards, the members recognized the need for the creation of a formal standard body that would take over the standardisation and commercialisation work within Auto-ID. A new entity was created in October 2003, the EPC Global as a joint venture between UCC and EAN. Whereas Auto-ID would continue to research RFID technologies, EPC Global focuses on standardisation activities, as well as their commercialisation.

In contrast with ISO RFID standards which are generic standards, EPC standards are specific. EPC standards describe the tag and the air interface depending on the data being carried. EPC standards prescribe the physical implementation of the tags and readers, rather then specifying their generic characteristics. The standards are also much more limited in their scope, for example where the ISO standards for air interface cover all the frequency range, EPC operates only within the UHF between 860-930MHz with one standard for 13.56MHz (http://www.infomax-usa.com/rfid.htm). The EPC standard activities, although taking advantage of the resources of the parent organisations in terms of expertise as well as potential users, is separate from the generic EAN UCC standardisation process. Such distinction is required due to the difference in the nature of standards and the need for a fast standard development process.

3.3. *ISO vs. EPC*

The table below compares the two standard settings in terms of their organisational characteristics (membership, procedures), and their approaches to RFID standardisation:

Characteristics	ISO	EPC
Membership	Driven by RFID manufacturers	Driven by large users (retailers and their large suppliers)
Resources	volunteers internal consultants from large companies external consultants that represent different smaller companies + national standard bodies	Full time people Academics (MIT) UCC – is a trade association funded by industry members (worked on bar codes)
Process	"Formal" standard body, characterised by openness, transparency, due process => slow, bureaucratic process	"Standard consortia", driven by the interests of its members => fast process
Approach	High level, generic approach, focusing not on the data itself, but on how to access it: ❑ the technical building blocks, not the applications ❑ air interface ❑ high level data access techniques, data object definitions Case level identification	Specific, focuses on the data itself: ❑ data carrier, data access and product mark-up language ❑ similar with the bar code system (central to EPC is the GTIN) => It can identify a specific item
Air interface	Cover the entire range of frequencies	Only UHV
Chips	Bigger, smarter, active chips => more expensive	Smaller chips => cheap enough to make economic sense for the package good industry

Table 1. ISO vs. EPC

Whereas ISO can claim that it reflects the global requirements into a legitimate process (equal footing and consensus based), EPC focuses on speed and emphasises the broad support it receives from the industry community. The ISO and EPC processes can be seen as complementary. However, for both EPC supporters and for ISO the need for a single, global standard is impetuous. The benefits coming from standardization would be lost if in different parts of the globe, multinationals would have to invest in different technologies for RFID.

4. RFID standards use

Today, RFID is used to track and identify parts/goods moving through shop floors or warehouses in order to get accurate data. Technologically, RFID has the potential to simplify the process of tracking parts, without any line of sight and with multiple tags that can be detected simultaneously. As such, RFID systems are a useful tool in improving the visibility in the supply chain, hence reducing time and costs. One major user of RFID technology is the retailing industry to track inventory and gather information at the point of sale about customers shopping behaviour. Among the early adopters is also the automotive industry which uses RFID technologies during manufacturing processes to track parts in the supply chain. Claimed benefits of RFID standardised technology include improved supply chain efficiency, for example significantly lower transport and operating cost, reduced capital, or the stop of misplaced packaging during transport when moved between suppliers, or the reduction in the incidence of fraud.

The actors involved in the use of RFID standards are component manufacturers, technology vendors, consultants, end user companies. Whereas technology vendors proclaim RFID as a huge market opportunity to sell their technology and promise huge benefits, the exact distribution of this benefits is not clear. Apart from unclear benefits, there are other factors that deter a widespread adoption of RFID technologies. For example, the standardised RFID technology seems not to be mature enough to satisfy the user requirements, or integration with existing IT systems. Additionally, as usually in the case of IS implementation, the challenges associated with internal organisational change required by the change in the business processes due to RFID use create massive problems. Under these conditions, the users care less about standards and more about the practical cost-benefit analysis of the technology.

The table below summarises the major concerns that the four categories of users included in our study have voiced regarding RFID standardisation.

Standardisation issues	RFID component provider	RFID system vendor	RFID consultants	RFID end user (auto industry)
Importance	(Very) important	Indirectly important, because of its relevance to customers	important	important
Perception (reasons why standards are considered important)	Significant in areas where company is market leader	Dual approach: standards and participation in standard setting is important to collaborate towards a common accepted standard to address customers needs, - but otherwise work to impose their product as a de facto standard - as their focus is on the application side, the hardware concerns their partners	There is a lack of commonly agreed standards which hampers RFID market diffusion, especially for external use (as currently most RFID project concern internal deployment) Standardisation is crucial for the deployment of RFID in inter-organizational relationships, but not so much for the internal use of RFID	The only concerns is that the technology (embedding the standards) has to work (anywhere)
Standardisation bodies	ISO	both	EPC global	none
Areas of standardisation considered relevant	Air frequencies ICs	Reader Air frequencies (indirect relevance, as the vendors focus on	Tag Reader Air frequencies	Applications Reader Data

		applications, not hardware)		
Participation Extent Reasons	Depending on the importance of application Exercise influence in market areas where double development is expensive	limited involvement, but visible member gain awareness, study the (potential) market, influence the standards	active involvement awareness	none

Table 2. RFID standardisation and RFID users

Standards are considered important by all four categories of actors for the reasons discussed at the beginning of this paper: the global diffusion of RFID technologies at low costs is not possible in the absence of common, global standards that prescribe the major components of the RFID system: the reader, the tag and the air interface. In addition to these generic components, the different actors are interested in specific areas of standardisation that directly affect their businesses: the chip manufacturer is interested in IC standardisation, whereas the user is concerned about data standards. The lack of direct interest of the vendors is justified by the fact that their businesses consist in providing the RFID applications to customers, whereas the hardware is provided by their partners. Consequently, their interest in RFID standardisation (tags, readers and interfaces) is only indirect, to the extent that it affects their customers' willingness to adopt their products embedding RFID applications.

The perceptions of RFID standardisation differ across the actors: the manufactures addresses only standards in areas where they position themselves as market leaders. Their interests concern data access, and not the data itself. Naturally, such interests determine their participation in ISO rather than EPC. The major reasons for participation are development cost reductions: lack of involvement would lead to duplication of efforts which is not only costly but it also increases the danger of higher competition.

The consultants working with large end users will naturally be involved in EPC which is a user driven consortium, however interestingly the particular user involved in our study is not involved in neither of the settings. The reason is the perceived retailing industry focus of the EPC, which means that users from other industry do not perceive EPC as being able to address their specific industry needs and requirements. A consequence of this might be either a proliferation of industry specific RFID standardisation efforts within industry specific standard consortia such as AIAG and ATA, or the enlargement of the EPC to include working groups addressing specific industry needs (for example EPC has already created a specific group for health care and life sciences).

RFID system vendors are involved in both ISO and EPC and the major driver is, according to them, the need for direct collaboration between companies involved in RFID development to address customer needs for interoperability. Additionally, participation is justified by a need to be aware of what is going on in the market, to identify (and therefore address) potential future trends, to keep an eye on competitors, and also to influence the development process to address their specific needs.

Finally, RFID technologies are not used as a common place technology to support every day business. In most of situations today, RFID is implemented internally, which means that standardisation is not high on the agenda. The major current concern for end users is that the technology "just has to work". Until the basic technological issues surrounding RFID development are not solved, standardisation will be only a remote concern for end users. However, driven by the large retailers mandate, RFID, at least in the retailing industry, became a must, and pushes standardisation to a more prominent role.

5. Conclusions

The RFID standards realm thus include two distinct and yet overlapping standardisation efforts – the ISO RFID standardisation which and the EPC Global. However, for both EPC supporters and for ISO the need for a single, global standard is impetuous. The benefits coming from standardization would be lost if in different parts of the globe, multinationals would have to invest in different technologies for RFID.

Today, from a user point of view, the implementation of RFID is in its infancy despite all the promising announcements of RFID technology vendors and consultancies predicting a boost in sales figures for RFID technology and related services. From the interview data gathered, this seems to be the case for about 5 years now. Due to market and cost pressures, some industries are more advanced than others, e.g. retail and the automotive sector.

Although organisations are well aware of the benefits RFID provides, a couple of questions remain still unanswered. As the barcode has a huge installed base, potential RFID users are on one hand aware of the benefits RFID can provide, but on the other hand complain about the lack of a concrete business cases. Apart from the question of cost and a respective investment in RFID systems (for example RFID tags are far more expensive than barcodes), the technology still shows weaknesses, e.g. antenna breakdown, small coverage and a lack of standardisation in the convergence of air interface protocols, performance and data structure. As most of the applications are only in use to support internal processes, the ROI of RFID in an internal so-called "closed-loop scenario" is mostly negative.

The RFID market/arena is populated by different actors with different interests in and approaches to the technology. Standardisation and/or the involvement in standard setting bodies depends on the role an actor takes up in the RFID game. There is definitely a gap between the development of RFID standards and their implementation. Whereas RFID vendors participate in EPC as well as in ISO, end users are primarily interested in the fact if a RFID solution fits their business requirements and work. Additionally, it appears that from the users perspective industry specific standard consortia should play a more significant role in RFID standardisation, otherwise the industry faces the danger that they voices will not be heard in the IT vendor dominated RFID standard bodies such as EPC.

6. Reference list

http://www.accenture.com, Access date: December 2004.

Brewin, 2003, "RFID users differ on standards", *ComputerWorld*, October 27, 2003.

http://www.rfidjournal.com, Access date: December 2004.

http://archive.epcglobalinc.org/aboutthecenter_oursponsors.asp, Access date: December 2004.

http://www.infomax-usa.com/rfid.htm, Access date: December 2004.

Connecting stakeholders and B2B standards life cycles

Eva Söderström

School of Humanities and Informatics, University of Skoevde
Box 408, 541 28 Skoevde
Sweden

eva.soderstrom@his.se

ABSTRACT: *In business-to-business (B2B), a standards-based approach to inter-organisational exchanges is becoming more and more common. These standards undergo a series of activities or stages during their existence, where this series is referred to as a life cycle. Often focus is kept on a small subset of the life cycle activities, even though the remaining ones are of importance as well. Furthermore, there are different stakeholders interested in standards that are necessary to pay attention to during the life cycle, not the least since they take on different roles around standards as the life cycle is progressing. This paper examines the combination of life cycle activities with stakeholder types. Results show great complexity in stakeholder type involvement around standards, as well as point to the importance of explicitly recognising life cycles and stakeholders as a means of facilitating management of organisational relationships.*

KEY WORDS: *B2B standards, life cycles, stakeholders.*

1. Introduction

Business-to-Business (B2B) is one of the areas getting more and more attention in terms of inter-organisational co-operation. In B2B, numerous transactions and communication flows take place between organisations and disparate systems. A standards-based approach is common in this respect. A B2B standard is defined as *guidelines for how communication and information sent between organisations should be structured and managed* (Söderström, 2004). Such standards are implemented between several partners as a means to achieve a common language, increased system integration, and automation. Standards undergo a number of activities and phases during their existence, much like regular software and information systems. The series of activities and phase are often referred to as life cycles. There are also different types of stakeholders interested in standards, how they are used and evolved. Attention to stakeholder types may indicate what organisations to keep in contact with during various parts of the life cycle. This paper deals with connecting life cycle phases to stakeholder types. Life cycles per se are useful for understanding standards and how they relate to surrounding complex contexts and activities. Stakeholder types may furthermore not only have varying interests in standards, but may also take on different roles around standards as the life cycle phases are progressing. Together, these aspects can point to how to deal with standards from different perspectives, as well as what organisations to pay attention to during e.g. implementation. The paper will be structured as follows: Chapter 2 presents a life cycle model for B2B standards. Chapter 3 introduces six stakeholder types, and Chapter 4 connects roles with life cycle activities, while Chapter 5 provides an example of how one organisation can take on different roles. Chapter 6 presents a summary of the findings.

2. A model for the B2B standards life cycle

The general life cycle model for B2B standards is structured as depicted in Figure 1. Each phase will be described briefly in a section each.

2.1. *Initiation*

Before development, there must be an *initiation* phase, during which the idea of the standard is born. This applies whether the standard-to-be precedes or follows on technology developments. The phase includes preparations for the standards development process. The need may stem from market requirements, technology developments or from the organisation itself. It may also include setting the scope of the standard and defining how to perform the development process. Initiation should be distinguished from development for several reasons. Firstly, the claimed standardisation need may not result in further actions, if the need is estimated to cost more than the anticipated return of investment. Secondly, the preparations made set the frames or conditions for the following standards development activities, and thus clearly affect the standard's final structure, content and application area.

2.2. Standards development

The second phase is *standards development*. Here, standards specifications are developed, defined, and negotiated. These are the essence of standards.

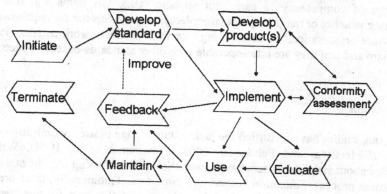

Figure 1. *The general standards life cycle model extended (Söderström, 2004).*

2.3. Product development

The cycle may proceed in two directions. One is by *creation of products* based on one or more standards. Product testing may be included before implementation, but we consider it a separate activity (see conformity assessment). Product development is a separate phase since it is not necessarily the way in which organisations implement standards. Software products are not a necessary requirement for standards implementations, even though it is a common approach.

2.4. Implementation

The second direction is to an *implementation* phase, where standards (and possibly standards-based products after creation) are implemented in organisations. Testing can be considered a part of implementation as well, in which case actual implementations of standards and/or products are tested and compared.

2.5. *Conformity assessment*

Since tests of different types are so important, they should belong to a separate phase referred to as *conformity assessment* (CA). CA can be applied in different ways, e.g. after completion of a standards-based product or after implementation of a standard or a standards-based product. Examples of techniques for testing are (ISO, 2003): *Testing*, for example calibration and measurement; *Inspection*, for example quality and suitability for use; *Certification*, for example written assurance from a first, second or third party that a product, service, system, process or material conforms to specific requirements; and *Accreditation*, for example giving formal recognition of competency to carry out specific tasks. CA helps e.g. users in determining whether or not their product/implementation meets the set requirements, and software organisations in determining that their products work as specified in the standard and that they are inter-operable with other standards-based products.

2.6. *Education*

Previous studies have identified the lack of knowledge in user organisations as a problem (Söderström and Pettersson, 2003; Premkumar et al, 1994). Without knowledge about standards, users have fewer chances of affecting e.g. the standards development process. *Education* is therefore important. Traditionally, there are few and weak efforts with regards to education. One potential reason for this "gap" is that the need to learn how to use complex standards brings a cost. A study by Amoako-Gyampah and Salam (2004) showed that training is essential for affecting the employees' beliefs in the benefits of Enterprise Resource Planning (ERP) systems. Besides employees currently working with standards, future standards workers need education as well. Education is an important matter if standards and their related products are to be used efficiently and effectively.

2.7. *Use*

Following implementation is actual *use* of standards and related products. The term "use" is often confusing, as many sources refer to this being equal to the use of software. We refer to use as all activities undertaken when utilising the standard and/or software in real-life business settings.

2.8. *Maintenance*

Maintenance in standards is a forgotten subject, e.g. concerning the sub-activity standards management (Boh et al, 2003). It is important, since buying new software each time e.g. an alteration is needed would mean immense financial effort. Maintenance is also difficult, since standardisation encompasses many elements, some of them not so obvious (Kemp, 1999). Technologies for using standards, particularly with the early technology such as Electronic Data Interchange – EDI, have required substantial financial investments. Therefore, many organisations cannot afford to throw out existing systems when new standards, versions of them, or new technology is introduced. As any other technology or system investment, maintenance is needed to keep the standard/system operating as intended, e.g. to monitor and improve quality and productivity (Fasolino et al, 2000).

2.9. Feedback

Feedback refers to users reporting back to product or standards developers what they think about the standard: what works or not, which problems have been experienced and so on. The feedback creates one possible input to evolving standards. Today, most standards development organisations are open to, and even encourage, user participation in their development activities. However, open participation does not mean free participation, and few users therefore have the financial resources required, nor the time for that matter.

2.10. Termination

There are occasions when standards are determined to be obsolete, and are taken out of use (*termination*). This should be explicit, in particular if there are international consequences. Consequences refer to the need to co-ordinate and communicate termination of international standards world-wide. Standards may also be terminated by a single company or group of companies that are not on an international level. Still, there may be consequences for the company environment. For example, any connection a company has with suppliers and/or customers will be affected by a change in or removal of a communication standard.

3. Stakeholders for B2B standards

Six stakeholder types have been identified: Standards User Organisations (SUO), Standards Development Organisations (SDO), Standards Adaptation Organisations (SAO), Standards Software Organisations (SSO), Standards Service Providers (SSP) and Standards Researchers (SR). Each will be described before connected to the life cycle processes in the next chapter.

3.1. *Standards developers*

Standards developers are by far the most commonly discussed role in literature. There is usually a distinction between formal and informal SDOs. Formal standards development can occur on several levels (combining Baskin et al, 1998; Slob and de Vries, 2002; Ollner, 1988; and Sivan, 2000): Individual; Organisational; Association; National; and International. Examples of formal SDOs are International Organisation for Standardisation (ISO), International Electrotechnical Commission (IEC), and European Committee for Electrotechnical Standardization (CENELEC). Informal SDOs are usually various industry consortia. An industrial consortium consists of a group of companies without formal standards setting accreditation. Often, the results are so called de facto standards. The market is the driving force, where companies join for a common purpose or need.

3.2. *Standards users*

Standards users are an essential stakeholder, since they ultimately decide the success of a standard, by using it or not. User requirements are today not being adequately taken into consideration by SDOs, and user participation is important for credibility (Jakobs et al, 1996; Jakobs et al, 2001; Fabish, 2003; Cargill, 1995). SUOs may also exist on several levels (combining Sivan, 2000; Jakobs et al, 1996; Cargill, 1995; Weiss and Spring, 2000; and Chauvel, 2003): End-user; Departmental; and Organisational.

3.3. *Standards adaptors*

Standards adaptors are a rather small stakeholder type. These organisations adapt standards to fit e.g. a specific industry sector or a specific company. In the first case, the role is often assumed by different types of trade associations and block alliances (Sivan, 2000; Cargill, 1995; Warner, 2003; Mähönen, 2000; Egyedi, 2000). In a way, SAOs and SDOs are comparable, since e.g. some consortia base their standards on an existing formal standard. We have chosen to make the distinction that an SDO develops standards from nothing, while an SAO attempts only to adjust a decided-upon standard to the industry's specific needs. It does not, in our opinion, attempt to create a new standard to be available for others.

3.4. *Standards software organisation*

Standards software organisations are becoming increasingly important. They take standard specifications and construct software based on them. In this way, users can buy the software product and automatically use the standard (Slob and de Vries, 2002). Inclusion of standards in software can be actual in both internal standardisation within a company, and in more formal standardisation. SSOs often participate in creating standards. SSO participation is natural in consortia since it is often these companies that initiate them.

3.5. Service providers

Service providers are organisations that provide services such as consultancy work, testing, and training and education. Such services are often either provided by the standards developers or by software organisations. One example is testing of conformance to standards. Users and SDOs both believe in third-party certification due to partiality and the costs of incompatible systems (Weiss and Spring, 2000).

3.6. Standards researchers

Finally, *standards researchers* (SRs) reside either in academic or in industrial settings. SRs are interested in various aspects of standards, and much literature has so far focused on technology or on the development process itself. Users are mentioned, but few case studies with this focus have so far been made. Often, SRs are "standards watchers" (Egyedi, 2000), which in this case means they take an interest in standards without being actively involved in them practically. This is, however, not always the case.

4. Connecting life cycle processes with roles

This chapter will describe how stakeholders may connect to life cycle processes. The role an organisation assumes depends on the interest at hand, and may change during the life cycle. The discussion will be structured according to each life cycle process. The discussion is summarised in Figure 2. SRs are not depicted in the figure, since they have an interest in all parts of the life cycle. The *initiate* process will not be included either, since any one of the roles may be responsible for creating ideas.

The responsible party for *developing standards* is always a SDO. However, the organisations making up an SDO can vary. SDOs may comprise either specifically dedicated organisations that assume no other roles during the life cycle, or of commercial organisations. These commercial organisations can be anything from users and service providers to software organisations. Basically any organisation that pays the membership fee to the SDO can take part in developing standards.

Product development is somewhat more limited than standards development in terms of which roles are involved. The responsible organisation is mostly SSOs, but advanced SUOs may also develop their own in-house products. The majority is regular, commercial SSOs. The resulting products often cater for more than one standard. The support for many standards is a means of achieving competitiveness, and enables SSOs to grasp larger pieces of the market cake. SDOs can also participate in the products development process, since many of them make reference implementations.

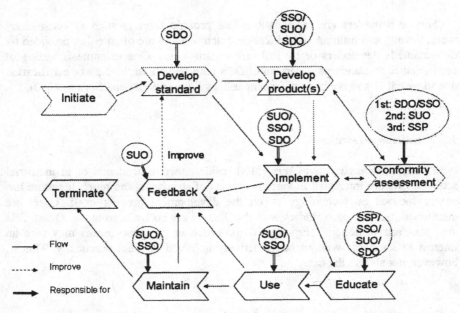

Figure 2. *Summary of the connections between processes and roles.*

The *implementation* process is one of the most complicated processes in the life cycle, since it has so many connections to other processes. The responsible party for implementation can either be a SUO, a SDO, or a SSO. Users are implementers when they themselves take the standards specifications and make changes to processes and products accordingly. SDOs are implementers when they make their reference implementations. This is often regarded as part of the development process, since it helps confirm that the standard works as intended. SSOs are implementers when they take their products and consult the users in how to implement them in the user organisations. This is one of the more common situations. Many SUOs do not want to get involved in technical details, and therefore outsource implementation to SSOs.

As with other processes, different roles can be responsible for making *conformity assessment* of standards-based products and implementations. SDOs can perform conformity assessment of their own standards, and SSOs can do the same for their standards-based products. In both cases, this is called first-party assessment (ISO, 2003). SUOs can also perform conformity assessment of the standards and/or products they obtain. If so, this is called second-party assessment (ISO, 2003). The third alternative is when SSPs conduct the assessment. Preferably, SSPs of this kind should not be involved in any of the standardisation work to allow their impartiality. If so, this kind of assessment is called third-party assessment (ISO, 2003).

Education is, as mentioned, an important matter if standards and their related products are used efficiently and effectively. One common role involved in education is the SSP, in terms of commercial and academic educational institutions. However, SDOs can help their users to learn more, as can SSOs. It is probably more common for SSOs to be the educators, since some education often is included in their consultancy work during implementation. Furthermore, there is an important distinction between SSOs and SSPs in this matter. SSOs focus on specific standards and situations, while SSPs often take a general view on education.

Only SUOs *use* standards in their daily work. However, e.g. SSOs and SSPs can also use standards in their daily work, which means that the same organisation can be both a SUO and a SSO/SSP. It depends on the viewpoint taken.

SUOs are the most common role responsible for conducting the *feedback* process, since they are the ones with real-life experience whether or not a standard and/or product works in practice. Feedback can thus be given to both SSOs and SDOs, depending on whether it was specifications or products the user implemented.

The party responsible for *maintaining* standards and standards-based products in SUOs is integrally related to who made the implementation. In the case of implementation maintenance, and if SUOs have consulted SSOs to install their implementation, it is more common that the maintenance of the product is outsourced to the same SSO. With regards to standards maintenance, SDO may be responsible in this matter for updates and versioning to changes in an existing and used standard.

At some point, many standards become obsolete and need to be replaced or removed. The party responsible for *termination* depends on whether the need is to replace or to terminate. Termination is managed by the same SDO that created the standard and has since maintained it. Replacement is mainly managed by the SUOs, and may be caused by market changes, technology developments or new demands from important partners.

5. Examplifying different roles in the life cycle

To further exemplify how processes and roles can be connected, and the complexity therein, we have constructed a simple, fictious example (Figure 3). Companies in a certain business area have discovered a need for common standards in order to communicate about the region's products and for overall communication and co-operation. Company A, as one of these companies and a member of a SDO initiates the creation of the standard by bringing the need to the SDO. The SDO members discuss the idea and decide to create the desired standard. Company A takes part in developing the standard, and communicates regularly with the other companies in the business area in question.

Another member of the SDO is Company B, a software organisation specialised in products that connect organisations and facilitates their communication. After completion of the standard, Company B decides to create a product that incorporates the new standard. In this way, Company B hopes to gain a large share of the market. At product completion, the product is handed over to Company C for impartial testing. Company C is a SSP managing third-party testing of new products. After clearance of the product for compatibility and connectivity, Company B receives approval for selling the product. Company A buys the product and hires Company B to conduct the implementation and to educate the staff in its usage.

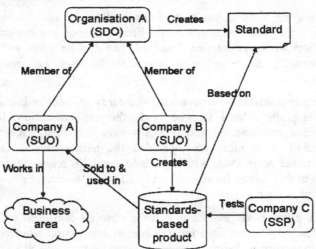

Figure 3. *Example of roles and how they relate.*

Following implementation, Company A outsources the management and maintenance of the standards-based product to Company B, which is a long term commitment. The business contract includes an assurance that Company B will update the product if new versions of the standard should be released. In this example, Company A is a SUO when buying and using the software created by

Company B. Company A is also a SDO when part of developing the standard. Company B has three potential roles: SDO when part of developing the standard; SSO when creating the product based on the standard; and SSP when managing staff education, usage and maintenance of their product in Company A. Company C is only an SSP in this example, when providing the testing services to Company B to assure their product follows the standard and that the companies by using the product are able to connect and communicate as intended.

6. Summary

When studying the life cycle phase, connections between included phases can be identified, for example in terms of input and output flows between them. This may serve as an indication of which phases affect each other and how. B2B organisations typically implement standards together with one or more partners. Some relationships are rather obvious, while others not. The identified stakeholder types illustrate a complexity in the roles, in particular in connection with life cycle phases for B2B standards. For example, one organisation may assume different roles at different points of the life cycle. The discussion presented in this paper points to the importance of paying attention to both the life of a standard, and to the parties that may take an interest in standards during this life. Explicit recognition of such aspects facilitates the management of organisational relationships in all parts of the life cycle.

As of today, knowledge about standards, their "life" and stakeholders is limited in most organisations. Future research should therefore focus on further elaborating stakeholder types, life cycle processes, and the connections between them in order to facilitate activities such as standards implementation, education to different stakeholders, and maintenance of standards-based implementations and software products.

7. Bibliography/References

Amoako-Gyampah, K. and Salam, A., An extension of the technology acceptance model in an ERP implementation environment, Information & Management, 41 (2004), pp.731-745

Baskin, E., Krechmer, K. and Sherif, M. (1998), The six dimensions of standards: Contribution towards a theory of standardization, In Lefebvre et al (eds), Management of Technology, Sustainable Development and Eco-Efficiency, Elsevier Press, Amsterdam, 1998

Boh, W.F., Yellin, D., Dill, B. and Herbsleb, J., Effectively managing information systems architecture standards: an intra-organization perspective, In King and Lyytinen (eds.), Standard Making: A Critical Research Frontier for Informatin Systems, MISQ Special Issue Workshop, Pre-conference workshop for International Conference on Information Systems (ICIS 2003), December 12-14, 2003, Seattle, USA, pp.171-187

Cargill, C., A Five-Segment Model for Standardization, in Kahin and Abbate (eds.), Standards Policy for Information Infrastructure, MIT Press, Cambridge, MA, USA, 1995, pp.79-99

Chauvel, Y., "Standards and Telecommunications Development: Where Are We Going?", International Journal of IT Standards & Standardization Research, Vol.1, No.1, January – June 2003, Idea Group Publishing, pp.50-53

Egyedi, T. (2000), "Institutional Dilemma in ICT Standardization: Coordinating the diffusion of technology?", in Jakobs, K. (ed.), Information Technology Standards and Standardization: A Global Perspective, Idea Group Publishing, ISBN 1-878289-70-5, 2000, pp.48-62

Fabish, G. (2003), "An Ambitious Goal – eEurope for All", International Journal of IT Standards & Standardization Research, Vol.1, No.1, January – June 2003, pp.57-61, Idea Group Publishing

Fasolino, A., Natale, D., Poli, A., and Quaranta, A., Metrics in the development and maintenance of software: an application in a large scale environment, Journal of Software Maintenance: Research and Practice, 12 (2000), pp.343-355

ISO, How conformity assessment works, available at: http://www.iso.org/iso/en/comms-markets/conformity/iso+conformity-02.html, as is: June 2, 2003

Jakobs, K., Procter, R. and Williams, R., "The Making of Standards: Looking Inside the Work Groups", IEEE Communications Magazine, April 2001, pp.2-7

Jakobs, K., Procter, R. and Williams, R., "Users and Standardization – Worlds Apart? The Example of Electronic Mail", StandardView, Vol.4, No.4, December 1996, pp. 183-191

Kemp, J., Economic Benefits of Transit Standards, Presentation at APTA Annual Meeting, October 12, 1999

Mähönen, P., The standardization process in IT – Too slow or too fast?, In Jakobs, K. (ed.), Information Technology Standards and Standardization: A Global Perspective, IDEA Group Publishing, USA, 2000, pp. 35-47

Ollner, J., The Company and Standardization, 3rd edition, Swedish Standards Institution, Stockholm, Sweden, 1988

Premkumar, G., Ramamurthy, K. and Nilakanta, S., Implementation of Electronic Data Interchange: An Innovation Diffusion Perspective, Journal of Management Information Systems, Fall 1994, Vol.11, No.2, pp.157-186

Sivan, Y., "Knowledge Age Standards: A brief introduction to their dimensions", in Jakobs, K. (ed.), Information Technology Standards and Standardization: A Global Perspective, Idea Group Publishing, ISBN 1-878289-70-5, 2000

Slob, F. and de Vries, H., Best Practices in Company Standardisation, ERS-2002-81-ORG, Erasmus Research Institute of Management (ERIM) Report Series, September 2002, Rotterdam, Netherlands

Söderström, E. and Pettersson, A., Adoption of B2B standards, In Jardim-Goncalves et al. (eds.) Concurrent Engineering: Enhanced Interoperable Systems, A.A.Balkema Publishers, Lisse, Netherlands, 2003, pp.343-350

Söderström, E., B2B Standards Implementation: Issues and Solutions, PhD Thesis, Department of Computer and Systems Sciences, Stockholm University, Akademitryck, 2004, ISBN 91-7265-942-4

Warner, A., "Block Alliances in Formal Standard Setting Environments", International Journal of IT Standards & Standardization Research, Vol.1, No.1, January – June 2003, Idea Group Publishing, pp.1-18

Weiss, M. and Spring, M., Selected Intellectual Property Issues in Standardization, in Jakobs, K. (ed.), Information Technology Standards and Standardization: A Global Perspective, IDEA Group Publishing, USA, 2000, pp.63-79

IPv6 versus Network Address Translation

A case study in standards adoption dynamics

J.L.M. Vrancken* — C.P.J. Koymans**

*Delft University of Technology

P.O. Box 5015, 2600 GA Delft, Netherlands

josv@tbm.tudelft.nl

**University of Amsterdam

Kruislaan 404, 1098SM Amsterdam, Netherlands

ckoymans@science.uva.nl

ABSTRACT: *This paper is a case study in standards adoption. It studies the adoption of alternative addressing schemes in the Internet. Currently there is a pressing need to replace the current addressing scheme of the Internet (IPv4), simply due to shortage of address space and increasing routing problems. The two most likely candidates are IPv6, the "official" successor to IPv4, defined by the IETF (Internet Engineering Task Force) and NAT (Network Address Translation), a technical solution to address space shortage within IPv4. In the absence of a worldwide authority to direct the endorsement of one standard, both standards depend on the uncoordinated initiatives of large numbers of users for their adoption. We call this bottom-up emergence. The case study leads to a number of criteria to assess a standard's chances in bottom-up emergence. Applied to Internet addressing schemes, the criteria lead to the conclusion that none of the two will prevail and addressing heterogeneity in the Internet will remain an unsolved problem for many years to come.*

KEY WORDS: *IPv6, Network Address Translation, Bottom-up Emergence, Addressing Schemes, Internet*

1.   Introduction

Traditionally addressing within the Internet is done by means of the IPv4 standard, developed in the period 1974 till 1979 (Tanenbaum 2002). Addresses in this standard consist of four bytes, allowing some 4 billion host machines to be addressed. This standard has done a great job in the past, allowing the emergence of the Internet, but the exponential growth of the Internet has come to the point where IPv4 address space is simply too small. For instance, one IPv4-address per person is not possible while nowadays presence on the Internet (both as consumer and as supplier of information and services; for this a personal IP-address is needed) can almost be considered a a basic human right, comparable to and closely related to the freedom of speech. The same can be said of the freedom of enterprise: nowadays it is virtually impossible to run a business without presence on the Internet.

In addition there is an important technological development which will stress the IPv4 scheme even further. In the early eighties there were in the order of 200 people per (mainframe) computer. In the early nineties this ratio had changed into one person per (personal) computer. The increase in computing power and storage capacity per cubic millimeter, and the decrease of chip prices, makes that within the coming decade we will move towards a ratio in the order of 200 devices per person (Sol 2004, Sol 2005). Not only mobile phones, PDA's and desktop-PC's but virtually any appliance or utensil will contain computing and (wireless) communication devices: cars, vacuum cleaners, refrigerators, clothes, etc. (Meloan 2003). All of these devices will communicate and therefore need an identification. This development goes by various names such as *ambient intelligence, ubiquitous computing* or *pervasive computing* (http://www.doc.ic.ac.uk/~mss/pervasive.html). It means that we become more and more surrounded by computing devices.

The ideal addressing scheme will allow fully functional end-to-end connectivity between any two communicating devices anywhere on the world. Among other things, this requires worldwide unique identification of all communicating devices. It can safely be assumed that an address space of 10 to the power 12 will be needed as a minimum in the coming two decades (Sol 2004). Further extensibility by several orders of magnitude would be welcome.

IPv4 will not be sufficient, so a new scheme will have to be adopted. In this paper we consider and compare the two most likely candidates for this new addressing scheme: IPv6 (www.ipv6.org), the "official" successor to IPv4, defined by the Internet Engineering Task Force (IETF), and NAT, a bottom-up emerging solution to address space shortage (Network Working Group 1994).

First the paper goes into the technicalities of addresssing and routing in general followed by a technical description of the two alternative addressing schemes. Then we consider properties of bottom-up processes, complexity and network effects that can be applied to the two alternative addressing schemes. This leads to criteria for the bottom-up emergence of standards. With these criteria the strengths and weaknesses of the two standards can be compared and their chances for adoption can be assessed.

2. Addressing and routing in general

The real problem about addressing schemes is not so much the unique identification of the network nodes (that's relatively easy, e.g. Ethernet addressing, IEEE Standards 802.3), but to have an efficient way to find a node in the network by its address and to find a path to reach it (Tanenbaum 2002, Kuiper 2004). In order to describe the routing problem, we will apply the following terminology, illustrated in fig. 1.

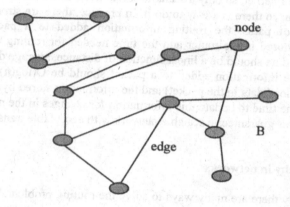

Fig. 1

In a network there are nodes and edges. In the Internet the nodes are actually applications running on so-called host machines. Host machines are connected to the Internet via a network device called *router*. When routers can find each other, applications can, because usually only few applications run on a host machine and only few host machines are connected to a single router. So without losing anything essential, we may restrict nodes to routers.

A router has connections or interfaces with the network. A router with only one connection makes little sense and can be omitted (virtual networks, in which single connection routers would make sense, can be omitted as well; routing in a virtual network is essentially the same problem as routing in a real network). A router with two connections makes sense (e.g. LAN protocol conversion), but is hardly interesting from the point of view of routing, as it can only transmit to one connection what it received at the other connection. Three connections and more is the interesting case for the routing problem.

A real network is dynamic: nodes may appear, disappear and re-appear at the same or at a different point in the network at arbitrary moments. If it re-appears, even at a different point, it retains its identity.

Edges are the connections between the nodes. They may also appear and disappear at arbitrary moments, but we do not consider edges that re-appear, preserving their identity, as we know of no situation in practice where this happens.

The routing problem is as follows: a arbitrary node A wants to send data to an arbitrary node B, known by its address. To that end, a path has to be determined from A to B, and all the routers in between have to be informed of this path, at least to the extent that they can take the right switching decision. From the router's point of view, it has to have this information for an arbitrary pair of nodes in the network. In a sizeable, dynamic network, this is far from trivial. Real networks tend to grow, especially the Internet, so only a scalable solution has much value. In principle it is a finite problem, so there is a way to do it. In practice, there are strong restrictions on the lengths of paths, the routing information added to a packet, the routing information stored in the router and the time needed for routing decisions. Ideally transmission time should be a linear function of distance, average distance should be $O(\log(n))$, the information added to a packet should be $O(\log(n))$ and small (less than the pay load data in the packet) and the information stored by routers should be $O(\log(n))$. The time to update this information for changes in the network should be $O(\log(n))$. This guarantees a scalable network with acceptable transmission times.

3.   Hierarchy in networks

Obviously there are many ways to solve the routing problem, but in practice we observe that one element is always present: network *hierarchy* (fig. 2). It is an interesting question wether hierarchy is necessary, but for our purposes we consider only hierarchy based solutions, as network hierarchy plays a very natural role in a bottom-up emergence process.

Hierarchy means that the network may be divided into domains (connected subnets of the network), and that the domains are connected via a so-called backbone network which is a small (in number of nodes and edges) subnet of the total network. This subdivision into domains can be repeated recursively. Moreover, this domain structure is reflected in the addresses. Routing then works as follows: for A and B within one domain, we may assume that there is an acceptable routing solution, otherwise the domains should be made smaller. For B not within the domain of A (which can readily be established whenlooking at B's address), the packet is handed over to the next higher level, where the process is repeated.

Again, the address structure is such that it can readily be established which one of the other domains on the same level applies or, if none applies, that the packet has to be handed over to the next higher level. Ideally, address information should be added and removed by the routers when moving up and down in the hierarchy. This reduces the amount of data needed for address information (of receiver and sender) in a packet.

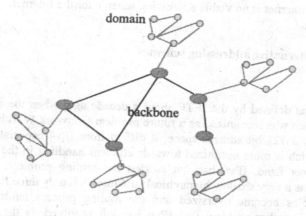

Fig. 2

One may easily verify that all of the desired order estimates mentioned above, can by achieved by hierarchical networks, on condition that new levels can be introduced as the network grows.

Examples of hierarchy

In telephony, there are three levels: local, national and international. The addresses in this case (telephone numbers) reflect this structure.

For the Internet, fig. 2 is somewhat too simple. Although it has a clearly hierarchical structure, it also has lots of shortcuts directly between domains. The Internet's hierarchy covers three levels: so-called autonomous systems at the highest level, then the domains and finally NAT-areas behind a single IP-number (to be explained below). The structure of IPv4 addresses reflects this network structure, although not in an obvious way. The mapping between domains and addresses has grown evolutionary over time (A, B, and C classes and CIDR (Network Working Group 1993)), and leaves much to be desired.

Apart from the complexities introduced by evolutionary growth, the real problem with Internet hierarchy seems to be that there are too few levels and that the partition into levels is not optimal. Neither is there an official way of introducing new levels and repartitioning the network.

Ethernet addressing

An third alternative for future Internet addressing might seem to be offered by Ethernet (more correctly called IEEE 802.3) addressing. The Ethernet address has a 48 bits address space, which can nowadays be found in virtually all network equipment. But the address structure is in no way related to network topology, such as hierarchy levels. Neither are there initiaves to introduce such a structure (other than the inclusion of Ethernet addresses in IPv6 addresses). This leaves the routing problem unsolved and as long as no practical solution turns up, hierarchical or otherwise, Ethernet is no viable addressing scheme for the Internet.

4.   Two alternative addressing schemes

IPv6

IPv6 was defined by the IETF about a decade ago, when the shortage of IPv4 address space was recognized as a future problem (Network Working Group 1998). Apart from a 128-bit address space, it differs from IPv4 especially in the header format, which is more optimized towards efficient handling in the routing process. On the other hand, IPv6 has not tackled the routing problem. As the Internet currently has a very shallow hierarchical structure with only three levels (see above), routing tables become oversized and the routing process tends to become too expensive. Another problem that IPv6 has left unsolved, is the so-called multi-homing problem. This problem is about having more than one Internet access provider while using different providers at different times. Organizations that do not want to depend on a single ISP (Internet Service Provider) would like to apply multi-homing.

Current status of IPv6 is that all major operating systems and a sufficient diversity of network equipment is ready to use it. From a technical point of view, the world could migrate to IPv6 within a very short period of time. Actual use of IPv6 however is most common in certain countries in Asia, where language boundaries have created communities (especially in countries like Japan or China) with far more internal interaction than externally with other communities. Another factor that plays a role here is that western industrialized countries started to use the Internet much earlier and got a much bigger share of the IPv4 address space. Until recently, some organizations in the US owned more IPv4 address space than the whole of China (APNIC).

A very serious drawback of IPv6 from the migration point of view, is that it is not in both directions compatible with IPv4. An IPv6 site can see (with some effort) the whole Internet, including IPv6 communities. This is because IPv4 addresses can easily be mapped into IPv6 addresses and gateways can be implemented to do this. Nevertheless a practical problem here is that there are many ways to do this. On the other hand IPv6 sites (or rather IPv6-*only* sites) are not visible from IPv4 sites, at least not without some effort on the side of the client. So trying to do worldwide business using an IPv6-only site is simply not a good idea (unless there is a special reason why only IPv6 sites are within the target group). In order to retain worldwide visibility, some of the many migration strategies from IPv4 to IPv6 (IETF on migration) include dual stacks, which means that a site is equipped with both an IPv4 and an IPv6 address. A dual stack strategy obviously cannot be a solution to address space shortage and is therefore not a strategy to migrate towards ambient intelligence.

NAT

A very different practical solution to IPv4 address space shortage, is offered by NAT (Network Address Translation (Network Working Group 1994)). NAT can be considered as adding another level to the Internet hierarchy at the lower end.

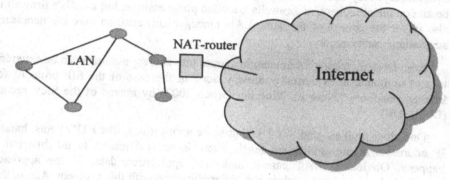

Fig. 3

In fig. 3, the LAN nodes do not have a worldwide unique (or *real*) IP-address but only a locally unique IP- address. Only the NAT-router has a real IP-address. From the point of view of the rest of the Internet, it looks as if all requests come from this node. In reality, requests from any host within the LAN are translated into requests from the NAT-router and marked by means of the TCP port number field (Tanenbaum 2002) in the packet. When the answer returns, this packet is retranslated into a packet with the right local IP-address and TCP port number. In this way, a host within the LAN initiating requests (a *client*) experiences no limitations. A host waiting for requests from others (a *server*) does experience limitations currently. This is because port numbers are now globally assigned to specific applications (80 to web servers, 25 to mail servers, etc.), so currently one cannot have two port 25 mailservers within a LAN behind a NAT router, both accessable from the Internet. But this can be remedied and this remedy can emerge evolutionary, as will be detailed below. Then the address space of port numbers (16 bits) adds to the address space of IPv4 numbers (32 bits), resulting in 48 bit addressing, coincidentally the same address space as Ethernet addresses.

NAT is currently being used very frequently. Home networks and Internet access by SOHO users is often implemented by means of one of the various forms of NAT.

5. Making NAT into a real addressing scheme

In order to make NAT into a real addressing scheme, the coupling between port numbers and types of applications has to be abolished. When publishing a mail server or web server, the IP address (of the NAT-router) is no longer sufficient: the port number has to be added as well. This is already technically possible and often done for various reasons. This way of addressing and publishing servers can grow evolutionary. Any LAN management team can do this on his own. Firewalls could be an complication here, as firewalls are often port-sensitive, but a LAN's firewall is also under the control of the same LAN management team, so here the necessary adaptations can be made.

Even DNS translation of mnemonic names into address numbers can be extended to port numbers, as is currently already done in the case of the SIP protocol for Internet telephony (Network Working Group 2002) by means of the SRV record (DNS SRV).

One other problem with NAT is that some applications, like FTP clients, handle IP addresses at the application level. There is no real reason to do this, but it happens. Obviously, NAT cannot look into application data, so the approach described above will not work in case of applications with this problem. Again, this is not hard to remedy, and this can be done application by application in an evolutionary way.

In case of client-server interaction, this way of extending the use of NAT works quite well with few changes needed in either servers or clients. The case of peer to peer interaction is somewhat harder, as current peer to peer applications tend to choose port numbers freely. Again there is no real reason to do this, but to remedy this will take an extra effort on the side of the application programmers.

NAT does allow recursive repetition (that means: several nested networks behind NAT routers), but this does not extend the address space any further. NAT extends the IPv4 address space such that this will be sufficient for a number of years. The ideal of fully functional worldwide connectivity cannot be achieved immediately, but NAT still has many options for further creativity.

6. Bottom-up processes and complexity

Bottom-up emergence is an example of a so-called bottom-up process. Bottom-up processes consist of the uncoordinated initiatives of large groups of actors, either individuals or organizations (Johnson 1992, Vrancken 1994). They contrast with so-called top-down processes that can be encountered in highly hierarchical organizations, where only the top has the right to take initiaves. Both types are theoretical extremes; in practice all processes are somewhere in between the two extremes.

In a bottom-up process, each actor considers his environment and takes decisions based on his own interests. In this sense one might say that there is some form of coordination, as each actor looks at other actors and his decisions can be influenced by other actors. This is the reason why bottom-up processes, without an explicit coordinating instance, can still produce structured, coherent results. Any de facto standard is an example of such a coherent result from a bottom-up process. IT, especially through the Internet, has made this self-organizing coordination effect in bottom-up processes stronger. Different actors can find each other and can exchange information far easier than before the Internet age. In addition, a successful solution made or chosen by one of the actors in the process, can spread easily to other users.

The content aspect of the Internet is one big bottom-up process. Other examples of bottom-up processes are science and art. The latter example illustrates that even without clear criteria or clear goals, a bottom-up process can achieve useful results.

An important distinction in a bottom-up process is the difference between local and global complexity. The effects of bottom-up processes can have very high global complexity, with the Internet as a prime example, but this complexity is of little concern to single actors who are only confronted with local complexity.

Another well-known distinction that is relevant in the comparison between bottom-up en top-down processes is the difference between user optimum and system optimum. In a bottom-up process each actor strives for a user optimum. This is not always the optimum for all users. Such an optimum is often called a system optimum, which is rather associated with top-down processes. This difference is also known by the name of *prisoner's dilemma* (Poundstone 1993).

Both top-down and bottom-up have their specific pros and cons, summarized in table 1. A proper understanding of these pros and cons is essential to understanding the future prospects of the different addressing schemes for the Internet.

Top-down processes are started and managed by a single person or a small group of people (the "top"), which favors the efficiency and goal-orientedness of the process and the predictability of the outcome.

Yet a small group of people has a limited work capacity, a limited group intelligence and a limited idea creation. Therefore top-down processes have difficulties in handling complexity and in generating and trying large numbers of different options. Moreover, responsibilities are often clearly defined in a small group, to the effect that top-down processes are often hampered by fear of taking risks.

Bottom-up processes consist of many actors, therefore are very creative, highly intelligent (due to todays communication facilities) and have the work capacity needed to try many different options. Efficiency, especially overall efficiency of the process, goal orientedness, and predictability of results is nobody's responsibility, so bottom-up processes are not strong in these aspects. Badly defined responsibilities on the other hand makes bottom-up strong in taking risks.

	Top-down	Bottom-up
Efficiency	+	-
Predictability	+	-
Goal oriented	+	-
Can handle global complexity	-	+
Can produce results in the absence of clear criteria (e.g. art)	-	+
Can try many different possible solutions	-	+
Daring to take risks	-	+
Creativity and group intelligence effects	-	+

Table 1.

Network effects in standards adoption

In a network, interaction between nodes can be such that communities of nodes can be distinguished with far more interaction within the community than with nodes outside of the community. Metcalfe's law holds especially in the case of homogeneous networks, that form a single community in this sense. Otherwise, cost/benefit considerations per actor in the network are more community related than network-wide. Changes in standards are obviously easier within a smaller community and can have satisfactory benefits when there is little interchange with the network outside of the community.

This kind of effects has been studied extensively in the case of payment mechanisms (Leibbrandt 2004).

7.   Criteria for bottom-up emergence

The considerations above lead to the following criteria for bottom-up emergence of a standard:

- It must solve enough problems to have good prospects as the single future standard. All individual actors that choose a standard, hope that it will gain exclusive acceptance.

- It must be locally beneficial in the short term, with a positive cost/benefit balance for a single actor, even if it does not gain wider acceptance.

- To this end, it must be sufficiently compatible with standards in current use.

- It must have low local complexity, thereby avoiding the need for high knowledge investments.

- Not only should it allow gradual growth actor by actor, but also functionally the standard should allow step by step growth.

8.   Comparing IPv6 and NAT

IPv6 is more of a top-down, "official" solution, although still dependent on a bottom-up implementation process, whereas NAT, used as an addressing scheme, is bottom-up and evolutionary, both in design and implementation. The strengths and weaknesses of both alternatives can therefore be derived from table 1 and their technical properties.

IPv6 benefits from its status as the official successor to IPv4, a very large address space and support by manufacturers of operating systems and network equipment. Drawbacks are the unsuitability of the standard in evolutionary, bottom-up processes (caused primarily by insufficient compatibility with IPv4) and the problems in routing and multi-homing left unsolved by IPv6. Moreover, it allows functionally no stepwise growth either, which makes its introduction a radical change that takes in addition a high knowledge investment.

NAT benefits from allowing gradual, evolutionary growth, both in number of implementations and functionally. It benefits from being beneficial locally and in the short term, and from being reasonably compatible with straight IPv4 addressing. Knowledge about NAT is currently abundant as it has already a large installed base. NAT's drawbacks are its low status as a standard and the fact that it offers only a limited extension of the address space.

9.   What will happen with addressing in the Internet?

Given the pros and cons of both alternatives, we may conclude that homogeneous addressing in the Internet is not to be expected within the foreseeable future. Both alternatives solve or sufficiently alleviate the address space shortage, but neither community of IPv6 or NAT users has a decisive incentive to change. NAT still offers many options for further extending it functionally, while retaining compatibility with the existing Internet. The existing communities of IPv6 users have no reason to switch either. Worldwide visibility makes little sense to them, as their target group is limited by language and cultural barriers.

10. Conclusions

This paper can be summarized by the following conclusions:

1. Worldwide adoption of a standard is always a bottom-up emergence process.

2. Properties of bottom-up processes can be translated into criteria for standards adoption.

3. In the case of Internet addressing, the criteria lead to the conclusion that addressing will remain heterogeneous in the foreseeable future, as neither of the two alternatives has a convincing cost/benefit balance for all actors involved.

11. Acknowledgements

This research was sponsored by EU project NOREST. We thank the following people for useful discussions: Hendrik Rood, Paul Allen, Wim Vree, Piet Van Mieghem, Egbert-Jan Sol and Kai Jacobs.

12. References

APNIC: IP-addressing in China, http://www.apnic.net/news/hot-topics/internet-gov/ip-china.html#ip-add-cn

Beijnum, I. van: BGP, O'Reilly, September 2002.

DNS SRV: http://www.voip-info.org/tiki-print.php?page=DNS+SRV

IEEE Standards: 802.3, Part 3: Carrier sense multiple access with collision detection (CSMA/CD) access method and physical layer specifications. http://standards.ieee.org/getieee802/802.3.html

IETF: www.ietf.org

IETF on migration towards IPv6: http://www.ietf.org/proceedings/02nov/I-D/draft-ietf-ngtrans-introduction-to-ipv6-transition-08.txt

IPv6: http://www.ipv6.org/

Johnson, H.Th.: *Relevance regained : from top-down control to bottom-up empowerment* , Maxwell Macmillan International, 1992. ISBN:0029165555.

Kuipers, F.A.: *Quality of Service Routing in the Internet: Theory, Complexity and Algorithms*, Ph.D. thesis, Delft University Press, The Netherlands, ISBN 90-407-2523-3, September 2004, http://www.nas.its.tudelft.nl/people/Fernando/papers/PhDthesiskuipers.pdf

Leibbrandt, G., Payment instruments and network effects. Adoption, harmonization and succession of network technologies accross countries, Maastricht, 2004.

Meloan, S: Toward a Global "Internet of Things": November 2003
http://java.sun.com/developer/technicalArticles/Ecommerce/rfid/

Network Working Group: RFC 1519 - Classless Inter-Domain Routing (CIDR): an Address Assignment and Aggregation Strategy, September 1993, http://www.faqs.org/rfcs/rfc1519.html

Network Working Group: RFC 1631 - The IP Network Address Translator (NAT), May 1994, http://www.faqs.org/rfcs/rfc1631.html

Network Working Group: RFC 2460 - Internet Protocol, Version 6 (IPv6) Specification, 1998.

Network Working Group, RFC 3261, SIP: Session initiation protocol: http://www.ietf.org/rfc/rfc3261.txt, June 2002.

Poundstone, W.: *Prisoner's Dilemma*, Anchor, 1993.

Sol, E-J., presentation at Delft Univerity of Technology, September 24, 2004.

Sol, E-J., personal communication, January 27, 2005.

Tanenbaum, A.S.: *Computer Networks*, 4-the edition, Prentice Hall, 2002.

Vrancken, J.L.M.: Bottom-up processen in de automatisering, *Informatie*, december 1994 (Dutch).

A bottom-up approach to build a B2B sectorial standard: the case of Moda-ML/TexSpin

Nicola Gessa* — **Guido Cucchiara**** — **Piero De Sabbata ***** — **Arianna Brutti *****

* University of Bologna, Department of Computer Science, Mura di Porta Zamboni 2, 40100 Bologna, Italy Times New Roman
gessa@cs.unibo.it

** Gruppo SOI, Via Brofferio 3, 10121 Torino, Italy
guidocucchiara@libero.it

*** ENEA, UDA-PMI, XML-LAB, Via Don Fiammelli 2, 40129 Bologna, Italy
piero.desabbata@bologna.enea.it
picicchia78@yahoo.it

ABSTRACT: This paper presents the experience realised building up a sectorial collaboration framework addressed to the Textile/Clothing industry, Moda-ML.

The experience of Moda-ML, started from the background of the EDI analysis but was developed looking to the ebXML specifications and with a great attention to the requirements arising from the industry. The requirements for an incremental approach and a vertical collaborative framework produced an original experience. The effectiveness of the approach is witnessed by the project contribution to the standardisation initiative CEN/ISSS TexSpin.

One of the main challenge arose from the large presence of SMEs in this sector that did not allowed, in the past, the diffusion of EDI technologies and that, presently, hampers the diffusion of integration systems.

On the other hand, there is a discussion about the capability of the standards, and of the standardisation processes, to effectiveness contribute to the development of the application level of the B2B integration.

KEY WORDS: Standard, EDI, interoperability, ebXML

1. Introduction

The complexity, relevance, and the heterogeneity of the commercial activities require the building of a common interoperability agreement upon which new business relationships could be established and inter-company data exchange can be carried out. These sets of document formats, structures and transmission protocols, usually are called "collaborative framework".

The adoption of standards in the B2B domain aims to facilitate the definition of such frameworks, but presents many non trivial issues.

While the availability of standards related to technological aspects, such as message exchanges, are not critical (i.e. SOAP or XML, that are free well recognised), the area of the standards related to the semantic, that are domain and application dependent, shows the weakness of the standardisation results (fig. 1).

One of the problems regards the process of standard definition and implementation: the standardisation process life-cycles are too long if compared to those of products and technologies that they should rule (Sherif 03). In other words, at the end of a standardisation process the released specifications may result obsolete when compared with the new enabling technologies: canonical standardisation processes (such as ISO, W3C, OASIS) may last many years, whereas practical solutions to face interoperability problems are needed immediately. These delays in the standardisation development, on one hand, damage the widespread adoption of the technologies and, on the other hand, discourage to undertake new standardisation processes for e-business.

In the 90's private consortia were setup to overcome the problem but the results are not so significantly different.

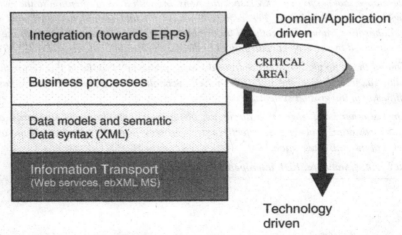

Figure. 1. *The stack of interoperability shows that critical area for standardisatin is that related with the semantic aspects, while the lower layers, related essentially to technology are not so critical*

Because of these difficulties, both technology suppliers and large final users, by themselves or through enterprises consortia, searched and developed ad hoc solutions based on the establishment of communities. This behaviour has led various initiatives to flourish out of the standardisation bodies, and to the birth of more and more abstract standard (or the definition of meta-model or meta-standard) with the objective to prolong the life of the released specifications beyond the life of a single enabling technology.

A second problematic aspect is that business documents are complex to define, adopt and maintain, and standardisation life-cycle could be very complex (and furthermore extensions of the standardisations life-cycle should be considered (Soderstrom 04)).

Generally, one (or some) de jure or de facto standard is born sooner or later in sectors dominated by few large companies as a result of an elitary standardisation process that involves the few dominant actors and their technological partners.

But in other sectors, characterised by the dominant presence of SMEs, such process is virtually impossible, since it becomes extremely difficult to reach the critical mass of actors needed (CEN/ISSS report 03).

Within such a complex scenario, the continuous research of a trade-off between the completeness and correctness of a standard and its rapid development has raised the proliferation of both horizontal and vertical standards. Whereas the so called horizontal standards belong mainly to the most recognized standardisation bodies (ebXML, UBL(Meadows 04),..), the vertical ones present a more heterogeneous panorama: some enterprise consortia have developed domain-based standards (e.g. RosettaNet, Papinet, Open Travel Alliance);   others based their standardisation activities on standardisation bodies (i.e. Eurofer within CEN/ISSS); nevertheless in many other sectors there is not a well-defined agreement on a common vision and, often, the needed critical mass to build a standard is lacking.

In the Textile-Clothing (T/C) sector, and also in other sectors related to the fashion industry, standardisation is even a harder task since the sophistication and specificity of the co-operation among enterprises of the supply chain (mainly based on human relationships instead of Information and Communication Technology means) are very high and represent a peculiar competitive factor.

Thus, in the T/C sector, B2B integration is needed but the tools (recognized standards) to achieve this objective cannot be developed for the sector

The eBusiness Watch report on B2B dedicated to the T/C sector (e-Business Watch 04) witnesses the difficulty of EDI based technologies in the sector: few installations, regarding only large companies and the relationships with large retail organisations rather than with suppliers and subcontractors.

In this context, can be notable how, and under which circumstances, the experience of Moda-ML (www.moda-ml.org (Moda-ML Public Final Report 03)) in defining, implementing and deploying an interoperability framework contributed to the definition of an European sectorial (pre-normative) standard (TexSpin (CWA14948 03)).

The EDITEX unsuccessful experience led to prefer a more user driven approach and this is the beginning of the history of Moda-ML and TexSpin.

In section 2 the paper presents some consideration about the EDIFACT technology that, anyway, represents one of the main efforts in the standard scenarios for e-Business and, surely, remains a relevant reference for Moda-ML. In section 3 the requirements for vertical frameworks are reported together with the relevant differences with EDIFACT and the most recent horizontal frameworks.

The Moda-ML initiative and its implementation process are described in sections 4 and 5; section 6 regards some customisation aspects considered; the final considerations about the feedback from the users are presented in section 7.

2. The EDI Approach in Short

The EDI, Electronic Data Interchange, was defined by a ONU Commission (ECE/Trade/WP4); it is focused on the simplification of the international com-merce and was based on:

- a document structure for the international electronic commerce, already known as UN-Layouts keys (they were conceived for the hard paper communications, before the diffusion of informatic tools inside the firms)

- the ONU dictionary of the words for the international commerce (UN/TDED) and the recommended codifications (Terms of Payment, INCOTERMS, ...)

- the ISO syntax for the electronic transfer of data within flat-files (ISO 9735).

The result was a complex and rigid technology, EDIFACT   (EDI For Administration, Commerce and Transport (EDIFACT)), where the applicative customisations (EDIFACT subsets) were obtained with the suppression of not used parts of a common general structure that was (in theory) the "least common multiple" of all the sectorial needs.

This approach was valuable because it conveys an "universal" standard, but its application found a great diffusion only in some market sector because its adoption was technically and economically justifiable only for large organisations and great amounts of data; however it represented a "cultural fracture" for the business world that was still unprepared.

In the period spanning '80s and '90s, the TEDIS project (namely EDITEX (TEDIS 92)) developed the EDIFACT subsets for the European T/C industry.

Despite the efforts, the diffusion of the EDITEX solution was bounded to few very large organisations.

The take over of the Internet dampened the growth capacity of this experience, with-out offering a final solution to the enormous problems that EDIFACT was facing.

These problems are tackled again with the diffusion of XML (eXtended Markup Language, well suitable to manage documents and contents on the Internet): tools to manage data structures and specifications (like XML Schema) have been developed in order to exploit the flexibility and human readability of the XML documents (a syntax much more flexible and quick than ISO 9735).

Internet, furthermore, solves the problem of the interoperability between different transmission networks (the EDIFACT approach was typically based on private value added networks) and offers a capillary widespread network infrastructure that makes XML and Internet a winning scheme.

On the other hand, the nature of "metalanguage", or "metastandard", of XML leads back to a sort of "linguistic relativity": now everybody has the tools to build infinite semantic representations compliant with XML; from a certain point of view the 'do it by yourself' approach appears to be encouraged.

From the market point of view, while the legacy applications are still based on EDIFACT, a new generation of XML based applications tries to establish new relationships with actors and in business areas that previously resulted impervious for EDI.

In this context the new Internet architectures, based on enterprise portals and/or Internet integration services (based on ASP paradigm and, usually, proprietary data formats), have known a wide diffusion and are directly competing with the Peer-to-Peer model of information exchanges of EDI.

Nevertheless the the new architectures and models show evident limitations when approaching complex networks of relationships that cannot be reduced to the hub-spoke model.

This is the reason for a renewed interest in the so called XML/EDI paradigms that are characterised by the Peer-to-Peer architecture and exchanges of standardised messages.

In the case on Moda-ML, after the failure of EDITEX, a strong user driven approach was adopted preserving some strong points of EDITEX, i.e. the transaction and information modelling and semantics. The same happened, parallelly, in other national based initiatives in France (eTeXML) and Germany (e-Visit).

3. General Considerations about the Construction of a Collaborative Framework

At this point could be helpful to identify the characteristics that distinguish vertical collaborative frameworks (a collaborative framework addressed to a specific do-main, i.e. an industrial sector) from the horizontal ones:

Horizontal frameworks (examples are UBL, EAN.UCC,...):

– are not specific to a domain;

– contain basic semantics (and processes), to be extended before a concrete application is developed;

– assign a relevant role (to design real word applications) to the implementation guidelines;

– are delivered by large organisations/bodies.

Vertical frameworks (examples are Papinet, OTA, Rosetta.net, ... Moda-ML):

– are restricted to a particular domain;

– are focused, i.e. they support a variety of highly specific business processes and messages and usually have a strong data typing;

– are ready to use;

– are, often, delivered by ad hoc consortia, with strong commitment of the final users.

Is to be noted that, from this point of view, ebXML is a META-framework that offer a methodology to establish both the kinds of frameworks.

Now, we will to focus on the experience of construction of a vertical collaborative framework (and its path towards a standardisation approach) in a context that is characterised by the fragmentation of the players (many firms of different kinds, large as well as small ones, with completely different inclinations to innovation).

From the re-examination of the EDI experiences, in this applicative context, some aspects have arisen:

- the problem of poor usability of the specifications (complex, addressed to few expert readers, non human-readable formats) (see also (Jacobs 04));

- the need for a support of an incremental adoption of the specifications, with low investments and low technological skills; this leads to an iterative approach where a core of transactions is the starting point and then, incrementally, fur-ther transactions (and business process) should be added to consolidate and extend the effectiveness of the framework.

A second group of considerations arises from the lessons learnt in various EDI adoption:

- when the adopting industries are SMEs, their technology suppliers might be SMEs in turn and the complexity of the software to validate and manage messages is an obstacle to the diffusion;

- the model of specifications based on few document templates to support many business should be substituted with many, very focused, document templates, each of them tailored for a specific type of transaction; they are easier to be checked with standard tools based on XML Schema and reduce the risk of misunderstanding and misalignment between partners;

- dealing with networks of industries comprising many SMEs, it is important to sim-plify the process of 'alignment' of the systems: each industry cannot afford excessive costs to join a new partner (Gessa *et al.* 04).

A third group of aspects resulted very important when the initial activity of frame-work construction became part of a standardisation process:

- the relationships with horizontal standardisation initiatives (e.g. ebXML and EAN.UCC; UBL in the near future);

- the formal representation of the specifications and the reorganisation of the back-office views of the dictionary (compliancy with ISO11179 and ebXML CCTS);

- the requirements and priorities along different rings of the supply chain may be different.

4. The Moda-ML Interoperability Framework

In this section we briefly introduce and outline the Moda-ML framework (Middleware tOols and Documents to enhAnce the Textile/Clothing supply chain through xML): the initiative started in April 2001 with the aim to define an interoperability framework for the Textile/Clothing sector, addressing both small and medium enterprises as well as large enterprises; the long term objective was to contribute to the establishment of an European standard for data exchange in the T/C sector.

At the beginning Moda-ML started as a project and collected various research organisations (ENEA, Politecnico di Milano, Domina, Gruppo SOI, Institut Francais Textil Habillement - IFTH) together with a representative set of leading Italian Textile/Clothing manufacturers. It has been supported by the Fifth Framework programme of the European Commission within the IST (Information Society Technology) initiative (more information can be found in http://www.moda-ml.org) and took part in the cluster of projects about Agents and Middleware Technologies (EUTIST-AMI IST-2000-28221, www.eutist-ami.org).

After the conclusion of the Moda-ML project, the consortia of partners continued to maintain a technical group assuming the denomination of "Moda-ML initiative"; this allowed the continuation of the activities.

To achieve the technical objective, both document structures and business process have been considered, but a special focus has been on the definition of the business documents (Gessa *et al.* 03).

Moda-ML did not produced a proprietary implementation, but has developed open specifications and open-source and free software implementations. This is surely a key point when aiming at encouraging a wide adoption to a large number of small and medium enterprises.

One of the first choices for the Moda-ML project was to employ a Peer-to-Peer architecture: we wanted each firm to communicate directly with its partners in the supply chain without using a central system or any form of service provider. For this purpose simple software modules and interfaces have been developed to allow users to access, define and deliver, in a friendly way, the documents needed for each step of the business process under consideration. The only central resource is a repository of document templates shared between the partners and used dur-ing the interchange processes.

The two most important points of the Moda-ML initiative have been the definition of a vocabulary of business components, expressed as Business Information Entities and their related XML implementation, and the design of a middleware architecture based on the ebXML messaging service specification.

5. The Moda-ML Standardisation Life-Cycle

To understand the experience of Moda-ML and the subsequent standardisation initiative TexSpin it is worth to examine the phases of the implementation (fig.3):

1.   Macro analysis phase: study of the main issues and requirements of the target sector (Textile/Clothing sector), to highlight key features. In this context existing solutions were criticized, cause of their poor usability. Choice of the main reference technologies.

2.   Organization phases: setting up a working team to carry out a project for the interoperability framework. In order to consider different perspectives and exploit different knowledge, the team was composed of:

a. Industrial leading firms, with the knowledge of practical and pragmatic vision of the sectorial issues.

b. Research institutes that contributed with the knowledge of proper technologies and solutions to tackle interoperability problems.

c. Technology suppliers (without a predominant role in the team).

The more relevant aspect at this stage consisted in a bottom-up approach for standardisation: rather than starting from an official standardisation body, the initiative got on with well-established industrial districts, where each actor knew the collaborative mechanism and was used to work with others.

3.   Document structure design phase: after a more specific analysis con-ducted in cooperation with all of the team components, two basic result were reached:

a. Definition (starting from the EDIFACT - EDITEXT experience) of the existing collaboration processes between the enterprises, and setting up of document structures and data models.

b. Definition of the transport mechanisms.

4.   Parallel consensus creation activity: since the beginning of the analysis and design activity, a campaign to involve potential users and their trade associations started (this included the creation of a public Web site as well as organisation of focus groups and technical events). On this Moda-ML worked hard with awareness meetings (about 20, with hundreds of participants in the industry and in the area of consultancy and solution providers), targeted visits and any other type of possible promotion, including scientific papers and participation to highly visible international Conferences dealing with e-Business or with the Textile-Clothing industry.

5.   Software support for the architecture design phase: definition of the document factory architecture to manage the interoperability framework. Instead of defining each business document as a single entity, we detected a large set of business components (near 300 terms) upon which the final business documents were built. In this manner we modularised the construction of the documents. Besides the definition of the component set, we specified a set of document types built upon those components.

6.   Implementing phase. Moda-ML provided a set of basic tools for both the users and the framework maintainers:

a. Demonstration software: implementation of a simple Message Service Handler (ebMS 1) to provide the users with a proper soft-ware to exchange business documents.

b. Managing tools: implementing tools to generate multilingual user's guides and UML diagrams.

7.   Standardisation phase. During this stage the project enlarged its horizons at European level, joining and facing other actors, initiatives and standards. In TexSpin

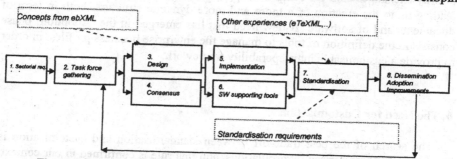

Figure 3. *Life Cycle of the Moda-ML combined with the TexSpin standardisation*

the results of Moda-ML and of eTexML were integrated and refined, and feedbacks were collected. Tackling the standardisation path of CEN/ISSS required acceptable efforts thanks to the simplified approach of CEN/ISSS (addressed to the construction of informal standards in a relatively short time) and to the early adoption of a general semantic framework (built on the past experiences of EDITEX and on the ebXML activities that were running at that time).

The involvement in the CEN/ISSS TexSpin activity aimed to contribute to a standard prenormative definition for data exchange in of the Textile/Clothing supply chain. The results were formalised in a CWA (CEN/Workshop Agreement 14948/2003). There were three main public events: the plenary sessions in Belgium, Italy and France which viewed strong participation of the industrial firms.

8.   Dissemination and evolvement phase:

a. Awareness setting up on the developed specification.

b. Integration with ERP products and developing of demos.

c. Comparison with other existing (not necessary standard) interoperability solutions adopted in the sector.

d. Fostering the adoption of the project results.

Presently about one hundred firms have declared their support to the specifications.

9.   Iteration. After the conclusion of the standardisation phase, further areas/relationships of the supply chain that require support were determined. As a result the activity of business analysis started again, produced a new set of specifications that has been prepared for a new standardisation activity.

The iteration of the cycle was completed on September 2003. The second iteration of the standardisation phase is starting with the CEN/ISSS initiative TexWeave. Within the life-cycles of the Moda-ML experience, phase 3 and the following ones can be considered as always "in progress", because of document and process structures need to be extended to cover new phases of the business processes. The result is a repeated iteration of the phases 3-8 (iterative life cycle), with the aim to expand the coverage of the specifications from a core of high priority exchanges until the complete supply chain. The evolvement of the project is leading us to the creation of a more and more dynamic structure, both in term of documents and of software. A new need that has emerged in the 'Adoption' phase consists in the definition of tools to manage the enterprise business profiles, in order to provide a customisable inter-operability framework.

6. The Need for Customisation

The search of the best trade-off between standardisation and customisation is continuously characterised by oscillations, and this rule is confirmed in our context. As soon as a common framework is established, it appears that the specificity of each couple of partners had to be managed (without destroying the framework). In fact e-business activities represent a very heterogeneous scenario: business processes can be more or less complex and dynamic, having to adapt to very different commercial circumstances. In this context standardisation initiatives must consider the necessity of the enterprises to personalize business processes and exchanged documents on the strength of the different relationships they hold: process and document structures should be customisable by the actors involved in the relation-ship in order to better fit the enterprise requirements.

In this perspective, Moda-ML framework is facing the problem of the definition of business profiles. Within the Moda-ML project several business processes related to the T/C sector have been defined and, adopting ebXML specifications, such processes have been formalized building proper BPSS document. At this stage BPSS documents represent the reference structure of the business processes that can be adopted by the enterprises to exchange business information (e.g. processes like Fabric Supply). The specifications of the business processes are flexible enough to allow different partners, with different roles in a specific business process, to specify how each one supports it. A business process in fact could be composed of many sub-activities, each of which requires the exchange of a specific document.

Together with ebXML BPSS, also ebXML CPP documents have been adopted by the framework to allow partners to express their own capabilities in supporting business processes.

Whereas this level of customisation represents a good starting point, complex relationships require that not only processes, but also exchanged document structures can be customized by the enterprises. CPP specifications do not allows this kind of customisation, so we have designed a first proposal to extend them introducing a mechanism to adapt document structure, and the information held, to different situa-tions within the same business process.

7. Conclusions

The focus of this paper is the experience realised with the Moda-ML initiative in the field of B2B standardisation, from the creation of an open community framework (Moda-ML) to the participation to a standardisation process in the context of the CEN/ISSS procedures (TexSpin). In our view the approach may apply to industrial sectors characterised by a large presence of small and medium enterprises, without few market leaders. As a conclusion of this paper we want mainly to point out three aspects:

- a bottom-up approach to B2B standardisation could be successful when it starts from a significant number of representatives of the different kinds of actors and a clear relationship with existing horizontal standards and enabling technologies.

- the EDIFACT experience is valuable, mainly from the point of view of the data semantics, but the simple translation into the XML paradigm is not sufficient without a clear identification of the target requirements (derived from SMEs participation and domain specific, i.e. fashion industry).

- machine treatable ways to customise the collaborative processes are needed to give to the standards enough flexibility to fit real world collaborations.

8. References

CEN/ISSS "Report and recommendations on key eBusiness standards issues 2003-2005", CEN/ISSS, Bruxelles, 2003

CWA 14948/2003, "Guidelines for XML/EDI messages in the Textile/clothing sector", CEN/ISSS Workshop Agreement, CEN/ISSS, Bruxelles, 2003.

e-Business Watch, sector report n. 01-11, August 2004, electronic Business in the Textile, Clothing and Footwear industries

"EDIFACT Application level syntax rules - ISO 9735" (1987)

Gessa N., De Sabbata P., Fraulini M., Imolesi T., Mainetti L., Marzocchi M. e Vitali F., "Moda-ML, an experience of promotion of a sectorial interoperability framework", pp. 350-357 in *Building Knowledge Economy: Issues, Applications, Case Studies*; Bologna October 23-24 2003, ISBN Ohmsha 2 274 90623 X C3055

Gessa N., Novelli C., Busuoli M., Vitali F., *"Use and extension of ebXML business profiles for Textile/Clothing firms"* pp. 186-195 in *"E-Commerce and Web Technologies"*, 5th international conference EC-Web 2004, Zaragoza, Spain, August/September 2004, Proceedings, ISBN 3-540-22917-5, Springer

Jakobs K., "Standardisation and SME Users Mutually Exclusive?", *Proc. Multi-Conference on Business Information Systems*, Cuvillier Verlag, 2004

Meadows B., "Universal Business language (UBL) 1.0" , cd-UBL-1.0, OASIS, September 15 2004; http://docs.oasis-open.org/ubl/cd-UBL-1.0/

Moda-ML Public Final Report, doc MG11-029, Bologna, september 2003, www.moda-ml.org/moda-ml/download/mg11-029-moda-ml_final_report.doc

Sherif M.H., "When is standardisation slow?", *International Journal of IT Standards & Standardistion Research*, vol. 1, N. 1, Jan.-June 2003

Soderstrom E., "Formulating a General Standards Life Cycle", *Proceedings of 16th International Conference of Advanced Information Systems Engineering - CaiSE 2004*, Riga, Latvia, June 2004.

TEDIS, Trade EDI Systems Programme, Interim report, 1992, Office for official pubblications of the European Community, ISBN-92-826-5658-6

Standards Dynamics:

Descriptive Statistics of Change in JTC1

Tineke M. Egyedi * — Petra Heijnen**

Faculty of Technology,
Policy and Management
Delft University of Technology
PO Box 5015
2600 GA Delft
the Netherlands
* *T.M.Egyedi@tbm.tudelft.nl*
***P.W. Heijnen@tbm.tudelft.nl*

ABSTRACT: *Standards might be presumed to be stable. But how stable are they in reality? This paper presents the first findings of a quantitative analysis of standards dynamics in ISO/IEC JTC1, the formal international standards body for IT standardization. It discusses among other things the volume of different types of change and developments over time..*

KEY WORDS: *dynamics, ISO, revisions, maintenance, stability.*

1. Introduction

One might assume that committee standards are stable and are not changed easily. Indeed, on the face of it 'stability' would seem to be an intrinsic, defining characteristic of standards. It is in most cases a precondition for interoperability between IT products and services, the area of technology addressed in this paper. Standards are signposts (Mansell & Hawkins, 1992). They are a point of reference for producers, suppliers and consumers, and reduce transaction costs (Kindleberger, 1983). They coordinate technology and market development (Farrell & Saloner, 1988). To effectively work as such, they need to be stable.

However, as we intuitively know, standards are not static entities. In practice they are revised, split and merged, withdrawn, succeeded, reinstated, etc. The changes which a standard undergoes after it has been developed and published, including its withdrawal, replacement and its possible after-life, we refer to by the term *standards dynamics*.

Although, exceptions aside[1], no systematic research has yet been done that takes standards dynamics as its core-focus, there is a fair amount of anecdotal evidence and evidence from specialist journals for IT practitioners. Moreover, there are also some case studies about post-hoc changes to standards. Usually these deal with more radical changes. Examples of such cases are,

- Telefax (Comité Consultatif International Télégraphique et Téléphonique, CCITT). The problem with Telefax standardization started when a Group 3 digital telefax standard was proposed. At the time, there already were two standards: the Group 3 for analogue networks and the Group 4 for digital networks. The main opposition against the new proposal came from the Group 4 supporters. To prevent the Group 3 digital telefax standard from being accepted, they came up with a compromise. In the ensuing stalemate, the CCITT decided to accept the compromise as well as the proposal for a Group 3 digital telefax, creating rival technologies that could well fragment the market. (Schmidt & Werle, 1998)
- Internet Protocol (Internet Engineering Task Force, IETF). To solve the lack of internet addresses in Internet Protocol version 4 (IPv4) the Internet standards body started working on a version 6 (IPv6) in 1990. It took a long time to develop (RFC 2460, 1998). The resulting protocol was not compatible with IPv4. In order to prevent the development of separate networks and to ease the transition to IPv6 and recreate compatibility, a separate standard on "Transition Mechanisms for IPv6 Hosts and Routers" (RFC 2893, 2000) was developed. (Van Best, 2001).
- Standard Generalized Markup Language (SGML) (ISO/IEC JTC1). The SGML (1986) standard, a standard for structuring information, was already amended in 1988, but thereafter remained stable until 1996. In 1996 a

---

[1] Apart from (Egyedi & Loeffen, 2002), we are not aware of other work in this area. NB: At the time of writing (December 2004) a European project is underway (NO-REST) of which one of its work packages, the one led by the first author of this paper, explicitly focuses on Standard Dynamics. See e.g. Gauch (2005) on DVD standards and Jakobs (2005) on IEEE 802.11.

Corrigendum was added (ISO 8879: 1986/ Cor 1:1996). In the same year work on Extensible Markup Language (XML) started in the World Wide Web Consortium (W3C). XML was to bring SGML functionality to the web.

Although XML developers originally aimed for compatibility with SGML, this point was not prioritized. In the end, despite additional measures to re-create compatibility - by means of non-binding recommendations in XML 1.0 (1998) and a second corrigendum by ISO (ISO 8879: 1986/ Cor 2:1999) – a fragmented practice resulted. XML partly replaced SGML, fragmented the existing market and created new markets. (Egyedi & Loeffen, 2002)

Radical changes such as the above but also smaller changes can lead to problems for standards users (implementors) and consumers (end-users). Some of the main problems are

- the lack of transparency that may arise and increased transaction costs (e.g. consumer unawareness of differences between versions or of the consequences for interoperability of products complying to different versions).
- the costs of update and loss of investments for standard implementors and IT consumers;
- interoperability is not self-evident anymore; that is, uncertainty may arise about the interoperability of new standard-compliant IT with ones own installed base and with the installed base of others.

In sum, standards dynamics is a problem.[2]

In this paper we aim to complement case study-based insights with more quantitative research into standards dynamics. We explore the scale of standards dynamics.[3] Our main research question is: *How stable are standards?* That is, which types of dynamics are at stake? How often do they occur? Etc.. We focus on international, formal IT standards, that is, on standards developed in JTC1, the Joint Technical Committee1 of ISO (International Standardization Organization) and IEC (International Electrotechnical Commission).

The paper is structured as follows. First, we summarize the terminology used and the procedures developed by JTC1 on standards maintenance, for standard maintenance defines its perspective on standards dynamics. Next, we describe characteristics of the dataset and the research methodology used. Two sets of analyses have been done, of which the first set is described in this paper. It gives an overall impression of the changes that have occurred. The paper closes with a summary of the main findings and conclusions.

---

[2] Standards operate in a changing environment, and may need to be adapted or replaced in response to evolving market and societal demands. That is, sometimes change is necessary. More will be said about this dilemma in an upcoming paper.

[3] Due to limitations to the number of pages, we present in this paper the first part of the analysis. For the second part we refer to Egyedi & Heijnen (2005) .

2. Standard Maintenance in JTC1

JTC1 was installed in 1987 to address the surge of work items in the field of information technology. JTC1 has a collaborative agreement with ITU-T, the part of the formal International Telecommunication Union that develops formal standards (i.e. recommendations) for telecommunications. Although JTC1 is officially one of ISO and IEC's technical committees (e.g. the ISO central secretariat administers JTC1 data), in certain respects it operates as an autonomous body. For example, it has its own website, its own directives, and currently 16 subcommittees. These produce International Standards (ISs) and standard-type documents, namely Technical Reports (TRs) and international standardized profiles (ISPs)[4]. Apart from developing and ratifying standards, they do maintenance work on standards. Standards maintenance starts with a periodical review. No more than five years after publication of the most recent edition of a standard, it is reviewed to decide whether it should be confirmed, revised, declared as stabilized, or withdrawn (JTCI, 2004, 15.3.1). To start with the first option, a standard is confirmed if it has been implemented at the national level and applied in practice[5].

A revision may involve supplementing a standard with a separate document called

- a *Technical Corrigendum* (Cor)[6] to correct a *technical defect* (i.e. a technical error or ambiguity in a standard that could lead to its incorrect or unsafe application; JTCI, 2004, 15.4.1);

- a *Technical Amendment* (Amd), which is a *technical addition or change*[7];

or it may consist of

---

[4] An IS is "a normative document, developed according to consensus procedure, which has been submitted for vote by all national bodies and approved by 2/3 of the P-members of the responsible technical committee with not more than ¼ of all votes cast being negative." (...) A TR is "an informative document containing information of a different kind from that normally published in a normative document (e.g. collection of data), approved by a simple majority of the P-members of a technical committee or subcommittee." An ISP is "an internationally agreed, harmonized document which identifies a standard or a group of standards together with options and parameters, necessary to perform a function or a set of functions." (ISO, 2004, p.2)

[5] See the Letter of Keith Brannon, ISO/IEC Information Technology Task Force, 2004-02-12, on Systematic review of International Standards. We have no information on whether this is decided based on hard data, on the impression of subcommittee members, or otherwise.

[6] Technical corrigenda are normally published as separate documents, the edition of the IS affected remaining in print. However, the ITTF shall decide (...) whether to publish a technical corrigendum or a corrected reprint of the existing edition of the IS. (op. cit. JTCI, 2004, ch.15.4)

[7] A technical addition or change is an alteration or addition to previously agreed technical provisions in an existing IS. (JTCI, 2004, 15.4.1)

- a next *Edition* (Ed.) (e.g. to correct editorial defects[8] or integrate supplements in the main body),

- a *Replacement* (e.g. standards A,B, and C may merge into standard D; or D may be split into A,B, and C), and acquire a new project number, or

- a *Change of document type,* e.g. from an IS into a TR.

For example, the set of standards and standard-type documents on Local and metropolitan area networks ISO/IEC 8802 consists of different parts (1- 12 parts, part 8 and 10 missing). All of them are ISs except for part 1, which is a TR. For most parts new editions have replaced old ones (e.g. part 3 four times). Some parts also have Corrigenda and/or Amendments. These are sometimes replaced by a new Corrigendum and/or Amendment (e.g. part 2), or are integrated into a new edition.

A standard might be withdrawn because a new edition replaces it, because it gets a new project number, or because it has become obsolete (no replacement).

Lastly, a standard may be declared to be stabilized. *Stabilized standards* are not subject to periodic review (JTCI, 2004, 15.3.1). "A stabilised standard (...) will be retained to provide for the continued viability of existing products or servicing of equipment that is expected to have a long working life." (JTCI, 2004, 15.6)[9] That is, other standards and/or in-use implementations depend on them. An ISO document ISO/TMB (2004) gives us two examples:

- The rationale to reinstate and stabilize the programming language Algol 60 (ISO 1538:1984), which was withdrawn in 1990, was that the standard and algorithms therein are still referenced to e.g. in textbooks and national standards.

- The rationale to reinstate and stabilize a standard for Basic mode control procedures (ISO 2628:1973; ISO 2629:1973), which was withdrawn in 1997, was that "there are many terminals in existence operating TPAD and other similar protocols (...) that are based on ISO 2628 and ISO 2629", and which are character-oriented.

Since their market is not expected to evolve anymore, no standards maintenance is needed (e.g. it is not necessary to keep a committee secretariat in place). In all, JTC1 has 193 such stabilized standard documents (i.e. ISs, TRs, Amendments and Technical Corrigenda (dd. 27th of April 2004).

The notion of 'stabilized standard' already suggests that other standards may not be stable. It already indicates that JTC1 also grapples with problems of legacy and standards dynamics. A second sign thereof is the notion of 'provisionally retained edition' (ISO, 2004, p.3). *A provisionally retained edition* is an edition, which has

---

[8] An editorial defect is "An error which can be assumed to have no consequences in the application of the IS, for example a minor printing error." (JTCI, 2004, 15.4.1)
[9] "(...) [H]owever, each Sub Committee shall periodically review a current list of its own stabilised standards to ensure that they still belong in stabilized status." (JTCI, 2004, 15.3.1)

been updated but is still valid – instead of being withdrawn, as is common procedure[10]. For example, one of the standards for quality management and quality assurance, ISO 9000-1 (1994) was revised in 2003. However, because the certification market still works with it, the 1994 edition has been retained. The 'provisionally retained edition' procedure is a double-edged sword. It allows parties who value compliance to international standards but cannot or do not wish to update their implementations, to preserve their investment. But the validity of successive editions may cause confusion and reduce the transparency of the standards market for newcomers.

If we take a closer look into what the procedures for *stabilized standards* and *provisionally retained editions* are used for, they are to a large extent used to reconfirm the current relevance of earlier Open Systems Interconnection (OSI) standards. For all 27 provisionally retained editions (ISO, August 15, 2004), and a majority of the stabilized standards (i.e. 101 out of 193) are OSI- related. This does not fit well with the widely shared feeling that OSI, because of a lack of market, is passé.

3. Methodology

The empirical results presented in the next section are based on quantitative analyses of the JTC1 database. The database was accessed in the period 12-15 July 2004[11], at the ISO secretariat in Geneva, Switzerland. Two types of queries were done. Firstly, because not all JTC1 data is public, some straightforward queries (lists and frequencies) were done for us by the central secretariat (i.e. not hands-on). For example, a list of revised standards was provided. Such data is in most cases not suitable for statistical analysis.

Secondly, permission was granted to directly query data that is also publicly available via ISO's website (www.iso.ch). At stake is a predefined subset of the database. This subset contains all JTC1 standards and standard-type documents (i.e. the whole population), but not all variables (data fields). It includes basic document features such as standard reference, date of publication, document number, document type, committee number, technical area addressed, and the most relevant fields in respect to standards dynamics such as the review stage of the document, the date, type and number of editions, and the number of amendments and corrigenda. According to the International Classification for Standards (ICS) level 1, the documents address the technical areas of *Telecommunications, Audio and Video*

---

[10] "Previous editions of standards (including their amendments and technical corrigenda) may be included in the ISO and IEC Catalogues on an exception basis as determined by the SC, noting that these documents should be used for reference purposes only." (JTCI, 2004, ch.15.1.5.)

[11] Some data was provided outside this period. Where this is the case, it is indicated. See Table 7.

Engineering (category 33) and in particular *Information Technology / Office Machines* (category 35).

The JTC1 database covers data from 1969 onwards. That is, it includes data from ISO TC97, the predecessor of JTC1. Data has been systematically and rigorously gathered since 1998. Earlier data can be conflicting or missing[12]. For example, during our research the edition number of a standard sometimes turned out to be incorrect (e.g. 8482 and 11801), was not included (e.g. 1155, 2593, 1860), or the same standards document was included twice because it was assigned to different ICS areas (e.g. 948, 962,1092-1). However, as far as we are aware, this is exception rather than rule. Moreover, due to the large number of documents the statistical significance of our results is not affected.

We mainly used SPSS 11.5 software as our statistical tool, sometimes next to and in combination with a spreadsheet program. To acquire overall insight in the scale and characteristics of standards dynamics, primarily descriptive statistics (e.g. frequencies and cross tabulations), variance analysis (e.g. ANOVA and Kruskal-Wallis test), and post-hoc tests (e.g. Tamhane test) were used. The reason for choosing specific analyses will be discussed on a case-by-case basis.

Lastly, some choices had to be made. As the reader will see, in all graphs the year 2004 is excluded because of the moment the data was gathered (mid-August). Furthermore, sometimes the area which a standard covers is addressed by a set of document parts. In the following these parts are treated as original, separate standards departing from the idea that for the purpose of examining standards dynamics it is irrelevant whether an area is addressed by different standards (different reference numbers) or by different standards parts (which share the same reference number).

4. Results

The JTC1 database contains 2752 documents. 2318 of them are international standards (ISs), 264 are international standardized profiles (ISPs) and 170 are technical reports (TRs). These are in the following referred to as standards unless explicitly stated. The 2752 documents consist of active and withdrawn documents, different types of revisions and replacements, original documents and supplements, and old and new editions.

Below, we examine these features of standards dynamics in a straightforward manner; i.e. by treating all documents on a par (level 1 analysis). This serves, in particular, to gain insight in developments over time. Some of the level 1 findings are later studied in more detail by aggregating the data on main documents (level 2 analysis; Egyedi & Heijnen, 2005).

---

[12] Private communication ISO Secretariat.

Dynamics Overall

The total amount of documents published per year increased considerably from 1990 onwards, peaks slightly in the year 1992 and more pronounced in 1995, and decreases after that. See Figure 1.

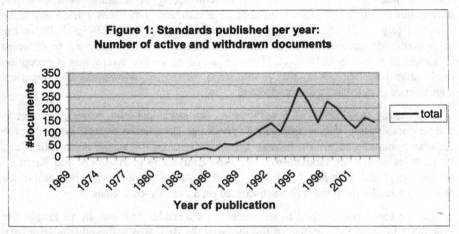

Figure 1: Standards published per year: Number of active and withdrawn documents

This can largely be explained by the following factors:

- a phase of Eurocentrism (1985-1992) in formal international standards bodies in the period leading up to 1992;

- support for the OSI standards trajectory by the formal SDOs and the market uptake of competing Internet protocols from the early 1990s onwards;

- a radical increase and competition from standards consortia in the field of ICT from 1995 onwards; and the possible emergence of a new equilibrium.

More specifically, the peak in 1992 coincides with the prior deadline of the European Commission to remove technical barriers to trade and achieve a harmonized Common Market. In the period leading up to December 1992, the Commission acquired the support of the European formal standards bodies for delivering the necessary standards in the given time frame (e.g. by means of mandates). European standardization gathered momentum. Ties with the international standards level were tightened. Formal international standardization passed through a phase of Eurocentrism (Egyedi, 1996). See box 1. That is, European developments could well explain the increase in international activity in and around 1992.

Taking a closer look at the peak in 1995 (N=286), 60% (N=172) of the documents published in that year are OSI-related (ICS 35.100). Many of them are

ISPs (N=104).[13] We assume that this flurry of OSI activity is at least partly caused by the rising popularity of a competing network solution: Internet (e.g. Abbate, 1994). From 1993 onwards implementations of Internet protocols (TCP/IP, SMTP, etc.) are fast gaining ground.

Lastly, we hypothesize that the decline in number of JTC1 standards published after 1995 is related to the exponential growth of the number of standards consortia in the second half of the 1990s (Hawkins, 1999). Where previously many newly founded fora and consortia adapted to or were assimilated in the overall formal structure (Genschel, 1993), they played a more competitive role from the mid-1990s onward. That is, they were pinned as competitors in the discourse about timely and effective standardization. Although perhaps too early to say, it seems as if the decline in the number of JTC1 standards published per year seems to have come to a halt. This suggests that an equilibrium has been reached between JTC1 and the IT consortia in respect to standards work. (NB: Possibly the argument can be extended beyond the number of consortium standards, relative to formal standards, to the number of consortia, relative to formal bodies. Indirect support is provided by Blind & Gauch (2005), who note that the number of consortia most relevant for European IT standardization (i.e. CEN/ISSS) is declining.)

Withdrawals

Currently, 1762 of the 2752 standards that have been published in the past are still active, while 990 have been withdrawn (see Table 1). Figure 1 shows the absolute number of standards published per year, part of which are still active and part of which have later been withdrawn. The withdrawal line follows the overall pattern of standards published and shows a 'bump' in the period 1992-1995. We have to keep in mind that, in general, older standards are more likely to have been withdrawn than standards just published – in absolute numbers. How many standards have been withdrawn per year proportionate to the total number of standards published? Figure 2 shows an irregular pattern in the period before 1989. Very few standards were published then (e.g. only one was published in 1969 and ultimately withdrawn). If we disregard this period, a clear trend emerges. This, too, is interesting. For one could expect that due to the extra time pressure and workload in 1992 and 1995 JTC1 might have developed less robust standards, that is, standards which would sooner require a new edition – and, thus, also a withdrawal of the old one. Moreover, a shortening of standards development time (see Table 5) also seems not to have impacted the withdrawal rate.

---

[13] E.g. the ISP 10609 on Connection-mode Transport Service over connection-mode Network Service (N=27).

Box 1: Eurocentrism and the Cooperation Agreements between formal European and International standards bodies.

In the period leading up to 1992 European Common Market deadline three cooperation agreements between European and International standards bodies were developed: the IEC-CENELEC *Agreement on exchange of technical information between both organisations* (1989), the IEC-CENELEC *Agreement on common planning of new work and parallel voting* (1991) and the *Agreement on technical cooperation between ISO and CEN* (Vienna Agreement, 1991). Two features in these agreements are of interest. Firstly, if a European body contemplates new standards work, it first ascertains that the work cannot be accomplished within an international standards body. Secondly, international draft standards (DIS) automatically become European drafts (prEN). The drafts are voted upon in parallel internationally and on the European level. Likewise a European prEN is put to a parallel vote at the international level.

The agreements offer the European partners the possibility to intervene in international standardization where work items of European origin show slow progress. In the IEC/CENELEC agreement (1991, p.6) a failure of planning is cited as grounds for withdrawing an item and proceeding its standardization at the European level. Between ISO and CEN, apart from timing reasons of technical and procedural nature are also noted as grounds for intervention. ("CEN reaffirms the primacy of international standardization work, (...) and use of international results wherever possible, (...). However, it is to be acknowledged that CEN (...) chooses, according to the advice of its interested parties, amongst (..) possibilities (...)."[14]. At stake is a conditional commitment of the European partners, a conditionality based on reference to European mandates and standards for European regulatory purposes.

Type of standard document	Stage in life-cycle		Total
	still active	withdrawn	
International Standard	1418	900	2318
Int. Stand. Profile	223	41	264
Technical Report	121	49	170
Total	1762	990	2752

Table 1. *Standard documents active and withdrawn*

[14] Revised "Guidelines for TC/SC Chairmen and Secretariats for implementation of the Agreement on technical cooperation between ISO and CEN", 1992, p.2.

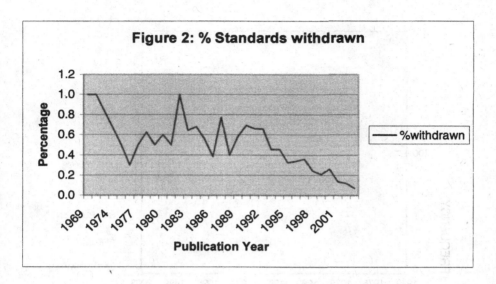

Figure 2: % Standards withdrawn

In the above, we focused on year of publication. If we look at the withdrawal line in figure 3, the number of withdrawn documents increases with periodic spurts, roughly proportionate to the overall number of publications, shows a sharp decline in 2001-2002, and a sudden increase again in 2003. Of interest is that two other features of standards dynamics share the dip in 2001, which is something to be examined further.

In respect to standards dynamics, the year of withdrawal is in most respects more informative than the publication year. It is e.g. a partial indicator of maintenance activity over time. In the following we will therefore focus on year of withdrawal unless explicitly stated otherwise.

Revisions

Revisions may concern new editions of single documents, changes of document type, integration of or a split into several documents, etc. Some documents *revise* previous documents and are later themselves *revised by* new documents. For example, part 4 of IS 7816 (7816-4), active since 1995, is in 2004 revised by a new part 4, a part 5, a part 8 and a part 9 (Table 2). Table 2 shows that the new part 9 of standard 7816, which is active since 2004-06-11, revises and integrates several other parts as well as part 4, including the amendments and corrigenda belonging to these parts.

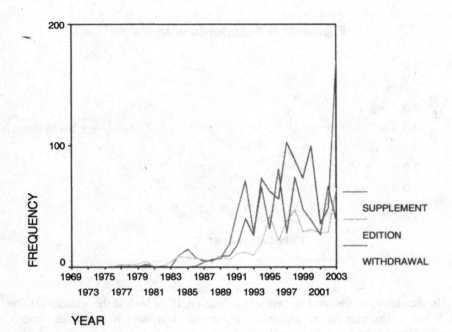

Figure 3. *Changes over time: Supplements (by publication date), Editions (by publication date) and Withdrawals (by withdrawal date).*

Reference	Stage Started	Revised by	Stage/Started	
ISO/IEC 7816-4:1995	9092	ISO/IEC 7816-5	6000	2004-10-21
(id 14738)	2001-02-23	ISO/IEC 7816-4	6000	2004-11-19
JTC 1/SC 17/WG 4		ISO/IEC 7816-8:2004	6060	2004-06-11
		ISO/IEC 7816-9:2004	6060	2004-06-11

Table 2. *Example of a forward document revision ("revised by"). (Source: ISO Secretariat, 26-11-2004)*

Reference	Stage Started	Revises	Stage/Started	
ISO/IEC 7816-9:2004	6060	ISO/IEC 7816-9:2000	9599	2004-06-11
(id 37990)	2004-06-11	ISO/IEC 7816-4:1995	9092	2001-02-23
JTC 1/SC 17/WG 4		ISO/IEC 7816-5:1994	9092	2000-02-10
		ISO/IEC 7816-6:1996	9599	2004-05-21
		ISO/IEC 7816-8:1999	9599	2004-06-11
		ISO/IEC 7816-4:1995/Amd 1:1997	6060	1997-12-18
		ISO/IEC 7816-5:1994/Amd 1:1996	6060	1996-12-19
		ISO/IEC 7816-6:1996/Cor 1:1998	9599	2004-05-21
		ISO/IEC 7816-6:1996/Amd 1:2000	9599	2004-05-21

Table 3. *Example of a backward document revision ("revises"). (Source: ISO Secretariat, 26-11-2004.)*

In all, 999 documents have been "revised by" another. 559 documents have revised one or more others. The difference between the two numbers indicates that integration and merging occurs more often than splitting up documents.

Replacements

From the administrative angle, there are two types of replacements[15]. Firstly, those standards which have been given a new document number but which are still of the same document type. There are 109 such cases, all published between 1980 and 2004. Salient is that 70 of them were published all in one year (i.e. 1994).

Secondly, some replacements keep their number but change document type: there are 23 of those, all published between 1988-2004.

Supplements

Of all documents one quarter (25.7%, N=708) is a supplementary document: Corrigendum (N=413), Amendment (N=278), or Addendum (N=17). See Table 4. (NB: Addenda were only published between 1977 and 1991. See figure 5.)

The use of supplementary documents really starts in 1990. From then on the amount of supplements remains rather stable over the years - although it can vary strongly per year. See Figure 3. Also in proportion to the total number of standards the number of supplements remains rather stable, the years 1992 (50%) and 1995 (10%) excepted. See Figure 4.

Supplement	Frequency	Percent
0	2044	74.3
Corrigendum	413	15.0
Amendment	278	10.1
Addendum	17	.6
Total	2752	100.0

Table 4. *Supplements*

---

[15] Source: Printout provided by the ISO Secretariat (26-11-2004).

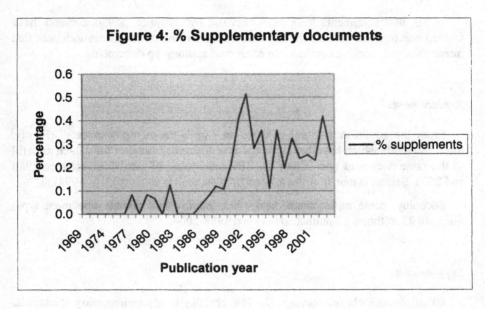

There are different explanations possible for the steep incline in 1991, explanations which have very different implications (see conclusion). Firstly, the steep incline partly coincides with the overall response to the challenge posed by the European 1992-Common Market requirements. That is, it roughly fits in with the general pattern.

Secondly, between 1989 and 1992 ISO/IEC procedures were adapted to hasten up the process from 7 to 3 years for a draft IS. See Table 5. Possibly the use of supplements has become a structural post hoc measure to compensate for 'too hasty' or, more positively formulated, 'efficient' standards development.

From date of inclusion project in program of work to	1989	1992
Working Draft stage	2 years	1.5 years
Committee Draft stage	5 years	2 years
Draft International Standard stage	7 years	3 years

Table 5. *Designated time for standards development (ISO/IEC, 1989, 1992)*

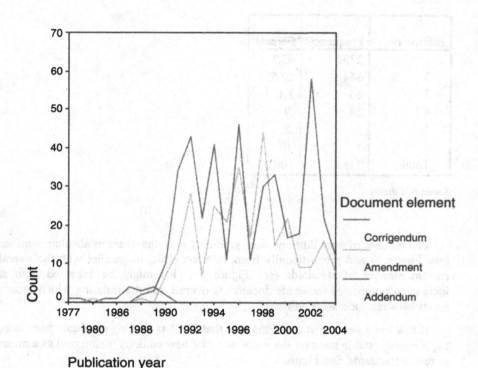

Figure 5. *Supplementary documents specified*

Thirdly, parallel to devising procedures that shortened the standards process, standards review and maintenance procedures may have been professionalized. This assumption needs to be checked. However, if so, where errors were dealt with in an implicit manner before (e.g., perhaps they were hidden in new editions, informally passed on by mouth, etc.), a more professional approach to maintenance would then suddenly uncover more problems, part of which may then have been addressed by supplementary documents.

Lastly, supplements are hardly re-issued as new editions. However, they do undergo change. Roughly an equal amount is active (46.8%) as is withdrawn (53.2%). This differs significantly from other documents, of which only 30.0% is withdrawn.

Editions

Of the 2752 documents most documents are first editions (N=2292). See Table 6 below. Only 16.7% are higher editions (edition 2-6).

Edition no.	Frequency	Percent
1	2292	83.3
2	344	12.5
3	86	3.1
4	24	.9
5	5	.2
6	1	.0
Total	2752	100.0

Table 6. *Edition*

The number of new Editions rises gradually over the years in absolute numbers (see Figure 3) and proportionally from 1990 onwards, in parallel with the overall rise in number of standards (see Figure 6). This might be expected with an increasing number of standards documents overall and the time lag which usually exists between successive editions.

If this trend persists, it could indicate that JTC1 is shifting emphasis from using supplements (stable use over the years) to using new editions (rising use) as a means to revise standards. See Figure 3.

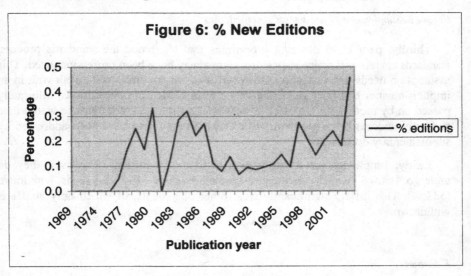

First editions are, as might be expected, more often withdrawn (N=861) (37.6%) than higher editions (N=129). About a quarter of all higher editions is withdrawn (28%).

Sum of Changes over Time

Table 7 summarizes the amount of change in absolute numbers per feature of standards dynamics.

Features of standards dynamics	Sub-category	N	Ref. date of data source
Withdrawals		990	14-07-2004
Revisions	Is revised by	999	26-11-2004
	Revises	559	26-11-2004
Replacements	New number/ same document type	109	20-07-2004
	Same number / new document type	23	20-07-2004
Supplements		708	14-07-2004
Editions 2-6		460	14-07-2004

Table 7. *Summary of amount of change at stake*

The figure 7 shows the sum of (the absolute number of) changes per year, including replacements but excluding revisions (see earlier explanation). If we contrast the number of changes (figure 7) to the number of documents that have remained stable (figure 8), we can conclude that the proportion of maintenance work done in JTC1 outruns pure standards development work in respect to the number of actions taken [16].

---

[16] This is the case even given the overlap between the number of new editions and the number of withdrawals which this mostly accompanies (the provisionally retained editions excepted). Whether the conclusion also applies for the volume of work done in JTC1 is a different matter, requires different data, but would seem less likely.

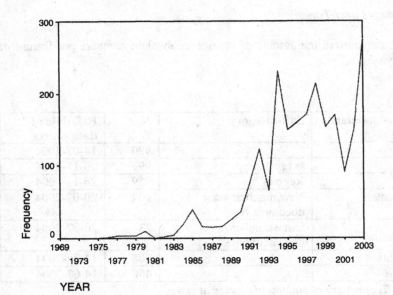

Figure 7. Sum of changes per year: withdrawals, new editions, supplements and replacement.

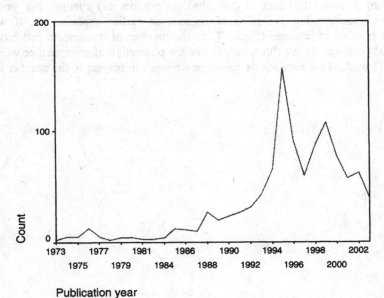

Figure 8. *Still active first editions of main documents (no supplements)*

5. Conclusion

In this paper we explored the scale of standards dynamics, or, worded differently, the degree of stability of standards. Standards bodies address such issues under the headings of 'standards maintenance'. For example, apart from the normal review procedures, JTC1 has procedures that specifically address the need for stable standards (*provisionally retained editions*) and implicitly refer to the lack thereof (i.e. *stabilized standards*). The latter procedure is largely used for securing the continuous availability of Open Systems Interconnection (OSI) standards.

Throughout the years JTC1 has published 2752 standard documents. Since 1995 there has been a steady decrease, a decrease which coincides with an increase of standards from standards consortia. This decline seems to have come to a halt, which suggests that a new equilibrium between the two standard setting environments is emerging.

If the number of changes to in JTC1 standards is anything to go by, maintenance work outruns initial standards development work. Most changes are due to withdrawals, revisions and supplements. There are relatively few replacements and new editions.

To highlight the main results of the analyses of dynamic features:

Supplements. Since the sharp increase in the relative use of supplements towards 1992, a development which corresponds to the 1992 deadline of the European Common Market, their use has been consolidated. Supplements are systematically used as a post hoc measure for correcting errors. For a certain category of work items standardization is becoming a two-step process: a rough main document developed in consensus followed later on by a supplement that clarifies ambiguities, etc. This is a point for follow-up research.

Withdrawals. One could expect that the time pressure of the 1992 deadline, changes in standards procedures and the radical cut-down of standards development time which this has led to, and the extra workload in 1995, together, this would have negatively affected the quality and appropriateness of the standards published in that period –and would have led to early withdrawals. However, the standards published in this period are not more prone to withdrawal than in other periods.

Editions. As noted, the (proportional) use of supplements has remained rather stable over the years. In 2003 it equals the proportional use of new editions, which has been rising steadily these last years. If both trends persist, it means that JTC1 is changing maintenance strategy and is shifting from using supplements to using new editions as a means to revise standards. Could this be the case? If so, it becomes of interest to determine whether new editions or supplements are the lesser problem of standards dynamics.

The paper provides some answers regarding the scale of standards dynamics. But at the same time it raises several new questions, new questions about the scale of standards dynamics (e.g. average age of standards, etc.), and about causes of standards dynamics (e.g. whether technology area determines dynamics, etc.). We address some of these issues in Egyedi & Heijnen (2005) , and hope to address others in ongoing work.

Acknowledgements

The work on which this paper is based was done in the framework of an EU project (NO-REST) and for Sun Microsystems. The authors would like to thank both the European Commission and Sun Microsystems for their financial support, and ISO for making the research possible at all.

References

Abbate, J. (1994). *From ARPANET to INTERNET: A history of ARPA-sponsored computer networks, 1966-1988.* Dissertation. University of Pennsylvania.

Best, Jan-Pascal van (2001). "IPv6 standardization issues", in: Dittrich, K. and Egyedi, T.M., eds. *Standards, Compatibility and Infrastructure Development. Proceedings of the 6th EURAS Workshop.* June 2001, Delft University of Technology, Delft.

Blind, K. & S. Gauch (forthcoming). *Trends in ICT Standards in European Standardization Bodies and Standards Consortia.*

Egyedi, T.M. (1996). *Shaping Standardization: A study of standards processes and standards policies in the field of telematic services.* Dissertation. Delft, the Netherlands: Delft University Press.

Egyedi, T.M. & P. Heijnen (forthcoming 2005). "Scale of Standards Dynamics: Change in formal, international IT standards", in S. Bolin (Ed.), *The Standards Edge: Future Generation.* Bolin Communications.

Egyedi, T.M. & A.G.A.J. Loeffen (2002). 'Succession in standardization: grafting XML onto SGML', *Computer Standards & Interfaces, 24,* pp.279-290.

Farrell, J. & G. Saloner, "Co-ordination through Committees and Markets," *RAND Journal of Economics,* vol. 19, no. 2, 1988, pp.235-252.

Gauch, S. (forthcoming). *+ vs. -: Impacts and Dynamics of Competing Standards of Recordable DVD-Media.* To be presented at the Interop-ESA conference, i.c. the Workshop on 'Interoperability Standards - Implementation, Dynamics, and Impact', Geneva, 22 February 2005.

Genschel, Ph. (1993). *Institutioneller Wandel in der Standardisierung van Informationstechnik.* Dissertation. University of Köln, Germany.

Hawkins, R. (1999). 'The rise of consortia in the information and communication technology industries: emerging implications for policy', *Telecommunications Policy, 23,* pp.159-173.

ISO (2004). *ISO Catalogue 2004*. Geneva, Switzerland.

ISO/IEC (1989). *ISO/IEC Directives*. ISO: Geneva.

ISO/IEC (1992). *ISO/IEC Directives*. ISO: Geneva.

ISO/TMB (2004). ISO Technical Management Board, 'Re-adoption of withdrawn standards and simultaneous transition into stabilized status', TMB Secretariat, Vote/Information-Form, 6/204, 2004-01-21.

Jakobs, K. (forthcoming). *Installation of an IEEE 802.11 WLAN in a Large University Setting: A Case Study*. To be presented at the Interop-ESA conference, i.c. the Workshop on 'Interoperability Standards - Implementation, Dynamics, and Impact', Geneva, 22 February 2005.

JTC1 (2004). *ISO/IEC Directives*. 5th Edition. ISO/IEC: Geneva, Switzerland.

Kindleberger, C. P. (1983). "Standards as Public, Collective and Private Goods", *Kyklos*, vol. *36*, 1983, pp. 377-96.

Mansell, R. & R. Hawkins (1992). Old Roads and New Signposts: Trade Policy Objectives in Telecommunication Standards. In: F. Klaver & P. Slaa (Eds.), *Telecommunication, New Signposts to Old Roads*. Amsterdam: IOS Press, pp.45-54.

Schmidt, S.K., & R. Werle (1998). Co-ordinating Technology. Studies in the International Standardization of Telecommunications. Cambridge, Mass.: MIT Press.

Abbreviations

Amd	Technical Amendment
CCITT	Comité Consultatif International Télégraphique et Téléphonique (predecessor of ITU-T)
CEN	Comité Européen de Normalisation
CEN/ISSS	CEN/Information Society Standardization System
CENELEC	Comité Européen de Normalisation Electrotechnique
Cor	Technical Corrigendum
DIS	Draft International Standard
Ed.	Edition
ETSI	European Telecommunications Standards Institute
ICS	International Classification for Standards
ICT	Information and Communication Technology
IEC	International Electrotechnical Commission
IEEE	Institute of Electrical and Electronics Engineers
IETF	Internet Engineering Task Force
IP	Internet Protocol
IS	International Standard
ISO	International Organization for Standardization
ISP	International Standardized Profile
IT	Information Technology
ITU-T	International Telecommunication Union – Telecom Standardization

	sector
JTC1	ISO/IEC Joint Technical Committee 1
OSI	Open Systems Interconnection
RFC	Request for Comments ("Internet standard" are also RFCs)
SDO	Standards Development Organization
SGML	Standard Generalized Markup Language
TCP/IP	Transmission Control Protocol/Internet Protocol
TR	Technical Report
W3C	World Wide Web Consortium
XML	Extensible Markup Language

Standards dynamics in the mobile communication area: Three cases

by: Eric J. Iversen* and Richard Tee**

* NIFU STEP, Norway
Hammersborg Torg 3, N-0179 Oslo, Norway
Eric.iversen@nifustep.no

** SMIT - University of Brussels, Belgium and TNO-ICT, the Netherlands)
Pleinlaan 2, 1050 Brussels, Belgium
Richard.Tee@Vub.ac.be

ABSTRACT

This paper addresses the changing role that standards play in achieving interoperability and stability. It starts with a discussion of what standards dynamics means in this context which it explores in terms of a drive towards dominant design in technology markets. Here, the paper distinguishes two main levels of standards dynamics. The first level involves adaptation of an individual standard when it is 'launched' and its subsequent interaction in the particular implementation environment. The second level involves higher order dynamics of the standard system in its adaptation to overall industry dynamics (involving technological factors, market factors, regulatory factors, etc). The paper goes on to look at three distinct cases of 'standards dynamics' in this light.

KEYWORDS
Standards dynamics, Dominant Design, Mobile Telephony, Mobile Communications

1. Introduction

It is commonly assumed that mobile communications— and the extensive standards that underpin them— develop in generations (1G, 2G, etc). The popular conception suggests an orderly development according to which standards are born and standards die, and in the meantime they develop in their interaction with their environment. This generational model builds on the conception that, "contrary to the often repeated slogans of a 'telecommunications revolution' changes in (the) information infrastructure business have come steadily, step by step, standard by standard, and not abruptly at all."(Wallenstein, 1990) At least since the last meeting of GSM created a Sub-Technical Committee to study UMTS in October 1991, a different set of standards dynamics has increasingly challenged the stability suggested by this model.

This paper analyzes the changing dynamics associated with mobile communication standards at three points. Starting with the GSM standards, the paper surveys the dynamics associated with Parlay, and Symbian, which involve different but poignant dimensions of standards dynamics. The cases represent very different types of standards representing very different modes of standardization at different points of time in the mobile communication area. The intention is to provide a triangulation of perspectives on standards dynamics. The purpose is that these perspectives can illuminate the relationship between standards dynamics and the changing business models of the actors involved, on the one hand, and, on the other, to suggest some types of impacts that standards have.

2. Flexibility and stability

Standards are an increasingly important broker of this tension between stability and the static, between flexibility and 'combinatorial explosion'. The important part is the *dynamic stability* standards contribute to the ongoing innovation. In this sense, "the question is not how things stabilize themselves in a 'static state', but how they endlessly grow and change." (Veblen, 1934: 8). On the other hand, not everything that changes is 'dynamic' in innovation. Schumpeter (1934) attached the question of 'dynamics' to the theory of economic development and thus raised it above the run of the mill changes observed during the normal running of the economy.

In this light we distinguish two levels of standards dynamics. The first level of standards dynamics involves adaptation of an individual standard when it is 'launched' and its subsequent interaction in the particular implementation environment (cf. Egyedi en Loeffen, 2001). The second level involves higher order dynamics of the standard system in its adaptation to overall industry dynamics (involving technological factors, market factors, regulatory factors, etc). This second level of dynamics includes new modes of organization of standards (e.g. competition between standards (e.g. Tetra versus Tetrapol), cooperation between standards-setting bodies (e.g. Parlay and ETSI), incorporated alliances emulating standards consortia (e.g. Symbian), as well as general tendencies to focus on middleware etc.

Such dynamics reflect a larger evolutionary process that arguably is reshaping the institutional basis for standardization within the volatile ICT markets.

3. Triangulating between three cases

The three cases demonstrate distinct aspects of the mobile environment and the role standards—broadly interpreted—play at different stages. To approach the dynamics of different modes of standards it is useful to distinguish between 'structural aspects' and 'process aspects' of the procedures that gave rise to (versions of) the standards. (Schmidt & Werle (1998):

- Where did the process take place? On markets, among firms, by committees.
- Why was standardization initiated? To establish technical compatibility, to promote competitive advantage, to fulfill a regulatory mandate, etc
- How different stakeholders were involved to influence or 'shape' the standard?
- What was the outcome? And what was its relationship to product (or service) structures?

We now go on to consider GSM, Parlay, and Symbian cases in terms of standards dynamics they demonstrate. Drawing on Schmidt & Werle, we review where the process took place, why standardization activities were initiated, how different stakeholders were involved to influence or 'shape' the standard, and what the outcome was and how it related to product (or service) structures.

3.1. Dynamics of the GSM standards

The relationship between the changing environment for mobile communications and the dynamics of standards is particularly pronounced in the case of the "Global System for Mobile-communications" (GSM). The standardization of GSM is often contrasted against the more fragmented US experience as a European success story for the coordinative power of the traditional committee-based standardization process. This comprehensive set of standards demonstrates particularly how this success played out in terms of second-level dynamics, influencing significant changes in the industry and, indeed, in society. The case also demonstrates significant first-level dynamics, as the GSM standards led to a two-phase release and an attempt to build in a hand-over to a follow-up 3G set of standards.

3.1.1 General dimensions

GSM is the widely known 'second generation' cellular radio-communications technology which was developed in Europe during the 1980s and 90s and which has since successfully spread to over a hundred countries. Our starting point is that GSM represents a product of the formal standardization regime in Europe. The initiation of GSM was firmly rooted in the monopoly-provider paradigm of European telecoms.

3.1.2 Involved Actors, Motives & General Strategies

Three main types of actors became involved in the standardization of GSM during the course of its decade-long evolution. One important feature of this evolution in fact is that participation changed fundamentally during the course of the process. In the formative stage, the PTTs (with the participation of their associated equipment manufacturers) were brought together by common interests as national monopolists. Their concerns were to reduce the uncertainty of which radio-communications technology would win, to increase the potential of a large European market, and to maintain monopoly rents.

Equipment manufacturers were first formally involved in the standards after the PTTs had agreed among themselves to a Memorandum of Understanding (MoU in 1987). At this point equipment manufacturers were invited to tender for equipment in a set of countries on the terms laid out in the MoU. Equipment manufacturers were attracted by some of the same motives as the PTTs; they wanted to avoid the uncertainty about the winning technology and they wanted to realize the scale economies promised by a European system. In several prominent cases, there were traditional allegiances between the equipment manufacturers and the national PTTs. (Ericsson, Nokia, Siemens, Alcatel) The fifth main equipment manufacturer (Motorola) held a wild-card position: its home-market was outside the EU, it had pioneered certain aspects of radio-communications, and the structure of its markets were different (technically and geographically) from the other actors. It was interested in strengthening its position in Europe while limiting the potential for competition with its other markets (for example the US).

The third main actor was the European Commission whose active support for the GSM standards became visible in the mid 1980s. This support began to materialize in the face of a variety of national strategies bent on taking a leading role in the standardization process. The Commission's interest in the GSM was primarily to promote a unified European market. During the de-regulation of telecoms in the late 1980s, it also became a vehicle to promote a tentative opening of markets to competition. In addition, the GSM system held a series of links to other technologies that the Commission had invested in: links with the chips industry (ESPRIT) and Integrated Services Digital Network (ISDN), an indirect link with the RACE program. European involvement sent a powerful signal about the importance of the system and its success.

3.1.3 The standardization process

In many ways the GSM case involved a very comprehensive standardization process. The process involved a wider systems-building project in which technical, political and institutional aspects of the system were engineered in great detail. The epicenter for this work was the committee-based standardization environment of CEPT and later ETSI, where the design for the digital mobile system was negotiated according to five basic sets of requirements. (cost aspects, network aspects, radio-frequency utilization, service, and quality of service and security) The process took more than a decade.

The specifications cover all aspects of the mobile-system, from switching (NSS), to radio transmission and reception, to channel coding, to terminal specifications to service recommendations etc. Further, they encompass two phases of the system's deployment (phase #1 and #2: see the timeline below) and include the specifications for a related PCS network at 1800MHz (DCS1800; 'delta specs').

Many actors became involved in the standardization process over time. The standardization process went from being a closed process (in CEPT), to an open multi-actor standard (in ETSI).

3.1.4 Split specifications

GSM actually consists of a set of specifications which evolved both during the initial elaboration and after. The GSM family is built up of a small set of members[1]. One dimension of the GSM standards was that it was not born fully formed but became a two-phase adoption which emerged under way. The dynamics of this comprehensive set of standards rather were changed during the considerable elaboration period to become a two phase process, based on the emergence of difficulties as well as new requirements. The family also involves a generational dimension which reaches back to some extent to existing systems, but which explicitly involved a succession to UMTS.

Several dimensions of the standardization process are important in order to understand the dynamics of the case. These include the circumstances of its initiation, its institutional grounding, its technological scope and degree of specification, its duration, its intended effect, and its impact.

3.1.5 First level Dynamics

The GSM case represents a comprehensive standardization process involving quite active first-level dynamics. The technological, the regulatory, and the commercial environment changed drastically from the early 1980s to the mid 1990s. Given the rate of change in the ICT area during this time, it was impossible for those involved to predict key dimensions of the final set of standards: capacity questions and the commercial demand for the technology was consistently underestimated. In this setting, a certain level of flexibility was necessary to provide the stability required for the GSM system to be successfully deployed and to spread. The list below consolidates salient aspects of the first-level dynamics of this important standard:
- Segmented original elaboration into phases in order to deal with contingencies while meeting deadlines
    - Coordination between phase 1 and 2 (freezing development in order to develop test specifications,

---

[1] The principal member of the family is the GSM-900 system (at 900 MHZ with a frequency allocation of twice 25 MHz). The GSM standards were extended in 1990 (the Delta Specs) to specify a system at 1800 MHz (with a frequency allocation of twice 75 MHz) for urban areas. In addition, the PCS-1900 and GSM-400 systems were adapted as well.

- o The rapid technological development (speech codecs) which ran concurrent to the long standardization process made
- Expansion of mandate under way (DCS 1800) with implications for other markets
- Developed organizational principles to coordinate launch (GSM MoU).
- Conclusion of GSM leads to the initiation of 'next generation' standards. These run into a set of contingencies themselves. The tail of GSM is seen in UMTS, TETRA, GPRS, GPP and beyond.

3.1.6 Second-level dynamics

The success of the GSM furthermore involved a unique case for second-level dynamics. The case is integral to the wider dynamics affecting the industry and involving the institutional organization of standardization.

- The evolution of the standards concurrent with the move from the 'monopoly provider paradigm' in Europe towards regional re-regulation.
- GSM had deep impacts for the global mobile market which has fundamentally affected market constellations, users and service providers, etc.
- Involvement of new players in the standardization process
- Links to other national markets, beginning with Australia
- Industrial renewal (especially the Nokia and Ericsson effect)
- Revenue reorientation and the basis for new services (including the SMS effect)
- Sparks the touchstone for conflict between standardization and IPRs

3.2 Dynamics of the Parlay Gateway standards

The Parlay case emerged at the end of the 1990s into a much different environment (in technological and market terms) than the changing environment in which GSM was initiated. This was a period that mobile communications, according to the generational model, should have been gearing up for the move towards 3G. The general proposition behind Parlay is the familiar concern of how to encourage the development of next-generation services and applications. The concern is common to IT vendors, network equipment providers, and application developers, as well as users. This concern is however particularly strong for the network operators who are already heavily invested in improving their networks (3G) but have not begun to see the new services that would generate new revenue.

3.2.1 General dimensions

The Parlay Group is a not-for-profit open multi-vendor consortium which was initiated by a community of operators, IT vendors, network equipment providers, and application developers in 1998-1999. The goal is to develop application programming interfaces (APIs) at the frontier between telecom and IT worlds that are open and technology- independent. The intention is to enable, "a wide range of actors to develop applications and technology solutions that operate across multiple networking platform environments the latest deployments of Next Generation services and applications, from Europe, Asia and North America."(source. http://www.parlay.org)

3.2.2 Involved Actors, Motives & General Strategies

Parlay was originally founded by a multi-vendor group in which network operators were central (number). The Board of Directors reflects a balance between network operators (BT, Orange/France Telecom, NTT) and different vendors (IBM, Ericsson, Alcatel). Its membership (2004-2005) consists of about 70 companies which it classes in the following way: independent software vendors (ISVs), software developers, network device vendors and providers, service bureaus, application service providers (ASPs), and other large and small companies.   It claims to have grown 10% during the last year.

The founders of the Parlay Group indicate that their objective of creating a gateway did not fit well with the existent standards development organizations, of which they were members (e.g. ETSI). The standards development organizations were reportedly more oriented towards platform standards, and this was one of the impetuses that led to the new consortium. The Group has however maintained and developed links with established standards development organizations, especially ETSI, as well as more recent consortia such as JAIN and the SIP forum. A chief way to actively link with other bodies is through the Parlay Joint Working Group (JWG), which collaborates in the elaboration of Parlay specifications. The JWG includes the Third Generation Partnership Program (3GPP), the Third Generation Partnership Program 2 (3GPP2), and the European Telecommunications Standards Institute (ETSI) Services and Protocols for Advanced Networks. Latest versions of Parlay 4.1, are developed jointly with ETSI and 3GPP, with cooperation from JAIN community member companies. The specifications are in fact co-published with ETSI.The linkages with standards suppliers are apparently strengthening, with ETSI collaborating and co-publishing the latest version of Parlay/OSA.   Parlay has implications for what at one time could protect network operator hegemony over developments of services and applications, but now seems more of a limitation. The APIs take pressure off operators to develop or co-develop the new traffic generating services. The gateway means among other things that development of these services no longer has to involve specialized programmers (telecom protocols), of which there are far fewer than IT programmers (human capital, below). This is one factor that lowers the cost of development.

3.2.3 Standards process

The Parlay/OSA (Open Service Architecture) standard defines API (application programming interfaces). The OSA is in its fourth consecutive version. These versions evolve after feedback from industry. A fifth version is on the table. This architecture acts as a gateway bringing together intelligent network services with IT applications at a 'secure, measured, and billable interface.' The gateway is technology neutral, and can work on services developed for fixed, mobile, as well as IP based networks. Examples of APIs include, account management, charging and connectivity managers under version 3.3., to interfaces for availability management etc under Parlay 4.0.

The OSA gateway allows developers to work in different programming language environments including C, C++, and Java. It also tries to compliment other standard protocols and technologies such as CORBA, IDL, UML, and Web Services (SOAP, XML and WSDL), SIP (Session Initiation Protocol) and JAIN (Java APIs for Intelligent Networks). The standardized gateway allows for the development of customized but secure telecom services for fixed and mobile operators.

3.2.4 First level Dynamics

The Parlay/OSA has reached version 5 in the course of 6 years. The first level dynamics of fairly rapid version turn-over is the need to expand into new areas (web services), to keep up with changes in the protocols with which Parlay gateways, and to meet more the evolving interest of implementers.

Level 1 standards dynamics
- Defining API (application programming interfaces) to gateway telecom protocols to IT platforms, spanning multiple networking platforms
- Group with broad member-base and links to other standards bodies/activities
- Institutionalizing an active and deliberate approach to evolve specifications through revisions and enhancements
  - Emphasis on rapid procedures and adaptability to environment: Parlay 4.1 and Parlay –x Web services 1 (2003), Parlay5 around the corner. (6 years)
- Focus on implementations as well as active marketing or 'educational' activities to actively encourage take up

3.2.5 Second-level dynamics

The Parlay Group represents an interest set of dynamics in the market for standards. The group first represents the drive to create a consortium, which have been a prominent mode for organizing standardization activities in the late 1990s. In this case, the founding companies went outside established standards development organizations avowedly because their objective of creating a gateway did not fit well with the more traditional route. The standards development organizations were reportedly more oriented towards platform standards, and this was one of the impetuses that led to the new consortium. Parlay also witnesses to a second side of the changing market for standards, namely the linking between activities in different standards environments. Parlay testifies to an active alliance building where the group has grown by embracing and developing links with established standards development organizations, especially ETSI, as well as more recent consortia such as JAIN and the SIP forum. A chief way to actively link with other bodies is through the Parlay Joint Working Group (JWG), which collaborates in the elaboration of Parlay specifications.

Level 2 standards dynamics
- Evolution of gateway standards leads to evolving the standardization environment
    - initiative reportedly not accommodated by existing SDOs, which were more oriented towards platform standards)
- Active linkages with other standards suppliers over time through the Parlay Joint Working Group (JWG).
- Cooperation with the activities of other bodies has become more active over time.
    - Latest versions of Parlay 4.1, are developed jointly with ETSI and 3GPP, with cooperation from JAIN community member companies, with ETSI collaborating and co-publishing the latest version.

3.3. Dynamics of the Symbian 'standards'

The final case represents a special type of dynamics in the market for standards which is significantly unlike the technological coordination involved in GSM. As with Parlay, the actors behind Symbian went outside the traditional standards environment. In this case, the founding actors—which compete in other markets—set up a company substantially based on the technology of one of the parties. The joint-venture mode to adapt an existing technology to the needs of a set of actors provides a distinct approach where the aim is to set a broadly applied standard. At base this mode attempts to provide maximum control over development (a company) while attempting to promote a high degree of coordination in very competitive environment (competitive companies inside the alliance, a larger competitor outside). The creation of alliances, although not new, illuminates an important area of the changing standards market. A defining aspect of this exclusive mode to standardize is partly due to the technology, an operating system for advanced mobiles which entailed a certain convergence of highly contested technology markets (PCs and mobiles). But the way the Symbian alliance was founded and the way it has developed since substantially reflects changes in the strategic landscape (the market regime). These changes lay basis for a different set of standards dynamics.

3.3.1 General dimensions

Symbian was formed June 1998, initially as a joint venture between Psion, Nokia and Ericsson. One of the main assumptions behind the alliance was that as mobile handsets were becoming increasingly more powerful, it would be beneficial to the actors involved to have a standardized technology (OS) on which it could further develop. Furthermore, it was envisaged that as mobile handsets and PDA's were thought to be converging, a strategic formation was considered a prerequisite to effectively compete against rival companies on the OS market (i.e. Microsoft).

The Symbian platform essentially consists of two components: the operating system (the Symbian OS which is currently in v9.0) and the User Interface (UI). By far the most important UI's are the Series60 UI, developed by Nokia and UIQ, developed by former Ericsson subsidiary UIQ. The separation between UI and base OS has, as commented on by certain analysts, shifted the competitional dynamics of the alliance, both inside it as well as with other platforms. The UI is by definition the direct interface (linkage) from the handset to the user. Also, since the UI can be separated from the OS, it could also be 'ported' (meaning that the source code will be partly rewritten to fit another OS) to be compatible with a different OS. Besides the separation of OS and UI, the emergence of middleware applications is also increasingly regarded as detrimental to the take-up of Symbian/smartphones. The traditional threats to the Symbian OS are traditionally regarded as competing OS's, which include Microsoft Windows Mobile, Linux, and Palm. Increasingly, other technologies which include middleware technologies, particularly Java for mobile devices (J2ME) and other middleware such as Flash Lite.

3.3.2 Involved Actors, Motives & General Strategies

The alliance has undergone a number of important changes in terms of member composition. Two events in particular are regarded as crucial events in the existence of the alliance. First, the departure of Motorola; besides giving up its financial stake, it subsequently announced a strategic partnership with Microsoft in licensing its Windows Mobile for Smartphones (WMS) platform. Next Psion opted to sell its stake, because of financial reasons. The subsequent plans of Nokia to take over Psion's part were received critically by the industry. It was taken as a sign that the alliance would evolve into a Nokia vehicle rather than a vendor neutral platform provider as was originally conceived. For Symbian as a supposedly handset neutral alliance, this is not necessarily an advantage, since it jeopardizes the idea of being vendor agnostic, and thus the willingness of other vendors to commit to or license the platform (on the other hand, the investments and commitment of Nokia have greatly benefited the alliance as well) Besides the ownership issue, Nokia has been most influential in terms of providing the UI technology for the OS.

The initial distribution of the shares was that Psion held 40 percent of the shares and the remaining 60 percent shared equally between Nokia and Ericsson. However, already at the company's launch Motorola had signed a memorandum of understanding to become a Symbian partner. When this was officially put into place Motorola's share taken from Psion's, with the three telecom vendors each having a 23.1% stake.[2] Later Matsushita (Panasonic) joined (May 1999), in April 2002 Siemens took part, and then Samsung joined as well (February 2003). Earlier on, questions were asked whether U.S. based software companies such as Microsoft or Sun would perhaps join in the future (30), but this was not foreseen, stating that all major markets (Europe, U.S., Japan and South Korea) were already represented. There were probably other motives behind this as well. From the start, Symbian was

---

[2]http://www.computerwire.co.uk/market.watch/5FF75ED112CF972380256BD50054C8DC?Open&Highlight=2,symbian

considered to be set up at least partly out of strategic reasons: for most of the vendors, having Microsoft supply a mobile operating system was not regarded as an attractive prospect.

Since its inception there have been several developments that have significantly influenced the viability of the alliance as it has been originally founded. First, one of the founders (Motorola) has sold its shares. It has not declined to release Symbian based phones but has released handsets working under the Microsoft Windows for Mobile Smartphone OS. Second, one of the main founders Psion has also announced to leave the alliance, resulting in a controversy regarding the redistribution of their shares, and also what this means for the proposed Symbian IPO that had been planned originally. Furthermore, Nokia's original proposal to take over Psion's shares has raised questions as to the vendor-neutrality of Symbian.

3.3.3 The commercial process mimicking a standard

In the case of the alliance, licensing becomes the vehicle to disseminate the product as widely as possible. Symbian has pursued this dissemination process almost as a standards consortium would. It has taking pains to disseminate the technology as widely as possible, while stressing openness and neutrality. The exact license fees of the UIs have not been officially disclosed but are said to be in the similar price range as the license cost of the OS itself. If true, this approach seems to downplay commercial concerns in favour of improving take-up.

Symbian's approach to licensing involves two dimensions: the first – relatively simple - one is getting its partners to use the OS in a range of their own devices. Since all have investments in the company, the vendors have an interest to use the product in a number of their handsets. The second, more difficult, task is getting the product licensed to other makers. The success in this area is perhaps a much better indication of the actual need for the Symbian OS. The company is gradually expanding its number of licensees, including most first tier vendors and a number of Original Device Makers (ODM), who supply the phones directly to network operators, who in turn brand the handsets themselves.[3]

In terms of licensing, there are two kinds of elements involved. The first is the Symbian OS itself, currently in its v8.0. Next to that, there is the User Interfaces (UI) a technical component that is required on top of the OS which gives the phone its 'look and feel'. As mentioned, there are two UIs of relevance here, UIQ and S60 (there are other proprietary UIs operating with Symbian, such as Nokia's S80, S90 and the Japanese FOMA Symbian phones). As mentioned, S60 is the dominant UI, estimated to drive around 85% of Symbian handsets.[4] The licensing fee of the Symbian OS is approximately $5.[5] In addition there are the costs of the UI. The costs of the license fee involved goes to the owner of the UI, which for Series60 is Nokia, and for UIQ it is Symbian (who fully owns the UIQ company). Alternatively, in non GSM markets like Japan, a device maker might consider to develop its own UI, like Panasonic has done for their FOMA handsets.

---

[3] http://www.theregister.co.uk/2004/08/04/symbian_h1_results/

[4] http://www.theregister.co.uk/2004/03/29/symbian_falters_in_battle/

[5] http://www.symbian.com/press-office/2004/pr040804.html

3.3.4 First level dynamics

As an alliance, Symbian demonstrates two notable types of first level dynamics. The first is that the 'standards' process builds on an existing proprietary technology owned by a single company. Psion's OS was in version 5.0 when Nokia and Ericsson entered the picture to create Symbian. The subsequent four versions developed within the alliance have co-developed as the membership of the Symbian alliance has substantially changed. The second type of dynamic, noted also in Parlay, is that the newer versions substantially reflect updates to interoperate with emerging standard applications and protocols. In this sense, Symbian represents a technology that strategically gateways with an increasing number of freely available standards.

-   Narrow and changing alliance membership building on top of proprietary OS (currently v9.0, starting with v5.0 developed by Psion)
-   Rapidly evolving versions of OS to strategically embrace existing and emerging messaging and connectivity standards.
-   Differentiation and branding of dependent User Interfaces on top of base OS: Series60 (Nokia) and UIQ (UIQ)

3.3.5 Second level dynamics

Symbian has some lessons to teach about the changing market for standards. This alliance can be seen as an attempt to capitalize on the coordinative capacity afforded by an open standard "consortium" while asserting ownership control of a company. This option was arguably taken under the original perception a potential 'standards war' between dominant players in the mobile handset market and in the PC market. This risk which would pit Nokia, Ericsson and Motorola in mobile handsets against Microsoft with its OS based position in the PC turned out not to be the VHS versus Betamax many feared.

The competitive dynamics turned out to be different (e.g. one competitor is coming from another non-native level of technology). As this became clear, the alliance evolved and major partners were lost. It also developed ways to coopt other interested parties and link with complementary resources through licensing conditions etc. One of the main things that the Symbian case does is to illustrate strategic questions in terms of what is happening in the 'implementation environment'.

Second level dynamics

-   Underlying standards war hypothesis:
    -   o   concerns that Microsoft would leverage dominant position onto the mobile
-   For-profit alliance involving actors who compete on other markets
    -   o   (originally Psion, Nokia, Ericsson)
    -   o   Evolving alliance involving considerable strategic behavior

- o   later joined by Motorola, Siemens, Samsung, Panasonic, SonyEricsson
- o   departure of Motorola (MS deal) and Psion (financial concerns)
- Competition from within (portable UI's) and outside Symbian via emerging middleware platforms such as J2ME and Flash Lite.

4. Conclusions

The paper explored the changing dynamics associated with mobile communication standards at three points. Starting with the GSM standards, the paper surveyed the dynamics associated with Parlay, and Symbian, which address standardization in different but poignant ways. The cases represent very different types of standards representing very different modes of standardization at different points of time in the mobile communication area. The point has not been to criticize the generational model, which after all is essentially a metaphor for successive success in establishing periods of stability through systemic standards. Rather, the cases are chosen to illustrate differences manifested in the standards themselves, which in turn reflect differences in the environments in which they were elaborated (or born) and differences in the environments in which they are implemented (or in which they are being attempted to be introduced). The three cases have demonstrated a variety of factors: the period of time that has elapsed since the technology originally stabilized or 'solidified' into a standard, the way this solidification took place, which setting it took place (and the relationship between it and the implementation environment), the degree and type of dynamics at play, the technological scope of the standard technologies, and their 'impact' where identifiable. This has provided a triangulation of perspectives on standards dynamics which illuminate the relationship between standards dynamics and the changing business models of the actors involved, on the one hand, and, on the other, suggest some types of impacts that standards have.

References

Abernathy, William J. and Utterback, James. M. (1978), *"Patterns of Industrial Innovation"*, Technology review, June-July.

Anderson, Philip and Tushman, Michael L. (1990). *Technological Discontinuities and Dominant Designs: a Cyclical Model of Technological Change.* Administrative Science Quarterly, 35:604-633.

Bresnahan, TF & Greenstein, S (1997). Technical Progress and Co-Invention in Computing and in the Use of Computers." Brookings Papers on Economics Activity: Microeconomics: pp. 1-78.

Clark, K. B (1985). *"The Interaction of Design Hierarchies and Market Concepts in Technological Evolution."* Research Policy, 14, no. 5: p235-251.

David, Paul A. (1995) Standardization policies for network technologies: the flux between freedom and order revisited. In Hawkins, R., R. Mansfield & J. Skea (Eds.). (1995) Standards, innovation and competitiveness: Edward Elgar.

Egyedi, T.M. and Loeffen, A.G.A.J.(2001) Succession in standardization: Grafting XML onto SGML. Standardization and Innovation in Information Technology, 2001 2nd IEEE

Gaillard, John. Industrial standardization: its principles and application. (H. W. Wilson Co. New York, 1934.

Haug, Thomas (2002). The Market Fragmentation in Europe and the CEPT Initiatives in 1982. in GSM and UMTS: the creation of global mobile communications. Hillebrand, F (ed)

Iversen, Eric (2001) Patenting and voluntary standards: the tension between the domain of proprietary assets and that of "public goods" in the innovation of new network technologies. Science Studies, 14. 2: 2001.

Marks & Hebner (2004). Government/Industry Interactions in the Global Standards System. In Bolin, S (ed) The Standards Edge: Dynamic Tension: 103-114.

Metcalfe, J. S. & Miles, Ian, 1994. "Standards, selection and variety: an evolutionary approach," Information Economics and Policy, Elsevier, vol. 6(3), pages 243-268, 12.

Murmann, J.P., Frenken, K. (2002). *Towards a systematic framework for research on dominant designs, technological innovations, and industrial change*, Papers on Economics and Evolution 0212, working paper, Max Planck Institute, Jena.

Rosenkopf, L. and M.L. Tushman. (1994) "*The Coevolution of Technology and Organization.*". In Baum, J. and J. Singh (eds.), Evolutionary Dynamics of Organizations, Oxford.

Schmidt, S (1992). Negotiating Technical Change through Standards: technical coordination in markets and committees, Cologne: MPLFG Discussion Paper.

Schumpeter, Joseph (1934) "The Fundamental Phenomenon of Economic Development," in Schumpeter, The Theory of Economic Development: 57-94. Schumpeter J.A. (1912), Theorie der Wirtschaftlichen Entwicklung, Leipzig: Duncker und Humbolt, English edition in 1934, The Theory of Economic Development. An Inquiry into Profits, Capital, Credit, Interest, and the Business Cycle, New Brunswick, NJ: Transaction Publishers (translated by Redvers Opie).

Tushman, M.L., and J.P. Murmann (1998) '*Dominant designs, technology cycles, and organizational outcomes*' in Research in organizational behavior. Anonymous, 231-266. Greenwich, CT: JAI Press.

Utterback, J., (1994) Mastering the Dynamics of Innovation. Harvard Business School Press, Harvard.

Veblen, Thorstein B. (1934) Essays on Our Changing Order. In Leon Ardzrooni (ed.) The Viking Press, New York

Vercoulen & van Wegberg, 1999. Standard selection modes in dynamic, complex industries: creating hybrids between market selection and negotiated selection of standards. SIIT Proceedings of the 1st IEEE Conference on Standardisation and Innovation in Information Technology SIIT '99, in Aachen, Germany, September 15-17, 1999.

Wallenstein, Gerd D (1990). Setting Global Telecommunications Standards: The Stakes, the Players and the Process. Norwood Massachusetts: Artech House.

Werle, Raymund (2000). Institutional aspects of standardizaiton: jurisdictional conflicts and the choice of standardization organizations. MPLFG Discussion Paper 00/1.

+ vs. - :

Impacts and Dynamics of competing Standards of recordable DVD-Media

Stephan Gauch
Breslauer Strasse 48
76139 Karlsruhe
Germany

stephan.gauch@isi.fraunhofer.de

ABSTRACT: *The following paper analyzes the impact and dynamics of competing standards and specifications with similar technological background by the concrete example of recordable and rewritable optical media based on Digital Versatile Disc technology. Special attention is paid to the structure of competitor networks as well as their strategic allocation of Intellectual Property assets and information flows in form of amount of specifications advanced from consortia specifications to formal standardisation bodies. Moreover, implications concerning timing of market entry and the role of installed base in the conflict are analyzed. Finally, problems of implementation and compatibility are discussed and the concept of "multiple implementation" is introduced as a strategy of stable coexistence in standards wars.*

KEY WORDS: *standards, competition, dynamics, DVD*

Every user of DVD recordable technology should by now have encountered the problem of choice among different kinds of DVD recordables and devices. Should he/she buy a device that is compatible with the official DVD-R standard or opt for a device capable of writing data to DVD+R or for a device writing both formats but at higher cost for the device? Even though these are relevant questions, the most striking question is: "Why are there two different standards for DVD recordables?". Even though this is not the main question of this paper it has to be discussed in order to answer a directly related question concerning the influence of coexisting standards on standards dynamics. The case of DVD recordable technology is in many ways a good example to analyze such questions concerning the dynamics of standards since it accounts for interesting constellations of boundary conditions: A) Competing standards with similar technological background. B) Competition among heavily networked actors involved in the development and standard-setting process. C) A diffused IPR structure among those actors that allowed two competing parties to emerge. D) Standard-setting processes on different levels of formality, ranging from specifications formed on consortia level to international ISO standards. E) Different time-to-market structures and influence of market competition on standardisation dynamics

One way of distinguishing DVD recording technology and standards is the way data is stored on the media and the consortia that back the underlying technology. The mode to store data on a medium can be differentiated into "Write Once Read Many" (WORM) by which data is stored once and then can neither be erased nor changed afterwards, and "read-write" (RW and RAM) by which data can be stored, changed or be erased at any given time. WORM media are DVD-R, DVD+R and DVD+RDL. The media with "read-write" capabilities are DVD-RAM, DVD-RW and DVD+RW. The second distinction stems from the fact that several different technological solutions for different forms of recording coexist, with two consortia producing rival specifications for DVD recordables. One consortium, the DVD Forum, produces and supports the "official" versions of the DVD recordable standards DVD-RAM, DVD-R and DVD-RW, and is in common discussions often referred to as the "slash"-camp, because of the "-" in the name of the standards. The other consortium is the DVD+RW Alliance, which supports the "inofficial" standards DVD+R and DVD+RW and is often referred to as the "plus"-camp for obvious reasons. One could assume that the different DVD recording technologies are closely related. On a very abstract level, this is even true. The DVD recording technologies for the different WORM media and the different RW media are comparable in nature. Mostly the same materials are used to build discs, laser diodes of comparable wavelength are used and physical appearance is, at least to the human eye, the same for different kinds of discs.

For an analysis of standards dynamics one of the foremost important aspects of the different standards is the constellation of IPR-holders of the competing camps and cooperation/competition structures prior to the forking of DVD Recordable standards. To understand the path dependencies that lead to that forking and to assess the consequences for dynamics of competing standards, it is essential to take a closer look at the history of the DVD standard itself.

When questions concerning a CD technology successor suitable for storing high-quality multimedia content arose in the early nineties, two competing parties both aimed at the development of a suitable medium. Two formats resulted from this. The Super Density (SD) digital video disc format developed by Matsushita, Toshiba and Time Warner and the MultiMedia Compact Disc (MMCD) format supported by the developers of CD technology: Sony and Philips. While the SD presented a double-side approach with 5GB of data to be stored per side, the MMCD could store 3.7GB of data, was single-sided in design. Apart from differences in storage capacity technical differences concerned the approach to either use a single substrate layer with a thickness of 1.2 mm or two substrate layers with a thickness of 0.6 mm bonded together by an adhesive. This approach resulted in the MMCD format being closer to CD Technology than the SD format. Apart from technical design both formats differed in support of actors that could influence the success or failure of either technology. Whereas on the one hand the motion picture industry supported SD, due to a foreseeable support by Time Warner and the higher storage capacity, the manufacturing industry on the other hand favoured MMCD, since the technology was closer to established CD technology, which meant that production facilities needed only slight modifications to produce MMCD media. This posed potential problems to both camps. In case the movie industry would stick to SD, while manufacturing industry would opt for MMCD, this could lead to a situation in which the supply of content stored on SDs (i.e. movies) would involve a shortage of playback devices or media. In the other scenario, which closely resembles the famous VHS/Beta story, MMCD devices sales would be low due to a shortage of content. Both situations could lead to effects of excess inertia (Farrel & Salooner, 1986) in sales of both devices and media. Being aware of those problems both camps initiated a working group consisting of mayor ICT players like IBM, Microsoft, Intel and HP to mediate a solution. By the end of 1995 this group, known as the Computer Industry Technical Working Group (TWG), proposed a merge of both specifications to circumvent problems resulting from two separate standards. The merged standard featured elements of both technologies, adopting the two-substrate approach proposed by SD while implementing the 8/16 modulation of MMCD and was termed "Digital Versatile Disc" (DVD).

Before we start to analyze the dynamics of DVD recordable standards, it is necessary to examine relevant actors involved in the standardisation processes of DVD Recordables. The actor constellation of the competing consortia reveals a distinct pattern that corresponds to structures in pre-DVD era, with the MMCD supporters backing the "plus"-standards (DVD+R and DVD+RW) and the former SD supporters backing the "slash"-standards (DVD-RAM and DVD-R). Four actor constellations are relevant for assessing dynamics of DVD Recordables standards. These four constellations are the DVD Forum, the DVD+RW Alliance, the DVD6C and the

Technical Committee 31 of the European Computer Manufacturers Association (ECMA TC31).

The DVD Forum, an industry consortium founded by IPR-holders of DVD and CD technology, is responsible for the approval of the official DVD specifications (books), including specification for file systems, discs but not for devices. Originally founded by ten companies holding assets in form of patents, the DVD Forum opened up in late 1997 for other companies like consumer electronics and computer manufacturers, as well as content providers to extend acceptance of DVD technology and legitimize their position as the standard-setting consortium responsible for DVD-related issues. The founding members do the DVD Forum are: Hitachi, Matsushita, Mitsubishi, Pioneer, Philips, Sony, Thomson, Time Warner, Toshiba, JVC

When in early 1996 the DVD Forum was about to decide on recordable DVD formats, the once unified position reached in the DVD-ROM standard-setting process crumpled. Even though unanimous agreement had been reached on DVD-RAM as the official standard for rewritable media, Sony, Philips, HP, Mitsubishi, Ricoh and Yamaha officially announced that they had another specification for a rewritable disc, which they termed DVD+RW. This specification had not been developed by the DVD Forum. So the DVD Forum announced, that there would be no support for DVD+RW, that the prefix "DVD" must not be used and that the format should be called Phase Change ReWritable (PC-RW) instead. So, in June 1998, the DVD+RW Compatibility Alliance, later to be renamed to DVD+RW Alliance, was founded by Philips, Sony, HP, Yamaha, Ricoh and Thomson while at about the same time Philips, Sony and HP started to offer joint licensing for their DVD relevant assets. A closer inspection of the key players reveals that the former supporters of MMCD are more or less congruent to the relevant IPR-holders of the DVD+RW Alliance. Apart from Sony and Philips, members like Ricoh, Thomson or Yamaha did not hold significant IPR, but qualified as important allies, since they could provide high manufacturing capacity, especially Ricoh and Yamaha who had a good reputation for producing CD-R devices. The patents included in the spin-off DVD recordable format proposed by the DVD+RW Alliance did partly stem from older assets of Philips and Sony – their patents concerning CD-R technology. Those patents held interesting aspects for Sony and Philips. With ongoing diffusion of DVD recordable technology and potential replacement of CD-RW technology as the main optical storage solution, Philips and Sony could position "old" IPR which otherwise might provide for less and less license revenues in the long run. So, by reimplementing old IPR assets into DVD recordable technology, they "relaunched" the value of their IPR by gathering license revenues from established CD-R technology and the upcoming DVD recordable technology as well. Even "if" CD-R technology would become less important and manufacturers abandoning the standard, they would still be left with revenues from +R(W) technology at the minor additional R&D expense they had to invest to bridge the gap from CD-R to +R(W). Another incentive to split the DVD recordable standard stemmed from the actors who actually hold no IPR assets in DVD technology – the manufacturers of blank media - as they could produce at much lower costs since the +R(W) technology was technically closer to CD-R(W) (Spath, 2003). Thereby the "plus" camp would have the chance to challenge the "slash" camp via the blank media producers entering the market at a lower price which in turn could spur the sales of the recording devices to be produced by Sony and Philips.

With the DVD+RW Alliance founded in 1998 and Sony, Philips and HP offering joint licenses, the position of the former SD camp shifted. To counteract the position of the DVD+RW Alliance, seven companies (Hitachi, Matsushita, Mitsubishi, JVC, Time Warner, Toshiba, IBM) established a patent pool for their assets. Notably, the DVD+RW Alliance and the DVD6C Patent Pool are completely disjunctive. Another interesting fact is that Pioneer is neither part of the DVD+RW Alliance nor the DVD6C, but is at the same time founding member of the DVD Forum and major backer of the DVD-RW technology. The DVD6C patent pool only covers patents for the "official" standards supported by the DVD Forum not covering IPR assets of Sony, HP and Philips. This meant that products concerning the original DVD Technology had to be licensed in both camps, while the patents for recordable DVD technology are licensed by either the DVD6C in case of the official "slash"-format or with the DVD+RW Alliance in case of the unofficial "plus"-format.

Another important factor for the analysis of dynamics of DVD recordable standards is the constellation of the Technical Committee 31 of the ECMA. The ECMA as an industry association dedicated to standardisation in ICT technologies plays an important role in the standard-setting processes of DVD recordables. This is due to the fact, that the standardisation processes of DVD recordables follow a unique pattern of consecutive information flows, with the ECMA acting as an intermediary between consortia level developing specifications and formal level represented by JTC1 of ISO. For all media types analyzed, the same unique pattern applies, regardless of the consortium the standard is proposed by. The process starts at the basic level of specifications. When agreement is reached the specifications are proposed to TC31 of ECMA and in some cases proposed to the SC 23 of JTC1 of ISO. This approach has some strategical implications, since ECMA is a liaison partner of JTC1 which holds the possibility of forwarding standards to ISO by using the Accelerated Approval Procedure (AAP) of the ISO. This "fast-track" allows for an ECMA standard to be placed directly at Enquiry Stage, leapfrogging early and sometimes time consuming stages of the ISO standard-setting procedure. Nearly all core members of the DVD6C and the DVD+RW Alliance are part of TC 31. Moreover all the founding members of the DVD Forum are represented in the TC31. This structure is important when considered along with regularities of ECMA concerning a freeze of a standardisation project, as the ECMA statutes stipulate that an ECMA standardisation project can not be stopped if three members of a technical committee keep supporting the project. As both camps are represented with at least 5 members, neither camp could stop the other from keeping an ECMA standardisation project running and establishing an ECMA standard. Once an ECMA standard is agreed upon, the camp can chose to fast-track it to the ISO. This means that at all times both camps had the chance to include their technological achievements in a formal ISO standard draft.

Before describing the actual changes in DVD recordable standards, it is necessary to further clarify the interdependence of a) membership structure of the four relevant groups, b) how the actors are linked to the different technologies and c) how the technologies are again linked to each other. In other words: The level of a) technology-standards relation (which technologies are similar and are incorporated in which standard), the level of b) standard-consortia relation (which standard is supported by which actors) and the c) consortia-actor relation (how are the actors linked in the consortia). All three levels are organized in Figure 1. The level of technology-standards relationship is given by the arrows that connect the different standards. On the level of the technology-standards relation we can see that both the MMCD and the SD technology are implemented in the DVD standard. Both technologies have, as mentioned before, been merged to form one standard. Technology used in the SD approach is related to the technology of DVD-RAM and DVD-R, MMCD technology, to be more precise old CD-R(W) technology, is implemented in DVD+R and DVD+RW standards. This accounts for a "merge-split"-relationship of the standards as SD and MMCD merge into DVD and then DVD splits into different DVD recordable standards that reflect the pre-DVD split into MMCD and SD.

Figure 1. Relationship of standards, consortias and actors in context of DVD recordable standardisation

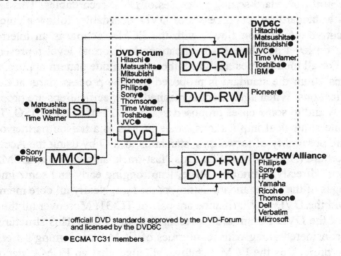

This merge-split scenario is reflected in the level of standard-consortia relations with the DVD Forum supporting DVD-RAM and DVD-R as well as DVD-RW, and the DVD+RW Alliance supporting DVD+RW and DVD+R. On the consortia-actor level we can see that the membership structure of the relevant DVD recordable consortia, at least to some considerable extent, represents the pre-DVD split into SD-

and MMCD-supporting actors with Sony and Philips, the former MMCD supporters, forming a separate consortium to promote their own standard of DVD recordables.

Now that the relations between underlying technology, actor groups and standards is described, the next step towards understanding the dynamics of DVD recordable standards is based on a complete and detailed history of DVD recordable standards developments. This historical timeline has to contain a) the changes of specifications on consortia level and b) which of those specifications are included in official standards and c) specific differences in timing on all levels of the process. In this case there are basically four different idealized conditions of interrelationship between horizontal dynamics (changes in specifications or standards) and vertical dynamics of standards (the transfer of specification content from one SSB to another). A very high level of vertical dynamics occurs for example when every change in specification is implemented into a new ISO standard or draft for ISO standard. This timeline is been synthesized in table 1.

On the horizontal dimension of standards dynamics two highly active phases of change can be isolated (see. table 1). The first occurs for DVD-RAM and DVD-R standard between 1997 and early 2000 with four major revisions of DVD-RAM and DVD-R. This phase of high activity is limited to the standards of the "slash"-camp. Strikingly, another highly active phase started in late 2002 and is limited to DVD-RW, DVD+RW and the two WORM-media types DVD+R and DVD-R. Considering market entry of devices conforming to the different standards horizontal dynamics of standards gathered momentum with the devices of the "plus"-camp entering the market but this is limited to the competitors DVD-RW vs. DVD+RW and DVD-R vs. DVD+R. This holds some interesting implications for the dynamics of standards, as in the light of competition, the horizontal dynamics of standards increases in this case. In contrast to the notion of the revision of standards as a reaction to problems of implementation, the dynamics of consortia standards in the case of DVD Recordables is driven by competition between the "slash"- and the "plus"-camp. This lends strong evidence that standards being used as part of competitive strategies play a dominant role for horizontal standards dynamics. This conforms to ideas that standards play a significant role in stabilizing competitors' market positions (Bonino & Spring, 1991). Horizontal standards dynamics is thereby influenced by competition fostered by technology races between competing parties. This corresponds to ideas of Anderson & Tushman (1990), by which an era of competing technologies, a so called "ferment", is characterized by extensive technology races. Considering a standard-setting process as an extension of a development process (Weiss 1990; also in detail: Blind, 2004) and the idea of technology races under competition, the consequence is that due to ongoing technology races, horizontal dynamics of standards should increase rather than decrease, as should be the case in absence of competition when standard revisions are due to implementation issues occurring at early stages of less mature technology. Key issue here is the need of both camps to distinguish their product from those of competitors to acquire higher market share. On the whole, two technology races can be identified in the DVD recordable standard-setting process. One is a technology race for storage capacity. This race occurred at early stages of DVD recordable standardisation and was limited to DVD-RAM and DVD+RW in late 1998 and has just recently gathered momentum with the first specification for DVD+RDL. The other technology race is for recording speed and has been a major force in horizontal dynamics of standards in the second phase of high dynamics since late 2002, as all revisions of specifications since then included changes in maximum recording speed. Generally, it can be derived that under competition horizontal standards dynamics increase as aspects of technical superiority become more important for securing or establishing market share.

Regarding vertical standards dynamic a stable pattern can be observed as the "slash"-camp only forwards basic specifications, while the "plus"-camp also includes matters of recording speed. This is a stable pattern applying to the DVD+R as well as the DVD+RW standard. The only exception to this pattern is the DVD-RAM 2.1rev1 specification included in the second draft of the ECMA-330 standard and contained triple recording speed specification. In the case of DVD-R standard, the commonly sold discs with a capacity of 4.7GB do neither muster a corresponding ECMA nor ISO standard. Even though on the whole this observed pattern is stable, there are still differences in vertical dynamics. Based on the condition that the ECMA standards propose an intermediary role in the vertical dynamics and all ISO standards stem from fast-forwarded ECMA standards, we can derive the number of specifications that included in any given ISO standard or draft. As both camps could at all times forward their specifications the question arises: Why did the "slash"-camp not forward specifications including information on the higher recording speeds while the "plus"-camp chose to do so?" Reasons cannot be explicitly deduced using the given data. Still there are a number of reasonable hypotheses that could explain vertical dynamics. One hypothesis could be that the "plus"-camp tried to compensate for the stigma of their standards not being approved by the DVD Forum and explored other mechanism of legitimization by transferring most of their specification to formal SDOs. Another possible hypothesis is that only "winners" of a technology race transfer information of recording speeds or capacity to other SSBs. This would explain the exception of the DVD-RAM rev 2.1rev1 specification in the revision of the ECMA-330 standard, as at that time DVD-RAM featured triple recording speed whereas other rewritable specifications only supported single speed recording. On the whole, the vertical dynamics of standards is high at the beginning of the standard war between DVD-RAM and DVD+RW between 1997 and 1999 with DVD-R, which was at that time the only WORM-media in the market showing little vertical dynamics and does not show any vertical dynamics after the first basic specification was published as an ISO standard. Vertical dynamics is generally higher when at competition is given and the competing parties have an incentive to be the first to produce a full-grown formal standard. This could be another explanation of the high vertical dynamics of the DVD+R standard between 2002 and the present, as the DVD+R standard hit the market comparably late in second half of 2002.

Another factor influencing horizontal and vertical standards dynamics is the implementation of competing standards in a single device as it helps assessing reasons for dynamic technology races and reduced tendency for markets to tip to either of the camps standards. Under competition Multiple Implementation can occur in two ways as a) Non-cooperative Multiple Implementation, referring to the implementation of standards not supported by competitors and b) Cooperative Multiple Implementation, by which standards supported by competing parties are implemented in one device. In our case the latter type of Multiple Implementation corresponds to the implementation of both DVD-RAM and DVD-R in early devices build by Panasonic (the LF-D321U) introduced to the market in 2001. The other type of Multiple Implementation was first adopted by Sony, a member of the "plus"-camp in late 2002 with the DRU-500A supporting both DVD+RW and DVD-RW. Though arguments for Non-Cooperative Multiple Implementation can easily be found we face the question, why Cooperative Multiple Implementation actually does occur. One answer could be that Sony by implementing its competitors standards could harvest the installed base of its competitor and reduce the perceived risk of the end users for taking chances with the "wrong" format. Cooperative Multiple Implementation proves to be a good strategy in a standards war as can be derived from the latest sales figures as "[n]early 50% of the DVD writers market is already for the models from the likes of Sony, Pioneer & NEC which are the dual drives (+ / - R)" (N.N, 2004).

The concept of Cooperative Multiple Implementation offers an explanation for special cases of continuation of high momentum technology races as it leads to stable structures of coexistence. This stable structure is due to the fact that neither of the camps that engaged in Cooperative Multiple Implementation can drop out of this strategy without risking the loss of market share. The explanation for this can be derived from diffusion theory as consumers at later stages in the diffusion process (i.e. late majority and laggards) tend to be more risk avers than their counterparts in early stages of the diffusion process (i.e. innovators, early adopters and early majority) (Rogers, 1999). Assuming that risk aversion increases parallel to adoption rate the strategy of Cooperative Multiple Implementation becomes the dominant strategy as it helps to keep the risk low for the end user. Apart from considering the revenues derived by sales of devices, the aspect of revenues from media sold keeps competition stable and prevents the competing parties from stopping innovation activities. For the dynamics of standards this leads to a stable structure as the probability of tipping markets is reduced while at the same time technology races keep momentum and foster dynamics standards on horizontal as well as vertical level.

Conclusions

Standards are not static. There are not isolated islands either. Standards exist and evolve in dynamic environments. One of the aspects of dynamic environments is competition among networking organisations, of which some are bound together in consortia. Under competition, some proportion of the dynamics of standards can be explained by diffused IPR structure, which enabled competing parties to engage in technology races. The outcome of those technology races lead to certain aspects of dynamics of standards on horizontal and vertical level. In contrast to other approaches which highlight aspects of dynamic standards as a solution to implementation problems, another explanation for dynamics of standards is given stemming from competition of rival consortia. Moreover Multiple Implementation can act as a catalyst for technology races under competition leading to dynamic standards.

References

Anderson, P. and M. Tushman (1990), "Technological discontinuities and dominant designs: a cyclical model of technology change" Administrative Science Quarterly; 35

Blind, K. (2004), "The Economics of Standards: Theory, Evidence, Policy", Edward Elgar, Cheltenham

Bonino, M.J. and M.B. Spring (1991), "Standards as Change Agents in the Information Tech nology Market.", Computer Standards and Interfaces,12(2), 97-107.

Farrell, J. and G. Saloner (1986), "Installed base and compatibility: innovation, product pre announcements and predation", American Economic Review, 76, 943-954.

N.N. (2004), "DVD+ / – RW Market Survey of Recorders + Discs", Optical Disc Systems, 2, http://www.opticaldisc-systems.com/2004march-april/market-survey90.htm   (last accessed on 30th of April 2005)

Rogers, E. M. (1999), "The Diffusion of Innovation", 4th ed., New York, The Free Press

Spath, M. (2003), "Why DVD+R(W) is superior to DVD-R(W)",   http://www.cdfreaks. com/article/113 (last accessed on 30th of April 2005)

Weiss, M.B.H. (1990), "The standards development process: a view from political theory", Standard View, 1 (2), 35–41.

Table 1: *Overview of DVD recordable Standardisation History*

Format		1997	1998	1999	2000	2001	2002	2003	2004
-RAM	Spec.	July 1.0	Oct 1.9	Sept 2.0	Feb 2.1		Jun 2.1rev1		Feb 2.1rev2
	ECMA		Feb 272	Jun 272/2		Dec 330	Jun 330/2		
	ISO		Apr 16824*	May 16824				Mar 17592*	Jul 17592
-RW	Spec.			Nov 1.0	Sept 1.1		Aug(2x) 1.1rev1	Nov (4x) 1.1rev2	
	ECMA						Dec 338		
	ISO							Mar 17342*	Jul 17342
+RW	Spec.	May 1.0				Mar 1.1	Dec 1.2		Oct 1.3rre
	ECMA		Apr 274	Jun 274/2			Dec 337	Dec 337/2	Jul 17341
	ISO		May 16969*	Oct 16969					
-R	Spec.	July 1.0	Nov 1.9		Feb (A) 2.0 / May (G) 2.0		Aug(G) 2.0r1	Nov (G) 2.0r2/r3	Jun (G) 2.1
	ECMA		Dec 279						
	ISO				Jun 20563*	Jul 20563			
+R	Spec.						Jul 1.0 / Dec 1.1	Jul 1.2	Jul 1.3
	ECMA							Dec 349	Jun 349/2
	ISO								Jul 17344*

* refers to ISO/DIS (Draft)

Open Standards and Open Source Software

Similarities and differences

Jack Verhoosel

TNO Information and Communicationtechnology
Colosseum 27
7521 PV, Enschede
The Netherlands
jack.verhoosel@tno.nl

ABSTRACT: *This paper is concerned with the similarities and differences between open standards and open source software. Both concepts are defined and their objectives, advantages and characteristics are discussed.*

KEY WORDS: *open standards, open source software, free of charge, licensees.*

1. Introduction

Standardization is already a fairly old means to reduce complexity and to simplify working procedures, communication protocols and so on. In the area of communication between ICT-systems, standardization has evolved very rapidly over the last ten years. This has led to standardization of networks on for instance the TCP/IP standard and web technologies. These standardization processes have been fairly open mainly thanks to the approach of organizations like IETF and W3C. The next challenge we face is standardization at the information level and the interfaces of software applications that exchange this information. Open standards in this area are generally accepted by the end-user organizations as a means to improve interoperability between their systems.

In the area of software applications for exchanging information, a related relatively new trend is the use of open source software. While many talk about open source software, the exact meaning of open source software is fairly unknown as are the advantages of using it. Open source software is for instance being built using a modular approach, because this simplifies control of the software developments in a large community of independent software developers. Another advantage of this approach is that extensions can be easily added without loss of stability and quality. In a nutshell, the most important pros for using open source software are: independence of software-vendors, usually lower implementation costs and easier coupling with other systems.

Important to notice is that the advantages of using open source software are almost equal to those for the use of open standards. Therefore, although open standards and open source software are entirely different concepts, they are often confusingly mixed. This paper briefly defines both concepts and discusses some similarities and differences between open standards and open source software.

2. Source code

The commonalities between open standards and open source software are mainly based on the similar objectives of both concepts, like the prevention or tackling of monopolies of software vendors, the decrease of cost of software and more freedom of choice for the end-user. In principle, however, open standards and open source software are entirely different concepts. Open standards are concerned with the content and meaning of information, while the subject matter with open source software is the source code, i.e. only the software and not the information that it operates upon. Of course, open standards can be used in open source software. In fact, open source development communities generally use rather a good open standard instead of a badly constructed proprietary one. Open source developers have no interest in keeping their standards private or closed, because this is against the principle of openness that they propagate for their software. Another reason for using open standards in open source software is the costs for using proprietary standards. On the other hand, there is also open source software that uses closed standards, mainly because there are no good open alternatives. In this context, it is hard to keep the specifications of the closed standard confidential and they will usually be publicly available. However, that doesn't make them completely open, because for instance they can still be maintained in a closed decision process.

Technically speaking, there is no difference between open source software and software of vendors of which the source code is not publicly available, also called closed source software. The technical components of both types of software do not differ. Therefore, open source or closed source software do not basically differ in quality, stability, security and functionality. This is mainly determined by the level of programming skills of software developers and the software development process they use.

The discussion about open source software is primarily a juridical one. The basis of a license under which an open source software product is being distributed is different from the usual software licensees. An open source software license guarantees a number of liberties. Sometimes a requirement is being used that guarantees that, if the software is changed and redistributed, the same liberties hold. The Open Source Initiative (OSI), a non-profit organization, has defined ten characteristics of open source software and its licensees. OSI certifies open source licensees and publishes a list of certified open source software. The most well-known examples of open source licensees are the GPL (GNU Public License), MPL (Mozilla Public License) and the BSD (Berkeley Software Distribution).

Summarizing can be concluded that a piece of software is called open source, whenever access to the source code and the application (target code) itself is free of charge and that the program can be adapted, used and under certain criteria be redistributed.

3. Free of charge?

There is a widespread mistake that open source software is completely free of charge because of the liberties laid down in open source licensees. Indeed, no fees have to be paid for the use of the software, whether the program is being installed on 1 or 10.000 computers. However, the use of open source software is never totally free. The software has to be installed, configured and managed, which of course also involves certain costs.

A well-known analogy that is often being used in this sense is "the car with the sealed hood". Whenever the motor of a usual car breaks down, the driver can open up the hood and try to repair the motor himself. Thus, the driver has a choice: with sufficient knowledge of mechanics, he can fix the motor himself or he can call the road-service for assistance. For the latter he will of course be charged. Whenever the motor of a car with a sealed hood breaks down, the driver has no choice and has to call for assistance and be charged.

With closed source software, there is usually only an executable program (byte-code or binary code) without access to the source code. The software can therefore not be easily changed and that is even prohibited by the vendor (the hood is sealed). The software usually comes with a license that only allows the use of the software and adaptation and redistribution of the software is prohibited. This is a problem unknown in the open source community

Open source software is about freedom and independence of monopolistic vendors. Open source software developers have the opinion that the knowledge (source-code) has to be shared and be freely available for everyone. However, the publishing of a book or CD with this knowledge and advising end-users can of course be charged for. By sharing knowledge we can achieve a lot more in the end. There is lots of proof of this in the form of projects in which hundreds of software developers in communities contribute to the development of open source software. Since everyone produces a part of the software, it can be developed towards a mature, stable and secure software product. The open source operating system Linux is living proof of this phenomenon.

4. Open standards

The label open source does not guarantee that the software also uses open standards. Standards make it possible to use software from different parties to work together, albeit vendors or open source communities. In order to make this interoperability work as much as possible, standards have to be as open as possible. There is no standard definition for the openness of a standard. Among those that can be found in literature and in use, the definition of the Dutch Program on Open Standards and Open Source Software is quite useful. This definition has also been adopted by the European Interoperability Framework of the European Commission. It consists of the following four criteria:

- The standard is adopted and will be maintained by a not-for-profit organization, and its ongoing development occurs on the basis of an open decision-making procedure available to all interested parties (consensus or majority decision etc.).
- The standard has been published and the standard specification document is available either freely or at a nominal charge. It must be permissible to all to copy, distribute and use it for no fee or at a nominal fee.
- The intellectual property – i.e. patents possibly present – of (parts of) the standard is made irrevocably available on a royalty-free basis.
- There are no constraints on the re-use of the standard.

This definition ensures good accessibility of a future-proof standard, optimal consensus about the standard and acceptable payment. In this way, there is no single party that can manipulate the standard for its own purposes. One of the reasons of confusion is that this definition of open standards can be easily applied to open source software. Thus, the openness of both concepts is also a similarity.

Open standards do not depend on whether the software in which they are being applied is open or closed source software. On the other hand, it is very well possible and from an end-users perspective very desirable to use open standards at the interfaces of closed source software. This is, however, strongly dependent on the market forces between end-users and software-vendors. In some sectors, the competition between different software-vendors is large enough to make them implement upcoming open standards fairly quickly. In other domains, however, there are only one or two software-vendors that dominate the market. In that case, the end-users have to strongly require the use of open standards in their tender towards the software-venders. When using open source software, this is not an issue at all.

5. References

OSOSS, *Dutch Program on Open Standards and Open Source Software*, http://www.ososs.nl

European Commission, *IDA Programme*, http://europa.eu.int/ida/en/home

European Commission, *European Interoperability Framework*: http://europa.eu.int/ida/en/document/2319

Belgium Government, *Belgium open standards definition*, http://www.openstandaarden.be

Bruce Perens, *open standards definition*, http://perens.com/OpenStandards/Definition.html

Ken Krechmer, *open standards definition*, http://www.csrstds.com/openstds.html

Towards Interoperability of Enterprise, Heterogeneous Enterprise Networks and their Applications: from Industries needs to ATHENA requirements

PC Chairs' message

The workshop aimed to present and discuss with the audience the current results of ATHENA programme related to industry short and long term needs and requirements regarding interoperability of enterprise software and applications.

In particular, the way industrial interoperability requirements are handled within the programme will be presented and specific examples of industry scenarios indicating interoperability needs and solutions will be provided. Nevertheless, the industry scenarios will be used also for testing the solutions provided by the R&D technology providers and for the development of the future scenarios with the needs of the industry in terms of interoperability. Also, under the ATHENA programme, a general model for determining the impact of interoperability on business will be provided by stating the strategic business challenges relating to interoperability.

The feedback provided from the assistants, with the presence of the Scientific/Technical Project Officer from the European Commission, for the INTEROP NoE and ATHENA-IP projects, six universities and two external companies, was considered by the workshop organizers very profitable for continuing the work performed to date.

Man-Sze Li, IC Focus Limited, UK
Maria Anastasiou, INTRACOM, Greece
Ruben Garcia, AIDIMA, Spain

ATHENA – Advanced Technologies for Interoperability of Heterogeneous enterprise networks and their applications

Rainer Ruggaber*

* SAP Research, SAP AG, Neurottstrasse 16
69190 Walldorf, Germany
+49 6227 747474
rainer.ruggaber@sap.com

ABSTRACT. *Organisations are engaging in more and more sophisticated business networks to improve collaboration. These business networks can range from more static relationships like Supply Chains to very dynamic networks like virtual organisations. A prerequisite to enable business networks is the interoperability of the participants systems and applications. ATHENA is an Integrated Project funded by the European Commission under Framework Programme 6 that addresses Interoperability of Enterprise Systems and Applications proposing a holistic approach. ATHENA will provide technical results like reference architectures, methodologies and infrastructures complemented by business results that provide ROI calculations and impact predictions for new technologies. This paper provides insights into ATHENA and how proposed approaches and expected results support business networks.*

1. Introduction

One of the trends in the global market is the increasing collaboration among enterprises during the entire product life cycle. This trend requires, that enterprise systems and applications need to be interoperable in order to achieve seamless business interaction across organisational boundaries, and realise networked organisations.

The European Commission considers the development of interoperability of enterprise applications and software as a strategic issue for European companies to strengthen their cooperation and gain competitiveness in the global market. In the context of the EU Framework Program 6 (FP 6) the integrated project ATHENA (Advanced Technologies for Interoperability of Heterogeneous Enterprise Networks and their Applications) has been funded (ATHENA 2004). It consists of a set of projects and is to lead to prototypes, technical specifications, guidelines and best practices that form a common European repository of knowledge.

ATHENA takes a holistic approach to solving the Interoperability problem taking a technical as well as a business viewpoint into account. Previous activities in that space led to fragmented solutions addressing only part of the problem. From a standards viewpoint in the B2B space there is rather a proliferation than a lack of standards.

ATHENA itself is driven by industry scenarios and requirements. Industrial users in the consortium provide examples from aeronautics, automotive, telecommunications and the SME space. The approach of ATHENA is to go from the specific scenarios provided industrial users to generic requirements applicable to a whole industry. ATHENA looks at the scenarios provided by industrial users in detail and then tries to abstract to industry scenarios common for an industry by identifying commonalities and differences. Currently users from the automotive, aerospace, telecommunication equipment and furniture industry are participating in ATHENA.

The main section of this document gives an introduction into ATHENA and discusses the research activities and the expected outcomes in detail.

2. ATHENA Integrated Project

The ATHENA IP (Integrated Project) (ATHENA Homepage) aims to enable interoperability by providing reference architectures, methods and infrastructure components. In ATHENA Research & Development will be executed in synergy and collaboration with Community Building: research will be guided by business requirements defined by a broad range of industrial sectors and integrated into Piloting and Technology Testing as well as Training. ATHENA consists of **three action lines** in which the activities will take place (Chen *et al.*, 2004). In Action Line A, the research and development activities will be carried out. Action Line B will take care of the community building whereas Action Line C will host all management activities (ATHENA Homepage). Relations between the three action lines are shown figure 1.

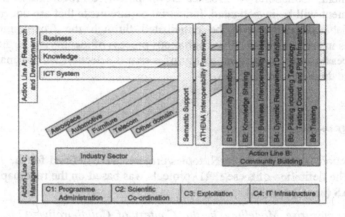

Figure 1. *Interaction of ATHENA Action Lines*

2.1. ATHENA Integrated Project

Scenarios play an important role in ATHENA as **sources of requirements** and for the **validation of results**. Scenarios represent the industrial sector-specific implementation of a process and capture industry-specific requirements of a given process. Industry-independent characteristics are described on the process level and are abstracted from the industry-specific scenarios. Scenarios used for validation of results need to be extended with business issues, software and infrastructure, and operational applications used in enterprises. Amongst other criteria, they will be selected based on their general relevance to current and future business paradigms, their general (i.e. industry-independent), industry specific and company-specific characteristics, and their coverage of the anticipated ATHENA approach, methods, and tools. These criteria apply to scenarios provided by partners before the start of ATHENA and to future scenarios.

For each selected business scenario, the partners will provide **detailed descriptions**. These descriptions will be analysed and compared in order to identify commonalities and differences. The description will be based on a common methodology to capture user requirements.

One of the initial tasks (Dynamic Requirements Definition) in Action line B is to provide this methodology to users in order to be able to systematically capture user requirements.

The selection of processes and industries identified in the initial phase will be **extended** during the course of the project. At first, the scenarios of Supply Chain Management, Collaborative Product Development, e-Procurement and Portfolio Management will be investigated. Industrial requirements that are not fully covered by available scenarios will be anticipated through the Community Building Activities in Action Line B. This continuous process of identifying further industries and processes ensures that the quality of scenario selection will be maintained for the whole duration of ATHENA.

2.2. R&D Projects

In Action Line A six research topics/projects were defined for the first stage of the IP. The definition of these R&D projects was based on the roadmaps elaborated by IDEAS (see Section 3.4):

– *Enterprise Modelling in the Context of Collaborative Enterprises* (A1) aims at developing methodologies for management and modelling of situated processes, flexible resource allocation and assignment. Furthermore, it investigates methodologies for work management and execution monitoring. For externalising the dynamic dependencies between participants and processes, methodologies of content based routing and collaborative processes will be developed. This project will enable scalable Enterprise Modelling methodologies and infrastructures, repository services and portal server services for "benefit driven Enterprise Modelling involvement".

– *Cross-Organisational Business Processes* (A2) deals with modelling techniques to represent business processes from different organisations on a level that considers the privacy requirements of the involved partners. Such models will have two perspectives: an enterprise modelling perspective that assigns a process to its context in the enterprise, and a formal aspect to perform computational transformations in order to allow for re-use of a process in a cross-organisational environment. Such models need to be enriched through ontological information and need to be executed through IT systems, such as workflow management systems.

These systems need to be enabled to operate efficiently in an architectural environment that adapts to particular business scenarios.

– *Knowledge Support and Semantic Mediation Solutions* (A3) aim at the development of methods and tools for the semantic enabled enterprise, with a focus on supporting enterprise and application software interoperability. A key objective is to build an integrated software environment that is able to manage the semantics of different abstraction levels that can be found in an enterprise. Focus is to use formal semantics, organised in domain ontologies, to annotate the business processes and the software components in order to reconcile the mismatches that may be encountered in unanticipated cooperation activities.

– *Interoperability Framework and Services for Networked Enterprises* (A4) is concerned with the design and implementation of the infrastructure supporting interoperability in scenarios adopting the Integrated Paradigm (i.e. where there is a standard format for all constituent sub-systems) by enriching existing state-of-the-art interoperability architectures with enterprise semantics and models derived from the Enterprise Interoperability Infrastructures of the organisations involved. The project will provide methodologies and develop seamless and configurable interconnection software components. The resulting toolset will be the basic set of software and engines that is to prepare any enterprise in the adoption and exploitation of interoperability support infrastructures.

– *Planned and Customisable Service-Oriented Architectures* (A5) is to develop the understanding, tools and infrastructures required for service-oriented architectures which can be achieved more easily through the planning and later customisation of solutions for better application to user scenario requirements. Although the project will consider available business services, an increasing emphasis will be given to the development of an environment for easier application development that natively provides better customisation.

– *Model-driven and Adaptive Interoperability Architectures* (A6) is to provide new and innovative solutions for the problem of sustaining interoperability through change and evolution, by providing dynamic and adaptive interoperability architecture approaches. The project aims to advance the state-of-the-art in this field by applying the principles of model-driven, platform independent architecture specifications, and dynamic and autonomous federated architecture approaches, including the usage of agent technologies.

2.3. Remarks

Though the programme as a whole adopts a holistic perspective on interoperability, there is an initial emphasis of individual projects on **individual building blocks** rather than on achieving solutions that address interoperability in a holistic manner. However, the individual results of the projects taken together will eventually be combined to an **integral solution**.

Four out of six initial research projects (projects A1, A2, A5, and A6) address relatively focused topics. Project A3 is rather supportive in its focus on semantic issues that will be evaluated and used by all other projects. Finally, project A4 integrates the results and methodologies reached in the other projects. This project is a first **reconciliation attempt** that will provide an integral solution resulting in the ATHENA Interoperability Framework.

Major impacting results from ATHENA could be stated as follows:

–   A generic, common platform for Networked Organisations, integrated by an open Infrastructure.

–   Interoperability services to assist enterprise designers, knowledge workers and system developers in composing and adapting executable solutions, reusing knowledge and software components.

–   Specific platforms built to support the research projects, the communities, use-cases, scenarios, test-beds, training and learning facilities, and collaborative experimentation.

2.4. Research Environment

ATHENA builds on results and experience of the thematic network IDEAS - Interoperability Development of Enterprise Applications and Software (IDEAS 2003). Goal of IDEAS was the definition of a roadmap for Interoperability of Enterprise Systems and Applications (Doumeingts *et al.*, 2003). This roadmap was used in ATHENA to define the R&D Projects described in the previous section.

Furthermore, besides ATHENA the European Commission approved a Network of Excellence addressing a similar problem space: INTEROP (Interoperability Research for Networked Enterprises Applications and Software) (INTEROP 2003) aims at integrating expertise in relevant domains for sustainable structuration of European Research on Interoperability of Enterprise applications. ATHENA is closely related to INTEROP.

3. Conclusion

This paper presented the EU project ATHENA that addresses Interoperability of Enterprise Systems and Applications. Its holistic approach and the individual research approaches and expected results were presented. Ongoing work focuses on research activities, building prototypes and applying them to pilot implementations.

Acknowledgements

This paper is partly funded by the European Commission through the ATHENA IP. It does not represent the view of the European Commission, and authors are solely responsible for the paper's content.

4. References

ATHENA - Advanced   Technologies for Interoperability of Heterogeneous Enterprise Networks and their Applications, FP6-2002-IST-1, Integrated Project – Annex I, 2004.

ATHENA Integrated Project, Homepage: http://www.athena-ip.org.

Chen, D.; Stevens, R.; Schulz, K.; Doumeingts, G.: *European Approach on Interoperability of Enterprise Applications – Thematic Network, Integrated Project and Network of Excellence*. IFAC04, Brazil.

Doumeingts, G.; Chen, D.: *Interoperability of Enterprise Applications and Software – An European IST Thematic Network Project: IDEAS*, e2003 eChallenges Conference, 22-24 October 2003, Bologna, Italy.

IDEAS Project Deliverables (WP1-WP7), Public Reports, www.ideas-roadmap.net, 2003.

INTEROP - Interoperability Research for Networked Enterprises Applications and Software, Network of Excellence, Proposal Part B, April 23, 2003.

Framework for training and education activities in interoperability of ESA

Ricardo Jardim-Goncalves* - Ricardo Saraiva* - Pedro Malo* - Adolfo Steiger-Garcao*

* New Univ. of Lisbon, UNINOVA,
Campus da Caparica, Quinta da Torre, 2829-516 Monte Caparica, Portugal
+351 21 294 8337
rg@uninova.pt

rss@dee.fct.unl.pt

pmm@uninova.pt

asg@uninova.pt

ABSTRACT. *The ATHENA Training Service offers high quality training in interoperability, aiming to generate an extensive impact in the field of interoperability. It allows students to understand the why's and how's of today's common problems at business level, which are directly or indirectly caused by interoperability problems. Having lecturers with international recognised expertise in interoperability, the ATHENA training courses and programmes are designed to meet the specific interests of different target-groups, which vary from academia to industry, from IT to business oriented, from software engineers to senior consultants, and from researchers in interoperability to university teachers. Thus, the curriculum is targeting everybody concerned with interoperability issues that affect today's business at several industry sectors. Each course has its own target audience, and students can choose from a large variety of courses, which focus different interoperability application areas, the ones that most suite their requirements and needs. A blended learning offering is provided, consisting of classroom, virtual classroom and e-learning training for the interested parties. Basic training is offered in different languages, while specific training is only offered in English. This paper presents the framework for training and education activities in interoperability of ESA, that is in development by ATHENA.*

1. Introduction

ATHENA comprises the leading European experts in the field of interoperability, allowing students to be in touch with a respected panel of internationally recognised experts, on interoperability areas.

ATHENA research results are transformed into appropriate training courses, allowing the students that enrol the courses to be in the state-of-the-art, and in a position to apply the gained knowledge in the improvement of existing and problematic solutions.

Beside the advantage as regards contents, the ATHENA training services have high didactical quality of the offered training courses. Expertise in research allied with training in an attractive form provides a strong guarantee of success. In this respect modern e-learning and virtual classroom trainings are an advantage, distinguishing the ATHENA training from its competitors.

2. Benefits for participants

With the help of the trainings offered by the current curriculum, students will be enabled to implement and operate interoperability technology. Moreover, they get insight into the methodology and techniques that are relevant in the field of interoperability. These measures will help enterprises to improve their relation to their business partners, reducing time and monetary efforts.

The training service should be understood as enabling for a reduction of costs and an increase of performance for interoperability. Designed to be inexpensive when compared with costly consulting services, which can be avoided while simultaneously achieving a long-term effect by transferring the required expertise to the relevant employees, getting maximum total value from the investments they've made. Thus the return on investment is achieved by the improved interaction opportunities with all business partners who possess the same expertise and ability of performance in interoperability. Such ability will represent a decisive factor in the competition with those that not dispose these capabilities.

3. Structure

The structure of the curriculum for training in Interoperability is depicted in Figure 1.

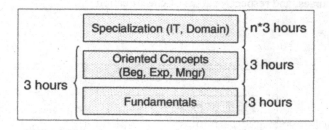

Figure 1. *Structure of the curriculum*

It consists of 3 blocks: Fundamentals, Oriented concepts and Specialization.

The block Oriented concepts is divided in 3 focused targets: Beginners, Experts and Managers, whilst the block Specialization is divided in 2: IT and Domain. For particulars about this division, please see section Target Groups.

The Fundamentals block endows the students with the basis and scope on Interoperability. This is a common block for all training programmes, with one unique module of 3 hours, in order to assure a common level of all students in class.

The Oriented concepts block, gives to the students the essential concepts needed to prepare them for a specialization. This block has 3 different orientations, depending of the background of the student, i.e., Beginner, Expert and Manager. In this way, specific matters are focally coursed to better approach the student and put him at the required stage. Such matters include essentially concepts that complement the students' background to enable them to have the same level of knowledge when starting coursing the Specialization. 3 modules of 3 hours are part of this block, where just one it is expected to be coursed to a student.

When it is recognised that students already have the basic knowledge in interoperability, these two blocks can merged, resulting in a compact course of 3 hours.

The Specialization block is a major block of the curriculum. The block is organized in clusters of modules, each one of 3 hours, representing each cluster a category of courses in a specific area of Interoperability.

Depending of the speciality of the programme to be executed under this curriculum, a set of modules, from one or more areas, is selected. Figure 2 depicts this structure of the curriculum. On section 4 is described in detail the list of available courses, and respective areas of classification.

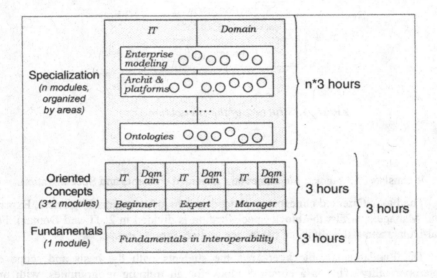

Figure 2. *Detailed curriculum structure*

4. Courses

Courses are the components for training programmes. The available courses are organized in 5 main categories, representing clusters of specialized modules in core interoperability areas. They are:

- Enterprise Modelling (EM)
- Architectures & Platforms (AP)
- Product data exchange (PDE)
- Ontologies (ONT)
- Concepts of Interoperability (CI)

5. The target groups

This is a large model with several relationships, and for this reason the relationships between objects are hidden. A possible query is to see what are the characteristics associated with a particular target group. Figure 3 shows a view of the model where is possible to see all the characteristics associated with the Academic Teacher of Computer Science target-group (the relationships are also hidden, being shown only three). Another example of a view is all the target-groups interested in Decision Making Support.

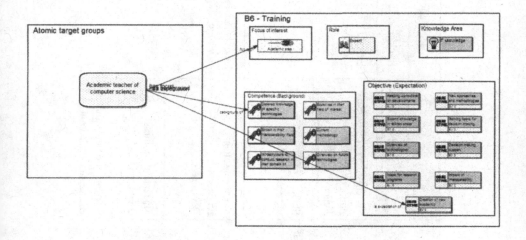

Figure 3. *Academic Teacher of Computer Science*

Focus of Interest	Target Groups	Profile	Beginners		
			Background	Expectations	
Industrial Area	IT Knowledge	SW engineers / developers; Junior consultants; Junior IT vendors.	General IT knowledge	Personal knowledge & skill; Personal promotion.	Becoming interoperability IT specialist; Gaining deeper knowledge of interoperability.
Academic Area		Students of computer science (Phd, Msc).		Better understanding of job opportunities; Thesis in interoperability fields.	
Industrial Area	Domain Knowledge	Junior consultants; Engineers; Developers; Vendors.	General domain knowledge	Gaining expertise for their job	
Academic Area		Students of business administration; MBA; Students of organizational engineering (industrial)		Complete their knowledge concerning interoperability	

Table 1. *Target groups (Beginners)*

Focus of Interest	Target Groups	Experts	
		Profile	Background
Industrial Area	IT Knowledge	SW specialists / architects; Senior IT vendors; Senior consultants; Project managers; Technical course authors / trainers.	Detailed IT knowledge of their infrastructure. Knowledge of other IT training courses (course authors / trainers).
Academic Area		Researchers in computer science; Academic teachers of computer science.	Experts in their interoperability field; Detailed knowledge of specific technologies.
Industrial Area	Domain Knowledge	Domain experts; Senior consultants; Domain course authors / trainers.	Detailed domain knowledge with respect to their focus area; Basic IT knowledge; Knowledge of other domain training courses (course authors / trainers).
Academic Area		Researchers in business administration; Academic teachers of business administration.	Detailed knowledge of applications, processes and industries

Table 2. *Target groups (Experts – Profile and Background)*

Focus of Interest	Target Groups	Experts
		Expectations
Industrial Area	IT Knowledge	Gaining overview of technical solutions; Information relevant for practical applications; Improvements of the IT infrastructure; Create elegant working technical solutions; Learn how to integrate new interoperability technologies; Improve capacity to monitor and manage interoperability IT infrastructure; Knowledge about standards; Deeper understanding of tools; Gaining knowledge for IT training courses on interoperability (course
Academic Area		Keeping up-to-date on developments; New approaches and methodologies for teaching; Extend knowledge in related areas.
Industrial Area	Domain Knowledge	Interoperability opportunities for their domain; Interoperability market requirements and standards; Domain problems well supported by technology; Interoperability solutions & their application at domain/business level; Gaining knowledge for domain training courses on interoperability (course
Academic Area		Keeping up-to-date on the opportunities of interoperability; New approaches and methodologies for teaching.

Table 3. *Target groups (Experts – Expectations)*

Focus of Interest	Target Groups	Managers	
		Profile	Background
Industrial Area	IT Knowledge	IT managers; IT training content administrators.	Knowledge of IT infrastructure; Overall business background; Basic business administration knowledge; Interest in future technologies; Overview of existing IT training courses on ...
Academic Area		Research managers of IT programs; Professors of ...	Expertise in their field of interest; Current methodology; Overview on future technologies; Infrastructure to conduct research in their domain of ...
Industrial Area	Domain Knowledge	Business managers; Business domain experts; Domain training content administrators.	Detailed business knowledge; Knowledge of business processes (e.g. BPM, BPR, EM); Understanding business governance; Basic IT knowledge; Knowledge about business ontologies; Enterprise integration approaches from management point of view (e.g. change management for a merging, ...
Academic Area		Research managers of business ...	Expertise in their domain

Table 4. *Target groups (Managers – Profile and Background)*

Focus of Interest	Target Groups	Managers	
			Expectations
Industrial Area	IT Knowledge	Gaining basis for decision making with respect to interoperability initiatives	Support for planning their IT strategy; Info about cost reduction potentialities of interoperability IT infrastructure; Learn to utilize current technologies and integrate new technologies in an organization for maximum impact and efficiency; Understand how to integrate IT infrastructure within enterprise strategy & models (from an Interoperability perspective); Cost reduction to monitor actual mngmt of interoperability IT...
Academic Area		Overview of technological trends and Decision	Ideas for research programs; Impact of interoperability trends on their field of research; Creation of new academic curriculum.
Industrial Area	Domain Knowledge	Informative basis for decision making; Overview of business trends.	Support business strategy; Improve company management; Optimization of business processes; Improve flexibility with respect to market needs; Understand technologies, which can overcome business challenges, maximize results, and provide return on investment; Reduce infrastructure costs; Create competitive organization and products; Identification of new business opportunities; Plan the process to move from the current way of making business to become a networked organization; Awareness of other commonly used business processes. Authority interest in adapting new technologies and methods;...
Academic Area			New aspects of business administration; Identification of research issues in the area of interoperability.

Table 5. *Target groups (Experts – Expectations)*

6. Training service plan

A detailed training service plan is being scheduled. The training service plan will focus on industry and research. The first will conduct training on industry sectors (automotive, furniture, telecom, aerospatial, B&C and software development), being the courses carried out at correspondent partner sites. On the research field, ATHENA aims to give courses at relevant international conferences, and events on the field of interoperability. Universities will play an important role, and courses should be rolled out to MsC at universities across Europe in the term 2006-2007.

Towards Interoperability of Heterogeneous Enterprise Networks and their Applications – Requirements Handling and Validation activities

Maria Anastasiou * - Maria José Núñez** - Òscar Garcia **

* INTRACOM S.A., Markopoulo Ave,
190 02 Peania Attika, Greece
+44 7974 811 497
mana@intracom.gr

** AIDIMA, C/Benjamín Franklin, 13,
Parque Tecnológico. Paterna. Valencia. Spain
+34 96 136 6070
mjnunez@aidima.es
osgarcia@aidima.es

ABSTRACT. *This paper presents the current results of ATHENA-IP programme. More specifically, the paper focuses on the programme's activities related to interoperability requirements handling and validation activities. The first part of the paper describes the ATHENA Dynamic Requirements Process that was defined to deal with requirements management within the different sub-projects, presents the Industrial sectors represented in ATHENA and their areas of interest as these are reflected in the industrial scenarios they are focusing on. The second part of the paper summarizes the current piloting activities and presents the validations methodologies that have been defined to support the pilots.*

1. Introduction

ATHENA (Advanced Technologies for Interoperability of Heterogeneous Enterprise Networks and their Applications) integrated project (IP) aims to be a comprehensive and systematic European research initiative in IT to remove barriers to interoperability, to transfer and apply the research result in industrial sectors, and to foster a new networked business culture.

This paper presents the current results of ATHENA-IP programme related to industry short-term needs and requirements regarding interoperability of enterprise software and application. In particular, the way industrial interoperability requirements are handled within the programme is presented and the scenarios used for extracting specific interoperability requirements are briefly described. The requirements handling in ATHENA is carried out within the context of B4 sub-project named Dynamic Requirements Definition.

The scenarios and the specific requirements form the basis for developing test cases and validation scenarios through which the evaluation and testing of the solutions provided by the R&D technology providers will be performed. Validation activities are performed under ATHENA B5 sub-project named *Piloting including Technology Testing Coordination and Pilot Infrastructure*. The methodology and the first test cases to be used for the validation are also presented in section 3.

2. Interoperability Requirements Handling

The management of requirements related to interoperability of enterprise applications and software in a networked organisation is a complicated activity. As it is illustrated in Figure 1, we have to deal with a compound system of independent subsystems, with different lifecycles, and with numerous stakeholders with conflicting interests. Classical requirements engineering approaches, used in IT projects, are not adopted to deal with these issues, as they address the specification of one system only.

Furthermore, ATHENA needed a requirements handling approach to support a programme of projects that in future a whole community, the Enterprise Interoperability Center (EIC), will adapt it.

In order to address the above issues, our work approach was to define a method and an associated process for enhanced requirement engineering taking into consideration classical requirement engineering methods. The objective was to provide a coherent and common way for the different projects to perform their activities concurrently and to integrate as soon as possible evolution in terms of solutions or needs coming from the market. This is the reason why we are talking about dynamic requirements definition process.

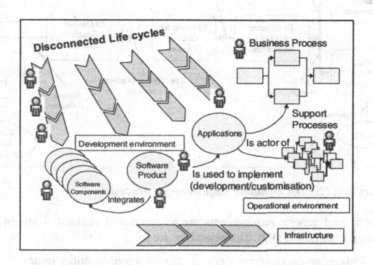

Figure 1. *Stakeholders, software and applications in an interoperability scenario*

2.1. ATHENA Dynamic Requirements process

This section presents the requirements process that was formed and adapted by ATHENA. The process is called the ATHENA Dynamic Requirements process and figure 2 provides an overview of it.

Requirements are gathered in Phases 1 (P1) and 2 (P2). Two origins of requirements are determined. The first one is the set of scenarios proposed by the industrial users in the ATHENA Programme. The requirements extracted from the scenarios are called **specific requirements** as they relate to specific industrial situations.

In phase two, **generic requirements** are gathered. These requirements come from external sources, such as the literature, other projects, in particular the Unified Enterprise Modelling Language (UEML) Project (IST–2001–34229) and IDEAS Thematic Network (IST–2001–37368).

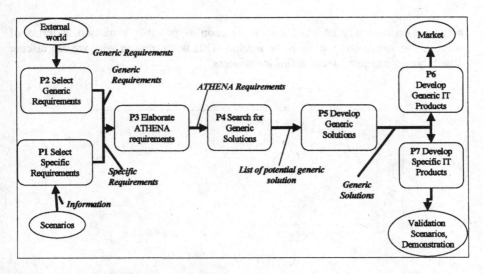

Figure 2. *ATHENA Dynamic Requirements process*

Specific and generic requirements are analysed and elaborated into ATHENA requirements in Phase 3 (P3). The objectives are to:

– Determine the requirements according to interoperability issues,

– Collect the additional information about requirements including a classification according to industrial needs, priority in terms of market, etc.

– Provide consistent requirements definition.

The elaborated ATHENA requirements give input to Phase 4, where the list of potential generic solutions is determined. Phase 5 is related to the development of the adapted Generic Solutions, which follows after an agreement inside the project. During Phase P6, generic Information Technologies (IT) Products[1] will be proposed by the Information Technologies (IT) suppliers.

Finally, in Phase P7, Specific Information Technologies (IT) products will be proposed to the ATHENA Industrial Users, in order to answer to the initial requirements deduced from their scenarios. Some specifics validation scenarios, in accordance of realized Test plans, will be the outputs of P7.

---

[1] In the context of ATHENA Dynamic Requirements Process, a product is considered as a concrete implementation of a given solution, in particular the tools that can be produced by solution providers.

2.2. Industrial Scenarios in ATHENA

As it has already been mentioned, specific interoperability requirements are extracted through the analysis of real life scenarios. The initial set of scenarios in ATHENA has been formed based on the needs and interests of the industrial users in the programme. The four industrial sectors and their representatives, currently inside the programme, are presented in table 1.

Sector	Company
Aeronautic and Aerospace **EADS CCR**	European Aeronautic Defence and Space Company (EADS) is Europe's premier aerospace and defense company and No. 3 worldwide. EADS comprises the activities of the founding partners Aerospatiale Matra S.A. (France), Construcciones Aeronáuticas S.A. (Spain) and DaimlerChrysler Aerospace AG (Germany). EADS CCR is the French part of EADS Corporate Research Centers. EADS CCR has a permanent staff of 250 people, 60% of which are senior scientists.
Automotive **Fiat CR**	Fiat Research Centre (CRF) is an industrial organization having the mission to promote, develop and transfer innovation providing competitiveness to its partners: Fiat Sectors, external SMEs, national research agencies and the European Commission. CRF fulfils its task by focusing on: development of innovative products, implementation of innovative processes (manufacturing and organization), development of new methodologies, and training of human resources.
Furniture **AIDIMA**	AIDIMA is a R&D association for the wood and furniture industries. It is a private, not-for-profit Spanish industrial association made up of more than 650 furniture manufacturers, many of which are small and medium size enterprises (SMEs). Founded in 1984, it has more than 70 employees and several offices across Spain.
Telecommunication **INTRACOM S.A.**	INTRACOM was established in 1977. Nowadays, it constitutes the largest Greek new technologies company with domestic and international activity. It engineers products, provides services and undertakes complex and integrated large-scale technology projects across the four basic economy sectors of: Telecommunications, Government, Banking and Finance, Defense systems.

Table 1. ATHENA Dynamic Requirements process

The industrial scenarios initially defined cover the four areas that are presented in the following subsections. Although these scenarios are identified and developed by the industrial users, their analysis, extraction of requirements and identification of interoperability solutions is performed through the collaborative work of multi skilled teams including industrial users, methodologists and solution providers. This collaborative work aims to close the gap between research and industry by facilitating users' deeper understanding of research trends, as well as researchers' deeper understanding of industrial needs. It will lead to the development of "realistic" ATHENA global to-be scenarios from which interoperability requirements will be derived and that will form the basis for the evaluation and piloting activities.

2.2.1. Product Data Management in a Virtual Networked Enterprise

The concrete case concerns sharing and exchange of technical information in the aeronautic sector for the change management process and for different types of supply chain relationships. Important factors specific to the Aeronautic and Defense sector are:

– The long lifecycle of an aircraft (around 50 years long). This means that information about the product should be useable during the whole lifecycle, which is longer than the lifecycle of an application, software product or even an organisation.

– The complexity of the product, due to the high level of reliability that is required, and the number of disciplines involved.

– Change management is very important; a product is defined as a set of ordered modifications.

This scenario highlights a family of cases mainly to deal with the first factor.

2.2.2. Collaborative Product Development

This scenario focuses on the Automotive sector and on the Product Development Process portion that prescribes the suppliers involvement on the objectives definition and on the product planning: Collaborative Product Development (CPD). CPD can be depicted as a three phases process that starts with the **Target Setting** and the nearly contemporary suppliers choice process or **Sourcing**. A third phase, once defined the suppliers' panel, consists in the real **Product Design**. Along the whole PDP process, the interaction between OEM and suppliers consists in a heavy exchange of information, sometimes conveyed through the net, and sometimes directly transferred face to face during meetings. Also although in most cases data are managed by suitable Enterprise Information System, human action is needed in order to carry out these data from a system to another. Some document management applications that guide the business processes exists (e.g. Open Plan application that support the sourcing execution), but most of the documents are sent by e-mail. Business logic is embedded within the applications, so every time the business model change it is not easy to update accordingly the software. A large number of stakeholders participate in this scenario and until now a shared format for data exchange has not been achieved.

2.2.3. e-Procurement

The objective of the e-Procurement scenario is to facilitate e-Business services interoperability and implementation of integration mechanisms by analysing the current e-Business implementation level in furniture sector and promoting multi-sector international agreements.

Product suppliers sell goods over the Internet through sell-side e-Commerce applications. Buying companies purchase goods over the Internet through buy-side e-Procurement applications. The scenario focuses on an e-Procurement application, through which members of a buying company purchase goods from multiple suppliers.

2.2.4. Product Portfolio Management

The focus of this scenario is on the management of the portfolio of new product development projects (NPD Projects), including also projects related to the development of new versions of already released products. The Product Portfolio Management is of significant importance especially to large enterprise with many business units and complex products.

The efficient performance of the product portfolio process requires federated information coming from marketing, project execution, as well as from the product life cycle management. It is also a knowledge intensive process, as it presupposes a very good and holistic view of the enterprise: strategy and objectives, skills and competences, as well as experience coming from previous projects. It requires therefore, many different aspects of interoperability to be covered: Business aspects, Knowledge Aspect and ICT aspects. The Product Portfolio Management scenario studied in ATHENA focuses on intra-enterprise level and on the telecommunication sector.

3. Pilot Activities and Validation Methodology

The validation tasks inside the ATHENA-IP Programme are carried out under the B5 sub-project named *Piloting including Technology Testing Coordination and Pilot Infrastructure*. Due to this sub-project, several pilots will be developed to test the solutions provided by ATHENA against the needs of the Industry.

3.1. ATHENA Pilot Cases

The pilots will cover the Aerospace, Automotive, Telecom and Furniture Industries. The piloting activities include the identification and implementation of test cases, test scenarios and test procedures in a real context of industrial users. The test cases and test scenarios are defined taking into consideration the to-be scenarios developed during phase P1 of the ATHENA Dynamic Requirements process. Currently, the following four use cases have been defined.

3.1.1. Product Data Management in a Virtual Networked Enterprise

The case is based on establishment of collaboration between two organizations, that use different specific change and configuration management processes, and nevertheless need to interconnect their process, in a way that allow interoperability between the heterogeneous Product Data Management Applications and software products. The federation of the processes, applications and software is based on the usage of consensual business (CMII, Manufacturing STEP application protocols) and technical standards at the level of the considered network. Integration of Product models is based on the usage of neutral information model related to several disciplines: AP233 for System Engineering, AP239-PLCS for customer support, AP214 for geometry, AP209 for calculation etc.

3.1.2. Collaborative Product Development Case

The essential test case is centred around the lifecycle of a Request for Quotation (RfQ) document and focuses on the management of process-critical events during the processing of the RfQ and allocated discussion and – if necessary – modification of the technical specification attached to the RfQ.

The test case is an integral part of collaborative product development and it is located in the early phase of the CPD, during which an OEM and its 1st and 2nd tier suppliers collaborate in order to verify (and where necessary to amend) a request for quotation (RfQ).

In the automotive sector, major portions of RfQ related input specifications are driven/owned by the OEM. A major problem and obstacle to interoperability between an OEM and its 1st and 2nd tier suppliers are modifications made to the specifications after publishing them together with the RfQ.

There are different reasons for these modifications:

–   Availability of new business-level information that change business parameters and may affect the technical specifications

–   Inconsistencies and technical problems observed as the RfQ is discussed between the OEM and its suppliers may force changes in the specification

–   In some cases, the availability of new technology may lead to changes being made

–   Sometimes, business relationships change during the process, and the specification needs to be adopted to the capabilities of new suppliers

3.1.3. e-Procurement Case.

The Test Case for the e-Procurement Scenario is based on a major Spanish office furniture manufacturer. Currently they are looking at implementing new technologies to assist its interactions with both customers and suppliers. The scenario is divided in two parts. In each case, apart from the manufacturer there is another company implied: either a Supplier or a Retailer.

The Supplier side of the e-Procurement scenario deals with the raw material procurement and the Client side deals with Quotations, Orders and Products delivery.

The points to be solved due to the case are the following:

–   Repetitive manual process for regular bulk orders
–   Confusion resulting from poor product descriptions
–   Missing information
–   Lag Time from product order to delivery could be shorter
–   Time spent rating supplier

3.1.4. Product Portfolio Management Case

The PPM case investigates into the use of Model Generated Workplaces to support simultaneous project, resource and results management, performance measurement through work management views, and the provision of shared project and work monitoring views. The overall objective is to support collaborative work by providing the actors in the enterprise with the tools, information and communication support they need to efficiently perform their work. This could be spitted down into the following expectations:

–   Ability of integrated applications execution via custom, adaptive and model generated environment

–   Provision of (near) real-time aggregated views of key business information. These aggregated views could be provided as services to the roles and actors required, accessing and integrating data in existing legacy systems. Such aggregated views will enable actors to take more accurate and timely decisions, exploiting to the full extend the capabilities of existing ICT systems.

–   Product related knowledge sharing within and between product life cycle phases

3.2. Validation Methodology

A set of different methodologies combining methods, procedures and evaluation criteria is proposed for evaluating preliminary, intermediate and final solutions. With these methodologies we intend to satisfy the basic characteristics of a method (clearness, completeness, coherence, impartiality, replicability) and to look at two complementary aspects: the Technical and Business aspects. Both aspects are relevant from an industrial perspective and will constitute the basis for a complete validation activity supported by two distinct methodologies.

3.2.1. Technical Validation

The methodology that will be used for technical validation is drawn from the ISO/IEC 9126 methodology "Information technology – Software Product Evaluation – Quality characteristics and guidelines for their use". The objective of this standard is to provide a framework for the evaluation of software quality. ISO/IEC 9126 does not provide requirements for software, but it defines a quality model that is applicable to every kind of software. It defines six product quality characteristics and provides a suggestion of quality sub-characteristics (Figure 3).

In ATHENA such sub-characteristics should be interpreted with respect to the identified reference architecture and Athena Interoperability Framework (multi cultural, multi-lingual, multi-standard).

The criterion used to evaluate the solution is based on the use of qualitative metrics, in order to facilitate the validation. The characteristics will constitute the base on which the testing scenario for the technical validation will be executed and are related to five different levels: Business, Knowledge, Application, Data and Quality.

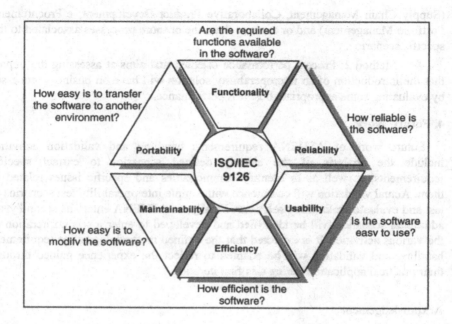

Figure 3. *ISO 9126 Quality Model*

3.2.2. Business Validation

The business validation methodology will be based on a business perspective and its main goal is to attempt to prove that interoperability has been reached and to identify and evaluate the real benefits deriving from the introduction of a solution in the enterprise.

Whereas it is relatively easy to identify the costs and evaluate the investment on IT, this is not the case with the identification and evaluation of benefits achieved by an organization deriving from the introduction of a new solution able to cover and solve interoperability issues.

For this reason a Business methodology should be tailored to the specific situation, in order to verify and assess the impact of an interoperability solution on the involved processes as described by industrial users and if necessary to extend the analysis to related processes.

The suggested methods to evaluate the interoperability from a business perspective and covering several aspects at different levels are:

–   Method 1 (Solution oriented) that aims to identify the applicability range of solutions. A solution can be usefully applied to one or more application scenarios

(Supply Chain Management, Collaborative Product Development, e-Procurement, Portfolio Management) and/or to more than one or more processes associated to the specific scenario.

–   Method 2: Process performance oriented that aims at assessing the impact that the introduction of an interoperability solution will have on business processes by evaluating some appropriate business performance.

4. Future Work

Future work of ATHENA requirements handling and validation activities include the analysis of the already defined scenarios to extract specific requirements, as well as to identify commonalties and specific issues related to them. Actual validation will commence with simple interoperability test scenarios to test and evaluate preliminary solutions. Finally, as ATHENA enters its second year, additional scenarios will be identified and developed to enter a second iteration of the various activities. It is expected that the defined methodologies for requirement handling and validation will be adapted to reflect the experience gained through their practical application during this first iteration.

Acknowledgement

This paper is partly funded by the E.C. through the Athena IP. It does not represent the view of E.C., and authors are responsible for the paper's content.

The authors thank and acknowledge the members of the Athena consortium:

SAP (D), AIDIMA (E), COMPUTAS (NO), CR FIAT (I), DFKI (D), EADS (F), ESI (E), FORMULA (I), FHG IPK (D), GRAISOFT (F), IC FOCUS (UK), INTRACOM (EL), LEKS (I), SINTEF (N), TXT (I), UNIV. Bordeaux I (F), UNINOVA (POR), IBM (UK), SIMENS AG (D).

5. References

ATHENA Deliverable D.B4.1 Dynamic Requirements Definition Principles, September 2004.

ATHENA Deliverable D.B5.1 Methodology & Technology Testing Report, November 2004.

ATHENA Working Document WD.B4.4.1 Starting Business Scenarios, July 2004.

ATHENA Working Document WD.B5.2.1 Use Case for test piloting, January 2005.

Towards Business Interoperability Research - Requirements Gathering and Analysis

Man-Sze Li* - Paolo Paganelli**

* IC Focus Ltd,
42 Clifton Road, London N8 8JA, UK
+44 7974 811 497
msli@icfocus.co.uk

** Gruppo Formula SpA, Via Matteotti 5,
40050 Villanova di Castenaso, Bologna, Italy
+39 051 6002 207
paolo.paganelli@formula.it

ABSTRACT. *This paper provides the context of ATHENA's activity in Business Interoperability Research. It describes the requirements gathering approach that has been adopted, discusses networked organisation views, proposes a "soft" networked organisation framework, documents the available preliminary findings, and identifies the main issues arising from the exercise.*

1. Introduction

ATHENA (Advanced Technologies for Interoperability of Heterogeneous Enterprise Networks and their Applications) integrated project (IP) aims to be a comprehensive and systematic European research initiative in IT to remove barriers to interoperability, to transfer and apply the research result in industrial sectors, and to foster a new networked business culture.

This paper presents the approach of the activity within the ATHENA-IP (Activity B3) to requirements gathering for interoperability research from a business - as opposed to a technical - perspective. Secondly, it provides the preliminary results of the research work that has been accomplished to date. Thirdly, it highlights some of the major issues identified.

The research work presented in the paper is expected to be completed in January 2007.

2. Objectives and scope

The overall context of this activity is the future company, creation and management of dynamic collaborative networks, knowledge management to support innovation, and evolution towards digital ecosystems.

The objectives of this activity are to:

- Determine the strategic business challenges relating to interoperability.
- Provide a general model for determining the impact of interoperability on businesses.
- Apply this model to ATHENA for assessing the business impact of the ATHENA results.
- Provide policy recommendations to the European Commission in respect of interoperability.

In terms of scope and temporal reach, we cannot simply refer to today's enterprise structures and business practices. ATHENA, especially through the B3 project, has to provide a strategic long-term vision, envisioning organisation forms and business models that will come of age by 2010.

In principle our analysis encompasses the whole business environment, including all intra- and inter-enterprise cooperative processes that will leverage interoperability technologies. Hence our approach must be model-independent, i.e., to look for interoperability problems/opportunities wherever they might arise, including:

– Co-operating enterprises (e.g., supply chain, virtual enterprise);

– Co-operating units within an enterprise (e.g., branch offices, production sites);

– Enterprise communities (e.g., marketplace, industrial district);

– Enterprises co-operating with other organisations (e.g., government organisations);

Similarly, our approach should be sector-independent, even considering cross-sector cooperation as one of the key issues in future, interoperability-powered business.

3. Approach to Requirements Gathering

The starting point of the research work is empirical. It gathers the business requirements for interoperability from a multitude of industrial sectors, using the following common analytical dimensions, at the organisation, sector, and cross-sector levels:

– Time.

– Value.

– Market structure.

– Role.

Requirements are further distinguished between those pertaining to the present situation and those relating to future scenarios (2010). The results are then consolidated and assessed for identifying the drivers that determine the choice and implementation of interoperability technologies, both now and in future.

4. Current Networked Organisations view

In parallel, ATHENA B3 is looking into networked organisation forms and related interoperability requirements, referring to the existing substantial body of work on the subject. The goal is to identify and assess new and emerging organisation forms that leverage interoperability technologies, for two main purposes:

– To map the networked business environment, taking into account the various interoperability contexts and dimensions.

–   To identify business-level requirements for design, management models and techniques of value networks.

To approach the subject with a balanced view, we must first of all consider it from the different points of view of the main interested players:

–   **The research community** sees collaborating enterprises as an undisputed reality, for which benefits are evident and organisation models have been on paper for at least 10 years. More sophisticated strategies are studied or new technologies (e.g., intelligent agents) are applied to well known scenarios.

–   **Industry initiatives** focus more on concrete solutions, immediately applicable by individual companies, than on innovative multi-organisation models. This is testified by the of work of important standardization consortia like VICS (VICS 2003) and RosettaNet (Kak *et al.*, 2002).

–   **IT Vendors**, despite the marketing hype that has almost any new (or renewed) software tagged as "Collaborative", only develop solutions that can be sold today to single enterprises - not tomorrow to multi-enterprise organisations. Business-to-business Integration platforms and on-line purchasing services are the main types of solutions currently found on the market.

This evident gap between theory and practice is not simply a matter of maturity but rather testifies that a common, comprehensive view of networked organisations is not yet available today. The different proposals concentrate on those aspects of collaboration that are more relevant to the proposer's research specialization or technological offering.

The risk in taking a unilateral approach to look at networked organisations is that of overlooking business interoperability requirements at any level, in particular:

–   Models based on advanced collaboration practices might not take into account lower-level requirements like, e.g., impact on the individual companies' existing strategies, organisation and infrastructure.

–   On the opposite side, point solutions to communication problems, although of limited impact and simpler implementation, might fail to achieve results on a proper scale due to lack of a strategic vision.

In answer to this situation, we intend to take a holistic, aggregating approach to find the broadest combination of requirements and organisational issues, addressing the following needs:

–   Our focus is not promoting a specific organisation model, no matter how innovative or valuable, but rather finding the organisational implications of interoperability technology. Our framework must be *inclusive* rather than exclusive, whereas the existing frameworks are always model- or even sector-biased (e.g., the VERAM framework (VERAM 2003) for one-of-a-kind manufacturing).

– Our major interest is in real experiences from the business community. None of these is the exact implementation of a theoretic model, but rather presents features common to several different models.

5. A "soft" framework for networked organisations

In accordance with the above principles, we will not try do build a taxonomy of networked organisation types. Constructs of this kind have often been used in the past, with the objective to arrive to a unique reference model where every possible networked organisation, within the model application scope, is precisely identified. The result is a "hard" framework, where each industry case is (or is not) characterized by its position in a pre-defined hierarchy of abstract organisations.

The scientific soundness of such an approach is not under discussion, but it is our opinion that it does not fit the objective of B3 and of ATHENA in general, for the following main reasons:

– No single, comprehensive networked organisation model is available, that would allows us to map all the requirements for any interoperability scenario. Attempts are currently in progress to arrive to a theory of Collaborative Networked Organisations, but research is still in an early stage (Camarinha *et al.*, 2004).

– Sufficient work has been done, respectively by Research, Industry Consortia and IT companies, to outline a wide spectrum of organisation models and interoperability situations.

– Each of the different approaches can be analysed from two main perspectives:

– The networked organisation **features** it assumes,

– The **interoperability requirements** it addresses or entails.

Features are the central element of our framework. They represent qualifying Networked Organisation aspects that characterize, to some extent, relevant organisation models found in state-of-the-art. A feature is not a fixed or discrete value; it is a range of values, with a minimum and a maximum. It allows the description of approaches when a certain organisational condition is partially fulfilled rather than either fulfilled or not. The range of values for the features indicates the degree to which a particular approach supports interoperability. This indication of the degree of interoperability facilitates the identification of requirements, which if fulfilled, will improve the level of interoperability of that approach.

The combination of different approaches mapped through the set of features, sets the boundaries of the Networked Organisations Space. Within this space, we can look for similarities, redundancies and juxtapositions between the different approaches that are analysed. Outside the Networked Organisation Space, we can look for innovations to be pursued or unidentified requirements.

This analysis framework can be considered as a "soft" framework for the following reasons:

‒ It is tolerant of approximated or partial definitions of approaches, allowing the indication of a degree of fulfillment for a certain organisation condition through the value of the corresponding feature.

‒ It can be enhanced to include approaches that were not known or not completely specified at the time the framework was designed.

‒ It allows the inclusion of new features as the list of features to cover all possible approaches at all times will never be complete.

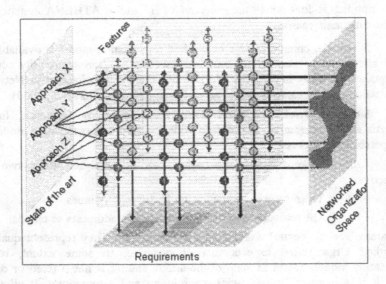

Figure 1. *Networked Organisation Analysis Framework*

The ATHENA B3 team is currently working with on an initial set of about 15 features but further can be added on demand, in line with the holistic nature of the framework.

By analysing the values of the features, it is possible to extract business interoperability requirements. For example, one of the approaches analysed in B3 is CPFR©, a standard promoted by the VICS Association[1] to "create collaborative relationships between buyers and sellers through co-managed processes and shared information". CPFR provides definitions and specifications for a set of collaborative processes between buyers and sellers in a consumer-oriented supply chain.

Some of CPFR features and requirements are shown in the following Table 1. For example, the feature "involvement" has a value 4, which indicates that the agreements among the partners in a CPFR (who are retailers and manufacturers) are closer to the strategic level rather than the transaction level and have a strategic value. However, this can be further improved by improving the ability of the partners to share their process logic, thus improving their collaboration at the strategic level. The value for the feature "association cost" is high indicating a threshold for CPFR adoption that could be lowered by removing some technical difficulties. One of these is the need for product data consolidation, hence the requirements for shared catalogue services like, e.g., UCC.NET provided by EAN.UCC[2].

Feature	Value	Business Interoperability Requirement	Requirement level / Interoperability area
Involvement	4	1. Shared Process Logic for collaboration.	Organisation / Processes
Interests balance	3	1. Shared Process Logic for collaboration.	Organisation / Processes
		2. Establish and share collaboration agreements.	Strategy / Objectives
Association cost	4	1. Consolidation of master item data through third-party service provider .	Infrastructure / Catalog management

Table 1. *Framework application results - example*

---

[1] The VICS consortium (http://www.vics.org/) is the entity promoting and maintaining the CPFR standard.
[2] The EAN.UCC System (http://www.uc-council.org) standardizes identification numbers, Electronic Data Interchange transaction sets, Extensible Markup Language Standard schemas and other supply chain solutions, presiding over several standardization initiatives like, e.g., RosettaNet and U.P.C. Bar Codes.

6. Preliminary Results

Preliminary results have been or are being gathered for the following sectors / organisational forms:

- Telecoms
- Software intensive organisations (small, medium, large)
- Manufacturing
- Building and construction
- Research organisations
- Furniture
- Industrial districts
- Automotive
- Public sector
- High tech industries
- Off-shoring organisations
- Textile

An initial set of Networked Organisation approaches is currently under examination, using the above described framework, in the following main categories:

- Industry standards for business interoperability, including, e.g.:
    - CPFR
    - RosettaNet.
- Supply Chain Management models, including features and requirements from:
    - SCM standards, like SCOR,
    - SCM experiences from industry and research, including significant EU projects in the field.
- Enterprise Networks and Virtual Enterprise, as defined in projects like GLOBEMEN, proposing a Virtual Enterprise life-cycle model.
- Marketplaces, subdivided in four main categories:
    - ...

A synthesis of the available preliminary results will be presented in a future version of this paper.

7. Main Issues

The main issues that have been identified are:

– A vast body of *related* state-of-the-art, but with little / insufficient concrete conceptual grounding in the specific subject of *business* interoperability.

– Considerable gulf between the business domain and the technology domain, and between actual market experiences and research efforts.

– The socio-economic aspects of interoperability are broad and wide ranging, and impact analysis must be based on a critical mass of empirical data, which is not always readily available or easily shared.

– Structural change in many sectors and markets leading to questions of:

    – How to find a common ground in interoperability?

    – How to move ahead with some degree of certainty?

– A long term timeframe is needed for achieving results - years not months.

Acknowledgements

The work published in this paper is funded by the European Commission through the ATHENA Integrated Project (www.athena-ip.org). It does not represent the view of European Commission or the ATHENA consortium, and authors are solely responsible for the paper's content. The authors would wish to thank various members of the ATHENA Activity B3 - Peter Mayer, Sobah Abbas Petersen, Nikos Pronios and Burkhard Schallock - for the many discussions concerning the substance presented in the paper.

8. References

ATHENA B3 Objectives, Results and Performance Indicators, May 2004.

ATHENA B3 Matrix on Business Requirements for Interoperability Technologies, Version 0.3, October 2004.

ATHENA B3 Matrices on Industrial Sectors - Various, July 2004 - January 2005.

Collaborative Planning, Forecasting & Replenishment (CPFR©), version 2.0, June 2003, Voluntary Interindustry Commerce Standards (VICS) Association (www.cpfr.org).

Kak, Rajeev, Sotero, Dave, *Implementing RosettaNet E-Business Standards for Greater Supply Chain Collaboration and Efficiency*, White Paper, © RosettaNet, 2002.

Luis M. Camarinha-Matos, Hamideh Afsarmanesh (editors), *Collaborative Networked Organisations: A Research Agenda for Emerging Business Models*, Kluwer Academic Publishers 2004.

Virtual Enterprise Reference Architecture and Methodology (VERAM), Deliverable, IMS Project IST-1999-60002, 2003.

INDEX OF AUTHORS

J. Abin	167
K. Ali Chatha	103
M. Anastasiou	319, 341
V. Anaya	31
A. Azevedo	77
P. Backlund	117
F. Bayer	127
M. Bergholtz	89
K. Blind	199
A. Brutti	249
R. Bunduchi	211
R. Camacho	19
C. Campos	65
L. Canché	19
R. Chalmeta	65
C.-M. Chituc	77
O. Coltell	65
G. Cucchiara	249
G. Doumeingts	53
T.M. Egeydi	261
L. Engel	153
R. D. Franco	31
O. Garcia	341
R. Garcia	319
S. Gauch	299

K. Geihs   153
M. Gerst   211
N. Gessa   249
I. Graham   211
R. Grangel   65
P. Heijnen   261
M. Henkel   119
X. B. Huang   147
E.J. Iversen   283
K. Jacobs   197
M. C. Jaeger   153
R. Jardim-Gonclaves   329
P. Johannesson   89
C.P.J. Koymans   235
H. Kühn. 117, 127
M.-S. Li 319, 353
P. Malo   329
R. Mejia   19
R. Molden   41
A. Molina 17, 19
J. Mueller   181
P. Mueller   181
M.J. Nuñez   341
M.-A. Ocampo   19
A. Ortiz. 17, 31
P. Paganelli   353
H. Panetto 13, 17, 103
A. Petzmann   127
F. Rodriguez   167
M. Roque   53
R. Rosas   19
R. Ruggaber   321
P. de Sabatta   249
R. Saraiva   329
R. Schlossar   127
G. Sindre   41
E. Söderström 117, 135, 223

A. Steiger-Garcao 329
J. Tang 147
R. Tee 283
B. Vallespir 53
J. Verhoosel 311
J.L.M. Vrancken 235
T. Wahl 41
L. Whitman 103
P. Wohed 89
J. Zdravkovic 119
G. Zhang 181